China's Road to the Korean War

The Making of the Sino-American Confrontation

THE U.S. AND PACIFIC ASIA:

Studies in Social, Historical, and Political Interaction

Carol Gluck and Michael Hunt, General Editors

THE U.S. AND PACIFIC ASIA:
Studies in Social, Economic, and Political Interaction

Carol Gluck and Michael Hunt, General Editors

ALSO IN THIS SERIES

Warren I. Cohen and Akira Iriye.
The Great Powers in East Asia, 1953–1960   1990

Charles W. Hayford.
To the People: James Yen and Village China   1990

Odd Arne Westad.
*Cold War and Revolution: Soviet-American Rivalry
and the Origins of the Chinese Civil War.*   1993

China's Road to the Korean War

The Making of the
Sino-American Confrontation

Chen Jian

New York
Columbia University Press

New York   Columbia University Press
Columbia University Press

New York   Chichester, West Sussex
Copyright © 1994 Columbia University Press
All rights reserved

Library of Congress Cataloging-in-Publication Data

Chen, Jian
  China's road to the Korean War : the making of the Sino-American
confrontation / Chen Jian.
    p.   cm. — (U.S. and Pacific Asia—studies in social,
economic, and political interaction)
  Includes bibliographical references and index.
  ISBN 0–231–10024–8 (acid-free paper)
  1. Korean War, 1950–1953—China.   I. Title.   II. Series.
DS919.5.C4513   1994
951.904'2—dc20   94–11240
                                                              CIP

Casebound editions of Columbia University Press books
are printed on permanent and durable acid-free paper.

Printed in the United States of America
c 10 9 8 7 6 5 4 3 2 1

To my Father and the memory of my mother.

Contents

Part Three
The Road to Intervention

Acknowledgments

In the course of completing this study, I have been indebted to many individuals and institutions. Professor David L. Wilson, my dissertation advisor at Southern Illinois University, advised and encouraged me at various stages of this book. Michael Hunt, Warren Cohen, Odd Arne Westad, and William Stueck read the entire manuscript more than once, and made constructive and critical comments. As a result, their influence can be felt on virtually every page of this book. I also wish to thank a number of friends, colleagues, and fellow scholars who have read all or part of the manuscript and offered critical comments: Charles R. Bailey, Thomas Christensen, William Derby, Cary Fraser, Immanuel Geiss, Sergei Goncharov, Torbjön L. Knutsen, Helena Lepovitz, Geir Lundestad, Joe McCartin, Niu Jun, Michael Schaller, Michael M. Sheng, David Tamarin, Marc Trachtenberg, William Turley, Xue Litai, Kathryn Weathersby, Philip West, Allen Whiting, Michael Winship, Marilyn Young, Zhai Qiang, and Zhang Shuguang.

Special thanks also go to Bao Shixiu, He Di, Hu Guangzheng, Li Haiwen, Liao Xinwen, Qi Dexue, Qu Ayang, Shi Zhe, Tao Wenzhao, Xu Yan, Yang Kuisong, Zhang Baijia, and Zhang Xi who offered invaluable assistance and/or advice during my four research trips to China in 1987, 1991, 1992, and 1993.

Support from several institutions allowed me to complete my study.

A 1991 SUNY-Geneseo Presidential Summer Fellowship facilitated my trip to China that year. A grant from Woodrow Wilson Center's Cold War History Project contributed to another trip to China in 1992. The Sponsored Research Office at SUNY-Geneseo, headed by Dr. Douglas Harke, provided several grants to cover research expenses related to this study. In Spring 1993, a Norwegian Nobel Institute fellowship not only released me from teaching and allowed me to devote several months to the revision of the manuscript but also, and more important, offered me a scholarly home replete of friendship and intellectual inspiration. My thanks go to Inger-guri Flögstad, Torill Johansen, Elisabeth Karesen, Anne Kjelling, Sigrid Langebrekke, and Arne Storheim.

A large portion of chapter 2 was published in the Summer 1993 issue of *Australian Journal of Chinese Affairs*, and part of chapter 4 appeared in the March 1993 *China Quarterly*. Both journals have graciously offered permission for me to reuse the published parts in this book. For both, I am very grateful.

The editors at Columbia University Press deserve great credit for their assistance in improving the original manuscript. In particular I would like to thank Kate Wittenberg for her encouragement at different stages of this project and Leslie Bialler for his skillful copyediting.

I would also like to thank Raymond Mayo of Computing and Media Services at SUNY-Geneseo for preparing the maps.

The greatest debt I owe to my father. In addition to his love and constant concerns for his only son's health, he devoted much of his after-retirement time to helping his son collect Chinese source materials. By now, even many of my Chinese colleagues are surprised by his knowledge of books and journal articles about China and the Korean War. I therefore dedicate the book to my father and the memory of my mother.

Abbreviations

Abbreviations Used in Text

CCP: The Chinese Communist Party
CIA: Central Intelligence Agency
CMC: The CCP's Central Military Commission
CMAG: Chinese Military Advisory Group
CPV: Chinese People's Volunteers
DRV: Democratic Republic of Vietnam
GMD: The Guomindang (The Nationalist Party)
JCS: Joint Chief of Staff
KPA: Korean People's Army
NEBDA: Northeast Border Defense Army
NSC: National Security Council
PLA: The People's Liberation Army
PPS: Policy Planning Staff
PRC: The People's Republic of China
UN: The United Nations

Abbreviations Used in Footnotes

CCA: Chinese Central Archives
CMA: Chinese Military Archives

FBIS: Foreign Broadcast Information Service
FRUS: Foreign Relations of the United States
MJWJ: Mao Zedong, *Mao Zedong junshi wenji* (A Collection of Mao Zedong's Military Papers)
MJWX: Mao Zedong, *Mao Zedong junshi wenxuan* (Selected Military Works of Mao Zedong)
MNP: *Mao Zedong nianpu* (A Chronology of Mao Zedong)
MWG: Mao Zedong, *Jianguo yilai Mao Zedong wengao* (Mao Zedong's Manuscripts Since the Founding of the PRC)
MXJ: Mao Zedong, *Mao Zedong xuanji* (Selected Works of Mao Zedong)
NA: National Archives
ZWJWX: Zhou Enlai, *Zhou Enlai waijiao wenxuan* (Selected Diplomatic Works of Zhou Enlai)
ZXJ: Zhou Enlai, *Zhou Enlai xuanji* (Selected Works of Zhou Enlai)
ZYWJXJ: *Zhonggong zhongyang wenjian xuanji* (Selected Documents of the CCP Central Committee)

China's Road to the Korean War

The Making of the Sino-American Confrontation

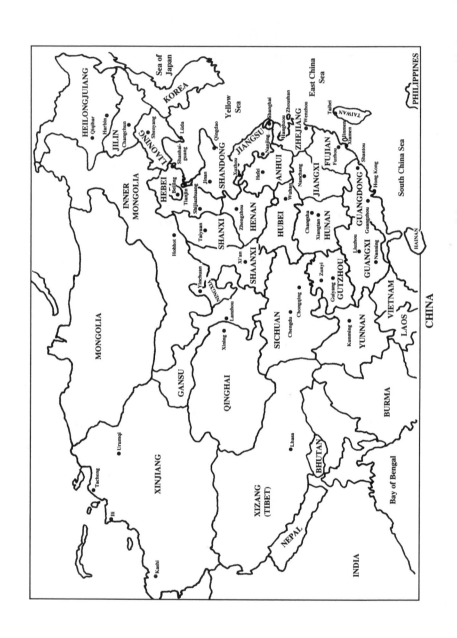

Korea and China's Northeast (Manchuria)

Introduction

In October 1950, one year after the establishment of the People's Republic of China (PRC), Mao Zedong and the Beijing leadership sent "Chinese People's Volunteers" (CPV) to Korea to fight against United Nations forces moving rapidly toward the Chinese-Korean border. Although China's intervention saved Kim Il-sung's North Korean Communist regime from imminent collapse, it was unable to fulfill the Beijing leadership's hopes of overwhelming the UN forces. Therefore, when the Korean War ended in July 1953, Korea's political map remained virtually unchanged, while America's military intervention in Korea and China's rushing into a conflict with the United States finally buried any hope for a Sino-American accommodation, and the Cold War in Asia entered a new stage characterized by a total confrontation between the PRC and the United States that would last nearly twenty years.

The newly established Chinese Communist regime faced enormous problems during its first year, including achieving political consolidation, rebuilding a war-shattered economy, and finishing reunification of the country. Why then did Mao decide to assist North Korea in fighting a coalition composed of nearly all the Western industrial powers? How was the decision made? What were the immediate and long-range causes leading to Beijing's decision to enter the Korean War? Finally, was there any opportunity that might have prevented the direct confrontation between the PRC and the United States? More than forty years after the end of the Korean War, scholarly answers to these questions are still limited and remarkably inadequate.

In the 1950s, Western scholars, strongly influenced by the intensifying Cold War, generally viewed China's entrance into the Korean War as a reflection of a well-coordinated Communist plot of worldwide expansion, believing that the entire international Communist movement was under the control of Moscow, and that neither Beijing nor Pyongyang had the freedom to make their own foreign policy decisions. The Korean conflict, therefore, was seen as an essential part of a life-and-death confrontation between the Communists on the one hand and the "free world" on the other.[1]

The North Korean invasion of the South, as viewed by President Harry Truman—and many later students of the Korean War—represented the first step in a general Communist plot to "pass from subversion" to "armed invasion and war" in their scheme of world conquest.[2] Correspondingly, Beijing's entrance into the Korean War was regarded as an action subordinate to Moscow's overall Cold War strategy. Scholars in the West widely believed that Beijing's policy was aggressive, violent, and irrational.

In 1960, Allen S. Whiting published his landmark study, *China Crosses the Yalu*,[3] which has strongly influenced a whole generation of scholars. Using Western intelligence sources and Chinese journal and newspaper information, Whiting argued that unlike the Soviet Union, Communist China had not directly participated in the planning for the North Korean invasion of the South. After the outbreak of the Korean War, Whiting believed, Beijing tried to terminate the conflict through political settlement, and only after the attempts for a political solution failed in late August 1950 did Beijing begin necessary military preparations in early September. Whiting emphasized that after the Inchon landing Beijing tried through both public and private channels to prevent UN forces from crossing the 38th parallel. Beijing entered the war only after all warnings had been ignored by Washington and General Douglas MacArthur and, therefore, in the Beijing leadership's view, the safety of the Chinese-Korean border was severely menaced. Whiting thus concluded that Beijing's management of the Korean crisis was based primarily on the Chinese Communist perception of America's threat to China's national security. Lacking access to Chinese archival materials, though, Whiting's study had to focus

more on the analysis of the environment in which the Beijing leadership made their decision to go to war than on a close examination of
the decision-making process.

In the late 1960s and early 1970s, a more critical perspective on the
Sino-American confrontation in Korea emerged in the wake of the
American debacle in Vietnam, the normalization of Sino-American
relations, and the declassification of new archival documentation.
Building on Whiting's thesis, scholars paid more attention to Chinese
Communist Party (CCP) leaders' concerns for China's national security as the decisive factor underlying their decision to enter the Korean War. They generally argued that Beijing did not welcome the Korean War because China faced difficult tasks of economic reconstruction
and political consolidation at home and gave priority to liberating
Nationalist-controlled Taiwan. Many of these scholars stressed that
Beijing's decision to enter the Korean War was simply a reluctant reaction to the imminent threats to the physical security of Chinese territory. And while most scholars believed that the American decision
to cross the 38th parallel triggered China's intervention, some speculated that if UN forces had stopped at the parallel China would not
have intervened.[4] A large majority of Chinese scholars seem to share
these assumptions, as can be seen in Chinese publications on the "War
to Resist America and Assist Korea" that appeared in the 1980s.[5]

As a lecturer at Shanghai's East China Normal University in the
early 1980s and then during my pursuit of doctoral studies in the
United States, I became increasingly interested in the emergence of
Sino-American confrontation in the late 1940s and early 1950s. In my
study I too believed in the standard interpretation of China's reasons
for entering the Korean War. Not until 1988-1990, when the work on
my dissertation led me to fresh Chinese sources, did I begin to feel
doubts. For example, to my surprise, I found that early in August 1950,
more than one month before the Inchon landing, Mao Zedong and
the Beijing leadership had been inclined to send troops to Korea, and
China's military and political preparations had begun even a month
earlier. I also found that the concerns behind the decision to enter the
Korean War went far beyond the defense of the safety of the Chinese-
Korean border. Mao and his associates aimed to win a glorious victory by driving the Americans off the Korean peninsula. It was no
longer possible to accept the well established view of Chinese and
American historians.

The reexamination of the Korean case led me into a broader question concerning the proper understanding not only of Communist China's foreign policy but also, probably, that of any sovereign country: is it appropriate to comprehend the foreign policy behavior of a country, especially one that had historically viewed itself as a "Central Kingdom," as totally reactive and without its own consistent inner logic? The assumptions underlying most of the existing scholarship on China's entrance into the Korean War, though seemingly critical of Washington's management of the Korean crisis, emerge ironically as American-centered in a methodological sense. Lacking a real understanding of the logic, dynamics, goals, and means of Communist China's foreign policy, they treat Beijing's management of the Korean crisis simply as a passive reaction to the policy of the United States. They thus imply that American policy is the source of all virtues as well as evils in the world—if something went wrong somewhere, it must have been the result of a mistake committed by the United States. It was time to rethink Beijing's entrance into the Korean War.

This study retraces China's road to the Korean War with insight gained from recently released Chinese materials. It argues that China's entry into the Korean War was determined by concerns much more complicated than safeguarding the Chinese-Korean border. To comprehend China's decision to enter the war, one must first examine the CCP leaders' perception of China's security interests and their judgment of to what extent and in which ways such interests had been challenged during the Korean crisis. This examination requires an extended analysis of a variety of basic factors shaping the CCP leadership's understanding of China's external relations. Among these factors, the most important ones include CCP leaders' perception of the outside world and China's position in it, the nature and goals of the Chinese Communist revolution and their impact on the CCP's security strategy and foreign policy, the influence of the CCP's domestic policies on the party's foreign behavior, and the leverage of historical-cultural factors (such as the Chinese emphasis of the moral aspect of China's external relations, Chinese ethnocentrism, and Chinese universalism) upon Mao and the CCP leadership. Only with a better understanding of the logic and dynamics of the CCP's outlook is it possible to construct the interactions that led China and the United States into a major confrontation in Korea.[6]

My three-part, seven-chapter study begins with an analysis (in chapter 1) of Communist China as an emerging revolutionary power. Focusing on the pre-1949 period, I discuss the domestic sources of the CCP's foreign policy, the party leadership's perception of the outside world and China's position in it, and Mao's central role in the CCP's policy-making structure. The second part (chapters 2-4), explains how the conflict between the CCP and the United States escalated and the strategic cooperation between Beijing and Moscow developed in 1949 and the first half of 1950—on the eve of the Korean War, Beijing and Washington had perceived each other as a dangerous enemy, and a stage for Sino-American confrontation had been set up. The third part (chapters 5-7) examines Beijing's management of the Korean crisis from late June to mid-October 1950, focusing on how the decision to enter the war was made and how it withstood both internal and external tests. Emphasizing that Beijing's decision to enter the war was based on the belief that the outcome of the Korean crisis was closely related to the new China's vital domestic and international interests, I argue that there was little possibility that China's entrance into the Korean War could have been averted.

A note on the Chinese sources used in this study is appropriate here. Since the mid-1980s, thanks to China's reform and opening policies, many fresh and meaningful materials concerning China's entry into the Korean War have been released, which offer the basis for this study. These new sources include personal memoirs by those who were involved in Beijing's intervention in Korea,[7] scholarly articles and monographs by Chinese researchers with archival accesses,[8] official academic publications using classified documents,[9] openly or internally published collections of CCP Central Committee's and regional bureaus' documents,[10] and the internally and openly published collections of Mao Zedong's papers.[11] While it is apparent that these sources have created new opportunities for fresh studies, it is also clear that they were released on a selective basis and, sometimes, for purposes other than a desire to have the truth known. Indeed, unless scholars, both Chinese and non-Chinese, are offered free and equal access to the original historical documentation, there is always the possibility that a study might be misled by its incomplete databases. Fully aware of this danger, I have made every effort to doublecheck my citations as much as possible (such as checking documents with information from interviews, and vice versa, and comparing Chinese materials with non-Chinese ones). Wherever necessary, I have pointed out what I consider to be dubious sources in the notes.

This study is also based on my four research trips to China respectively in 1987, 1991, 1992, and 1993. During these trips I established and updated my research databases, and interviewed those who were involved in Beijing's policy-making during the late 1940s and early 1950s, and those who have access to classified CCP documents (because of the political sensitivity involved in the issues under discussion, unless authorized by the interviewees, I will not identify their names, but I will restrict using unidentified interviews only if it is absolutely necessary). I have not been able to get close to Beijing's CCP Central Archives (which, by the way, is located in the city's remote western suburb). But by a combination of effort and good luck, I accessed some important classified documents (including correspondences and telegrams of Mao Zedong, Zhou Enlai, and other CCP leaders, and a few minutes of CCP leaders' decision-making conferences) for the 1948-1950 period. To compromise the need to protect my sources with the general practice of Western scholarship, I cite them in this study by pointing out their forms (telegram, correspondence, or minute), dates, and where their originals are maintained (the Chinese Central Archives or Chinese Military Archives). I believe that this is the best one can do in the current circumstances. It is my hope that China, my motherland, will follow the internationally accepted practice of declassifying historical documents on a legal basis, so that all researchers, including myself, will soon be able to get free access to them.

Part One

The Emergence of a Revolutionary Power:
1948-1949

1 | Revolutionary Commitments and Security Concerns: New China Faces the World

By the end of 1948, Mao Zedong and his comrades realized that China's three-year civil war would soon end with a Communist victory. The Guomindang (the Nationalist Party or GMD) regime, suffering from political corruption, economic collapse, and a series of military failures, had little chance to save itself from a final defeat.[1] Mao proclaimed with full confidence in his new year message of 1949 that "the Chinese people will win final victory in the great War of Liberation, even our enemies no longer doubt this outcome." In his report to the enlarged Politburo meeting on January 6, he further alleged that "the Chinese revolution will achieve final victory in the whole country in 1949 and 1950."[2] Mao and his party would now have to govern China and devise a foreign policy for the new Chinese Communist state.

In September 1948, the CCP Politburo held a five-day meeting at Xibaipo (CCP headquarters at that time), to analyze the international situation as well as other tasks facing the CCP in the last stage of China's civil war.[3] In January 1949, Mao chaired another enlarged Politburo meeting of top leaders at Xibaipo; and two months later, the CCP held its Second Plenary Session of the Seventh Central Committee. The main purpose of these two meetings was to thrash out basic strategy and policy after securing nationwide victory.[4] Out of these meetings was to emerge a security strategy and foreign policy geared to consolidating the achievements of the Communist revolution, preparing for a thorough transformation of the old Chinese society, serving China's security interests as defined by the CCP, and changing completely China's humiliating relationship with the outside world. Mao and his comrades decided that "making a fresh start," "cleaning the house first before entertaining guests," and "leaning to one side (the Soviet Union)" would become the principles guiding Communist China's external relations.[5] Consequently, the "new China," as Mao and the CCP called it, was to emerge as a revolutionary power in a world that had been rigidly polarized by the Cold War.

The Domestic Agenda

The CCP's foreign policy-making was in the first place influenced by the party's domestic agenda, especially by the tasks of achieving political consolidation, rebuilding a war-shattered economy, and, in a deeper sense, maintaining the inner dynamics of the Chinese Communist revolution after nationwide victory. These problems conditioned CCP leaders' consideration of the new China's foreign policy, driving them to adopt a radical approach toward the outside world.

The first aspect of the CCP's domestic agenda involved the need to establish a new revolutionary regime. To Mao and his associates, this was first of all a question concerning the elimination of the GMD regime and its remaining influence in China. Mao always believed that "the fundamental problem of a revolution is that concerning political power."[6] A primary goal of the Chinese Communist revolution, as often expressed by Mao and other CCP leaders in overt ways, was to destroy completely China's old political structure and at the same time, with the support of the new state power, to build in China a "New People's Democratic Dictatorship," which, according to Mao, was the Chinese form of "proletarian dictatorship."[7]

In Mao's view, this political transformation was extremely important because it would serve as the basis for the CCP's plans to conduct a thorough transformation of Chinese society. In terms of the contents of this political transformation, Mao and his fellow CCP leaders believed that they had to "eliminate all reactionary forces in China through revolutionary means" so that the GMD and the Chinese "reactionaries" would have no hope of returning. As the first step, they needed to dismantle the old constitutional system and state apparatus of the GMD regime and replace them with the CCP's own revolutionary government. Considering the importance of these tasks, Mao argued that, with the disintegration of the GMD's military forces, political struggle would replace military engagement as the main form of the CCP-GMD confrontation, and that it was crucial for the CCP to demonstrate no mercy for the GMD, now on the verge of collapse.[8] Understandably, these revolutionary commitments would push the CCP leadership to take a harsh attitude toward those countries that still maintained active relations with the GMD regime.

In 1949, the CCP also faced the problem of economic reconstruction. After wars and chaos lasting for nearly half a century, China's economy was in a shambles. Compared with the standard of 1936, the year before Japan's invasion of China, the country's general industrial production had decreased 50 percent, with heavy industry dropping almost 70 percent. All main railroads were severely damaged. Agriculture also suffered from grave problems; compared with the pre-World War II period, grain production had fallen by 22.1 percent and cotton production by 48 percent. Runaway inflation caused additional economic and financial problems that were difficult to cure.[9] Mao and his fellow CCP leaders realized that the challenge of economic recovery and reconstruction would be daunting. During both the January enlarged Politburo meeting and the March Central Committee meeting, Mao spent considerable time discussing strategies, policies, and tactics the CCP would need to revitalize the economy. Mao understood that a failure in China's economic recovery and reconstruction would jeopardize the prospect of the continuous success of the Chinese Communist revolution.[10]

However much China might need foreign support for economic reconstruction, Mao was unwilling to compromise the CCP's revolutionary principles to get that assistance. He believed that the economic challenge China had to face was in its essence a political problem. While Mao realized that the CCP should not refuse to pursue or accept economic assistance from abroad, especially if the assistance was from the Soviet Union and other people's democratic countries,[11] he also emphasized that the party should never forget its final goal—the construction of a socialist society in China—and should always combine its policy for economic recovery and reconstruction with its strategy for the realization of socialist transformation of the old economic structures. At the Central Committee's Second Plenary Session, Mao stressed that the CCP should restrict the existence and development of private capitalism in China through limiting its sphere of activity, defining and restricting its working conditions, regulating its price system, and imposing taxes on it. Mao also made it clear that the process of economic reconstruction would be put under the absolute control of the CCP in order to "consolidate the leadership of the proletariat in the state power" and to promote China's development "from the new democratic society to the future socialist society."[12] In short, Mao viewed China's economic reconstruction as a pivotal aspect of the Communist revolution.

Mao, who also believed that China's economic reconstruction had to be carried out mainly by the Chinese themselves, did not feel that large-scale economic assistance from Western capitalist countries was either possible or necessary. Mao assumed that Western countries would be unwilling to maintain positive economic ties with Communist China as the latter posed a profound challenge to the Western-dominated "old world." Chen Yun, the CCP leader in charge of economic affairs, followed Mao's ideas to anticipate that Western capitalist countries, the United States in particular, would impose an economic blockade by "refusing to buy from China while not selling to China" after the CCP's nationwide victory.[13] Mao, unfrightened by such a prospect, believed that China—with its huge land area, abundant resources, vast domestic markets, and a large population, could be self-reliant in economic matters. As early as 1938, he had argued that China could survive a protracted war with Japan because of the self-sufficient nature of the Chinese economy. The CCP's experience during the Yanan period further strengthened Mao's belief in self-reliance.[14] In late 1948 and early 1949, Mao and the other CCP leaders stressed on a series of occasions that the CCP should strive for economic self-reliance so that the new China would stand the challenges of Western imperialist countries.

This profound confidence in China's ability to live independently strengthened the CCP's unyielding attitude toward Western capitalist countries. In a document about the new China's foreign trade policy dated February 16, 1949, the CCP Central Committee stressed that "The basic guideline of our foreign trade is that we should export to and import from the Soviet Union and other new democratic countries so long as they need what we can offer or they can offer what we need. Only in the situation that the Soviet Union and other new democratic countries are not in a position to buy from us or sell to us will we do some business with capitalist countries."[15] Mao summarized the CCP's economic strategy: "The two basic policies of the state in the economic struggle will be regulation of capital at home and control of foreign trade."[16]

Zhou Enlai later summarized the CCP's calculus of the relationship between the party's revolutionary doctrine and its attitude toward trade with the West. He stated that as "the old China had been dependent on the imperialists not only in the economic sphere but also in the sphere of culture and education, "China was therefore "exploited economically and polluted politically." In order to "expose and eradicate the evil influence of imperialism," Zhou emphasized, "we should neither rely on the imperialists nor be afraid of them." Zhou concluded that the CCP's foreign trade policy should be based on the assumption that "most of those materials we need could be supplied by ourselves and some by our friends" and that "we should never count on our enemies."[17]

Mao and the CCP leadership attached even greater importance to the problem of maintaining the inner dynamics of the Chinese Communist revolution after victory than they did to political consolidation and economic reconstruction. This emphasis was to play a decisive role in shaping Communist China's foreign policy. Mao titled his 1949 New Year's message "Carry the Revolution through to the End." According to him and other CCP leaders, the "end" of the revolution must be understood at two different levels. First, the CCP was determined to eliminate the GMD military forces and to overthrow the GMD regime so that "the Chinese reactionaries would not be able to come back, by taking advantage of the compromise of the revolutionaries, as had happened during the 1911 revolution and the North Expedition [of 1927]."[18] Second, Mao was contemplating how to push the revolution forward after its victory. In his report to the Central Committee's Second Plenary Session, Mao pointed out that the CCP's seizure of power was only the completion of the first step in the long march of the Chinese Communist revolution, and that "the road after the victory would be longer, the work greater and more arduous." Mao warned the members of the party:

> It will not require much time and effort to win the nationwide victory, but to consolidate it will. The bourgeoisie doubts our ability to construct. The imperialists reckon that eventually we will beg alms

from them in order to live. With victory, such moods as arrogance, self-styled heroism, inertia and unwillingness to advance, preoccupation with pleasure-seeking, and distaste for continued hard struggle may grow within the party. With victory, the people will be grateful to us and the bourgeoisie will come forward to flatter us. It has been proved that the enemy cannot conquer us by force of arms. The flattery of the bourgeoisie, however, may conquer the weak-willed in our ranks. There may be some Communists who were not conquered by enemies with guns and were worthy of the name of heroes for standing up to these enemies, but who cannot withstand sugar-coated bullets; they will be defeated by sugar-coated bullets. We must guard against such a situation.[19]

This emphasis on "carrying the revolution through to the end" was a long-standing preoccupation in Mao's thinking. As early as 1939 and 1940, Mao stated in *The Chinese Revolution and the Chinese Communist Party* and *On New Democracy*, two of his most important works, that the Chinese Communist revolution would be divided into two stages: the stage of new democratic revolution and the stage of socialist revolution. During the first stage, the revolution had to overthrow the rule of the bureaucratic-capitalist class, wipe out foreign influence, eliminate remnants of feudal tradition, and establish a Communist-led regime that would unify all patriotic social classes in China. The second stage of the revolution would transform the Chinese society, including the economic system, political structure, and social life, under the leadership of the Communist regime. This transformation would lay the foundation of China's transition into a socialist and later Communist society. In Mao's view, the two stages in the revolution were closely linked: without the first stage, the second stage of the revolution would be impossible; without the second stage, the first stage of the revolution would become meaningless.[20] When Mao called for "carrying the revolution through to the end" in 1949, he was thinking about leading the revolution into its necessary second stage.[21]

How could, then, the inner dynamics of the great Chinese revolution be maintained and enhanced after the Communist seizure of power? This question concerned Mao in 1949–50 and would occupy his primary attention during the latter half of his life (In a sense, here lies one of the most profound origins of the "Great Proletarian Cultural Revolution"). When Mao first touched upon the problem of how to push the revolution forward in 1949, he would try all the means he had been familiar with, especially mass propaganda and mass mobilization, and his train of thought developed in terms of the continuous existence of outside threats to the revolution. In actuality, starting in early 1949, Mao constantly stressed that enemies of the revolution had not disappeared with its victory. On the contrary, he claimed that victory had created greater internal and external threats. A brief examination of the CCP leadership's changing assessment of the "American threat" will help expose Mao's train of thought.

During the first two years of the 1946–1949 civil war, the CCP leadership acted on the assumption that direct American intervention was unlikely. Mao and his comrades believed that because American strategic emphasis lay in Europe and that the "reactionary American ruling class" was in nature vulnerable, it would be difficult for Washington to send significant numbers of military forces to China to support the GMD.[22] Nearing complete victory in late 1948 and early 1949, however, CCP leaders began to demonstrate great concerns about direct American intervention in China's civil war. During the January 1949 enlarged Politburo meeting, American intervention was a central topic. In spring 1949, CCP leaders and military planners continued to emphasize the danger involved if Washington should decide to send its troops to China to rescue the GMD regime.[23]

In addition to its conviction that Washington was profoundly hostile toward the Chinese revolution, the CCP leadership's vigilance against American intervention at the last stage of the civil war was caused by the fact that the People's Liberation Army (PLA) attacked coastal commercial centers like Shanghai, where the Western presence had been significant.[24] But in a deeper sense, the CCP leadership's emphasis on the danger of direct American intervention in early 1949 had to be understood in the context of Mao's deep concern for maintaining the inner dynamics of the Chinese revolution after nationwide victory.

When Mao and the other CCP leaders tried to define "American threat" in early 1949, they never restricted their vision to the immediate danger involved in direct American intervention in China. Rather, they emphasized long-range American hostility toward the victorious Chinese revolution, as well as the U.S. imperialist attempt to sabotage the revolution from within. At the January Politburo meeting, Mao noted the possibility of American direct intervention in China; but he believed that well-prepared Chinese revolutionary

forces could defeat American military intervention.[25] Mao emphasized that an American strategy of sabotage could be a more serious
threat than military intervention. Both at the January enlarged Politburo meeting and the March Central Committee's Plenary Session,
Mao spent considerable time discussing the threat of American sabotage of the Chinese revolution and "the danger of winning the victory." He stressed that "after the destruction of the enemies with guns,
the enemies without guns were still there, and they were bound to
struggle desperately against us." He therefore warned the entire party:
"If we fail to pay enough attention to these problems, if we do not
know how to wage the struggle against them and win victory in the
struggle, we shall be unable to maintain our political power, we shall
be unable to stand on our feet, and we shall fail."[26]

Not surprising at all, an important gap would emerge between the
CCP leadership's real assessment of the nature of the "American
threat" and the party's open propaganda about it when Communist
forces occupied Shanghai, Qingdao, and other major coastal areas in
mid-1949. In internal correspondences, Mao and his comrades were
by then convinced that the danger of American direct intervention
had disappeared.[27] But in the party's open propaganda, they would
continue to emphasize the "American threat." On one occasion, for
example, Mao warned the whole country that the United States and
Chinese reactionaries were unwilling to "resign themselves to defeat
in this land of China" and would "gang up against the Chinese people in every possible way," even by sending "some of their troops to
invade and harass China's frontiers."[28]

Given that the Chinese revolution was at a crucial juncture in
1949, Mao's warnings could be understood in two ways. First, as a
revolutionary, Mao hoped that his comrades would maintain revolutionary vigilance at the time of victory so that the achievements of
the revolution would not be lost. Second, as a revolutionary strate-
gist, Mao looked into the future. Many revolutionary movements in
history have lost their momentum after the victory because their
objectives disappeared. Mao did not want to see this to happen in
China. When he stressed the continuous existence of external threat
to the Chinese revolution after its victory, he had actually issued the
most powerful appeal for maintaining its inner dynamics. It is apparent that this approach made it easier for Mao and his fellow CCP
leaders to emphasize conflict, rather than reconciliation or accom-

modation, with the Western countries, particularly with the United States.

International Outlook

In the late 1940s, when Mao and his comrades focused their vision on the outside world, they encountered an international environment that had been divided by the Cold War. The deteriorating relationship between the Soviet Union and the United States drove the world into incessant crises, making the world situation replete with elements of instability and conflict. In the meantime, with the declining influence of the old European powers in international politics, national liberation movements developed rapidly in the non-European world, especially in East Asia.[29] Facing such a situation, Mao and his fellow CCP leaders defined the nature of the emerging Cold War in light of the Marxist-Leninist theory of international class struggle, as well as of the CCP's need to win the war against the GMD. In the meantime, they demonstrated a strong desire to come to the fore in the international arena and to make China a significant actor in the changing world. All of this was clearly manifested in the late 1940s by the CCP's introduction of the theoretical concept of the "intermediate zone."

After the Second World War, Mao and the CCP leadership initially believed that the American-Soviet contradiction was the "main contradiction"[30] in world politics and that the conflict between the CCP and the GMD was subordinate to the confrontation between the two super powers.[31] The disclosure of the secret agreement on China between Roosevelt and Stalin at Yalta challenged this view. Mao and the other CCP leaders found that between Moscow and Washington there existed not only confrontation but also areas of compromise.[32] With the development of China's civil war, especially after Mao and the CCP leadership became convinced that the United States would not use its military forces directly in China because its strategic emphasis lay in Europe, Mao's understanding of the "main contradiction" in the world underwent a fundamental change, becoming more complicated. Beginning in late 1946, Mao and the CCP leadership introduced a series of new ideas about the postwar world situation and China's position in it, known as the theory of "the intermediate zone."

In an August 1946 interview with Anna Louise Strong, an American leftist journalist visiting Yanan, Mao asserted that sharp differences existed between the United States and the Soviet Union and that "the U.S. imperialists were preparing to attack the Soviet Union." However, he did not believe that the United States was ready to start a new world war. He observed that the United States and the Soviet Union were "separated by a vast zone including many capitalist, colonial and semi-colonial countries in Europe, Asia, and Africa," and it was therefore difficult for "the U.S. reactionaries to attack the Soviet Union before they could subjugate these countries." He speculated that the United States now controlled areas in the Far East larger than all the former British spheres of influence there, including Japan, the part of China under GMD rule, half of Korea, and the South Pacific. As a result, it was not the Soviet Union but these countries that became "the targets of U.S. aggression." Mao concluded that America's anti-Soviet campaign was designed to oppress the American people and to expand U.S influences in the areas between the United States and the Soviet Union, including those capitalist countries.[33]

Underlying these speculations was the belief that the United States was by nature a "paper tiger." In a long conversation with Zhou Enlai and Liu Shaoqi on November 21, 1946, Mao stressed that the CCP should not overestimate the strength of the United States and other Western countries, which he felt were on the verge of a new destructive economic crisis. Furthermore, the competition for raw materials and potential markets between major imperialist powers would cause serious problems between the United States and such imperialist countries as Britain and France, thus weakening the strength of the "reactionary ruling classes" in these countries. As a result, leftist forces in Western countries would further develop in the wake of the economic crisis. Mao therefore concluded that the "reactionaries" in the United States and other Western countries were vulnerable.[34]

Mao introduced here the CCP leadership's unique comprehension of the nature of the emerging confrontation between the two superpowers: although the postwar world seemed to be characterized by the sharp confrontation between the Soviet Union and the United States, the Cold War at the present stage was nevertheless in its essence a struggle between, on the one hand, the American people and peoples in the "intermediate zone," of which China occupied a crucial position, and, on the other hand, the reactionary American ruling class. This struggle would determine not simply the direction of the emerging Cold War but actually the fate of the entire world. In early 1947, an important article entitled "Explanations of Several Basic Problems Concerning the Postwar International Situation" offered a more detailed analysis of the "intermediate zone." Published in the name of Lu Dingyi, the CCP's propaganda chief, the article had been discussed by top CCP leaders and personally revised by Mao.[35] It argued that the postwar confrontation was between the "anti-democratic forces" headed by the United States and the "peace-loving and democratic forces" headed by the Soviet Union. In this sense it is true that the international scene after the Second World War had been bipolarized. As the strength of the Soviet camp far surpassed that of the American, it was erroneous to believe "that a new world war was inevitable or that a lasting world peace was impossible." Stressing that the United States was separated from the Soviet Union by the vast intermediate zone in Asia, Africa, and Europe, the article repeated Mao's view that Washington's anti-Soviet campaign was designed for "internal oppression and international expansion in the intermediate zone." The article continued to analyze the "main contradiction" of the postwar world. It emphasized:

> After the end of the Second World War, the main contradiction in world politics exists not between the capitalist world and the socialist Soviet Union, nor between the Soviet Union and the United States, but between the democratic and anti-democratic forces in the capitalist world. Or more concretely speaking, the main contradiction in today's world is that between the American people and American reactionaries, that between Great Britain and the United States, and that between China and the United States.[36]

It can thus be seen that in the view of Mao and his fellow CCP leaders, sharp differences did exist between the Soviet Union and the United States. The real thrust of the Soviet-American confrontation, however, lay in the competition over the intermediate zone, and the fate of the competition would be decided by the struggle between the peoples of the intermediate zone and the "reactionary" U.S. ruling class, rather than between the two superpowers themselves. As China occupied a crucial position in the intermediate zone, Mao and his comrades believed that China would play a central role in determining the result of the Cold War.

The CCP leadership's introduction of the intermediate zone theory came at a time when China's civil war had been escalating. Mao and his fellow CCP leaders obviously hoped to use this theory, especially the part about "all reactionaries were paper tigers," to encourage the whole party to pursue a victorious end in the war against the American-backed GMD regime. In this sense, the theory served the party leadership's need to mobilize the party to win the civil war.

In a broad sense, the theory of the intermediate zone reflected CCP leaders' fundamental perceptions of China's position in the postwar world. First, it mirrored the CCP's commitment to transform the existing international order by challenging the United States as a dominant power in the Asian-Pacific area. In Mao's view, since the American intention to control the Asian-Pacific area served the interests of "the dark reactionary forces," the CCP's challenge to the existing order was just and necessary. And since the reactionary forces headed by the United States faced themselves a variety of internal and external crises, such a challenge was feasible. The Chinese people and other peoples in the Asian-Pacific should have the courage to challenge American domination in international politics.

Second, the theory of the intermediate zone demonstrated that the CCP's postwar policy had a strong "lean-to-one-side" tendency from the beginning. Although Mao stated that China belonged to the "intermediate zone" between the Soviet Union and the United States, he opposed China to take a middle ground between the two superpowers.[37] Lu's article made it clear that China belonged both to the "intermediate zone" and the Soviet camp. In a report on domestic and international relations in December 1947. Mao placed the United States squarely as the head of the imperialist camp with the Soviet Union as the leader of the anti-imperialist camp, of which China should become a member.[38] In December 1948, Liu Shaoqi published a lengthy article, "On Internationalism and Nationalism" (again, a collective work of the CCP leadership). He postulated that sharp confrontation did exist between the Soviet-headed "new democratic" camp and the U.S. headed "reactionary" camp, which involved "all the peoples of the world—of all countries, classes, sections of the population, parties and groups." Therefore one must "line up with one side or the other.... If one is not in the imperialist camp ... one must be in the anti-imperialist camp."[39] It had never been a problem for the CCP leadership that China belonged in the Soviet camp.

Third, the theory of the intermediate zone reflected a strong tendency toward Chinese ethnocentrism in Mao's and the other CCP leaders' perception of the postwar world. Mao and his fellow CCP leaders stated vigorously that the American-Soviet competition over the intermediate zone would be finally determined by the result of the struggles between China and the United States, and that the "main contradiction" in the postwar world was thus of a Sino-American nature. This emphasis upon China as a critical front in the postwar world may have been part of an attempt to win more Soviet assistance to the CCP. It indicated also that the CCP leaders' thinking was strongly influenced by the desire to pursue China's worldwide influence, even during the time when the party was still fighting for a dominant position in China.

Within this context the CCP leadership's concept of revolution, especially its understanding of the relations between their own and the world proletarian revolution, evolved during the civil war. Mao and his comrades had consistently viewed the Chinese revolution as part of a world proletarian revolutionary movement initiated by Russian Bolsheviks. As the Chinese revolution progressed, however, a different model from that of the Russian revolution emerged: instead of concentrating on urban areas the Chinese revolution was largely rural-oriented. Mao and the CCP leadership now had second thoughts about the nature and significance of the Chinese revolution. During 1948–49, they began to think in terms of a much broader anti-imperialist Asian and world revolution. They had come to believe that their model of revolution transcended China. They concluded, first, that the Chinese revolution offered an example of universal significance to other peoples struggling for national liberation and, second, that the victory of the Chinese revolution was the beginning of a new high tide of revolutionary movements of oppressed peoples in Asia and in the world. Consequently, Mao and his comrades believed it their duty to assist Communist revolutionaries and national liberation movements in other countries in order to promote a worldwide revolution.[40]

Ironically the desire to make a total break with the "old world" reveals the CCP's inheritance of a heavy cultural-historical burden. In the CCP leaders' eagerness to make the Chinese revolution Asian-wide or even worldwide, we see the reemergence of a familiar Chinese ethnocentrism and universalism, an age-old tradition seriously challenged during modern times by the Western invasion of China. "China's standing up among the nations of the world," according to Mao's logic, would be realized through China's promotion of Asian and world revolutions, thus bringing about the rejuvenation of China's central position in the international community, that is, the cultural and moral superiority of the "Central Kingdom," now represented by Mao's revolutionary China, would achieve an international recognition.

We have encountered at this point a key rationale underlying the CCP's foreign policy: Mao's and his comrades' revolutionary nationalism. China has a long history and a profound civilization. The traditional Chinese were deeply convinced that Chinese civilization and the Chinese way of life were the most superior in the known universe. Indeed, the Chinese during traditional times had only a vague impression of the "world" or the distinction of nation-states; they would be more comfortable using the concept "*tian xia*" (all under the heaven), which implied that the "Central Kingdom" was the only civilized land in the world; or in other words, China was civilization *in toto*.[41]

This Chinese view of the world had been severely challenged when China had to face the cruel fact that China's door was opened by the superior forces of Western powers, and that the very survival of the Chinese nation was at stake. Mao's and his comrades' viewpoints of China's international status and foreign connections were deeply influenced by the unequal exchanges between China and the foreign powers. They became indignant when they saw Western powers, including the United States, treat the old, declining China with arrogance and a strong sense of superiority. They also despised former Chinese governments, from the Manchu dynasty to the regimes of the warlords, which had failed to protect China's national integrity and sovereignty. An emotional commitment to national liberation provided a crucial momentum in Mao's and his comrades' choice of a Marxist-Leninist style revolution. As Mao expressed it, China's national crisis early in the twentieth century had a decisive impact on his decision to join the revolutionary movement aimed at transforming Chinese society.[42] For Mao and his comrades, the final goal of their revolution was more than the total transformation of the old Chinese society they saw as corrupt and unjust; they would pursue at the same time changing China's weak power status, to prove to the other parts of the world the strength and influence of Chinese culture, and to redefine the values and rules underlying the international system.[43] We certainly can call Mao and his fellow CCP leaders Chinese nationalists. But their nationalism had not only a strong revolutionary orientation but was also interwoven with the deep-rooted image of a "Sinocentric world order," as once defined by John K. Fairbank.[44]

This revolutionary nationalism, under the Cold War environment, led Mao and his comrades to emphasize persistently that the Chinese Communists would not tolerate Washington's disdain of China and the Chinese people. While Washington's hostility toward the Chinese Communist revolution offended Mao and his fellow CCP leaders, the perceived American disdain for China as a weak country and the Chinese as an inferior people made them angry. When the Chinese Communist revolution approached nationwide victory, Mao would personally initiate a series of propaganda campaigns calculated to expose the "reactionary" and "vulnerable" nature of U.S. imperialism and to encourage the Chinese people's national self-respect. Although Mao and the CCP media frequently used Marxist-Leninist terminology in these campaigns, how to face the "U.S. imperialists" was to the CCP a problem concerning values and beliefs, which was related to their feelings as Chinese.

Under the influence of the same revolutionary nationalism, the CCP's relationship with Moscow was close but never completely harmonious. Around the time of the establishment of the People's Republic, conditioned by both ideological considerations and practical interests (the Soviet Union was more than a Communist friend; it was also the only great power that was willing to back the PRC), Mao and the CCP leadership would adopt the policy of allying China with the Soviet Union. Mao and his fellow CCP leaders, however, would be extremely sensitive to being treated by Stalin and the other Soviet leaders as the "little brother."

In sum, underlying the CCP's perception of the outside world were not only political ideological considerations, but also, and more important, profound historical-cultural factors: the conceptual world of Mao and his fellow CCP leaders as twentieth-century Chinese revolutionaries was consciously or unconsciously dominated by the age-old "Central Kingdom" mentality. The international goal of the revolution therefore mirrored its domestic tasks. Just as it would destroy traditional Chinese society and establish a new China, so too it would challenge and destroy the old world order, and create a new one.

Defining China's Security Interests

The CCP's domestic agenda, its perception of the postwar world and China's position in it, and its revolutionary nationalism carried Mao and the party's leadership to an exceptionally strong sense of insecurity and, correspondingly, the pursuit of special means for security. Consequently, the CCP leadership's definition of China's security interests was deeply penetrated by the party's revolutionary commitments.

In a general sense it is understandable that, in a divided world in which the balance of power had been severely threatened by such factors as the emergence of nuclear weapons and the increasing confrontation of the two superpowers, any country had reasons to feel less secure than ever before. The sense of insecurity on the part of Mao and the CCP leadership, however, was special in several respects in comparison with the typical considerations of insecurity during the early Cold War period. It was not so closely related to fear of America's nuclear power since Mao emphasized that the Chinese Communists would not be intimidated by it.[45] Nor would Mao believe, as the result of his deep conviction of China's ability to rely on its own resources for survival and development, that revolutionary China could easily be knocked down by the "imperialist plot" to isolate it from international society. Rather, the CCP leadership's deep sense of insecurity had a close connection with its understanding of the nature and influence of the Chinese Communist revolution. Three hypothetical observations might be made here. First of all, the ambitious hope on the part of Mao and the other CCP leaders to change China into a central international actor conflicted with China's weak power status at the time of the PRC's formation—in 1949, as Frederick C. Teiwes once put it, "China's fundamental economic and military backwardness created monumental impediments to the [Communist] elite's goals of national wealth of power."[46] As Mao and his fellow CCP leaders would not give up the effort to chart their own course in the world and to make China a leading world power, they would continue to feel insecure until China's weakness had been turned into strength.[47]

Second, since Mao and the CCP leadership emphasized the significance and influence of the Chinese Communist revolution and regarded the struggles between revolutionary China and the United

States as the "main contradiction" in the world, they would logically feel that they faced a very insecure world. One could find here a mutually restrictive or mutually promotive relationship in the CCP leadership's security concerns: the more they stressed the significance of the Chinese Communist revolution, the less secure they would feel in face of the perceived threat from the West and the United States.

Third, the continuous emphasis by Mao and the CCP leadership on the necessity of maintaining the inner dynamics of the Chinese Communist revolution would represent another constant source of insecurity. In order to use the continuous existence of the foreign threat to mobilize the Chinese masses, Mao and his comrades enhanced anti-foreign-imperialist propaganda. This propaganda, in turn, might lead to a deepening sense of insecurity on their own part. Allen Whiting's analysis certainly makes good sense in this regard: "Perhaps Mao spoke propagandistically while retaining more sophisticated judgments privately. The consistency of the bias in his erroneous forecasts, however, makes probable his wholehearted acceptance of Communist assumptions of world affairs."[48]

Consequently, when defining China's security interests and the threats to them, Mao and his fellow CCP leaders would not restrict their vision to China's physical security. Rather, they perceived China's national security interests at three different yet interrelated levels. First, as noted earlier, they emphasized that one threat to the Chinese revolution and the Communist regime came from within. In Mao's opinions, the imperialists would try to use representatives within the revolutionary camp to sabotage the revolution; and some revolutionaries could shift their revolutionary stand as the result of being unable to meet the challenges brought about by the revolution's nationwide victory. In both cases the vital interests of revolutionary China could be in danger.

Second, Mao and his fellow CCP leaders paid special attention to the connection between the safety of China's neighboring areas and the security of China itself. In this regard, following China's modern experiences (especially those of the 1884 Sino-Franco War over Vietnam and the 1894 Sino-Japanese War over Korea and Manchuria), CCP leaders placed great value on defending the suzerain spheres of traditional China, the Korean peninsula and the Indochina area in particular. Believing that these two regions had special connections with China's overall security interests, the CCP leaders endeavored to

promote revolutionary movements there in the early days of the
PRC, and would treat them, together with Taiwan, as the most possible sites for a direct confrontation with the United States.[49]

Third, Beijing leaders believed also that China's security interests
were linked with the scenario in the entire Asian-Pacific area or even
the entire world. Viewing China as an emerging power in the international arena, CCP leaders were concerned about the possible influence of major changes in Asia and other parts of the world upon
China's security status. Starting in early 1949, the CCP demonstrated
strong interests in the internal and external affairs of countries in
Southeast Asia, Indonesia, the Philippines, India, and Japan. The party
emphasized that the development of revolutionary movements in
these countries was closely related to the fate of the Chinese revolution—while their failure would create greater pressure on the Chinese revolutionaries, their success would strengthen the new China's
international position.[50] On a global scale, CCP leaders believed that
the changing world situation was in one way or the other connected
with the status of China's security. In accordance with the Marxist-
Leninist rules of social progress and the CCP's understanding of the
postwar situation, Mao and the CCP leadership were convinced that
Communist China's security would be guaranteed only when the
outside world was no longer dominated by hostile capitalist-imperi-
alist forces.[51]

These specific considerations and, as a result, the unique definition
of China's security interests led Mao and the CCP leadership to
believe that special means were required to maintain China's national
security. In pursuing China's security interests, Mao and the CCP
leadership would often resort to such conventional means as allying
China with other powers, trying to split China's enemies (often combined with the Chinese tradition of "utilizing barbarians to check barbarians"), pursuing effective means of deterrence, and "preparing for
the worst while at the same time pursuing the best." However, strongly influenced by the party's successful experience of mobilizing the
masses in the confrontation with the GMD, they would emphasize the
importance of maintaining China's security interests through a total
and continuous mobilization of the party and the Chinese people.
Mao believed that if the Chinese nation, which was composed of
almost one quarter of the world's population, could be fully mobilized
under the CCP's strong central leadership, China's national security

interests would be best maintained.[52] For Mao, the question of the best means to maintain China's security interests had thus turned into the question of how to achieve full mobilization of the Chinese nation under the Communist leadership.

Mao at the Center

By the late 1940s, Mao Zedong had established himself as the CCP's indisputable leader. His comrades became increasingly accustomed to echo his judgment, rather than to challenge his wisdom. The revolutionary features of the CCP's foreign policy reflected Mao's ideas and, in a sense, epitomized his rebellious character, his consciousness of challenge, and his devotion to Chinese revolutionary nationalism. In order to understand better the CCP's revolutionary foreign policy, we need to comprehend Mao as a person and his dominant position in the CCP's decision-making structure.

Born in 1893, Mao was from a peasant family in Shaoshan, a village in Xiangtan County, Hunan Province. During his childhood, he had a frequently conflicting relationship with his father, which, as many scholars believe, contributed to the making of his rebellious character. As a schoolboy, he read Confucian classics, but only to the tales of rebelling peasants fighting against the exploitative and corrupt bureaucracy (such as the popular novel *Water Margin*) would he devote his heart and soul. As he left Shaoshan to pursue more advanced studies in Changsha, Hunan's capital city, all of this was reinforced by the rebelliously oriented cultural environment in Hunan Province. The result was his deep conviction that "rebellion was by nature legitimate" (*zaofan youli*).[53]

When Mao further touched upon the realities of Chinese society and China's declining status in the world, his rebellious and challenge-oriented character began to combine with the strong desire of "transforming China and the world," leading to a profound and persistent consciousness of challenging the "old world." In Mao's conceptual realm, there existed little respect for the existing rules or regulations in either Chinese society or the international community; rather, Mao's way of thinking was dominated by "the philosophy of struggle," which emphasized that "only through struggle was progress in human history possible."[54] In Mao's mind, the very dynamics of his revolution lay in the constant needs of defining and redefining the objec-

tive(s) that the revolution was to challenge. These ideas, in the late
1940s, became the spiritual backbone of the CCP's revolutionary foreign policy.

Mao's central position in the CCP's policy-making structure in the
late 1940s allowed him to change his opinions into the party's policies
without much checking and balancing by other top party leaders. As
a Communist party, the CCP had long taken the Leninist principle of
"democratic centralism" as the basis of its decision-making framework, which meant that only before the decision had been made
would different opinions be allowed to exist and that in no circumstance would factional activities within the party's leading circle be
tolerated. In practice, the CCP's policy-making procedures following
"democratic centralism" were steeped in the deep-rooted patriarchal
tradition in China's political culture, allowing the party's paramount
leader to act as the head of the party "family." Indeed, since Mao's
emergence as the CCP's top leader in the mid-1930s, his authority in
the party's decision-making structure had increased continuously. A
decision by the Politburo in March 1943 made Mao the party's undisputed leader and granted him the power of "making the final judge-
ment for important decisions."[55] The party's seventh congress in 1945
further established "Mao Zedong Thought" as the party's guiding ideology. In the wake of the CCP's victory in China's civil war, Mao's
credibility and authority within the party leadership rose further; so
did his confidence in his own political wisdom. With the emergence
of the "Mao cult" that was to characterize Communist China's political and social life, Mao's leadership role became of a patriarchal
nature—it was no longer possible and meaningful to distinguish his
voice from the party's.

Until late 1948, domestic affairs dominated the CCP's agenda. The
nationwide victory, however, made Mao feel an urgent need to place
the party's diplomatic affairs under tighter control of the party's central leadership and himself. He could see that most of the CCP's local
and provincial cadres were from rural areas. While familiar with military and domestic political matters they had little experience in foreign affairs. As the CCP emerged as the ruling party, it encountered
new problems (especially in the field of diplomacy) that did not fit
into the party's previous strategies and policies. Mismanagement of
foreign affairs by local party cadres might undermine the CCP's
whole foreign policy. Furthermore, Mao's understanding of the deci-

sive role the new China's foreign policy was to play in continuously promoting the Chinese revolution prevented him from releasing his decision-making power on diplomatic affairs—he believed that his direct leadership would best guarantee the party's foreign policy to serve his grand revolutionary designs. Under these circumstances, Mao emphasized repeatedly in late 1948 and early 1949 that "there existed no insignificant matter in diplomatic affairs, and everything should be reported to and decided by the Central Committee," and, particularly, by Mao himself.[56] There is no doubt that Mao Zedong was the single most important policymaker in Communist China's foreign affairs—the other CCP leaders, including Zhou Enlai and his staff, were more policy-carriers than policymakers.[57]

Mao in 1949, though, was not an experienced master at foreign affairs in a conventional sense. As of 1949, he had never been abroad. His knowledge of other parts of the world was based largely on his highly selective reading, which focused more on Chinese history, Chinese politics, and Chinese translations of Marxist-Leninist classics than on world politics or international relations.[58] In addition, Mao's direction of the CCP's foreign policy was strongly influenced, as noted earlier, by a preoccupation with the ongoing Chinese revolution. These factors generated misperceptions and improper initiatives and responses in Communist China's foreign policy.

But Mao also brought strength. Deeply convinced of the just nature of his cause, Mao was determined to challenge and destroy the unjust and exploitative "old world." He was not alone; a nation with a population equal to one quarter of that of the world would be under his rule. He had learned to be a master at mobilizing the party and the revolutionary peasantry to realize the revolution's domestic tasks; now, as China's ruler, he was more than willing to apply the same strategy to mobilize the Chinese nation in pursuing the revolution's international aims. To underestimate the determination and potential of a China led by this man would be a fatal misperception.

Toward the end of the 1940s, China had emerged as a revolutionary power. In domestic affairs, Mao and the CCP leadership placed extraordinary emphasis on the need to maintain the inner dynamics of the Communist revolution, so that the revolution would eventually produce a profound transformation of China's state and society. In international politics, Mao and his comrades were determined to break with the legacies of the old China, to "make a fresh start" in China's foreign affairs, and to lean to the side of the Soviet-led socialist camp. Indeed, Mao's new China challenged the Western powers by questioning and, consequently, negating the very legitimacy of the existing "norms of international relations," which, as Mao and his comrades viewed them, were of Western origins and inimical to revolutionary China. In order to pursue their domestic and international goals, the Chinese revolutionaries would in no circumstance allow themselves to be restricted by the rules of the "old world."

To be sure, the foreign behavior of Communist China appeared to have its own language and own theory, and would follow its own values and codes of behavior. In a world that had been divided by the Cold War, the adoption of a new and revolutionary discourse by the world's most populous country inevitably brought about factors of instability and demands for radical change in both East Asian regional politics and the worldwide political scenario. What made the situation even more complicated is that at the time of its formation, Communist China's ambitious international aims were yet overshadowed by the prevailing images of China as a weak country. While this cognitive gap turned out to be one of the most important sources for foreign misperceptions of China's intention and capacity, it also caused an extraordinary sense of insecurity on the part of the Chinese leaders. In retrospect, indeed, it would be surprising if Communist China's emergence as a revolutionary power had not been followed by its confrontations with the Western powers in general and the United States in particular.

Part Two

Friends and Enemies:
A Stage Set for Confrontation

November 1948–June 1950

2 | The Recognition Controversy: The Origins of Sino-American Confrontation

When Chinese Communist troops entered Shenyang, the largest city in China's Northeast, on November 2, 1948, their commanders discovered with surprise that among foreign diplomats remaining in the city was Angus Ward, the consul general of the United States. While suspecting Americans' motives for staying on in the "liberated zone" (especially given Washington's hostility toward the Chinese revolution), they sensed proudly that even the "U.S. imperialists" now could not avoid direct contact with the Chinese revolutionaries. Ward, however, had only a vague knowledge of his tasks: the State Department ordered him to remain not because of any willingness to reach an accommodation with the new Chinese Communist regime, but only in order to observe the Communist controlled zones without arousing misunderstandings about formal recognition.[1] Lacking an understanding of the profound potential confrontation between the CCP's and Washington's perceptions of each other's stance, Communist cadres and American diplomats in Shenyang failed to anticipate that the contact between them would create a point of serious conflict, finally leading to a direct Sino-American military confrontation in late 1950.

The Ward Case: The Beginning of Confrontation

Local CCP cadres' contacts with American diplomats started shortly
after the Communist occupation of Shenyang. After receiving a letter
from Western diplomats asking for proper protection, Zhu Qiwen, the
new Communist mayor, summoned the American, British, and
French consuls general to his office on November 5, promising that
the Communist authorities in Shenyang would protect the foreigners
remaining there and that he would issue identity cards to consular
motor vehicles. Four days later, Zhu visited the three Western consuls
and had cordial talks with them. Meanwhile, Ward received "several
communications from local [Communist] authorities" addressed
either to him "as Consul General or to the office as the American
Consulate General."[2] It seemed that Zhu and the Shenyang Communist authorities were willing to deal with these Westerners in their
official capacity.

Zhu's actions were not without grounds. On November 1, the
CCP Central Committee summarized the party's general stand
toward Western diplomats in a cable, drafted by Zhou Enlai, to the
party's Northeast Bureau. The cable instructed that given the special
situation in the Northeast, foreign banks should not be closed after the
liberation of Shenyang. Under the martial law, according to the cable,
the U.S., British, and Soviet consulates should be protected by troops;
and when the martial law was lifted these consulates should be guard-
ed by police. Under no circumstance should body search be imposed
upon foreign diplomats entering and leaving the consulates; neither
should the consulates be searched. The cable stressed that as diplomatic practice and international custom were new to the CCP, the
party should "consult with Soviet diplomatic personnel," and that
while the opinions of the Soviets should be carefully considered,
"[their ideas] should be treated as no more than suggestions, and any
matter related to policy should be reported to the Central Committee for instructions before action."[3]

Several leading members of the CCP Northeast Bureau, including
its secretary and deputy secretary, Gao Gang and Chen Yun, who were
also CCP Politburo members, as well as Zhu Qiwen, failed to pay
enough attention to the last point of these instructions. Without asking for instructions from the central party leadership, Zhu contacted
Western diplomats in his official capacity, believing that this was in

tune with the CCP's long-time policy of international "united front" as well as helpful for improving the CCP's international image.[4] Ward, taking this as a sign that the Communists were willing to maintain official contacts with the United States, concluded in a report to the State Department: "It was obviously the intention of the Communist authorities at the time to recognize us and permit us to function as an official United States Government establishment."[5]

The situation changed suddenly. On November 15, the CCP's Municipal Military Control Commission of the Shenyang City informed all "former" Western consulates in Shenyang, including the Americans, that no foreigners could possess a radio transmitter without special permission of the commission, and that all radio transmitters should be handed over to the commission within 36 hours.[6] In reality, this order affected only the Americans, as the British and French relied instead on regular Chinese communication channels.[7]

The changing attitude of the Shenyang authorities was in the first place caused by the CCP leaders' determination to eliminate the old China's diplomatic legacies. Unwilling to treat Western establishments and personnel accredited by the GMD government as formal diplomats, the CCP Central Committee found it necessary to clarify its stand by correcting the "wrongdoings" of the Shenyang authorities. In a November 10 telegram to the Northeast Bureau, the Central Committee directed that because the British, American, and French governments had not recognized the Chinese Communist authorities, the CCP would not recognize their official status either, and that Western diplomats should be treated as common foreigners without diplomatic immunity. Criticizing the Shenyang authorities for their failure to ask instructions beforehand, the telegram emphasized that CCP local authorities should not respond to any diplomatic questions without guidance of the Central Committee. They should request instructions from the party leadership and in the meantime keep open their options.[8] After receiving this telegram, the Northeast Bureau immediately stopped treating Western diplomats according to their official status.

Shenyang's change was also the result of the advice from Soviet representatives in the Northeast, which, as is well known, had long been viewed by the Russians as in their sphere of influence. With the Chinese Communist victory in the Northeast, the Soviets did not want the CCP to allow Western diplomats to remain there in either official or unofficial capacity. I. V. Kovalev, the Soviet representative who was then helping the Chinese Communists restore railroad transportation in the Northeast, advised members of the CCP Northeast Bureau that the CCP should keep a distance from Western countries. He suggested strongly that the CCP should treat American diplomats remaining in Shenyang in the same manner as the GMD treated Soviet commercial representatives in the Northeast in 1946, that is, to cut off their external communications. He particularly mentioned that the CCP should "take control of the radio stations in those places where the Chinese comrades were sure they were operating." Leading members of the Northeast Bureau, especially Gao Gang, who had a particularly intimate relationship with the Soviets, decided to follow the advice of the Soviets to drive Western diplomats out of the Northeast by creating difficulties for them.[9]

Security considerations played an additional role in the Northeast Bureau's order to requisition radio transmitters of Western consulates in Shenyang. The PLA's Fourth Field Army was then preparing to move south from Manchuria to enter the Beiping-Tianjin Campaign, a decisive military showdown between the CCP and the GMD, and CCP military planners in the Northeast worried that the remaining American diplomats might use their radio transmitters to send information about the PLA's movement to the GMD. In fact, CCP leaders in the Northeast already believed that American diplomats in Shenyang were "actively engaged in" collecting any available information about the PLA.[10] Later, in a report to the Central Committee on November 24, the Northeast Bureau concluded that U.S. consulate in Shenyang had been involved in espionage activities on behalf of the GMD regime.[11]

The combination of these factors caused the Northeast Bureau to order all foreign consulates to hand over their radio stations within 36 hours. After the issuance of the order the Northeast Bureau reported it to the CCP Central Committee for the central leadership's approval. The Bureau also reported that they planned to cut off the three Western consulates from outside communications and to restrict the movement of members of these consulates so that they would be driven out of Shenyang.[12]

Mao and the CCP central leadership quickly approved the Northeast Bureau's actions. In a telegram to Gao dated November 17, Mao agreed in principle to the Bureau's ideas of "driving the American,

British, and French consulates out of [Shenyang]." At the same time, Mao sternly criticized Zhu Qiwen (but not Gao Gang): "Several of Zhu Qiwen's actions are ridiculously naive, such as notifying foreign consulates for the mayor's inauguration, returning visits of foreign consuls, newspapers in Shenyang publishing the information that the U.S. consulate apologized for the enemy's bombardment, and promising without careful consideration to issue passes for American motor vehicles." Mao ordered that Chen Yun and other leading CCP Northeast Bureau personnel, who were supposed to be responsible for the above mistakes, to make "profound self-criticism." Mao also directed Gao Gang to inform the Soviet Union: "So far as our foreign policy in the Northeast and the whole country is concerned, we will certainly consult with the Soviet Union in order to maintain an identical stand with it."[13]

The CCP's order to requisition radio transmitters possessed by Western consulates in Shenyang immediately challenged the status of American diplomats. Following instructions of the State Department, Ward refused to hand over the transmitter, arguing that it was an "integral part of consulate establishment."[14] The Chinese Communists interpreted Ward's noncooperative response as intentionally disregarding Communist authority and violating Chinese sovereignty.

In a telegram to the Northeast Bureau on November 18, Mao further dictated the party's strategy. This time he sternly criticized the Shenyang Military Control Commission for its failure to request instructions from the party leadership before setting the 36 hour deadline. He ridiculed his comrades in Manchuria: you set the deadline and informed the three Western consulates before you reported to the Central Committee, and then you waited for the instructions from the Central Committee, allowing the deadline to be passed. Did you think you might take back the order if the Central Committee disagreed with you? Mao believed that the Northeast Bureau should execute the order immediately in the name of the Shenyang Military Control Commission. Mao also agreed that the Northeast Bureau should follow the suggestion of the Soviets to isolate the three Western consulates "so that the members of the British, American, and French consulates would evacuate in the face of difficulties and our purpose of driving them away could be reached." Criticizing once again Zhu's treatment of Western diplomats in their official capacities, Mao explicitly emphasized that "a certain foreign consul should be called as Mr., not his official title."[15]

Following Mao's instructions, the Shenyang Military Control Commission cut the American consulate off from outside contacts during the afternoon of November 18. Two days later, PLA soldiers cordoned off the consulate's offices and residential compound, and Ward and his colleagues were placed under house arrest without advance warning.[16] In a letter to "Mr. Ward," the Shenyang authorities emphasized that because of his "failure [to] surrender [the] radio transmitter constitutes intentional defiance personnel [of] former American Consulate General [would] hereafter [be] forbidden intercourse with [the] outside." In addition to Ward and his wife, twenty Americans and Europeans were confined in the consulate, including two vice consuls, six clerks, one mechanic (with his wife and four children), two staff employees (and the wife of one of them), and one "stateless women."[17] Ward and his staff would not be allowed to leave China until the end of 1949.

"We Should Not Hurriedly Pursue American Recognition"

The CCP's management of the Ward case demonstrated clearly the party's deep hostility toward the United States. It also caused Mao and the party leadership to place the party's external activities under tighter central control, as well as to further clarify the party's policy principles toward the United States.

Mao found it intolerable that the Northeast Bureau had acted on its own without asking instructions from the party center, and the chairman used his criticism of Zhu's mistake as a warning to the entire party. In the following months, he emphasized repeatedly to local and provincial party authorities that they should report to the Central Committee on any matter concerning foreign affairs. In a telegram to the CCP's Tianjin Municipal Committee on January 20, Mao stressed: "Before taking any concrete step in dealing with foreign nationals, you should ask the opinions of the Central Committee, and act with the approval of the Central Committee." After the Communist occupation of Nanjing, the capital of the GMD government, in April 1949, Mao reiterated in two cables to Su Yu, then the director of the Nanjing Municipal Military Control Commission, that "you should request instructions from the Central Committee in advance in all diplomatic matters, large or small alike. . . . Otherwise you might commit huge mistakes."[18]

In order to guarantee that all party organs would "request instructions beforehand in diplomatic matters, large or small alike," the CCP Central Committee ordered in January 1949 that in every large city a special group for diplomatic problems should be established within the party's military control commission, which should be commanded by one of the leading members of the party municipal committee. The task of the group was to "study problems concerning foreign residents and diplomatic affairs, collect relevant materials, report periodically to the Central Committee and the party's regional bureau, and put forward questions and ideas for instructions."[19] Not surprising at all, diplomatic affairs had become the field most tightly and directly controlled by Mao and the CCP Central Committee even before the establishment of the People's Republic.

The events in Shenyang also drove Mao and his comrades to further contemplate the principles underlying the CCP's policy toward the United States. The central questions involved here, as Mao perceived them, were that the CCP should never compromise itself with the old China's diplomatic legacies, and that the new China should not hurriedly pursue diplomatic relations with the Western countries in general and the United States in particular. On November 23, 1948, right after Ward's detention, the CCP Central Committee cabled to the Northeast Bureau, emphasizing again that the party's basic policy toward Western countries was that it would not recognize the diplomatic relations between the GMD and those countries.[20] In a Central Committee "Instructions on Diplomatic Affairs," dated January 19, 1949, Mao further defined the principles the whole party had to follow: "With no exception, we will not recognize any of those embassies, legations, and consulates of capitalist countries, as well as the diplomatic establishments and personnel attached to them, accredited by the GMD government. We will treat them only as common foreigners and give them due protection." As for the party's attitude toward the United States, Mao stressed: "As American military attachés have been involved in direct support to the GMD's civil war efforts, we should dispatch our soldiers to supervise them and give no freedom of movement to them." In contrast, the directive stressed that diplomats from the Soviet Union and other new democratic countries should be treated differently, as "the foreign policy of the Soviet Union . . . had been thoroughly different from that of capitalist countries."[21]

At the Central Committee's Second Plenary Session in March 1949, the CCP leadership reached the consensus that the new China should neither hastily seek recognition from, nor pursue diplomatic relations with, the United States and other Western countries. "As for the question of the recognition of our country by the imperialist countries," asserted Mao, "we should not be in a hurry to solve it now and need not be in a hurry to solve it even for a fairly long period after country-wide victory."[22] Consequently, the decision not to recognize any foreign diplomatic establishment and personnel accredited to the GMD government was firmly established in early 1949 as one of the most important principles of the CCP's foreign policy. During 1949–1950, the CCP leadership stressed on nearly every occasion that the party would put the emphasis on pursuing strategic cooperation with the Soviet Union, and that establishing diplomatic relations with the United States and other Western countries was not a priority.[23]

There were profound causes underlying the CCP leadership's negative approach toward establishing relations with the United States. In the context of the escalating Cold War, it is easy to see that this stance correlated with the CCP's perception that the world had been divided between a socialist camp headed by the Soviet Union and a capitalist camp headed the United States, and that no middle ground existed between the two camps. These fundamentals left an indelible stamp on the CCP's attitude toward the recognition problem—when CCP leaders decided to lean to the Soviet-led socialist camp it is natural that they would have no illusion of an early Western recognition of the new China or establishing diplomatic relations with Western countries.

Underlying the CCP's suspicion of the United States was also the conviction that the United States had been historically hostile toward all revolutionary movements, including the Chinese revolution. Mao and other CCP theorists particularly noticed that in the twentieth century the United States had demonstrated an extreme hatred for revolutionary changes, especially those related to communism. For example, the United States had sent its troops to interfere with the Russian civil war after the 1917 Bolshevik Revolution, and the United States was the last major Western country to give diplomatic recognition to the Soviet Union. In the case of China, the United States was unsympathetic toward both the 1911 Revolution and the Great

Revolution from 1924 to 1927, as well as the Chinese Communist movement.[24]

Washington's continuous support of the GMD regime in China's civil war further confirmed the CCP's perception that the United States was the enemy of the Chinese revolution. Ever since the outbreak of the Chinese civil war, the CCP had constantly criticized Washington's pro-Jiang Jieshi (Chiang Kai-shek) approach. Mao and his fellow CCP leaders were further angered by the fact that U.S. Congress had passed appropriations in 1948 and 1949 to buttress the GMD's economic and military position. In the Central Committee's "Instructions on Diplomatic Affairs" of January 19, 1949, Mao and Zhou justified their policy of not recognizing diplomatic representatives accredited by the GMD regime by stating that "as many governments of imperialist countries, the U. S. imperialist government in particular, had supported the reactionary GMD government in opposing the liberation cause of the Chinese people, it would be very logical for us not to recognize their representatives in China as formal diplomats." So long as the United States still stood by Jiang's regime, CCP leaders would not agree to a diplomatic relationship with the United States.[25]

Mao's concerns over the impact early Western recognition might produce on China's domestic situation was another reason for the CCP's unwillingness to pursue relations with Western countries. To maintain revolutionary momentum after victory, Mao and his comrades believed it necessary to slow down the establishment of diplomatic relations with the West, the United States in particular. Party leaders concluded at the Central Committee's Second Plenary Session that in order to prevent imperialist countries from sabotaging the revolution from within the new China must not establish diplomatic relations with imperialist countries until imperialist privileges, power, and influence in China had been eliminated.[26] Mao's belief that economically China could live on its own further convinced him that Western recognition would not play a crucial role in reconstructing the new China.[27]

In a deeper sense, the CCP's attitude toward the recognition problem reflected the CCP leaders' comprehension of the history of China's century-old humiliating relations with the West. What dominated the thinking of Mao and his comrades here was again the revolutionary nationalism deeply rooted in China's history and modern experience.

China's modern exchanges with the West were to Mao and his comrades most humiliating and painful. China had lost its historical glory as the result of Western incursions after the 1840 Opium War. In the eyes of Mao and his fellow CCP leaders, the United States and other Western Powers had never treated China equally in modern history, and they thus had a strong suspicion whether the Western Powers in general and the United States in particular would treat the new China as an equal. Mao explained at the Second Plenary Session: "We are willing to establish diplomatic relations with all countries on the principle of equality, but the imperialists, who have always been hostile to the Chinese people, will definitely not be in a hurry to treat us as equals. As long as the imperialist countries do not change their hostile attitude, we should not grant them legal status in China."[28]

The key concept here is the idea of "equality" as defined by Mao. The CCP based their dealings with the United States in 1949–1950 on this concept and emphasized it repeatedly as the prerequisite for accommodation. Mao viewed "equality" basically as a historical problem pointing out that Sino-American relations had been dominated by a series of unequal treaties since China's defeat in the Opium War. He believed that in a moral sense the United States and other Western Powers owed the Chinese a heavy debt. As the first step toward establishing an equal relationship, he argued, the United States had to end as well as apologize for its unequal treatment of China. Only when the historical phenomenon of unequal exchanges between China and the West ended would it be possible for the new China to establish relations with Western countries.[29] So, Mao's definition of "equality" not only meant a total negation of America's roles in China in modern times; it also posed a crucial challenge to the existing principles of international relations followed by the United States and other Western powers. In Mao's opinion, America's willingness to change its attitude toward China represented a pass-or-fail test for American policymakers; and he believed that the United States could not pass the test.

This specific definition of "equality," however, was unacceptable to the Americans. President Truman, Secretary of State Dean Acheson and other American policymakers of their generation came to the political scene in an age when America had become a world power. Compared with their predecessors, they had much more aggressive and extensive an understanding of the concept "American interests."

This fact, combined with a long-existing belief in the superiority of American institutions and values, made this generation of American policymakers often exaggerate the power and influence of the United States, thus confusing their own definition of "principles of international relations" with the universal principles that should be obeyed by everyone in the world. They were therefore neither in a position nor willing to comprehend the real meaning of Mao's concept of "equality." In the final analysis, this reflected the divergences in political interests and ideologies of the two sides, as well as a profound confrontation of a cultural-psychological nature.

Mao and his fellow CCP leaders led their revolution toward victory through practical efforts. They certainly had the sense to fit their policies to reality. Least of all would they want to see China totally isolated in the world. As long-time players of the "united front" strategy, Mao and his fellow CCP leaders were more than willing to weaken the threat of the enemies and potential enemies toward revolutionary China. While facing Western countries on the recognition problem, Mao and the other CCP leaders tried to distinguish between primary and secondary enemies. Strongly influenced by the Chinese diplomatic tradition of "utilizing the barbarians to check the barbarians" (*yi yi zhi yi*), they hoped to treat with certain Western countries differently to counterbalance the United States, perceived as their most dangerous enemy. Zhou Enlai stressed at the enlarged Politburo meeting in January 1949 that the CCP should not only distinguish between the "international democratic front" and "imperialist front" but should take advantages from contradictions among imperialist countries as well.[30] Mao and Zhou reminded their comrades that the CCP needed to treat "concrete diplomatic cases differently in light of the real nature of the problem and the circumstance" in order to "show flexibility while staying firm on problems concerning principles."[31] In July 1949, when CCP organs in Shanghai reported that there were signs that problems existed between British and Americans remaining in Shanghai, Mao stated in a telegram to the CCP East China Bureau that "as contradictions existed between the United States and Great Britain on the China problem, we should be ready to take advantage of these contradictions."[32] Mao and the other CCP leaders did not want to become ideological diehards.

The question involved here, however, is how to assess the limits of flexibility of the CCP's external policy in the late 1940s. Since the early 1970s, many scholars have argued that the CCP's hostility toward the United States was basically a response to American hostility toward the CCP, and that if Washington's China policy had been more flexible, the CCP's policy toward the United States could have been less hostile. Consequently, these scholars believed that the CCP's foreign policy was in its essence "situational," and that with a different American policy an accommodation could have emerged between the revolutionary China and the United States in the late 1940s.[33]

These scholars have exaggerated the flexibility of the CCP's foreign policy while at the same time neglecting the party leadership's determination to adhere to the party's fundamentals. In fact, almost every time Mao mentioned that the CCP should maintain flexibility in its dealing with Western countries, he always emphasized that under no circumstance should the party sacrifice its basic revolutionary principles. For example, when Zhou talked at the January 1949 Politburo meeting about taking advantage of the contradictions among imperialist countries, he emphasized particularly that while doing so the party should never waver from its own principles.[34] In the telegram to the CCP East China Bureau in July 1949, Mao called on to the possibility of utilizing the contradictions among the imperialists, but he stressed at the same time the need for the party to adhere to diplomatic principles established by the central leadership.[35] Mao and the CCP leadership thus created a situation allowing little space for a flexible foreign policy, let alone an accommodation with the United States.

Washington's Nonrecognition Strategy

For Washington's policymakers, the Ward case posed serious challenges on how to deal with a revolutionary regime. For a period, they were unclear what had occurred in Shenyang. The State Department tried to use diplomatic channels to reestablish contact with the Shenyang consulate, while at the same time limiting publicity in order not to complicate the situation.[36] Starting in early December 1948, George Hopper, U.S. consul general in Hong Kong, repeatedly contacted Qiao Mu (Qiao Guanhua), head of the Hong Kong branch of the Xinhua News Agency, to regain communication with the Shenyang consulate. Qiao, refusing to assist the Americans in reestablishing contact with the Shenyang Consulate, responded in

January 1949 that the Ward case "was part of a larger question of U.S. attitude toward new government and toward the KMT [GMD]."[37] In the following months, the State Department continued to instruct Hopper and O. Edmund Clubb, U.S. consul general in Beiping, to convey the message that the U.S. government took the CCP's mistreatment of American diplomats in Shenyang as "a violation of international law and custom." As of May 1949, however, the Americans achieved no progress toward the solution of the Ward case. They were told only that the CCP's regulations would not permit official contact with American diplomats in Shenyang "owing to the absence of recognition."[38]

Under the shadow of the Ward case, policymakers in Washington found it more difficult than before to discuss the recognition problem with the CCP. Confident in America's values, strength, and influence, they saw recognition (or the threat of nonrecognition) as a possible weapon to put pressure on the CCP. From the beginning, they linked America's recognition of Communist China to the CCP's willingness to fulfill China's obligation in established treaties and agreements with foreign countries. For example, on February 3, 1949, Secretary of State Dean Acheson instructed Clubb to make it clear on an "appropriate occasion" that the CCP's acceptance of Chinese treaty obligations was the basis for American recognition of the Communist regime.[39] On May 13, 1949, three weeks after the Communist occupation of Nanjing, mentioned earlier, Acheson cabled to Stuart three basic conditions for American recognition: "a. de facto control of territory and administrative machinery of state, including maintenance public order; b. ability and willingness of govt to discharge its international obligations; c. general acquiescence of people of country in govt in power."[40] The key here was that the CCP should prove to the United States that it had the ability and willingness to "discharge its international obligation." He implied that the United States would not recognize the Chinese Communist regime until it adjusted its attitudes in line with the diplomatic heritage of the old China and adjusted its foreign policy to the standards set by the Americans.

The Ward case certainly played a role in Washington's adoption of a nonrecognition policy toward the new Chinese Communist regime. Indeed, it is inconceivable that Washington would have given positive consideration to a revolutionary regime at a time when it was detaining American diplomats. In this sense, the CCP's management of the

Ward case, as Acheson viewed it, precluded the possibility of any American recognition of Communist China.[41]

However, Washington's nonrecognition policy had a background much broader and more complicated than the gloomy impact of the Ward case. First and foremost, this policy was the product of the emerging Cold War and America's global strategy of containment. To understand this problem, we need to review briefly the American economic-political strategy toward China aimed at preventing "China from becoming an adjunct of Soviet power."

After the Second World War, the Soviet Union emerged as the main adversary of the United States in the world. In order to meet the challenge of the perceived Soviet threat on a global scale, policymakers in Washington made the containment of the expansion of Soviet influence in the Far East a primary goal of U.S. policy toward China. In the final analysis, it was the desire to contain Soviet expansion that determined America's generally pro-Jiang policy during China's Civil War.[42]

Jiang's impending defeat in China forced policymakers in Washington to reexamine the means and goals of American China policy in late 1948 and early 1949. Preoccupied with a series of crises with the Soviet Union in Europe, especially the one caused by the Berlin blockade, the Truman administration's review of its China policy focused on the possible impact of the rise of a Communist China upon the overall confrontation between the two superpowers. President Truman, Secretary of State Acheson and others in Washington wanted to prevent the triumph of the Chinese Communist revolution from causing an irreparable reversal of the strategic balance of power in the world.

After a series of deliberations, the State Department initiated in late 1948 a comprehensive review of America's China policy, prepared by the department's new Policy Planning Staff (PPS) headed by George Kennan. The resulting document, PPS 39, was candid and explicit. Recognizing that the GMD was "on the verge of losing their long struggle with the Chinese Communists," PPS 39 asserted that it would be unwise for the United States to use its military strength to "reverse the course of the civil war" because China was not for anyone to gain or to lose. PPS 39, however, did not recommend accepting the new political realities created by the CCP-GMD struggle in China. Instead, the document set up three immediate aims for America's China policy: "to continue to recognize the National Government as now constituted"; "with the disappearance of the National Government as we now know it, make our decision regarding recognition in the light of circumstances at that time"; and, most important, "to prevent so far as possible China's becoming an adjunct of Soviet politico-military power."[43]

A crucial assumption underlying the PPS's proposals was that China was not a military and industrial power and that the rise of a Communist-controlled China did not impose a direct threat to vital American interests in the Asian-Pacific area, let alone on a global scale. The loss of China was undesirable, but not unendurable. PPS 39, for example, emphasized that there was no reason to overestimate China's power potential because "in any war in the foreseeable future China could at best be a weak ally or at worst an inconsequential enemy."[44]

This low estimation of China's strategic potential was originally introduced by Kennan and widely shared by many other key figures in the State Department, the Pentagon, and Congress. It served as the basis of the State Department's China policy after Dean Acheson became secretary of state in January 1949. Acheson then oversaw the drafting of a series of policy papers based on the premises of PPS 39. In these papers, which presented a series of comprehensive, yet urgent, political-economic considerations that would guide the Truman administration's China policy throughout 1949 and 1950, Acheson shifted the focus of American strategy from direct support of the GMD to more subtle political and economic methods, including the nonrecognition policy and economic pressures, in order to influence the direction of the Chinese revolution and preserve American interests in China and the Far East.[45]

Among these papers regarding China, the two most important are National Security Council (NSC) 34 and NSC 41, which further clarified American policy goals. Admitting the virtual defeat of the GMD and longing for a possibility of eventual alienation of the Chinese Communists from Moscow, the drafters of NSC 34 recommended that the United States "continue to recognize the National Government until the situation is further clarified"; meanwhile, Washington should "avoid military and political support of any non-communist regimes in China" and "maintain so far as feasible active official contact with all elements in China." The drafters emphasized that Washington should not anticipate short term gains of this policy:

"The Kremlin waited twenty-five years for the fulfillment of its revolution in China. We may have to persevere as long or longer."[46]

NSC 41 focused more on available means to implement these
goals. Realizing that the United States had limited options, NSC 41
asserted that manipulating trade policy through "moderate restriction" might effectively pressure the CCP. Acheson, who supervised
the drafting of the document, believed that full-scale economic warfare, "through intimidation or direct economic pressure," might have
only a minimal effect on China's "subsistence economy" and could
possibly drive the Chinese into "a position of complete subservience
to the USSR." Instead, a policy of encouraging and, at the same time,
controlling nonstrategic trade with China through a licensing system
would "serve to indicate United States ability and intention to deal
drastically with China's foreign trade if necessary." This policy represented, accordingly, "the most effective strategic leverage to create rifts
between China and the Soviet Union."[47] Acheson believed that by
creating trade difficulties for the Chinese Communists the West could
make them understand the deficiencies of the Soviet Union, thus
turning China back to the West.

In accordance with the general policy of "making difficulties for
the [Chinese] Communists," Acheson decided that the United States
should not take positive steps to recognize the Chinese Communist
regime. Acheson and others in Washington realized that this stand
would not improve American-CCP relations. In the long run, however, they believed that nonrecognition would cause changes in Chinese Communist policy and create conditions for a rapprochement
between the United States and China on American terms. American
policymakers might be willing to accept reluctantly the failure of the
American-supported GMD regime in China but could not accept the
rise of a revolutionary China in the East. Unless the CCP clearly distanced itself from the Soviet Union and the international communist
movement, the United States would not recognize the new China.[48]

To increase leverage on the Chinese Communists, Acheson further
instructed American diplomats in Atlantic Treaty countries to discourage any attempt by Europeans to recognize or reach accommodation with China. In the summer and fall of 1949, Western countries
were urged to take common ground with the United States on the
recognition problem.[49] As a result, the hostility between the United
States and the CCP deepened.

The State Department's nonrecognition policy was deeply embroiled in America's domestic politics. In the late 1940s, as Cold War sentiments grew in the United States, the China lobby and the "China bloc" on Capitol Hill, raised a public outcry for the continuation of material assistance to Jiang even as the GMD suffered spectacular setbacks in the civil war. Many influential people, such as publisher Henry Luce of Time-Life, columnists Joseph and Stuart Alsop, former head of the "Flying Tigers" General Claire L. Chennault, China expert George Taylor, and Senators William Knowland (R-California), Kenneth Wherry (R-Nebraska), H. Alexander Smith (R-New Jersey), and Pat McCarran (D-Nevada), vociferously opposed the State Department's attempt to disengage the U.S. from the GMD. Some extreme members of the "China bloc" in Congress even charged that the GMD's defeat was a result of the treason within the State Department.[50]

At the same time, Jiang's boosters in Congress and in the State Department also insisted on the notion of a "monolithic communism" and challenged the idea of pursuing Titoism in China. They strongly questioned the wisdom of Acheson's policy to attempt to drive a "wedge" between the CCP and the Soviet Union.[51] Acheson and his advisers became very sensitive to public and congressional opinions on the China problem. They understood that while it was not easy to convince the public and leading legislators of the necessity to reduce support for Jiang, it was even more risky politically to discuss establishing relations with a Chinese Communist regime.[52] Consequently, the inflexible political approach of the "China blocs," backed by the vagaries of public opinion during the emerging Cold War, made accommodation with Communist China an unlikely choice for the Truman administration.

In a deeper sense, American policy toward political relations with a Chinese Communist regime was linked to concerns for maintaining American prestige and credibility in the world in general and in East Asia in particular. Most American policymakers in the early Cold War period had first gained their experiences in foreign affairs in the 1930s and they would never forget how Hitler pushed the world one step after another toward a global catastrophe. Acheson's experience, for example, convinced him that it was meaningless to try to come to terms with an enemy like Hitler, who would be willing to compromise only if his armed forces had been outstripped.[53] From this experience, American policymakers were convinced of the necessity to stand firm in the face of an international aggressor, believing that any concession would eventually lead to increased aggression and undermine the prospect of international peace and order.

When the United States became the leading world power after the Second World War, the traditional American sense of self-superiority was further reinforced by the newly emerged sense of "a world leadership responsibility." Policymakers in Washington were convinced that to preserve American interests in the postwar world the United States had to demonstrate to other actors in the international arena—friends and enemies alike—that it would always honor its international obligations. In the case of China, this perspective encouraged continuation of assistance to the GMD, an old friend of the United States, and discouraged the prospect of reaching accommodation with the Chinese Communists, a perceived threat to America's security interests in East Asia.[54]

The above factors caused Washington's nonrecognition policy toward Communist China, and the CCP's management of the Ward case further justified this policy. The American perception of the Chinese Communists combined hostility with contempt, which demonstrated typically the mentality of a dominant Western power in the face of a rising revolutionary country. Mao, angry about America's hostility toward the Chinese revolution, became extremely indignant when he sensed America's contempt of China as an inferior nation. The confrontation between the United States and the CCP would thus become far more than of a purely political nature.

The Failure of the Huang-Stuart Conversations

In May and June 1949, the fundamental differences between the CCP and the United States were further exposed in one of the most important direct contacts between them in 1949–50: the Huang Hua-Stuart conversations. After the Communist occupation of Nanjing in April 1949, Ambassador Stuart received permission from the State Department to stay.[55] Stuart had several goals in mind, believing that he could protect established American interests in China as well as those of American citizens remaining. He was also convinced that he could maintain a channel to communicate with CCP leaders, and, if possible, to influence the CCP leadership. In Stuart's view, the CCP's increasing "anti-American sentiment" was "a substantial residuum of genuine misapprehension." By approaching the Chinese Communists, Stuart believed that he could "remove or to some extent reduce" such misapprehensions. He asked Acheson for permission to meet top CCP leaders on an appropriate occasion to explain American policy and to convince them of the value of cooperating with the United States. Stuart believed that his long-time achievements in China as a devoted educator, as well as his acquaintance with many Chinese Communists, would enable him to have a frank and, possibly, fruitful contact with CCP leaders.[56] On April 6, Acheson authorized Stuart to have discussions with Communist leaders, but reminded him that "every care should be taken to avoid any publicity regarding your approach to the Chinese Communist leaders and the nature of such an approach."[57] After the PLA occupied Nanjing, Stuart quickly expressed his desire to contact representatives of the CCP and even proposed making a trip to Beiping to meet with CCP leaders.[58]

CCP leaders were originally puzzled to find Stuart in Nanjing. Almost immediately, however, they realized that this could serve as an opportunity to further explore America's attitude toward the CCP while making clear the CCP's own stand. In a telegram to the CCP's General Front-line Committee on April 28, one week after the Communist occupation of Nanjing, Mao speculated that the United States was now "contacting us through the third person to ask for establishing diplomatic relations with us" and that Great Britain was willing "to do business with us." Mao believed that this was because the old U.S. policy of supporting the GMD had failed, forcing the United States to change its policy. Mao stated that "if the United States (and Great Britain) cut off relations with the GMD, we could consider the problem of establishing diplomatic relations with them."[59] On April 30, Mao, in the name of the spokesman of the General Headquarters of the PLA, publicly suggested that the CCP would be "willing to consider the establishment of diplomatic relations with foreign countries" if such relations could be "based on equality, mutual benefit, mutual respect for sovereignty and territorial integrity and, first of all, on no help being given to the GMD reactionaries."[60]

Had Mao changed his basic attitude toward the recognition problem? Certainly not. What should be particularly noted here is that Mao emphasized once again the CCP's precondition for any possible accommodation with the United States: Washington should first abandon the GMD regime and its old China policy. If the United States did not cut off its connections with the GMD, Mao made it very clear that the CCP would not yield at all on the recognition issue.

Mao, however, did not reject contacts with the United States. One of the main purposes of the April 30 statement was to offer a basis for any possible discussions between the CCP and the United States. Meanwhile, following the established principles of the CCP leadership, the Military Control Commission of the Nanjing City refused to recognize the official status of American diplomats, although it agreed to protect them as common foreigners. After the PLA occupied Nanjing, some soldiers of the PLA's 35th Army entered Stuart's residence. Mao, after learning this, angrily criticized the 35th Army for its failure to ask instructions from the CCP Central leadership and ordered the Nanjing Municipal Military Control Commission to take responsibility for the matter immediately.[61] In addition, the CCP Central leadership ordered Nanjing authorities to allow all Western embassies and legations to maintain cipher communication with their governments.[62]

In late April, the CCP leadership appointed Huang Hua to be director of the Foreign Affairs Bureau under the Military Control Commission of Nanjing.[63] Huang was a graduate of Yenching University, where Stuart was once the president. He joined the CCP in the 1930s and later became Zhou's assistant. During Marshall's mediation in China in 1946–1947, he acted as Marshall's interpreter. His appointment to the post in Nanjing was evidently related to CCP's wish to deal with the Americans. Among other things, such as "taking over the Foreign Ministry of the GMD government and transforming foreign affairs," his tasks included "personal contact with Stuart."[64]

The CCP's interest in the Huang-Stuart contact was in the first place based on military considerations. As the Chinese civil war was still in progress, CCP leaders believed that they needed to pay special attention to the possibility of American military intervention, especially during the PLA's march toward Shanghai, the largest port city in China and commercial center in East Asia, "because the U.S. imperialists had deep roots in Shanghai."[65] This worry of direct American intervention was further strengthened by Stalin's advice that the CCP should not exclude "the danger of Anglo-American forces landing in the rear of the main forces of the PLA."[66] The Stuart-Huang contact, in the eyes of CCP leaders, would serve as a practical channel for them to convey messages to and get information from the Americans, thus pinning down the military movement of the Americans through diplomatic activities. Mao therefore instructed Huang Hua that the purpose of his meeting with Stuart was "to explore the intentions of the U.S. government."[67] When Stuart informed Huang that the United States would not militarily intervene in China's civil war and that American naval vessels in Shanghai had received orders to leave the combat zone, CCP leaders were greatly relieved and ordered the PLA units attacking Shanghai to act resolutely against GMD ships staying in the Shanghai port.[68]

The CCP leadership also believed that contact with Stuart offered an opportunity to press Washington to cut off its connections with the GMD and to stop "interfering with China's internal affairs." In a telegram to the CCP Nanjing Municipal Committee on May 10, 1949, Mao set forth a series of guidelines for Huang. He instructed Huang to "listen more and talk less" while meeting Stuart. Whenever expressing his own ideas, Huang should follow the tones of the PLA spokesman's April 30 statement. Huang needed to make it clear to Stuart that the meeting between them was informal because diplomatic relations did not exist between the CCP and the United States. Mao asked Huang to be "cordial to Stuart while talking to him if Stuart demonstrated also a cordial attitude," but Huang should avoid being "too enthusiastic." If Stuart expressed the desire to remain American ambassador to China, Huang should not rebut him. In response to the CCP Nanjing Municipal Committee's request to ask "the United States to do more things beneficial to the Chinese people" as part of the CCP's conditions to establish relations with the United States, Mao criticized that this "implied that the U.S. government had done something beneficial to the Chinese people in the past" and that it would "leave the Americans an impression as if the CCP were willing to get American aid." Instead, Mao dictated the following principles as Huang's guidelines for discussions with Stuart:

> Our request now is that the United States should stop supporting the Guomindang, cut off its connections with the GMD remnants, and never try to interfere with China's internal affairs. . . . No foreign country should be allowed to interfere with China's internal affairs. In the past, the United States interfered with China's internal affairs by supporting the GMD in the civil war. This policy should stop imme-

diately. If the U.S. Government is willing to consider establishing diplomatic relations with us, it should stop all assistance to the GMD and cut off all contacts with the remnants of the reactionary GMD forces.[69]

Mao had thus defined the fundamentals for Huang Hua's conversations with Stuart. Huang could be personal, gentle, and even touch upon such sensitive questions as establishing diplomatic relations with the United States. Under no circumstance, however, would he deviate from the determination "to make a fresh start" for the new China's foreign policy. Unless the United States was willing to follow the CCP's conditions, Mao left no doubt on this point, the CCP would not consider recognizing America's "rights" in China.

In early May, Stuart and Huang Hua began a series of secret meetings. Their hoped-for conversations, however, proved quickly to be no more than monologues stating the policy principles of each side. Stuart emphasized the legitimacy of American interests in China and tried to convince the Chinese Communists that they had to change their behavior and accept widely recognized international regulations and principles. Huang, on the other hand, stressed repeatedly that the new China viewed America's cutting off relations with the GMD as the precondition for establishing formal relations. Huang also pointed out that relations between the two countries, including economic exchanges, had to be placed on an equal and mutually beneficial foundation, implying that Sino-American relations in the past had not been equal and thus placing the Americans in the position of a criminal facing trial.[70]

CCP leaders showed interest in Stuart's request to visit Beiping. They believed that by entertaining Stuart there, they could further test American policy toward China and, possibly, drive a wedge into the American-led international alliance against Communist China. But they would handle Stuart's visit very carefully, without creating any illusion of a CCP-American accommodation. After careful consideration, Zhou Enlai arranged for Lu Zhiwei, president of the Yenching University, to write to invite Stuart to visit Beiping, informing Stuart at the same time through Huang Hua that he could meet top CCP leaders during his Beiping trip.[71] Zhou, in a telegram to the CCP Nanjing Municipal Committee on June 30, stressed that whether Stuart came to Beiping or not, the CCP "would have no illusion of U.S. imperialism changing its policy"; and that it should be made clear that

Stuart had not come to Beiping at the invitation of the CCP, so that the Americans would not use this as "an excuse for propaganda."[72]

When the Stuart-Huang contacts were still underway, Mao outlined China's foreign policy at the Preparatory Session of the New Chinese Political Consultative Committee in mid-June. He emphasized that the new China was "willing to discuss with any foreign government the establishment of diplomatic relations on the basis of the principles of equality, mutual respect for territorial integrity and sovereignty."[73] Mao's statement has been taken by many scholars as an indication that the CCP leadership was willing to reach an accommodation with the United States.[74] The key, however, was the two preconditions: to sever relations with the GMD and to treat the new China in an equal and mutually beneficial way. In the same speech, Mao also stressed that if certain foreign governments wanted to establish relations with the new China they must "sever relations with the Chinese reactionaries, stop conspiring with them or helping them and adopt an attitude of genuine, and not hypocritical, friendship toward People's China." What was implicit in these words was the necessity for the Americans to say farewell to the past before they could discuss establishing relations with the new China. Therefore Mao's statement was no more than another expression of the CCP's determination not to trade basic revolutionary principles for the recognition of Western countries.[75]

Not surprisingly, at the same time that Mao issued the above statement the CCP escalated their charges against Ward. On June 19, 1949, the CCP alleged through its media that the American consulate general at Shenyang had links with an espionage case directed by an American "Army Liaison Group." The Xinhua News Agency published a lengthy article reporting that "a large American espionage bloc" had been discovered in Shenyang. According to the article, "many pieces of captured evidence show clearly that the so-called Consulate General of the United States at Shenyang and the Army Liaison Groups are in fact American espionage organizations, whose aim was to utilize Japanese special service as well as Chinese and Mongols in a plot against the Chinese people and against the Chinese people's revolutionary cause and world peace."[76] On June 22, Mao instructed the Northeast Bureau not to allow any member of the American consulate to leave Shenyang before the espionage case had been cleared up.[77] Two days later, Mao personally approved an article,

entitled "The British and American Diplomacy, an Espionage Diplomacy," prepared by the Xinhua News Agency, calling on the whole
party to mobilize to expose the "reactionary nature" of American and
British diplomacy, and to maintain a high vigilance against it.[78]

Recent studies by Chinese scholars in the PRC indicate that the
espionage charge against Ward and the U.S. Consulate in Shenyang
was probably an exaggeration of the situation and no convincing Chinese evidence has ever been released to prove the charge.[79] To Mao
and CCP leaders, irrespective of the extent to which they believed in
this charge, the new accusations against Ward and his colleagues
offered the opportunity to further an anti-American mood among
Chinese population and also justified their management of the Ward
case.[80] Most important of all, Mao and the CCP leadership used this
to send the Americans a clear message: if necessary, the Chinese Communists did not fear a confrontation with the United States.

On the American side, the Huang-Stuart conversations failed to
mitigate Washington's reluctance to reach an accommodation with
the Chinese Communists. On June 3, it was reported to the State
Department that Zhou Enlai had expressed an extraordinary
démarche to the U.S. consul general in Beiping that China was "on
the brink of complete economic collapse" and desperately needed
assistance "from the U.S. and the U.K." Trade relations between China
and the United States, according to this message, "would have a defi-
nite softening effect on the Communist party's attitude toward the
Western countries."[81] Years of investigation have provided no evidence to prove that Zhou authored this message and it is now widely agreed by historians both in China and in the United States that
this message may have been fabricated.[82] Nevertheless, the State
Department accepted the message as genuine at the time. Although
Consul General Clubb, who received the message in Beiping, strongly urged the State Department to give a positive response, policymakers in Washington acted slowly. Not until two weeks after the "Zhou
message" reached Washington was Clubb authorized to contact Zhou,
and then Zhou's "spokesman" had disappeared.[83]

The escalation of the Ward case made it less possible for policymakers in Washington to favor Stuart's plan to visit Beiping. In the
judgment of Truman and other top American policymakers, Stuart's
proposed trip to Beiping would inevitably cause a massive attack on
the administration by pro-GMD factions in Congress and in the press.

Furthermore, they were afraid that "the Communists would try to make as much capital as they could out of such a visit," and that the United States would lose a strong means to pressure CCP leaders. Consequently, at the end of June, Truman vetoed Stuart's proposal.[84]

Before he heard that Stuart would not come to Beiping, Mao issued his "leaning to one side" statement, announcing that the new China would support the Soviet Union in international affairs. Then a CCP delegation led by Liu Shaoqi secretly visited the Soviet Union, which proved to be an important step toward the formation of a strategic cooperation between Communist China and the Soviet Union.[85] One month later, in response to the *China White Paper* published by the State Department, Mao initiated a country-wide anti-American propaganda campaign. He wrote five articles criticizing America's China policy from both historical and current perspectives and denounced the United States as the most dangerous enemy of the Chinese people.[86]

On the American side, the State Department made further efforts to consolidate a "common front" on the nonrecognition policy. In meeting with Ernest Bevin, the British foreign minister, in September 1949, Acheson insisted that "the Communists recognize international obligations in full as a prerequisite to recognition." He also strongly urged Great Britain and other Atlantic Treaty countries to "consult fully and carefully and concert policies on recognition of the Chinese Communist Government."[87] Meanwhile, the Truman administration supported the GMD's decision to block Chinese coastal areas by naval forces, hoping that this would cause economic problems for the CCP and strengthen America's bargaining power.[88] The gulf between the CCP and the United States widened.

A Diplomatic Impasse

On October 1, 1949, the People's Republic of China was formally established; the same afternoon, Zhou Enlai notified foreign governments of the formation of People's China. A copy of this notification was sent to "Mr. O. Edmund Clubb" to convey to the U.S. government. Zhou stated in the letter of transmittal that "it is necessary that there be established normal diplomatic relations between the People's Republic of China and all countries of the world."[89] Meanwhile, as a practical step toward building the new China's diplomatic framework, the PRC government decided to treat the problem of establishing diplomatic relations with foreign countries with the following distinctions: while relationship with communist countries could be established without negotiation, diplomatic relations with "nationalist countries" and "capitalist countries" would be formed only after the other countries clarified their attitude toward the GMD regime through the process of negotiation.[90]

The State Department believed that "the announcement of the establishment of the Chinese Communist 'government' would not add any urgency to the question of recognition."[91] On October 3, a State Department spokesman announced that because the Chinese Communist regime did not promise to "recognize international obligations" the United States would not recognize it.[92] Different opinions concerning recognition did exist both inside and outside the State Department. For example, at a State Department-organized round-table conference, which comprised mostly scholars, in early October 1949, many participants stated that the United States should recognize China, and some even believed that recognition should come immediately.[93] The mainstream in Washington, however, believed in nonrecognition. On October 12, Acheson told the Senate Foreign Relations Committee that the State Department would continue to follow those guidelines he had set up earlier in the year on the recognition of the Chinese Communist regime. The same day, Acheson informed American diplomats around the world that American policy toward recognition remained "unchanged" and he asked "friendly governments" to "maintain common attitude" toward the recognition of Communist China.[94]

Mao and his fellow CCP leaders, now certain that prospects for an American recognition of Communist China were remote, again emphasized that Communist China would not pursue early diplomatic relations with Western countries. In an internal instruction to its regional branches on October 19, 1949, the Xinhua News Agency, expressing the ideas of the CCP leadership, stressed that it was the British and Americans, not the CCP, "who were eager to establish diplomatic relations," and that the CCP "should maintain an attitude of waiting and seeing toward the [recognition] problem." The instruction particularly warned that "it is a big mistake to make people believe that we are eager to establish diplomatic relations with Britain and America."[95] In a speech to cadres of the Ministry of Foreign

Affairs on November 8, Zhou Enlai made it clear that the CCP's view of the recognition problem had not changed. He stressed that "in order to open the [new China's] diplomatic front, we must first distinguish enemies from friends."Therefore, emphasized Zhou, the new China needed to "establish brotherly friendship with the Soviet Union and other People's Democratic Countries," as well as "to be hostile to the imperialists and to oppose them."[96]

As Mao acted to translate the "leaning to one side" policy from rhetoric to reality by visiting the Soviet Union in December 1949, the CCP leadership decided to take further measures to expose the "imperialist nature" of American policy, to strike at the "arrogance" of American attitude toward China, and to cut off any remaining illusion about a Sino-American accommodation among Chinese people, Western-educated intellectuals in particular. On October 24, 1949, Ward and four other consulate employees were arrested by the Shenyang Public Security Bureau under the pretext that Ji Yuheng, a Chinese messenger at the American Consulate, had been mistreated and "seriously injured" by Ward.[97] *Dongbei ribao* (Northeast Daily), the Shenyang based party newspaper, editorialized on October 25 that "we Chinese people sternly protest against this violent act and will back up People's Government in meting out to the criminals headed by Ward legal sanctions due them."[98] CCP authorities wanted to emphasize that Ward's arrest was within the sovereign authority of Communist China.

The arrest of Ward and his colleagues caused indignant reaction in the United States. The *New York Times* claimed, "We cannot afford, if we are to retain a shred of prestige anywhere in Asia, to let such men as Angus Ward . . . suffer any further as martyrs to our inability to decide what can and should be done. If the Chinese Communists are illiterate in the language of international diplomacy and decency, we will have to draw them a picture they can understand." The *New York World Telegram* further suggested that the picture be drawn by America's Pacific fleet.[99]

Policymakers in Washington had to respond. The State Department instructed Clubb to meet Zhou Enlai or other high-ranking Chinese officials to present an American protest against the "arbitrary action" of the Chinese Communist authorities. But Clubb was unable to find a way to reach CCP leaders.[100] President Truman expressed the desire to see if the United States could "get a plane in to bring these people out." He also indicated that the United States should consider blockading coal transportation from ports in northern China to Shanghai.[101] The president instructed the Joint Chiefs of Staff to consider using force to free the diplomats, but the latter recommended working for Ward's release through negotiations.[102] At the same time, Acheson, Stuart, and others believed that an economic blockade, rather than military forces, could be used as an effective means to force the CCP to release Ward and his colleagues.[103] Facing the new tension in Sino-American relations, Acheson announced at a news conference on November 16 that the United States would not consider diplomatic recognition of the Chinese Communist regime until the Americans held at Shenyang were released.[104]

The CCP leadership paid little attention to these American threats. One month after Ward's arrest, he and his colleagues were tried by a People's Court at Shenyang. The trial followed the CCP's tight procedures: the Americans were denied any defense, nor were they able to question witnesses or plaintiffs. On November 21, they were convicted and sentenced to a year's probation and expelled from China. At the same time, the Shenyang People's Court announced the expulsion of the remainder of the non-Chinese staff at the former American Consulate at Shenyang because of their involvement in "spy activities." On December 11, 1949, Ward and his staff left China.[105]

The CCP was willing to escalate the confrontation with the United States. On January 6, 1950, when Mao Zedong was in the Soviet Union, the Military Control Commission of Beijing City ordered the requisitioning of the former military barracks of the American diplomatic compound in Beijing, which had been transformed into regular offices.[106] The CCP carefully prepared their rationale for action. The Xinhua News Agency argued that the legal basis of these barracks was the "unequal" Chinese-American treaty signed by the GMD and the United States in 1943. The new government had announced its determination to abolish these unequal treaties between the old China and the Western powers, leaving no reason to allow these barracks to be controlled by an "imperialist country." Requisitioning these military barracks was therefore a crucial step in enforcing "complete abolition of all imperialist privileges in China and all unequal treaties imposed on China [by Western powers]."[107] The CCP leadership used this move to send the message that the party was determined to maintain its principles, even at the risk of provoking a confrontation with the U.S.[108]

Beijing's decision further irritated policymakers in Washington. To protest Beijing's "violation of its treaty obligations," Acheson declared in mid-January his intentions to pull out American diplomats from mainland China.[109] This did not bother CCP leaders because they had long prepared for this eventuality. On January 13, 1950, Mao Zedong cabled from Moscow to Liu Shaoqi, in charge of the party's affairs during Mao's absence: "I agree to . . . the requisition of foreign military barracks, and we have to prepare for the United States to retreat all consulates in China." Several days later, Mao stressed in another telegram to Liu: "It is extremely favorable to us that the United States withdraws all diplomats from China."[110] In a statement issued by the Xinhua News Agency on January 18, 1950, the CCP declared that "on problems concerning the maintenance of the interests of the Chinese people as well as the safeguarding of China's sovereignty, the Chinese people will never consider the will of imperialists." The statement reiterated that "all unequal treaties made by imperialists and their privileges of aggression should be abolished," particularly emphasizing that "whether the imperialists will withdraw from China or not, whether they will shout or not, whether they will treat us as equals or not, will have no influence on the just stand of the Chinese people."[111]

Policymakers in Washington were now fully convinced that there existed no prospect for an American recognition of the Chinese Communist regime. But Acheson did not want to give up the last opportunity to make clear to Beijing the American view of the causes of the friction between the two countries. In late March, he instructed Clubb to try to meet Zhou Enlai informally before his departure from China. Clubb should tell the Chinese that the American public did not understand the CCP's management of the Ward case and a series of other similar affairs. Clubb should not leave the Chinese with the impression that the discussion would lead to American recognition of the Chinese Communist regime.[112] However, Clubb was unable to meet Zhou. On April 10, an official of Beijing's Alien Affairs Office reiterated to him that the termination of all American support to the GMD was the prerequisite for the discussion of any other issues between the new China and the United States.[113] Deeply disappointed with and, even angered by, his dealing with the CCP leaders, Clubb wrote to George Kennan on April 25, shortly before his departure from China, claiming that the CCP had "oriented its own program to Moscow's and attached China to the Soviet chariot, for better or worse." He concluded that Beijing leaders "do not think like other men," and that they were prepared to risk world destruction in pursuit of their goals.[114] Clubb's words indicated clearly that the gulf between Beijing and Washington had further widened.

The Ward case and the recognition controversy demonstrate the profound gap between the CCP and the United States. On the one hand, CCP leaders took American recognition as a test of America's willingness to accept the great changes brought about by the Communist revolution in China (as the first step the U.S. should cut off its connections with the GMD). The American charge that the CCP's management of the Ward case was "a violation of the basic international concept" had little appeal to the Chinese revolutionaries who were anxious to throw off all vestiges of Western influence. Indeed, CCP leaders believed that the Americans were using the "basic concept of the international law" to control subordinate countries, which had nothing to do with such a revolutionary country as Communist China. On the other hand, American policymakers, driven by the strategy of containment, confined by America's domestic setting, and influenced by considerations about preserving "American prestige," emphasized that the key to recognition lay in the CCP's acceptance of basic principles of international relations as defined by the United States. Policymakers in Washington (especially Acheson) did try to understand the CCP's behavior, but these conditions prevented them from appreciating the CCP's intense revolutionary nationalism, and they seldom considered the possibility of a compromise between the CCP's devotion to its understanding of China's national independence and the American adherence to "widely-accepted international custom and principles."

At this stage, the two sides did not lack channels of communication; they lacked, however, mutually understandable political language and common codes of behavior essential for communication. The Americans stressed the importance of individual liberty, international law and custom, and responsibility to maintain treaty obligations. The CCP claimed that "any struggle on the part of the oppressed people to oppose the oppressors was a just one." Both sides believed that they were correct; neither of them was able to place itself in the other's shoes. Consequently, the more they contacted each other, the greater the conflict became. Such a pattern, as we will see, would dominate the development of Sino-American relations throughout the 1949–1950 period.

3

"Leaning to One Side": The Formation of the Sino-Soviet Alliance

On June 30, 1949 Mao issued his famous "lean-to-one-side" statement. In a long article entitled "On People's Democratic Dictatorship," broadcast by the CCP's radio service and reprinted by all major CCP papers, Mao announced the new China's special relationship with the Soviet Union:

> Externally, unite in a common struggle with those nations of the world which treat us as equal and unite with the peoples of all countries. That is, ally ourselves with the Soviet Union, with the People's Democratic Countries, and with the proletariat and the broad masses of the people in all other countries, and form an international united front. . . . We must lean to one side.[1]

Mao's statement demonstrated that the CCP and the Soviet Union shared a common political ideology. But ideology alone does not offer a complete answer to the origins of the CCP's lean-to-one-side approach, especially given the CCP's frequently inharmonious relations with Moscow in the past. In order to understand the making of this policy, we need to examine the CCP's historical exchanges with the Soviet Union, to explore the interactions between the party's Soviet policy and its general domestic and international strategies, and to define the relations between Beijing's decision to ally with the Soviet Union and Communist China's increasing confrontation with the United States.

Background

Mao's lean-to-one-side statement, viewed in the context of international politics, can be seen as a logical outgrowth of the CCP's longtime revolutionary policy of attaching itself to the "international progressive forces" led by the Soviet Union. By the late 1940s, CCP leaders had clearly perceived the postwar world order as divided into two camps, one headed by the Soviet Union and the other by the United States and viewed their revolution as an inseparable part of the Soviet-led international proletarian movement. Mao's statement is consistent with this view of the postwar world structure. The political implications of Mao's decision are straightforward: in an international confrontation between the Soviet-led progressive camp and the American-led reactionary camp, the CCP had to ally itself with the Soviet Union against the United States.

The lean-to-one-side approach also grew out of the CCP's assessment of the serious nature of America's threats to the security interests of Communist China. As the CCP neared final victory in China's civil war in early 1949, Mao and his fellow CCP leaders became very concerned about the prospect of direct American intervention in China. Although the American military had never intervened, CCP leaders, given their belief in the aggressive nature of U.S. imperialism, continued to view the United States as a dangerous enemy. In the eyes of Mao and the CCP leadership, "it was the possibility of military intervention from imperialist countries that decided the necessity of China allying itself with socialist countries."[2] By allying China with the Soviet Union, Mao and the CCP leadership hoped to be in a stronger position to face a potentially hostile America.

The CCP's lean-to-one-side decision had also domestic roots. Sources now available indicate that the CCP leadership differed on the direction of the new China's domestic and foreign policies with some pro-Communist "democratic parties." Mao Zedong and Zhou Enlai argued that these people "still had illusions about U.S. imperialism" in the sense that they wanted the new China to maintain a less radical stand in international politics.[3] The opinion of General Zhang Zhizhong, a former close associate of Jiang Jieshi who had just joined the Communist side, was typical in this regard. In a discussion with Mao in May 1949, Zhang suggested that China, while uniting with the Soviet Union, should seek accommodation with the United States and other Western countries. He believed that such a policy would be in the interests of the Chinese nation. Mao disagreed, arguing that the attempt to pursue the "doctrine of the mean" [*zhong yong zhi dao*] in international politics would be dangerous to the cause of Chinese Communist revolution because it would weaken the revolution's dynamics and blur the distinction between revolution and counter-revolution.[4] In order to promote the Chinese Communist revolution at home, Mao believed it essential for Chinese foreign policy to lean to one side.

As a practical policy choice, Mao's policy has to be understood within the context of the CCP's efforts to adjust relations with the Soviet Union during the last stage of China's civil war. When Mao issued his statement on June 30, 1949, he apparently had in mind the fact that a high-level CCP delegation, headed by Liu Shaoqi, would travel to the Soviet Union in two days.[5] Considering the frequently unpleasant history of CCP-Soviet relations, Mao hoped to send a strong signal of his willingness for friendship and cooperation.

The development of the CCP-Soviet relationship had been tortuous during the long course of the Chinese Communist revolution. In the 1920s and early 1930s, the CCP, as a branch of the Soviet-controlled Comintern, had to follow Soviet instructions. Among the party leadership, sharp disagreements existed between the native section headed by Mao and the international section headed by Wang Ming (Chen Shaoyu), a Soviet-trained orthodox Communist. Mao had long been stifled by the international section, which was supported by Stalin and the Soviet party. Mao never forgot this experience. After Mao emerged as the top CCP leader in the late 1930s, he continued to face pressures from the Comintern and the Soviet Union on several occasions. Between 1940 and early 1943, when he refused to follow the Soviet order to use the CCP's military forces to attract the main Japanese forces in China "to protect the Soviet Union," the Comintern severely criticized Mao and the CCP leadership.[6] In the early 1940s, the CCP's rectification campaign, a political movement designed to consolidate Mao's leading position in the party, was viewed suspiciously by the Soviet party and the Comintern, which suspected that the campaign represented an attempt to suppress the pro-Soviet section within the CCP.[7]

Even after the dissolution of the Comintern in 1943, the CCP continued to find its policies, especially its management of the unit-

ed front with the GMD, occasionally the target of Moscow's criticism.[8] At the Yalta Conference of 1945, Stalin promised Roosevelt
that he would not support the CCP in the internal conflict in China
in exchange for Roosevelt's agreement on the independence of
Outer Mongolia and other concessions in China. This promise was
obviously a severe offense to the CCP.[9] After Japan's surrender at the
end of the Second World War, Stalin cabled Mao twice in late August
1945, warning the Chinese Communists not to risk a civil war with
the GMD because "it would bring the danger of the complete
destruction of the Chinese nation." Mao was very unhappy with
these warnings.[10]

During the course of the 1946–1949 civil war, CCP-Soviet relations were again inharmonious. While contingently offering the CCP
assistance in its confrontation with the GMD, especially in the Northeast, Soviet leaders generally doubted the CCP's ability to win. Even
though the GMD insistently took a pro-American stand as the Cold
War intensified, the Soviet Union remained neutral.[11] Stalin even
pressured the CCP to compromise with the GMD, and Soviet media
kept a strange silence as CCP forces won a series of crucial military
victories.[12] Several Chinese sources contend that in early 1949, Stalin
advised Mao and the CCP leadership not to cross the Yangzi River in
order to avert triggering a direct Soviet-American confrontation.
Mao firmly rejected this suggestion.[13] Even by late February 1949,
after the PLA had forced the GMD government to move from Nanjing to Guangzhou, the Soviet ambassador remained with the GMD
government, transferring to Guangzhou. All this must have made it
difficult for the CCP to establish a close strategic cooperation with
the Soviet Union.[14]

All the above, however, gives only one side of the picture. After all,
Mao and his followers were Communists. In the long revolutionary
process, the CCP leadership kept or tried to keep an intimate relationship with Stalin and the Soviet party. Except for a short period
during the Chinese Red Army's "Long March" from southern to
northwestern China, the CCP Central Committee maintained daily
telegraphic communication with the Comintern and the Soviet
Communist party. Mao and the CCP leadership kept Moscow well
informed of nearly all their important decisions.[15] Even when the
CCP leadership strongly disagreed with Stalin and the Soviet party,
they avoided any open disputes with Moscow. Mao and the CCP

leadership believed that the divergences between themselves and the Soviets were no more than the ones that would sometimes emerge between brothers.[16]

When the tide of China's civil war turned in favor of the CCP, Mao showed a stronger willingness to seek a closer relationship with the Soviet Union. In mid-May 1948, Mao cabled Stalin, stating that the CCP lacked the experience for running China's national economy and asking the Soviet party to send experts to assist the CCP in economic recovery and reconstruction. In response, the Soviet Politburo sent, among others, I. V. Kovalev.[17] After the Soviet-controlled Cominform, successor to the Comintern, announced that Communist Yugoslavia and its leader Josip Tito were "traitors" to the communist world in late June 1948, the CCP immediately decided to stand on the side of the Soviet Union. A series of the party's internal documents emphasized that "if the Chinese people hope to win a complete victory in the revolution, they had to pursue a solid brotherly alliance with the Soviet Union."[18]

Believing it necessary to consult with Stalin about the strategic cooperation between the CCP and the Soviet Union, in the spring of 1948 Mao began to plan a visit to Moscow to meet Stalin. In order to concentrate on preparations for this visit, Mao stayed at a small village called Chennanzhuang from mid-April to late May (other members of the CCP Central Committee were then staying at Xibaipo).[19] In a report about the CCP's Politburo meeting to Stalin dated September 28, 1948, Mao mentioned that he had a series of questions to discuss with Stalin and the Soviet party's Central Committee and he planned to visit the Soviet Union in November. Then in another telegram to Stalin on October 16, Mao further clarified that he would be willing to hear Stalin's opinion about "convening the new political consultative conference and establishing the provisional central government (in China)." On December 30, 1948, Mao informed Stalin that the CCP Politburo would convene an enlarged meeting to discuss the party's strategic tasks of 1949, after which Mao planned to visit the Soviet Union.[20]

For whatever reason, however, Stalin was not interested in such a meeting at that time. He cabled Mao on January 14, 1949, stressing that since China's civil war was at a crucial juncture, it would be improper for Mao to leave China. Stalin offered to send a Politburo member as the representative of the Soviet party to China to listen to

Mao's opinions. Mao agreed.[21] Anastas Mikoyan, a Soviet Politburo member, was chosen to carry out this mission, which proved to be a crucial step toward the formation of the Sino-Soviet strategic alliance.

Mikoyan Comes to Xibaipo

From January 31 to February 7, 1949, Mikoyan secretly visited Xibaipo, the location of the CCP headquarters. Mao, with the other four members of the CCP Central Secretariat, Liu Shaoqi, Zhu De, Zhou Enlai, and Ren Bishi, held formal meetings with Mikoyan. At the beginning of the first meeting, Mikoyan explained to Mao why Stalin had not earlier agreed to receive Mao at Moscow. Stalin, according to Mikoyan, did not want Mao to leave his position during a critical stage of the war, and he was also concerned about Mao's safety and health. So, rather than invite Mao to the Soviet Union, Stalin sent Mikoyan to China. Mikoyan also stressed that Stalin had asked him merely to listen to the opinions of Mao and the Chinese Communists, but not make any important decision.

Dominating the meeting, Mao tried to neutralize what he thought might be Stalin's worries. He used almost three days to introduce the Soviets to the CCP's thinking on important domestic and international issues. Mao's central topic was the CCP's political design for the new China. He stated that the CCP, together with other anti-GMD democratic parties, would establish a Communist-led coalition government after the Communist victory. The main task of the government would be to lead China to a socialist society. Obviously aimed at easing Stalin's suspicion that Titoism was involved in the CCP's advocacy of such an idea, Mao emphasized that the government would be Marxist-Leninist in nature. While some government positions would be reserved for non-Communist "democratic figures," Mao made it clear that the CCP would firmly control the leadership of the government. Probably responding to Stalin's suggestion that CCP forces should not cross the Yangzi River, Mao pointed out that crossing the Yangzi was absolutely necessary for the CCP to destroy the remnants of the GMD and to "carry the revolution through to the end."

The new China's foreign policy was another focus of Mao's talks. He stressed repeatedly that it was the firm determination of the Chinese Communists to destroy totally the old China's diplomatic legacy. The new China, according to Mao, would adopt the strategy of "cleaning the house before entertaining guests" in its foreign affairs, meaning that the CCP would not pursue diplomatic relations with Western countries until the entire country had been "cleaned up." Mao clarified also that "true friends" of the Chinese people were welcome to stay in China, "helping us in the big cleaning." Mao thus implied that the Soviets would be such true friends.

Mao, touching upon the sensitive problem of the "American threat" to the Chinese revolution, also noted that the United States up to this point had avoided direct involvement in China's civil war. As he saw it, the United States' international obligations were too extensive and Western allies were unwilling to take risks in China. Thus, Mao stated, the Chinese Communists were truly in a favorable situation to win a nationwide victory, and were determined to do so. Mao, however, emphasized that it was yet unforeseeable if the United States would intervene directly when the PLA crossed the Yangzi River. By introducing the problem of "American threat" in such a way, Mao argued skillfully that the CCP needed the support of the Soviet Union without scaring the Russians away.[22]

Although Mao was eager to seek the Soviets' support of China's economic reconstruction and military buildup, he made no concrete request for Soviet assistance. This task was left for Zhou Enlai. After the formal meetings, Zhou met with Mikoyan separately. He further explained the plans for the construction of China's political and diplomatic framework and discussed problems such as the recovery of the transportation system and the reconstruction of China's economy after the formation of the new China. He made it clear that the CCP wanted active Soviet participation in China's post-revolution reconstruction.[23]

From the CCP's perspective, Mikoyan's trip to Xibaipo was important because it was the first formal contact between the CCP leadership and the Soviet Communist leaders in many years. Mao's systematic introduction of the CCP's domestic and international strategies offered the Soviets an opportunity to understand the CCP's stand and created an atmosphere conducive to discussion between equals. Mikoyan's visit thus served as the first step toward a new mutual understanding and cooperation between the CCP and the Soviet Union, which would finally lead to the formation of the Sino–Soviet alliance.

Liu Shaoqi in Moscow

After the PLA crossed the Yangzi River and occupied Nanjing in April 1949, the CCP had final victory firmly in its grasp. While constructing the domestic and international policy framework for the new China, Mao and the CCP leadership wanted to further promote relations between the CCP and the Soviet Union. In early May, CCP leaders decided that the time had come to send a delegation headed by a top CCP leader to Moscow. Liu Shaoqi and Zhou Enlai were placed in charge of preparations for the visit. Wang Jiaxiang, a senior CCP Central Committee member and former CCP representative to the Comintern in the 1930s, was summoned back from his post as party secretary in Manchuria to assist planning the visit.[24]

The preparations were ready by late June and the CCP Central Committee decided to assign Liu Shaoqi to lead the mission, authorizing him to discuss with Stalin all important problems concerning the international situation and Sino-Soviet relations. He would introduce to Stalin the considerations underlying the CCP's policy line (especially the CCP's policy of including non-Communist democrats into the CCP-led People's Political Consultative Conference), convince Stalin that the Chinese Communists were not Titoists, and lead the Soviets to a better understanding of China's situation and the nature of the Chinese revolution. He would also pursue practical Soviet support of the Chinese Communist regime, including a guaranteed Soviet recognition of the new China and Soviet military and other assistance. If everything moved smoothly, this mission would open the way for a personal trip by Mao to the Soviet Union in the near future.[25]

Mao and the CCP leadership saw Liu's visit as a crucial step in establishing strategic cooperation with the Soviet Union. Following Wang Jiaxiang's suggestion, the CCP Central Committee prepared a long memo for Liu to present to Stalin, which summarized the new China's domestic and international policies. The memo made it clear that the CCP would win China's civil war, and that the complete liberation of the whole of China was only a matter of time. The CCP leadership believed that it was now almost impossible for imperialist countries to intervene in large scale on the GMD's behalf. The imperialist countries, though, might send troops to disturb China's coastal areas or to carry out an economic embargo against China. This, however, would not change the outcome of China's civil war.

The memo gave a detailed introduction to the CCP's domestic policy, particularly the party's design of the new China's government structure. While emphasizing that the new China would adopt a system of "people's democratic dictatorship," the memo argued that such a system was in nature compatible with Lenin's ideas about "the dictatorship of workers and peasants."

Regarding the new China's foreign policy, the memo made it clear that the CCP would firmly stand on the side of the Soviet Union and other "new democratic countries" while at the same time "fighting against imperialist countries as well as maintaining the complete independence of the Chinese nation" in international affairs. The memo explicitly stated that "the relationship between the Chinese and Soviet parties and the consolidation of the friendship between the Chinese and Soviet nations were extremely significant for the two countries as well as to the whole world." The memo also mentioned that Mao planned to visit the Soviet Union when the new China and the Soviet Union established diplomatic relations.[26] To guarantee the success of Liu's trip, Mao knew that he had to do something significant and noticeable. His lean-to-one-side statement was apparently the signal introduced to catch Stalin's attention. When Mao praised the Soviet Union as the undisputed leader of the international progressive forces, he sent an unmistakable message to Stalin: now Stalin had no reason to suspect that the CCP leadership shared the thinking of Titoism.

Liu's delegation left Beijing on July 2. After an eight-day journey, the delegation arrived in Moscow on July 10. Among members of the delegation were Gao Gang, Wang Jiaxiang, Deng Liqun, and Ge Bao-quan. Shi Zhe was Liu's interpreter and Xu Jiepan was Gao Gang's. I. V. Kovalev, the Soviet general adviser to China, accompanied the delegation to Moscow.[27] During the CCP delegation's stay in the Soviet Union, they held four formal meetings with Stalin and other top Soviet leaders, in which they touched upon a series of crucial themes.

First, to the surprise and satisfaction of Liu and his comrades, Stalin apologized for having failed to give sufficient assistance to the CCP during the civil war. According to Shi Zhe's recollection, Stalin asked Liu at the second meeting: "Have we disturbed you [in China's civil war]?" Liu replied: "No!" Stalin answered: "Yes, we have been in the way of hindrance to you because our knowledge about China is too limited."[28] Although Stalin's apology came in a private meeting, it deeply impressed Mao and his fellow CCP leaders. Most important, CCP leaders viewed this as a clear sign of Stalin's willingness now to treat his Chinese comrades as equals.[29] Later, many top CCP leaders, including Mao, Liu, and Zhou, mentioned Stalin's apology on different occasions, using it as a strong justification for the CCP's lean-to-one-side approach.[30]

Second, the discussion focused on Soviet support of the newly established Chinese Communist regime. Around the time of Liu's visit, CCP leaders were concerned about the problem of international recognition of the Communist regime in China. While convinced that the United States and other Western countries would not offer quick recognition to the new regime, Mao and the CCP leadership were not sure if Moscow and the "new democracies" in Eastern Europe would do so either. Liu spent much time explaining to Stalin the CCP's domestic and international policies. He emphasized that the system of people's political consultative conference, which the CCP would adopt in China, followed China's specific situation, especially the fact that the CCP had a united front with several "democratic parties" in the struggle against the GMD. Under no circumstances would the CCP give up its leadership in post-revolution China. Stalin's response was again very positive and explicitly approved the CCP's domestic policy.[31] When Liu told Stalin that the CCP planned to establish a central government on January 1, 1950, Stalin advised the Chinese to take this step even earlier, stressing that "a long period of anarchy in China should not be allowed." He also promised that as soon as the CCP established a central government the Soviet Union would recognize it. Encouraged by Stalin's attitude, the CCP leadership decided to hasten the formation of the central government, and the CCP's confidence in Soviet support was thus bolstered.[32]

Third, Liu's visit produced a CCP-Soviet cooperation on the settlement of the Xinjiang (Sinkiang) problem, which was a substantial achievement for the CCP. As a strategically important region located in northwestern China next to Russian Kazakh, northern part of Xinjiang had long been viewed by the Russians as within their sphere of influence. In the late nineteenth and early twentieth centuries, several bloody disputes took place between China and Russia in northern Xinjiang. After the triumph of the Bolshevik revolution in 1917, Lenin's Soviet Russia acknowledged China's sover-

eignty over Xinjiang, but the Soviet Union had never fully relin-
quished its claim of interests there. In November 1944, a pro-Communist rebellion backed by the Soviet Union erupted in Tacheng,
Ili, and Ashan (the three northernmost counties in Xinjiang) and the
rebels had since controlled that area. When the CCP achieved decisive victory against the GMD in China's civil war in 1949, Xinjiang
became one of few regions still controlled by the GMD. During
Liu's visit to the Soviet Union, Stalin told Liu that, according to
Soviet intelligence reports, the United States planned to use Muslim
GMD forces in northwestern China to establish an independent
Islamic republic in Xinjiang, which he believed would be extremely harmful to both the CCP and the Soviet Union. He offered to
use the Soviet-supported revolutionary forces in northern Xinjiang
to check the GMD so that it would be easier for the PLA to enter
Xinjiang.[33] Then Moscow helped the CCP Central Committee to
establish direct contact with the revolutionary forces in northern
Xinjiang by assisting Deng Liqun, the CCP Central Committee's
liaison person, to travel from Moscow to northern Xinjiang. Before
the PLA finally took over Xinjiang in October 1949, the Soviet
Union and Outer Mongolia became the main link of communications and transportation between the CCP Central Committee and
CCP agents in Xinjiang.[34]

Most important of all, Liu's conversations with Stalin produced a
crucial consensus: while the Soviet Union would remain the center of
international proletarian revolution, the promotion of Eastern revolution would become primarily China's duty. Stalin stressed that the
world revolutionary forces were marching forward and much stronger
than ever before. He expressed the hope that the CCP would play a
more active role in advancing the rising tide of world revolution,
especially in East Asia. Stalin stressed that he was not flattering the
Chinese. He believed that since the Chinese had greater influence in
the colonial and semi-colonial countries in the East, it would be easier for China to help promote Eastern revolution than the Soviet
Union. Liu, on the other hand, emphasized to Stalin that the Chinese
viewed the Soviet Union as the undisputed leader of the progressive
forces of the world. He seemed very cautious in acknowledging
before Stalin that China would become the center of the Eastern revolution. Indeed, when Stalin toasted "the center of revolution moving
to the East and China," Liu refused to respond. But Liu agreed that

Communist China would try to contribute more in promoting revolutionary movements in Asia.[35]

Such an agreement on "division of labor" between the CCP and the Soviet leaders was based on their fundamental assessment of the world situation in the late 1940s. According to both Shi Zhe and Kovalev, when Liu asked Stalin's opinion about the possibility of a new world war, Stalin made it clear that the United States was not in a position to start a new world war against the Soviet Union at the moment and that this offered the Communists an opportunity to develop their own strength.[36] Shi Zhe recalls that when the Chinese were in Moscow, Stalin invited them to a documentary film which allegedly had recorded the Soviets testing an atomic bomb.[37] The film recorded the whole process of the test and the Chinese were told that they were the first group of foreigners to be allowed to share the information. By showing the Chinese this film, in Shi Zhe's view, Stalin was relaying to his Chinese comrades not only that the Soviet Union possessed the bomb but also the hope that China "would be protected by the bomb owned by a friend."[38]

There is no indication in available Chinese materials that the Korean problem came up in Liu's talks with Stalin.[39] We do know now, however, that in the summer and fall of 1949, right around the time when Liu Shaoqi was in the Soviet Union, the 164th and 166th Divisions of the PLA's Fourth Field Army, the majority of whose soldiers were of Korean nationality, were sent to North Korea.[40] Considering the close relationship existing between the Soviet Union and Kim Il-sung's North Korean regime and that the problem of promoting revolutionary movements in East Asia was one of the central topics of Liu-Stalin conversations, we have no reason to exclude the possibility that members of the Chinese delegation (such as Gao Gang, who had his own interpreter and had a much closer connection with North Korea as the CCP's head in the Northeast) and the Soviets had discussed such matters as sending PLA soldiers back to Korea during their stay in the Soviet Union.

As the conversations between Liu and Stalin were progressing smoothly, the CCP and the Soviet Union quickly entered discussions for establishing military and other cooperation between them.[41] On July 26, 1949, the CCP Central Committee cabled Liu, instructing him to explore with Stalin whether the Soviet Union would be willing to supply the Chinese with 100 to 200 Yak fighters and 40 to 80 heavy bombers, to help the Chinese train 1,200 pilots and 500 technicians in Soviet air schools, and to send air force advisers to China. If the Soviets agreed to the first two requests, the CCP Central Committee stated, Liu Yalou, commander of China's newly established air force, would visit the Soviet Union immediately to work out the details.[42] Following the CCP Central Committee's instructions, Liu Shaoqi met with Stalin, Bulganin, and other Soviet leaders on July 27 to discuss these CCP requests. The Soviet response was positive. Instead of accepting Chinese trainees in the Soviet Union as suggested by the CCP, they offered to assist the Chinese in establishing pilot schools in Manchuria. They also agreed to receive Liu Yalou in Moscow for more detailed discussions. Stalin promised Liu Shaoqi that he would authorize the Soviet Ministry of Armed Forces to give the Chinese requests favorable considerations. Liu Shaoqi telegraphed Stalin's promise to the CCP Central Committee immediately.[43]

After receiving Liu Shaoqi's report, the CCP Central Committee decided at once to send Liu Yalou to the Soviet Union. On July 29, Zhou Enlai informed Liu that he and three other Chinese air force officers should prepare to leave Beiping for the Soviet Union in three days.[44] On July 31, Mao Zedong, Zhu De, and Zhou Enlai received Liu, and instructed him to pursue Soviet support in establishing the new China's air force. Both Mao and Zhu emphasized that the main task of the CCP's air force was to help land forces to liberate Taiwan. It should therefore take the United States and the GMD as its primary enemies.[45]

The Chinese air force delegation arrived in Moscow on August 11. Liu Shaoqi was originally scheduled to return to China in early August. To await the Chinese air force delegation and personally introduce them to the Soviets, Liu stayed in Moscow until mid-August. On August 13, led by Liu Shaoqi and Wang Jiaxiang, Liu Yalou and his fellow Chinese air officers met with Marshal Aleksander Mikhailovich Vasilevskii, the Soviet minister of armed forces. The Chinese side, introducing to the Soviets the details of their own plans, requested the Soviets to help them establish an air force composed of 300–350 planes within one year. Marshal Vasilevskii made it clear that Stalin had already ordered the Soviet air force to do its best to assist the Chinese. This meeting concluded with an agreement leaving the details to air force officers of the two sides to work out.[46]

Liu Shaoqi left Moscow on August 14, accompanied by 96 Russian experts who were to assist China's economic reconstruction and military build-up. Altogether more than 200 Soviet experts would come to China in weeks as the result of Liu's visit.[47] The Chinese and Soviets set up a joint committee, headed by Mikoyan on the Soviet side and Liu Shaoqi and Gao Gang on the Chinese side, to handle Soviet loan and material assistance to China (Stalin agreed to offer China loans of $300 million).[48] Negotiations between the Chinese air force delegation headed by Liu Yalou and the Soviets also developed without difficulty. The two sides reached an agreement on all details of Soviet assistance to China by August 18. The Soviet side agreed to help the CCP to establish six aviation schools, including four for fighter pilots and two for bomber pilots, so that the training of 350 pilots would be completed within a year. The Soviet Union also agreed to sell 434 planes to China, and 878 Soviet air experts would come to work in China.[49] Stalin approved these details in early October.[50] On October 15, the Soviets delivered the first group of Yak-12 planes to China. Nine days later, the first group of 23 Soviet air force experts arrived in Beijing. On December 1, all of the six aviation schools were established with the assistance of the Soviets. By the end of 1949, China had received 185 planes of different types from the Soviet Union.[51]

In late September, another Chinese delegation, headed by General Zhang Aiping, came to Moscow to work out the details of establishing China's navy with Soviet assistance. They quickly reached agreement with the Soviets. The Soviet Union would now take responsibility for assisting the new China's naval construction. In October and November of 1949, the first group of 90 Soviet naval advisers arrived in China.[52]

As CCP–Soviet relations developed, Sino–American relations deteriorated. Mao responded to the *China White Paper* by starting a nationwide anti-American propaganda movement to criticize America's China policy while at the same time praising the Soviet Union. After Liu Shaoqi returned from the Soviet Union, he addressed a party conference attended by high-ranking cadres on September 3, 1949. He emphasized that the new China's unity with the Soviet Union represented the "most important interests" of the Chinese people and was thus crucial to China's national security and reconstruction. "While assistance from imperialist countries was an act of aggression," according to him, "the support from the Soviet Union was designed to change China into a strong power." He expressed the firm belief that if the new China and the Soviet Union could establish a close alliance, "the world will be ours."[53]

Liu could easily find evidence to support his statement. Indeed, less than two months after Mao's issuance of the lean-to-one-side statement, substantial Soviet support began to arrive in China. Mao and the CCP leadership, knowing Stalin's attitude, became more confident in dealing with the United States and other "imperialist' countries. To further change the lean-to-one-side approach from rhetoric to reality, the CCP leadership now had every reason to base China's foreign policy and security strategy on a close alliance with the Soviet Union.

The Mao-Stalin Meetings

The next six months were to see further dramatic development of Sino-Soviet relations. On October 1, 1949, the People's Republic of China was formally established. The next day, the Soviet government informed Zhou Enlai of its decision to establish diplomatic relations with the PRC and to break relations with the GMD.[54] A pleased Mao personally composed the Xinhua News Agency release on the establishment of diplomatic relations between the PRC and the Soviet Union.[55] Accordingly, CCP leaders decided to establish diplomatic relations with all "new democratic countries."[56]

To continue the construction of Communist China's lean-to-one-side diplomatic framework, the CCP Central Committee decided in early October that it was time for Mao to travel to Moscow and began laying grounds for this visit immediately. On October 20, Mao informed Stalin of the appointment of Wang Jiaxiang, deputy minister of foreign affairs in charge of relations with the Soviet Union and East Europe, as China's first ambassador to the Soviet Union. Mao emphasized to Stalin that Wang, as a member of the CCP Central Committee, would not only be responsible for "general affairs concerning those new democratic countries in East Europe" but also represent the CCP Central Committee "to contact with you and the Central Committee of the Soviet Communist party for affairs between our two parties." The naming of Wang Jiaxiang as ambassador indicated Mao's determination to promote cooperation with the Soviets.[57]

Mao hoped that his visit would result in a new treaty with the

Soviet Union, one that would replace the 1945 Sino-Soviet treaty between the GMD and the Russians.[58] This, as Mao saw it later, "would place the People's Republic in a favorable position by forcing those capitalist countries to fit themselves to our principles; foreign countries would be forced to recognize China unconditionally as well as to abolish those old treaties and sign new treaties with us; and those capitalist countries would dare not to take rash actions against us."[59]

While a new alliance with the Russians was Mao's first priority, he was still uncertain about how Stalin would receive him. He considered bringing Zhou Enlai with him to negotiate the treaty with Zhou's counterpart on the Soviet side, so that he himself could remain in the background. Mao decided to let Stalin determine if Zhou should come, probably to sound out Stalin's intentions. On November 9, Mao cabled Wang Jiaxiang, asking him to inform Stalin that he planned to leave Beijing in early December. He stated: "As to whether Comrade [Zhou] Enlai should come with me, or whether his coming should be decided after my arrival in Moscow, please ask Stalin to make a decision." Stalin, perhaps not understanding Mao's request, reaffirmed his invitation only for Mao. On November 12, Mao replied to Stalin that he would leave Beijing for Moscow in early December without mentioning concrete plans for the forthcoming visit.[60]

Mao left Beijing by train on December 6, 1949. Among Mao's delegation were Chen Boda, a member of the CCP Central Committee and Mao's political secretary, Shi Zhe, the interpreter, and Luo Ruiqing, minister of internal affairs. I.V. Kovalev, then the Soviet general adviser to China, accompanied the Chinese delegation.[61] After a ten-day journey across the Eurasian continent, Mao arrived at the central train station of Moscow on December 16 to a warm welcome by V. M. Molotov, Nikolai Bulganin, Andrei Gromyko, and other Soviet leaders.[62] The same evening, Stalin and nearly all members of the Politburo received Mao at the Kremlin, a gesture demonstrating high respect for Mao. According to Shi Zhe, immediately after the greetings, Stalin said to Mao: "Great! Great! You have made tremendous contributions to the Chinese people. You are their good son. I wish you good health." Mao replied: "I have been oppressed [within the party] for a long time. I even did not have a place to complain . . ." Before Mao could finish, Stalin said: "Now you are a winner, and a winner should not be criticized. This is a common law." He also observed: "The victory of the Chinese revolution will change the balance of the whole world. More weight will be added to the side of international revolution. We wholeheartedly congratulate your victory and wish you to achieve greater victories."[63] Stalin seemed strongly interested in developing a new relationship with China.

When Mao and Stalin began to touch upon substantive issues, however, communication between them became uneasy. During their first meeting, Stalin cautiously asked Mao about his goals for the trip. Mao evasively replied: "For this trip we hope to bring about something that not only looks nice but also tastes delicious." A cautious Mao wanted a new Sino-Soviet alliance, but he intentionally remained ambiguous to gauge the Soviet response. Shi Zhe further explained in his translation of Mao's remark that "looking nice means something with a good form and tasting good means something substantial." Stalin and other Russian leaders, however, did not seem to understand Mao's meaning. Shi Zhe recalled that Lavrenti Beria, a Soviet Politburo member, laughed at Mao's expression. Stalin might have sensed Mao's real purpose, but he would do nothing until Mao clarified himself. So, when Mao asked if he should call Zhou to join him in Moscow, Stalin replied: "If we cannot make certain what we really want to work out, what is the use to call Zhou to come here." Mao, again, made no direct answer.[64]

We may never know why Mao did not make his points in a straightforward manner. One possible answer is that Mao adopted a tactic common in ancient Chinese diplomatic practice, "not to release your real intention until your adversary fully expresses his intention." In addition, there is another hypothetical explanation—one concerning Mao's complicated mentality in face-to-face meetings with Stalin. An examination of this mentality helps understand Mao's later complaints about his visit to the Soviet Union and meetings with Stalin,[65] as well as Mao's management of China's relationship with the Soviet Union during the Korean crisis.

There is no doubt that both Mao and Stalin, as fellow Communists, had similar ideological beliefs. It is also apparent that the new China and the Soviet Union, in the face of the escalating Cold War, had many common interests. Mao therefore had strong reasons for pursuing an intimate personal relationship with Stalin, which, as he could clearly see, would greatly strengthen the foundation of the strategic cooperation between his country and Stalin's. Mao, however, was also a revolutionary leader from the "Central Kingdom," who aimed not only to realize a Communist transformation of the Chinese nation but also to reestablish China's central position in international society. Against this background it is understandable that Mao would view Stalin's attitude toward him, especially Stalin's willingness to treat him, his revolution, and his country as equals, with extremely sensitive eyes.[66] In a sense, it became more important to Mao for Stalin to treat him equally than for the Soviet Union to offer substantial material aid to China. In fact, according to Shi Zhe, Mao longed for a personal apology from Stalin for the mistakes the Soviet Union had committed during the Chinese revolution.[67] Psychologically this would certainly put Mao and Stalin on an equal basis and clear the history of unequal exchanges between the CCP and the Soviet Union. In Mao's view, Stalin's praise for Mao himself and the Chinese revolution was important, but not enough, because such praise could also betoken the relationship between a father and a son or an elder brother and a younger one. Mao wanted more. Stalin, however, deeply disappointed Mao as he never demonstrated any willingness to have a profound discussion with Mao about the unpleasant episodes between the CCP and the Soviet Union.[68] This led Mao to suspect that Stalin still viewed China as the inferior "younger brother."[69] Mao therefore would not give Stalin his full trust.

Because neither Mao nor Stalin was willing to take the initiative, Mao's visit achieved little progress in the following two weeks. On December 24, 1949, I.V. Kovalev further complicated the situation by sending Stalin a written report entitled "Several Policies and Problems of the CCP Central Committee." This report pointed out that some CCP Central Committee members, who had been anti-Soviet and pro-America in the past, were now backed by top CCP leaders; that Liu Shaoqi organized groundless criticism of Gao Gang, a pro-Soviet CCP leader in the Northeast; and that non-Communist "democratic figures" possessed many important positions in the Central People's Government of PRC, making the government virtually a united association of different political parties. Influenced by this report, Stalin regarded Mao more dubiously. Mao finally complained to the Soviets that he came to the Soviet Union not just for Stalin's birthday celebration but also to accomplish things more substantial and significant. At this point, Stalin handed this report to Mao.[70] Stalin had unknowingly probed Mao's sore point.

Seeing that no substantial progress had been achieved during Mao's visit, Stalin telephoned Mao twice in late December, urging him to articulate his plans and intentions. Mao remained ambiguous. Finally, Wang Jiaxiang hinted to A.Y.Vyshinsky, the Soviet foreign minister, that Mao intended to abolish the 1945 Sino-Soviet treaty and to negotiate a new Sino-Soviet alliance.[71] Stalin understood that a new treaty with China would strengthen the strategic position of the Soviet Union in its deepening confrontation with the United States, and he welcomed Mao's initiative and suggested that the two leaders themselves sign the treaty. Mao, however, believed that the treaty, as a matter between the two governments, should be signed by Zhou Enlai, the Chinese prime minister and foreign minister, and Vyshinsky, the Soviet Union's foreign minister. In the last week of December, Stalin agreed to invite Zhou to Moscow to work out a Sino-Soviet alliance and related agreements.[72]

On January 2, 1950, Tass, the official Soviet news agency, published "Mao's interview with a Tass correspondent in Moscow," in which Mao stated: "Among those problems [I have in mind] the foremost are the matters of the current treaty of friendship and alliance between China and the Soviet Union, and of the Soviet Union's loan to the People's Republic of China, and the matter of trade and of a trade agreement between our two countries."[73] That same evening, Molotov and Mikoyan visited Mao and they had an important discussion. The two Soviet leaders made it clear that they were authorized by Stalin to hear Mao's opinions and to decide what the two sides should do to make Mao's visit fruitful. Mao then expressed three considerations:

> (1) We may sign a new Sino-Soviet alliance treaty. This will be very favorable to us. [By doing this], Sino-Soviet relations will be consolidated on the basis of the new treaty; China's workers, peasants, intellectuals, and leftist nationalist bourgeois will be greatly encouraged while rightist nationalist bourgeoisie will be isolated; internationally we will have more political strength [*zhenzhi ziben*] to deal with imperialist countries and to examine all treaties signed by China and imperialist countries in the past. (2) We may ask our news agencies to issue a joint communiqué, only mentioning that our two sides have exchanged views on the old Sino-Soviet Friendship and Alliance Treaty and other problems, and we have reached a consensus on all important problems. . . . (3) We may sign an open statement, but not a treaty, to list the principles underlying our relationship.

Mao made it clear that only if the first choice was implemented would Zhou be called to Moscow. Molotov confirmed immediately that he believed the first choice was the best and Zhou should come. Mao then asked if a new treaty would be signed to replace the old treaty, and Molotov's answer was again affirmative. After the meeting, Mao directed Zhou Enlai to come to Moscow. Not wanting to give the Russians the impression that they were in a hurry to negotiate the treaty, Mao instructed Zhou "to prepare for five days . . . and come here by train not by airplane." Zhou followed Mao's instruction and did not leave for the Soviet Union until nearly two weeks after receiving Mao's telegram.[74]

Zhou and a large Chinese delegation arrived in Moscow on January 20, 1950.[75] Two days later, Mao and Zhou had a formal meeting with Stalin and Vyshinsky. This time Mao made it clear that he favored a Sino-Soviet treaty of alliance. Mao emphasized that the treaty should guarantee close political, military, economic, cultural and diplomatic relations between China and the Soviet Union, so that the two countries could stop the aggression of imperialist countries. Stalin immediately expressed his willingness to sign a treaty of alliance with China. Mao and Stalin then worked out an agenda for further negotiations for details of the treaty by Zhou and Mikoyan and Vyshinsky. They agreed that besides the treaty, the two sides would also discuss problems related to the Soviet use of the Manchurian railroad and Port Arthur, Sino-Soviet trade, and Soviet financial aid to China. This meeting paved the way for the Sino-Soviet alliance treaty.[76]

The next day, Zhou, joined by Wang Jiaxiang, Li Fuchun, Ye Jizhuang, and Wu Xiuquan, started negotiations with Vyshinsky, Mikoyan, and other Soviet officials. Zhou focused on making the forthcoming treaty a solid military alliance. According to Wu Xiuquan, one of Zhou's top assistants, Zhou insisted that the treaty should clearly state that if one side was attacked by a third country the other side "must go all out to provide military and other assistance."[77] This persistence paid off, and the treaty included a clause of explicit mutual military commitment.

In exchange for Soviet support to strengthen China's security position, Mao offered to recognize the independence of Outer Mongolia and allowed the Russians to maintain their privileges in Manchuria, including control of Port Arthur (Lüshun) for several more years.[78] After a long and uneasy bargaining process, the Sino-Soviet alliance

came into being on February 14, 1950. At a ceremony attended by
Mao and Stalin, Zhou and Vyshinsky signed the Sino-Soviet alliance
treaty. According to the treaty, the two sides would "make every effort
possible to stop Japan's aggression and the aggression by a third state
which is directly or indirectly associated with Japan's act of aggression." And "in the event of one of the High Contracting Parties being
attacked by Japan or states allied with it, and thus involved in a state
of war, the other High Contracting Party will immediately render
military and other assistance with all the means at its disposal."[79] Zhou
and Vyshinsky also signed an agreement granting China a loan of
$300 million at an annual interest of one percent.[80] With an under-
standing reached by the two sides, the money was largely designated
to cover China's purchase of Soviet military equipment.[81] The Soviets agreed also that they would transfer the Southern Manchurian
Railway to China by the end of 1952, and withdraw Soviet forces
from Port Arthur following the signing of a peace treaty with Japan
and no later than the end of 1952.

     Both Mao and Stalin were greatly relieved. On the evening of Feb-
ruary 14, Stalin, who usually did not attend banquets outside the
Kremlin, personally attended Mao's farewell banquet. Three days later
Mao and Zhou left Moscow. They returned home with Stalin's
promise to support the Chinese revolution and Moscow's military
commitment to China's national security. During Mao's visit to the
Soviet Union, China ordered 586 planes from the Soviet Union,
including 280 fighters, 198 bombers, and 108 trainers and other planes.
On February 15, 1950, two days before Mao left for China, he wrote
to Stalin to order another 628 planes. From February 16 to March 5,
1950, a mixed Soviet air-defense division, following the request of the
PRC government, moved into Shanghai, Nanjing, and Xuzhou, to
take responsibility for the air defense of these areas. From March 13 to
May 11, this Soviet division shot down five GMD planes in the Shanghai area, greatly strengthening Shanghai's air defense system.[82]

     These achievements were not easy for Mao to obtain, but he ulti-
mately got them and he was generally satisfied.[83] In his departure
speech he called the Sino-Soviet alliance "permanent and inviolable,"
anticipating that it would "not only influence the prosperity of these
two great countries, China and the Soviet Union, but would surely
affect the future of humanity and the triumph of peace and justice all
over the world."[84] Zhou Enlai also stated in his departure address that

"these treaties and agreements made the Chinese people feel that they were no longer isolated"; on the contrary, "they were now much stronger than ever before."[85]

Mao and Zhou aimed their statements largely at the enemies of the new China, especially the United States. With the making of the new Sino-Soviet alliance, both Mao and Zhou believed that Communist China now occupied a more powerful position in the face of the long-range American threat. On March 20, Zhou emphasized in an internal address to cadres of the Foreign Ministry that the Sino-Soviet alliance treaty made it less likely that the United States would start a new war of aggression in East Asia.[86] One month later, in a speech to the sixth session of the Chinese People's Government Council, Mao further claimed that the victory of the Chinese revolution had "defeated one enemy, the reactionary forces at home." But, the chairman reminded his comrades, "there are still reactionaries in the world, that is, the imperialists outside China." China therefore needed friends. With the making of the Sino-Soviet alliance, the chairman emphasized, China's external position had been strengthened. "If the imperialists prepare to attack us, we already have help."[87]

In fact, even without Mao reminding them, American policymakers understood that the Sino-Soviet alliance represented a big blow to America's strategic interests in the Far East. The alliance symbolized the failure of "driving a wedge" into Chinese-Soviet relations, a primary State Department objective during the 1949–1950 period. As we shall see, the fact that China had now become a close Soviet ally would lead to further escalation of the Sino-American confrontation.

The Chinese-Soviet Green Light for Kim Il-sung

One of the most mysterious aspects of Mao's visit to the Soviet Union has been its connection with the Korean question. Did Mao and Stalin discuss the Korean problem during Mao's visit? Was the coming of the Korean War in any way related to the Sino-Soviet alliance? Scholars have long been unable to answer these questions because of the scarcity of reliable sources. The only clue was from the memoirs of Nikita Khrushchev, former prime minister of the Soviet Union.[88] According to Khrushchev, Stalin and Mao had a discussion about Kim's plan to unify the Korean peninsula through military means in late 1949 or early 1950:

About the time I was transferred from the Ukraine to Moscow at the
end of 1949, Kim Il Sung arrived with his delegation to hold consultation with Stalin. The North Koreans wanted to prod South Korea
with the point of a bayonet. Kim Il Sung said that the first thrust
would touch off an internal explosion in South Korea and that the
power of the people would prevail. . . . Stalin persuaded Kim Il Sung
to think it over again, make some calculations, and then come back
with a concrete plan. Kim went home and then returned to Moscow
when he had worked everything out. He told Stalin he was absolutely certain of success. I remember Stalin had his doubts. He feared that
the Americans would jump in, but we were inclined to think that if
the war were fought swiftly—and Kim Il Sung was sure that it could
be won swiftly—then intervention by the USA could be avoided.
Nevertheless, Stalin decided to ask Mao Zedong's opinion about Kim
Il Sung's suggestion. . . . Mao Zedong also answered affirmatively. He
approved Kim Il Sung's suggestion and put forward the opinion that
the USA would not interfere since the war would be an internal matter which the Korean people would decide for themselves.[89]

Khrushchev's testimony was certainly important. However, since
the publication of *Khrushchev Remembers* in the early 1970s, scholars
have had little opportunity to prove or disprove his story. The emergence of new Chinese, Korean, and Russian materials in recent years
places historians in a position to check the accuracy of Khrushchev's
recollections and draw a more comprehensive (though still far from
complete) picture of Chinese-Soviet involvement in Kim Il-sung's
plan to unify his country by military means.

First of all, recently released Chinese, Russian, and Korean sources
demonstrate that Khrushchev's story about the Korean War, though
sometimes ambiguous and inaccurate on details, is generally consistent with these new sources. Khrushchev's description of Zhou Enlai's
secret visit to the Soviet Union after the UN landing at Inchon, for
example, is compatible with new Chinese sources even in small
details.[90] Khrushchev's recollections concerning the Korean problem
should thus be treated much more seriously than those sections dealing with himself in his memoirs.

Khrushchev's recollections of Kim's discussions with Stalin about
his plan to attack the South have also been proved to have their
grounds. Now we know, since early 1949, Kim had made constant
efforts to get Stalin's support for attack on the South. In March and
April 1949, he made a highly publicized visit to the Soviet Union,

during which he had extensive meetings with Soviet leaders and signed an economic and cultural agreement with the Soviets.[91] He also brought to Stalin's attention the need to liberate the entire Korean peninsula in the near future. But Stalin, worried about the American reaction, did not agree with him.[92]

Kim's desire to liberate the South grew more acute by the end of 1949. The victory of the Chinese Communists strongly encouraged Kim to believe that he could make the same thing happen in Korea.[93] Moreover, in late 1949, Communist guerrilla forces in South Korea had suffered heavy losses to the Rhee regime, possibly convincing Kim that he needed to act swiftly.[94] Consequently, throughout late 1949, Kim tried to achieve Stalin's backing for "his idea of military unification of Korea." Stalin, however, remained uncertain about United States reaction. He therefore asked Kim to reconsider his plan.[95]

According to Khrushchev, it was Mao who convinced Stalin that the United States would not interfere militarily if Kim attacked the South because "the war would be an internal matter."[96] Chinese sources now available differ on this problem. Chen Boda, Mao's political secretary who accompanied Mao to visit the Soviet Union in 1949–1950, claimed that Mao was not informed of Kim's plan during his stay in the Soviet Union, nor did he discuss any such plan with Stalin.[97] Two Chinese authors, Hao Yufan and Zhai Zhihai, assert that Mao and Stalin did discuss Kim's plan but differ from Khrushchev's account. "Mao was more cautious than both Kim and Stalin," they suggest, "he raised the possibility of American military intervention during his talk with Stalin in Moscow."[98] Shi Zhe offers a more detailed account of Mao's discussion with Stalin about Kim's plan:

> During Chairman Mao's visit to the Soviet Union, Stalin did talk with him about Kim Il-sung's plan to liberate the whole of Korea. Stalin told Chairman Mao that Kim had come to him with the ideas [of the plan] and he asked Kim if there existed any condition unfavorable to his plan, such as whether the Americans would intervene. He found that Kim was in a high mood. "He will only listen to the voice for his ideas, not the voice against his ideas; he was really young and brave," commented Stalin. Then Stalin asked Chairman Mao's opinions about Kim's plan, especially if he thought the Americans would intervene. Chairman Mao did not answer immediately. After a while, he said: "The Americans might not come in because this is Korea's internal

affairs, but the Korean comrades need to take America's intervention into account." As a matter of fact, Chairman Mao held reservations about Kim Il-sung's plan. Chairman Mao had anticipated that Kim Il-sung would attack the South no matter what happened.[99]

Despite the different opinion offered by Chen Boda, strong grounds exist to conclude that the Korean problem was part of Mao's discussions with Stalin and that Mao at least did not challenge Kim's plan. In addition to Khrushchev's and Shi Zhe's recollections, we have another piece of highly reliable evidence supporting this conclusion: the information concerning a high-ranking North Korean officer's visit to Beijing in early 1950 offered in the memoirs of the late Marshall Nie Rongzhen.

While Mao was still in the Soviet Union, Kim Il-sung sent Kim Kwang-hyop[100] to visit China, asking the Chinese to release all remaining Korean-nationality soldiers in the PLA's Fourth Field Army. According to Nie Rongzhen, acting general chief of staff of the PLA, the Chinese agreed to this request after discussions between himself and Kim Kwang-hyop. On January 19, 1950, Kim asked the Chinese to send these soldiers to Korea with their equipment. Nie, sympathetic to the request, had to ask instructions from the CCP Central Committee. He reported this matter to the CCP Central Committee on January 21, and the Committee approved the Korean request the next day.[101] Then, according to Nie, 14,000 Korean-nationality PLA soldiers, with their equipment, returned to Korea in the spring of 1950.[102]

The CCP Central Committee had given an unusually expeditious approval of the second Korean request. Since late 1948 and early 1949, Mao had stressed on several occasions that "in diplomatic affairs nothing was small" and everything should be reported to him and the party's Central Committee. It is thus unlikely that Nie or even Liu Shaoqi, who was in charge of CCP's daily affairs during Mao's absence, would have failed to report to Mao about such a matter which was by no means small. And if Mao could approve this request so quickly or Liu believed that he could authorize the request by himself, this indicates that both within the CCP leadership and between China and the Soviet Union there had existed a well defined consensus on the Korean problem, that is, it was the duty of the Beijing leadership to support the North Koreans' "just struggle" to unify their country.

Another key issue is Mao's assessment of the possibility of American intervention in Korea. Khrushchev emphasized that Mao believed that the Americans would not interfere militarily; Hao and Zhai stressed that Mao called Stalin's attention to the possibility of American military intervention; and Shi Zhe showed us a balanced Mao—while he thought an American intervention in Korea unlikely, he believed it unwise to ignore such a possibility. These accounts are not totally exclusive, as all agree that the possibility of American military intervention was the focus of the Mao-Stalin discussion. Shi Zhe's account seems to be most convincing. This is not only because when Mao and Stalin discussed the issue Shi Zhe personally witnessed it; it is also because Shi's account of Mao's responses to Stalin's inquiry is consistent with the well-known dialectic feature of Mao's way of thinking. Furthermore, Shi's account of Mao's response is also compatible with our knowledge of the CCP's general assessment of American intentions and capacities in East Asia in late 1949 and early 1950.

The CCP leadership, since late 1949, began to downplay the danger of American intervention in East Asian affairs. Mao and the CCP leadership did prepare for direct American military intervention in the mainland in the spring and early summer of 1949. When American intervention did not materialize as the PLA mopped up GMD forces in China's coastal areas, the CCP's perception of the "American threat" changed in late 1949. Convinced now that the prospect of an American invasion of the Chinese mainland no longer existed, CCP leaders concluded that it would take at least five years before the United States would be ready to engage in major military operations in East Asia. U.S. vulnerability in the East seemed more obvious to the CCP in January 1950 when Secretary of State Dean Acheson excluded Taiwan and South Korea from the U.S. western Pacific defensive perimeter.[103] What Mao told Stalin, if Shi Zhe's recollections are accurate, is compatible with the general CCP assessment of the American position in East Asia.

In the winter and spring of 1949–1950, however, the Beijing leadership was accelerating the preparations for liberating GMD-controlled Taiwan. As previously discussed, an important purpose of Mao's visit to the Soviet Union was to pursue additional Soviet support for the PLA's Taiwan campaign. Mao may not have wished to see the CCP's Taiwan campaign plan become entangled with Kim's invasion of the South. In other words, although Mao, Kim and Stalin shared common interests in promoting Communist revolutions in East Asia, they had at the same time held their own priorities. It was therefore reasonable that Mao did not give Stalin too affirmative an answer on the possibility of American intervention in Korea.

In short, the Korean problem was a part of Mao-Stalin meetings. Mao did not give active support to Kim's plan, but nor did he oppose it. As Kim had been taking Moscow as the main patron for his attack on the South, such a Chinese attitude would not impede his war preparations. And from Stalin's perspective, Mao's approach would be enough to allow him to back Kim's further war preparations. In fact, on January 30, 1950, for the first time Stalin informed Kim Il-sung in a telegram that he was now ready to discuss with Kim the plan for unifying Korea by force, and "willing to help Kim in this affair."[104] Mao-Stalin meetings produced a Chinese-Soviet green light for Kim's plans to attack the South.

The Sino-Soviet alliance served as a cornerstone for the PRC's foreign policy during its early years. In order to pursue a close strategic relationship with the Soviet Union, the CCP leadership adopted the lean-to-one-side approach. Since Liu Shaoqi's visit to the Soviet Union in July and August 1949, political, economic, and military cooperations between Beijing and Moscow had developed rapidly. Meanwhile, CCP and Soviet leaders divided spheres of responsibilities between them, leaving the promotion of revolutionary movements in East Asia primarily as China's duty. Mao's visit to the Soviet Union from December 1949 to February 1950 further promoted the Sino-Soviet strategic cooperation, resulting in the Sino-Soviet alliance treaty. It was within this context that Beijing and Moscow offered Pyongyang de facto approval for Kim Il-sung's plans to attack the South.

Shared ideological commitment to Marxism-Leninism, as well as to the "world proletarian revolution," certainly played an important role in the alliance's making. The CCP's need to maintain the inner dynamics of the Chinese revolution and Mao's desire to change China's weak-power status by defying the "old world" served as additional causes for the lean-to-one-side decision. A more direct cause, though, could be found in the two leaders' concerns over the threats from the United States. While Stalin needed Beijing's support for strengthening its position in a global confrontation with Washington,

Mao and his fellow CCP leaders regarded the alliance with the Soviets an effective means to check America's "ambition of aggression" against China, as well as to challenge the presence of U.S. influence in East Asia. The Sino-Soviet alliance treaty had greatly enhanced the CCP leadership's confidence in confronting the United States.

The high level of unity between Beijing and Moscow in 1949–1950, however, did not mean an absence of problems. In addition to the usual troubles between any partners (such as the differences in each other's strategic emphasis, and the gap between one's need for support and the other's ability to offer aid), an important source of differences between Beijing and Moscow lay in the conflicting personalities of Mao and Stalin. The reality created by the lean-to-one-side policy became particularly uneasy for Mao when he had to play the role as Stalin's junior in direct exchanges with the Soviets, especially in face-to-face discussions with Stalin himself. One finds here the early clues of the divergence between Beijing and Moscow during the Korean crisis and, in the long-run, of the process leading to a Sino-Soviet split.

4

Taiwan, Indochina, and Korea: Beijing's Confrontation with the U.S. Escalates

In late 1949 and early 1950, the Sino-American confrontation reached a pivotal point. As the PLA mopped up GMD stragglers on the mainland and occupied all important strategic regions except for Tibet and Taiwan, CCP leaders now believed that there was no immediate threat of an American invasion of the Chinese mainland. Sino-American relations, however, continued to deteriorate at deeper levels. The CCP's tough attitude toward the recognition problem, the anti-American propaganda tide following Mao's open criticism of the *China White Paper*, and the incarceration of American diplomats and requisition of former military barracks of the American diplomatic compound fully demonstrated the CCP's unyielding stand toward the United States. Washington's refusal to recognize Communist China and continuous support for Jiang's regime, on the other hand, further intensified the hostility between Beijing and Washington. Meanwhile U.S. policymakers had to face the reality of the buildup of a close relationship between China and the Soviet Union, reflected in the Sino-Soviet alliance treaty. Combined with the shock wave caused by Soviet explosion of an atomic bomb in summer 1949, these developments changed significantly the strategic balance in the Asian-Pacific area as well as the ways in which Beijing and Washington perceived each other. Consequently, on the eve of the outbreak of the Korean War, Beijing's policy toward the United States and Washington's policy toward China became increasingly hostile and aggressive.

The Concept of Confronting the U.S. on Three Fronts

In late 1949, Beijing leaders began to base their policy toward the United States on more complicated considerations than before. In the short run, they believed that the United States, restricted by its limited strength and confined by a variety of internal and external problems, was unable to invade the Chinese mainland or to engage in major military operations in East Asia.[1] From a long-term perspective, however, CCP leaders were firmly convinced that sooner or later revolutionary China had to face a direct military confrontation with the imperialist United States. Because of the growing international influence of the Chinese revolution, as the CCP leaders perceived it, revolutionary movements following the Chinese model would develop in other Asian countries. The United States, as the "head of the reactionary forces" in the world, would then resort to the most desperate means to prevent revolutionary changes in East Asia. As a result, a showdown between China and the United States would eventually occur.[2]

China's domestic situation also contributed to its maintaining a tough policy toward the United States. With the establishment of the People's Republic, Mao and the CCP leadership needed to expend considerable energy on political consolidation and economic recovery. Meanwhile, driven by his perception of the nature of the Chinese revolution, Mao was eager to create among party members as well as the general population support for the CCP's grand plans of transforming Chinese society. Mao and the CCP leadership sought by emphasizing the historical significance and international influence of the Chinese revolution and by igniting the anti-American imperialist propaganda to mobilize that support.

Correspondingly, in late 1949 and early 1950, three ideas appeared consistently in Communist-controlled media in China. First, all CCP writers emphasized that the victory of the Chinese revolution represented a breakthrough in the struggle against international imperialism and would cause a rising tide of revolution in other Asian countries and regions. Second, they postulated that the model of the Chinese revolution would spread far beyond China and inspire the

liberation of all oppressed peoples and nations, thus making China
the center of revolutionary movements in the East. Last, they stressed
that it was the duty of the Chinese people to assist in every way possible those peoples who were striving for their own liberation and
independence.[3]

Under these circumstances, the CCP's perception of the "American threat" and the PRC's strategy vis-à-vis the United States subtly
evolved in late 1949 and early 1950. While CCP leaders previously
had prepared for a direct American invasion of the mainland, now,
they viewed Sino-American relations in the much broader perspective of a long-range Chinese-American confrontation in all of East
Asia. Accordingly, a significant transition occurred in the emphasis of
the CCP leadership's security strategy: the focus of Beijing leaders'
concerns now moved from mainland China and problems concerning China's civil war to Taiwan, Vietnam, and Korea, and the three
areas came to occupy a central position in Beijing's security strategy
and foreign policy in late 1949 and early 1950. While putting Taiwan
at the moment as the priority, especially because the "liberation of Taiwan" was a crucial step in completing the CCP's unification of
China,[4] CCP leaders believed that developments in the three areas
were interrelated. Zhou Enlai later referred to this "the concept of
confronting the United States on three fronts."[5]

In light of the need to prepare for a long-term confrontation with
the U.S., the Beijing leadership started in late 1949 to restructure
China's military forces and to establish a central reserve force. After
months of deliberations, in the spring of 1950, the CCP leadership
decided to start a large-scale demobilization of the PLA's vast ground
force by cutting its size from 5.4 million to 4 million.[6] Many scholars, both in China and the West, have thus concluded that the CCP
leadership hoped to focus on economic recovery and reconstruction
and that Beijing's stand on the eve of the Korean War was much less
belligerent than that of Washington's. A few scholars even use the
CCP's demobilization plans to argue that the CCP leadership wished
to improve relations with Western countries, including the United
States.[7] A close examination of available sources about the CCP's
demobilization plan, however, leads to a very different conclusion.

We need first to analyze carefully the causes underlying the CCP's
demobilization plan. According to top CCP leaders and PLA commanders, the introduction of the plan was based on three considera-

tions. First, the size of the PLA's land force had reached almost 5.7 million by the end of 1949, placing too heavy a financial burden for the newly established PRC. As fighting against the GMD forces on the mainland ended, there was no need to continue to maintain such a huge land force.[8] Second, a large portion of PLA soldiers were either former GMD prisoners or members of defecting GMD units. In order to enhance the PLA's strength and weaken the GMD's, as Nie Rongzhen put it, "Chairman Mao had instructed that they should all be absorbed into the PLA." And now, "rectification and demobilization were necessary so that the quality of our combat units could be improved."[9] Third, with the annihilation of the GMD's main force, the PRC needed to establish an air force and a navy to fulfill such tasks as the "liberation of Taiwan" and the defense of China's air and sea against, most probably, the "American threat." By reducing the size of the land force," emphasized Nie Rongzhen, "we can use our limited money to construct our air force and navy."[10]

As CCP leaders viewed the demobilization plan as a step to restructure China's military power so that the PRC's military forces would be in a position to meet "the need of future wars,"[11] they emphasized from the very beginning that while the size of the land force would be reduced through the demobilization, its quality should be improved, and that in the meantime both the air force and the navy would be significantly expanded.[12] The final goal of the demobilization plan, in Nie Rongzhen's words, was "neither to reduce nor to weaken our military forces; rather, it was designed to strengthen our military forces."[13] It is apparent that this plan was compatible with the CCP leadership's need to prepare for the long-range Sino-American confrontation, not the first stage in an attempt at diplomatic accommodation with the United States.

Not surprising at all, when top CCP leaders were considering the demobilization plan, they made another crucial decision in the winter and spring of 1949–1950: to establish a national central reserve force with the United States as the perceived primary enemy. After the 13th Army Corps under Lin Biao's Fourth Field Army, one of the PLA's best units, completed military operations in southern China at the end of 1949, the CCP's Central Military Commission (CMC) ordered them to move to Henan province in central China, deploying along railroads within easy reach of Shanghai, Tianjin, and Guangzhou. The CCP leadership instructed the central reserve force to maintain a high degree of mobility, so that it could be available to meet any crisis situation caused by the Americans in Taiwan, the Korean peninsula, or Indochina.[14]

The real nature of the CCP's demobilization plan made it more of a restructuring of China's military forces. This restructuring, together with the establishment of the central reserve force, reflected Beijing leaders' concerns over a possible showdown with the United States.

The Taiwan Problem

In late 1949, as military operations ended on the Chinese mainland, Taiwan became increasingly important in the CCP leadership's perception of China's relationship with the United States. Taiwan, long a part of China, had become a Japanese colony after China's defeat in the 1894 Sino-Japanese War. After the Second World War, the island was returned to China. When the GMD lost the civil war, Jiang Jieshi moved his regime to Taiwan, converting the island into the GMD's last political and military bastion.

CCP leaders viewed the liberation of Taiwan as the "last campaign to end China's civil war."[15] In the eyes of CCP leaders, a successful Taiwan campaign would complete destruction of the GMD regime and conclude a century's political division and internal turmoil in China. A unified new China would then emerge as a significant actor in East Asia and the world.

From the beginning, CCP leaders feared that a hostile America might jeopardize their plans. In March 1949, before liberating Taiwan became a part of the CCP's immediate agenda, the Xinhua News Agency published an editorial criticizing the United States for its attempt to interfere with the Taiwan problem. The editorial observed that at the time "the colonial rule of U.S. imperialists and their GMD lackeys had approached its grave," and they were "envisioning holding Taiwan, part of China's territory, as the springboard for aggressive operations against mainland China in the future." The editorial called on the Chinese people to smash the plot of the U.S. imperialists, thus guaranteeing that Taiwan would "be liberated and returned to the hands of the Chinese people."[16]

In late May 1949, soon after Shanghai fell into the hands of the PLA, Jiang Jieshi arrived in Taiwan. Almost immediately he ordered the GMD's naval and air forces to harass the coastal areas now occupied by the Communists. On June 21, the GMD regime announced a naval blockade of all CCP controlled coastal ports, and GMD air forces started bombing coastal cities, especially important industrial and commercial centers like Shanghai. CCP leaders viewed this as evidence of the GMD's "desperate resistance before death" and also the result of Washington's continuing support of the GMD. Otherwise, CCP leaders believed, the GMD would have neither the strength nor the courage to challenge the CCP on the mainland.[17]

Mao and the CCP leadership decided to put the task of "liberating Taiwan" at the top of their agenda. On June 14, in a telegram to commanders of the Third Field Army and the CCP's East China Bureau, Mao urged his officers to "pay attention to the problem of seizing Taiwan immediately." Mao asked them to make suggestions on "whether Taiwan could be seized in a relatively short time, in which way Taiwan could be seized, and how the enemy troops in Taiwan could be divided and a part of them might switch to our side and cooperate with us from within." Stressing that "if we failed to solve the Taiwan problem in a short period, the safety of Shanghai and other coastal ports would be severely threatened," Mao instructed his officers to respond to his questions immediately.[18]

A week later, before receiving a reply from the Third Field Army, Mao telegraphed to Su Yu and the CCP East China Bureau again, stressing the urgent importance of a quick settlement of the Taiwan problem. Mao pointed out that despite the crucial importance of Taiwan, "you have so far ignored it, but you must pay sufficient attention to it immediately." To clarify his reasoning Mao told his officers: "If Taiwan were not liberated and the GMD's naval and air bases not destroyed, Shanghai and other coastal areas would be menaced from time to time. If Taiwan were not liberated, we would not be able to seize hundreds of thousands of tons of vessels [still controlled by the GMD]. Our coastal and inland water transportation would thus be controlled by foreign merchants." Mao asked the Third Field Army to overcome the "pessimistic mood" that resulted from viewing "the Taiwan problem as difficult to be solved." Rather the commanders should take a positive view by "completing all preparations during summer and autumn and occupying Taiwan in the coming winter."[19]

After carefully considering the problems involved in organizing a Taiwan campaign, Mao found that the summer of 1950 might be more reasonable a deadline. He understood that a successful Taiwan campaign depended on the CCP's ability to secure defection of GMD forces and sufficient Soviet naval and air support. In a letter to Zhou Enlai on July 10, 1949, Mao pointed out that to prepare for a successful Taiwan campaign, the CCP forces "needed to rely on internal cooperations and the support of an air force." Mao believed that "our plan would succeed if we could meet one of the two conditions, and our hope would be even greater if both conditions could be satisfied." Mao suggested that 300 to 400 PLA men be sent to study in Soviet air schools for six to eight months and to purchase 100 Soviet planes. He believed that the Soviet support would provide the CCP with "an offensive air unit to support the cross-strait campaign to seize Taiwan next summer."[20]

During Liu Shaoqi's visit to the Soviet Union in July and August 1949, winning Soviet air and naval support had the highest priority on his agenda. Liu made it clear to the Soviets that the Chinese Communists needed to expand their air and naval forces quickly to make it possible to conduct a successful amphibious campaign against Taiwan in the near future.[21] The Soviets responded positively to the CCP's request. In August, a Chinese air force delegation and a naval delegation came to Moscow to discuss with the Soviets the details of Soviet air and naval support to China. As a result of the agreement reached at these talks, Soviet air and naval aid, which was at this moment largely designed to strengthen the PLA's amphibious combat power for the Taiwan campaign, began to arrive in September and October 1949.[22]

Mao's eagerness to wage the Taiwan campaign in the shortest possible time was based on two fundamental assumptions. First, the PLA's expeditious victorious march after crossing the Yangzi River convinced Mao and the CCP leadership that the GMD forces were too weak to endure a single major blow. As the morale of GMD troops had virtually collapsed, CCP leaders and military planners believed that the PLA would be able to conquer the GMD-controlled islands, including Taiwan, without much difficulty.[23] Second, because the United States had not interfered militarily when the PLA crossed the Yangzi River and attacked Shanghai and other important coastal cities, Mao and other CCP leaders believed that, most probably, the Americans would not send in their troops if the PLA attacked GMD-controlled islands. Mao thus ordered the Third Field Army to accelerate its march toward coastal areas in Zhejiang and Fujian provinces and to complete preparations for the Taiwan campaign as soon as possible.[24]

Much to the CCP leaders' surprise, the PLA suffered two significant defeats in their attempts to occupy Jinmen (Quemoy) and Dengbu, two small islands controlled by the GMD. These defeats made CCP leaders aware of the tremendous difficulties involved in attacking the offshore islands and Taiwan, and forced Mao and the CCP leadership to change their original schedule for the Taiwan campaign.

Late in October 1949, when three regiments of the PLA's 28th Army of the 10th Army Corps tried to occupy Jinmen, located east of Xiamen, about five and half miles from the mainland, they encountered fierce resistance from GMD forces, who were equipped with American-made artillery, airplanes, and gunboats. The PLA troops succeeded in landing on Jinmen island on October 24, but the GMD forces, controlling both sea and air, quickly separated the PLA landing force from their supplies and surrounded them on Jinmen Island. After three days of bloody fighting, about 10,000 PLA troops were either destroyed or captured.[25]

Before CCP military planners could fully assess the meaning of the Jinmen defeat, the 61st Division of the PLA's Seventh Army Corps suffered another setback in its attempt to seize Dengbu Island in early November. Dengbu Island is part of the Zhoushan Islands off Zhejiang Province. On the evening of November 3, as part of the efforts to attack Zhoushan, three battalions of the PLA's 61st Division landed on Dengbu. After fierce fighting, by early next morning, these troops had occupied almost the entire island. The situation, however, suddenly changed. The GMD, still in control of the air and the sea, sent in four regiments of troops. Meanwhile, hindered by the changing ocean tide, the PLA was unable to reinforce its troops. As a result, the PLA had to retreat from Dengbu during the evening of November 5.[26]

These setbacks, especially that of Jinmen, were the worst defeats of the PLA in China's civil war. They shocked Mao and the CCP leadership. On October 29, 1949, Mao, in the name of the CMC, issued a circular suggesting that his commanders should "overcome the tendency of taking the enemy lightly and doing things impatiently" by drawing "deep lessons from the Jinmen defeat."[27]

The Jinmen and Dengbu defeats influenced the CCP's Taiwan strategy in at least three respects. First, these operational failures made clear to the CCP leadership the difficulties involved in amphibious operations. In a telegram to Su Yu and other commanders of the Third Field Army on November 4, Mao asked them to take a "more cautious approach" in organizing further campaigns aimed at GMD-controlled offshore islands. They should, in Mao's opinion, "concentrate a superior force, make sufficient preparations in advance, and overcome the tendency of assessing the enemy lightly."[28] Ten days later, Mao instructed Su Yu in another telegram to further consider "the lessons of the Jinmen defeat and the recent setback in Laidao [Dengbu] Island nearby Dinghai [the capital of the Zhoushan Islands]." Mao believed that Su had "to pay close attention to such problems as military deployment, preparedness, and timing for starting the attack while waging operations aimed at Dinghai." And if Su found that preparations had not been completed, Mao emphasized, he should "postpone the deadline for operations."[29]

In early December, before his trip to the Soviet Union, Mao conferred with Xiao Jinguang to obtain a more detailed knowledge of the naval and air needs for a major cross-strait campaign.[30] During Mao's two month visit to the Soviet Union, he did his best to win more Soviet naval and air support for the forthcoming Taiwan campaign. Even during the busy days of dealing with Stalin and other top Soviet leaders in Moscow, Mao remained concerned about the PLA's amphibious operations against offshore islands in Zhejiang, Fujian, and Guangdong. In telegrams of December 18 and 31 to Lin Biao, who was then in charge of a major amphibious campaign aimed at Hainan Island, Mao asked Lin to study carefully the lessons of the Jinmen defeat, reminding him of the importance of following "the principle of taking action only after full preparation and victory being certain."[31] With the change of Mao's and top CCP leaders' attitudes, PLA commanders in coastal areas began to take a more cautious approach in planning amphibious operations aimed at GMD-controlled offshore islands. In a telegram to Mao and the CMC on November 22, Su Yu reported that the Third Field Army would not conduct the attack against Dinghai until January or February of 1950, so that they would have more time to prepare for the campaign.[32]

A second result of the Jinmen and Dengbu defeats was a change in the CCP policymakers' original assumption that the PLA could seize Taiwan in a single major effort. On November 22, 1949, Su Yu summarized a new Taiwan campaign plan in a telegram to Mao and the

CMC. He predicted that the Jiang regime, encouraged by the GMD forces' success in Jinmen and Dengbu, would further strengthen their position in Zhoushan, Jinmen, and other offshore islands. While this would inevitably increase the difficulties involved in attacking these islands, it also provided an opportunity for the PLA to eliminate substantial enemy forces by concentrating on these relatively easier targets, and thus creating favorable military and political conditions for the Taiwan campaign in the future.[33] Mao and the CMC quickly approved this new plan.[34] From this moment to the outbreak of the Korean War, the PLA's military operations focused on Hainan, Zhoushan, and several other offshore islands with Taiwan as the ultimate target. Accordingly, the deadline for carrying out the Taiwan campaign was postponed several times. On the eve of the outbreak of the Korean War, the CCP leadership had already decided that the Taiwan campaign would not be implemented until the spring and summer of 1951.[35] Meanwhile, Mao reconsidered the Taiwan problem, sending General Zhang Zhizhong, a former high-ranking GMD official who had switched to the Communists shortly before the PLA's Yangzi River campaign, directions to explore "liberating Taiwan in peaceful ways."[36]

Third, the aftermath of the Jinmen and Dengbu battles also influenced CCP leaders' judgment of America's hostility toward the new China. CCP leaders could see that one of the most important reasons for the PLA's defeat was that the GMD forces, supported by American-made airplanes and gunboats, dominated the sea and the air. Without American support, CCP leaders believed, GMD could not survive the PLA's offensive operations.[37] This experience, combined with GMD naval and air forces using American-made bombers and warships to bomb Shanghai and other coastal areas and to blockade major mainland ports, further convinced CCP leaders that the United States was their primary enemy. They now viewed the liberation of Taiwan from the perspective of a long-range Sino-American confrontation in East Asia, and the CCP-GMD struggle in the Taiwan Strait became a part of the broad Sino-American confrontation.[38]

While the CCP leaders could not ignore Washington's hostility toward Communist China, they were still convinced that the United States was strategically too vulnerable to send in American troops to stop the PLA's attack against Taiwan. Two of Su Yu's reports are extremely revealing in this regard. In a report to a military conference held on January 5, 1950, Su Yu argued that it was unlikely that the United States would provide its troops to protect the GMD. In a diplomatic sense, Su emphasized, the United States had recognized Taiwan to be part of China and thus had no ground to interfere militarily if the PLA attacked Taiwan. Politically, according to Su, policymakers in Washington would meet great difficulty in reaching a consensus with their allies in Great Britain, the Philippines, and Japan, if the United States were to enter "the last campaign of China's civil war." From a military perspective, Su saw a vulnerable America. He believed that the United States needed at least five years to mobilize enough troops to enter a major military confrontation in the Far East. Su's conclusion was that "in terms of their attitude toward Taiwan, the Americans would not send troops to Taiwan but might send in planes, artillery, and tanks."[39]

Washington offered further evidence to confirm this assessment. On January 5, 1950, President Truman proclaimed that the United States would not challenge the notion that Taiwan was part of China. One week later, Secretary of State Acheson openly excluded Taiwan and South Korea from the U.S. western Pacific defensive perimeter. CCP leaders paid heed to both statements. In a report to a conference discussing the Taiwan campaign plan on January 27, 1950, Su Yu was now confident that Washington would not risk a third world war by sending its military forces to protect Taiwan.[40]

Viewing the United States as simultaneously a hostile enemy and a "paper tiger," Mao and the CCP leadership adopted a more aggressive strategy vis-à-vis the United States in East Asia, to challenge the existing international order in the Asian-Pacific area in which China had little voice, as well as to expand the influence of the Chinese revolution. Such an approach became the background of Beijing's policies toward Indochina and Korea in late 1949 and early 1950.

Indochina as a Test Case

Immediately after the establishment of the PRC, Beijing leaders began to give special attention to Indochina (Vietnam, Laos, and Cambodia). The CCP and Vietnamese Communists had historically enjoyed close connections. Early in the 1920s, Ho Chi Minh and other Vietnamese Communists initiated contacts with their Chinese comrades. Ho himself often came to China and spoke fluent Chinese.

In the late 1930s and early 1940s, he was even a member of the CCP-led Eighth Route Army.[41] After the end of the Second World War, Ho's Indochina Communist Party[42] led a national uprising and established the Democratic Republic of Vietnam (DRV) with Ho as president. When the French returned to reestablish control, Ho and his cohorts moved to mountainous areas to fight for independence with little outside assistance between 1946 and early 1950.

The Chinese Communist victory in 1949 offered Vietnamese Communists backing. Both sides were eager to establish close cooperation. In late 1949, the Indochina Communist Party sent Hoang Van Hoan, a member of its central committee, to China to strengthen ties between the two parties.[43] In early January 1950, Liu Shaoqi, then in charge of the CCP's relations with the Indochina Communist Party, decided to send Luo Guibo, director of the CMC's Administration Office, to be the CCP's liaison in Vietnam. Liu made it clear that Luo's appointment had been approved by Mao and the CCP Central Committee. His task in Vietnam was to establish good communications between the two parties as well as to provide the CCP Central Committee with first-hand information on how to assist the Vietnamese Communists in their struggle for independence. Liu stressed to Luo that "it is the duty of those countries which have achieved the victory of their own revolution to support peoples who are still conducting the just struggle for liberation," and that "it is our international obligation to support the anti-French struggle of the Vietnamese people."[44] In mid-January 1950, the PRC granted formal diplomatic recognition to the DRV so that it could participate in international society. CCP leaders, who understood that recognition of Ho's government would inevitably make an early French recognition of the Chinese Communist regime unlikely, still believed that establishing relations with the DRV was in the fundamental interests of revolutionary China. Following the example of China, the Soviet Union and other Communist countries quickly recognized the DRV, which would later name January 18 as the day of "diplomatic victory."[45]

Before Luo arrived in Vietnam, however, Ho Chi Minh, after walking for seventeen days, secretly arrived in China in late January 1950.[46] Liu Shaoqi immediately received him and reported his visit to Mao Zedong, who was then in Moscow. Meanwhile, the CCP Central Committee established an ad hoc commission composed of Zhu De, Nie Rongzhen, and Li Weihan, director of the United Front

Department of the CCP Central Committee, to discuss with Ho his mission in China.[47] Ho made it clear that he came to obtain a substantial Chinese commitment to support the Vietnamese Communists.[48] He also wished to meet Stalin and Mao in Moscow and obtain Soviet and Chinese military, political, and economic assistance. Through arrangements made by the CCP and the Soviet Communist Party, Ho arrived in Moscow in early February.[49]

Ho's secret trip to Moscow brought mixed results. While the Soviet Union decided to recognize Ho's government, Stalin had international priorities in Europe and was unfamiliar with, and to a certain extent even suspicious of, Ho's intentions. He was therefore reluctant to commit the strength of the Soviet Union directly to the Vietnamese Communists and turned Ho to the Chinese.[50] To Ho's great satisfaction, Mao and Zhou, first in Moscow then Beijing (to where Ho returned), promised that the CCP would do its best "to offer every military assistance needed by Vietnam in its struggle against France." When Ho returned to Vietnam he was certain that he could now rely on China's support.[51]

The CCP's attitude toward Vietnam was first and foremost the logical result of the Chinese Communist perception of an Asian revolution following the Chinese model. Because CCP leaders took the victory of the Chinese revolution as the beginning of "a new wave of revolutionary movements of oppressed peoples" in Asia and in the world, they felt obliged to assist Communist revolutionaries and national liberation movements elsewhere. The CCP's policy of supporting the Vietnamese Communists was also consistent with Mao's lean-to-one-side approach. When Liu and Mao visited the Soviet Union, the Chinese and the Soviets agreed that the promotion of revolutionary movements in East Asia was primarily China's duty. It is natural that Beijing leaders were willing to commit to the support of their comrades in Vietnam.

CCP leaders also believed that standing by their Vietnamese comrades would serve their goal of safeguarding China's security interests. Significantly, Mao, though a Marxist-Leninist revolutionary, demonstrated an approach similar to many traditional Chinese rulers: the safety of the "Central Kingdom" could not be properly maintained if its neighboring areas fell into the hands of hostile "barbarian" forces. In 1949–50, this view was further strengthened by the fact that some Chinese Nationalist units who were still loyal to Jiang Jieshi had fled to the Chinese-Vietnamese border area, making it a source of trouble for the newly established CCP regime.[52] Mao and the CCP leadership concluded that a Communist Vietnam would enhance the security of China's southern borders.

When the CCP made the decision to support the Vietnamese Communists, it moved forward immediately. On March 13, 1950, Liu Shaoqi cabled Luo Guibo, who had arrived in the Viet Minh's bases in northern Vietnam four days earlier, instructing him to start his work in two stages. He was first to deal with urgent problems, including providing the CCP Central Committee with a clear idea about the way in which Chinese military, economic, and financial aid would be given to the Vietnamese and how the aid could reach Vietnam. Secondly, Luo was instructed to carefully investigate the overall situation in Vietnam so that he could offer the CCP Central Committee suggestions for the long-term goal of defeating the French colonists.[53] The CCP obviously took the cause of the Vietnamese Communists as if it were their own.

In April 1950, the Central Committee of the Indochina Communist Party formally asked for military advisers from the CCP. The CCP leadership responded immediately. On April 17, the CMC ordered each of the PLA's Second, Third, and Fourth Field Armies to provide advisers at battalion, regiment, and division levels for a Vietnamese division. The Third Field Army organized the headquarters of the Chinese Military Advisory Group (CMAG) while the Fourth Field Army set up a military school for the Vietnamese. On April 26, the CMC instructed the PLA Northwestern, Southwestern, Eastern, and South-central Military Regions to offer another thirteen cadres over battalion level to join the CMAG to work with the Vietnamese at the top commanding positions of their Communist forces.[54] The military advisers gathered in Beijing during May and received indoctrination courses for the CCP's international policy. They would also meet top CCP leaders to receive instructions. General Wei Guoqing, political commissar of the Tenth Army Corps of the Third Field Army, was put in charge of the preparation work.[55]

By mid-1950, Beijing leaders had committed important military and financial resources to support their Vietnamese comrades. They fully understood that their intervention in Indochina would further intensify China's confrontation with the United States as well as complicate Beijing's relationship with Paris. But they were determined to go their own way, because Indochina was to them a test case for the promotion of the new China's international prestige and influence, as well as for inevitable confrontation between revolutionary forces and the imperialists in East Asia.

China and Korea: A Special Relationship

In accordance with the concept of confronting the United States on three fronts, Korea became another focus of the CCP's East Asian strategy in early 1950, and Mao and the CCP leadership demonstrated an intense interest in the Korean peninsula.[56] The Korean Communists were happy to have the backing of a Communist China, and relations between the CCP and its North Korean counterpart were generally intimate. Factors such as factionalism among the Korean Communists and Kim Il-sung's strong nationalism did create problems between the CCP and the North Koreans. Consequently, Chinese-North Korean relationships manifested a special dual character before and during the initial stage of the Korean War.

Historically, the Korean Communists had close ties with their Chinese comrades. In the 1920s, many Korean Communists began their revolutionary activities in China, and some even joined the newly established Chinese Communist Party.[57] During the 1930s, Kim Il-sung, who would later become the leader of Communist North Korea, joined the Anti-Japanese United Army and waged an anti-Japanese guerrilla struggle first in northeastern China, and then from the Soviet Union. Kim spoke fluent Chinese and was for a time a member of the Chinese Communist Party. In the late 1930s and early 1940s a group of Korean Communists, such as Pak Il-yu, who would become North Korea's vice prime minister, came to Yanan, the CCP's "Red Capital," to join China's War of Resistance against Japan.[58] In the last stage of the war against Japan and during China's civil war, around 100,000 Korean residents in China joined Chinese Communist forces, especially in the Northeast. In the late 1940s, the PLA's 156th, 164th and 166th Divisions, three of the best divisions of the Fourth Field Army, were mainly composed of Korean-Chinese soldiers.[59]

During China's civil war from 1946 to 1949, Communist North Korea served as the strategic base for Chinese Communist forces in the Northeast. In September 1945, the CCP leadership adopted a grand strategy of "maintaining a defensive posture in the south while waging the offensive in the north" in its confrontation with the GMD.[60] Accordingly, the Northeast became the CCP's main theater in China's civil war. Mao and other CCP leaders made this decision because they believed that, with the Northeast bordering the Soviet Union to the North and North Korea to the East, the CCP would be in a more favorable position to counter the GMD in the Northeast than in China's other regions.[61]

Jiang Jieshi and the GMD high command also understood Manchuria's strategic importance and committed the GMD's best troops to compete for it with the CCP. In late 1945 and early 1946, a series of fierce battles occurred between the CCP and GMD forces in Manchuria. Better equipped and outnumbering the Communists, the GMD troops occupied almost all important cities and transportation lines in central and southern Manchuria. When the full-scale warfare erupted in June 1946, Communist forces there were confined to a few small cities and rural areas. GMD forces succeeded in cutting the CCP's communication and supply lines within the Northeast as well as their connections with Communist bases in other parts of China. The CCP faced an extremely difficult situation in southern and central Manchuria.[62]

Confronting these difficult circumstances, the CCP's Northeast Bureau decided in June 1946 to use North Korea as the strategic rear and supply bases for Communist forces in southern Manchuria and that with North Korea's help, they would try to maintain communication and transportation between southern and northern Manchuria as well as between Manchuria and the CCP Center.[63] In July 1946, Zhu Lizhi and Xiao Jinguang, two members of the CCP Northeast Bureau, traveled to Pyongyang and established the Northeast Bureau's special office in North Korea. The CCP Northeast Bureau assigned three main tasks to the office: "(1) To evacuate [CCP's] wounded and sick soldiers as well as to transfer strategically important materials to North Korea; (2) via North Korea, to maintain transportation and communication between CCP forces in southern and northern Manchuria as well as to establish connections with the Soviet military bases in Dalian and, through Dalian, with CCP bases in other parts of China; and (3) to gain assistance and to purchase war materials from North Korea."[64]

The North Korean Communists cooperated in all three tasks. In

addition to ideological considerations, they must have sensed, as Bruce
Cumings points out, that by supporting the CCP they would eventually be able to enjoy "the immense strategic blessing of a Chinese
Communist victory."[65] North Korean territory quickly changed into
the strategic rear for Chinese Communist forces in the Northeast. In
July 1946, CCP forces, under great pressure from GMD offensives,
retreated from Andong and Tonghua, two of the last cities under their
control in southern Manchuria. Thousands of wounded CCP soldiers,
family members of CCP troops, and other noncombat personnel
crossed the Yalu River to take refuge in North Korea. Several CCP
combat units moved into North Korea to regroup. Meanwhile, the
North Koreans helped the CCP forces to move more than 20,000
tons of strategic materials into their territory. Without the assistance
of the North Korean Communists, CCP forces in southern
Manchuria could have been totally destroyed by the GMD.[66]

While the military confrontation between the CCP and the GMD
in the Northeast continued, North Korea's role further increased.
With the North Korean assistance, the CCP established two land
transportation lines on North Korean territory, linking together
Communist forces in southern and northern Manchuria. Through
Rajin and Nampo, two Korean ports located on Korea's east and west
coasts, the CCP established sea-communication with Soviet naval
bases in Dalian, and then, through Dalian, with CCP-controlled areas
in other parts of China. According to the statistics offered by two Chinese sources, in the first seven months of 1947, the CCP transported
210,000 tons of materials, including food, coal, salt, cloth, medicine,
and industrial raw materials, along these routes; in 1948, the total
weight of materials transported through North Korea reached more
than 300,000 tons.[67] The North Korean help allowed the CCP forces
in the Northeast to avoid being isolated.

North Korean Communists also offered material and human support to CCP forces in the Northeast. According to Cumings's study, in
early 1947, Kim Il-sung "began dispatching tens of thousands of Koreans to fight with Mao and to swell the existing Korean units to division size."[68] Chinese sources available now confirm that many Korean
"volunteers" joined the CCP, fighting to "liberate China."[69] In the
meantime, the North Korean Communists provided the CCP with a
large quantity of material support. According to one Chinese source,
during the two-year period 1946–1948, the North Koreans provided

the CCP with more than 2,000 railway cars of war materials left by the Japanese. In most cases, the North Koreans did not charge the Chinese for these supplies, and in some cases, they allowed the Chinese to exchange Korean supplies for Chinese-manufactured goods.[70]

North Korea's backing dramatically strengthened the CCP's strategic position in China's civil war. CCP leaders understood this and did not forget the "brotherly support" they had received from North Korean Communists. In fact, CCP leaders later used the North Korean support of the Chinese revolution to justify their decision to send Chinese troops to "resist America and assist Korea."[71] Cumings's statement certainly makes good sense here: "These ties [between Chinese and North Korean Communists] were strong enough such that, in retrospect, what a historian would have trouble explaining is why the Chinese did *not* intervene in the Korean War."[72]

Between September and November 1948, the CCP forces destroyed the main body of GMD forces in the Northeast. The Communist victory in China, in turn, made the Northeast a safe strategic rear for the North Korean Communists, and encouraged the North Korean Communists to liberate the entire Korean peninsula through military means. American intelligence sources and the GMD and South Korean sources have long maintained that during the spring and summer of 1949, China, North Korea, and the Soviet Union conducted a series of secret exchanges on military cooperation in northeastern China and Korea. In January 1949, these sources allege, the CCP and the North Korean Communists, in the presence of Soviet military advisers, held a meeting in Harbin and discussed the problem of returning Korean soldiers in the PLA to North Korea. Reportedly, those participants included Defense Minister Choe Yong-gon, Artillery Commander Mu Chong, and others from the North Korean side, and Zhou Baozhong, Lin Feng, and Li Lisan from the Chinese side. Several Korean commanders in the PLA, such as Pang Ho-san, commander of the 166th Division, also attended the meeting. The result was a decision to send some 28,000 Korean soldiers in the Fourth Field Army back to Korea by the end of September 1949.[73] In mid-March 1949, according to one GMD source, the North Koreans and the Chinese signed a secret mutual defense pact, affirming that the CCP would send PLA soldiers of Korean nationality back to North Korea and that the Chinese and Korean Communists would coordinate their reactions to "imperialist aggression."[74]

No Chinese sources can prove the existence of the January 1949 meeting or the alleged March 1949 pact. Yao Xu, a Chinese authority on the history of the Korean War, firmly denied the possibility of such a "mutual defense pact" as reported by the GMD source.[75] Two young Chinese military researchers whom I interviewed believed that the January 1949 meeting seemed to be more possible, although they could not confirm such a meeting by sources available to them. They did confirm, though, that "in the spring of 1949 China and North Korea held a series of contacts at different levels to discuss the problem of how China could support the Korean revolution, and they reached the agreement that PLA soldiers of Korean nationality would be sent back to Korea."[76]

Against this background, in the summer and fall of 1949, two PLA divisions, the majority of whose soldiers were Koreans, returned to North Korea. In July 1949, the PLA's 166th Division, headed by Pang Ho-san, crossed the Yalu and was transformed into the Korean People's Army (KPA)'s Sixth Division. The same month, the PLA's 164th Division, also made up mostly of Korean soldiers, entered Korea and became the KPA's Fifth Division. Both divisions later played a crucial role in the North Korean invasion of the South.[77] Several other smaller groups of Korean PLA soldiers also returned to Korea during the same period, and by the end of 1949, the total number of returnees from China is estimated to be between 30,000–40,000.[78]

In January 1950, when Mao and Zhou were visiting the Soviet Union, Kim Il-sung sent Kim Kwang-hyop to China to ask the return of all remaining Korean PLA soldiers together with their weapons. The Chinese quickly agreed to the North Koreans' request. Following the agreement between the Chinese and North Korean high commands, starting in February 1950, another 23,000 Korean PLA soldiers, mainly from the PLA's 156th Division and also other units of the former Fourth Field Army, returned to North Korea. They were later organized as the KPA's Seventh Division, which would be deployed in an advanced position near the 38th parallel and would become another of the KPA's main combat division in the early stage of the Korean War. The offensive capacity of North Korean Communists was thus tremendously increased.[79]

All the above proves that the relationship between Chinese and North Korean Communists was close. The simple fact that the CCP leadership decided to send as many as 50,000–70,000 (if not more)

Korean PLA soldiers back to Korea together with their military equipment from late 1949 to mid-1950 made it clear that CCP leaders would not forget the assistance they had received from their North Korean comrades during China's civil war, and that they were more than willing to reward the North Korean Communists with similar assistance.

This, however, does not necessarily suggest that problems, or even serious ones, did not exist between Beijing and Pyongyang. Cumings emphasizes in his study that the North Korean Communists followed basically the Chinese revolutionary model and that Beijing had more powerful influences on Pyongyang than Moscow did. This judgment becomes one of the cornerstones of Cumings's analysis of the origins of the Korean War.[80] Chinese evidence, however, challenges Cumings's argument in this regard, supporting the historian Roger Dingman's comment that Cumings may "have gone too far in magnifying Mao's and shrinking Stalin's contribution to what became the Korean War."[81]

What Cumings has ignored, interestingly and ironically, is something he frequently discussed himself: the influence upon the North Koreans' external policy of the profound factional division among Korean Communists and of Kim Il-sung's strong nationalism. After decades of investigation (including Cumings's own study), it is a widely accepted consensus among scholars of the Korean War that the Korean Communist Party had been divided deeply prior to the outbreak of the Korean War. Kim Il-sung's authority within the party encountered challenges from both the southern section headed by Pak Hon-yong and, to a lesser degree, the Chinese section headed by Pak Il-yu, Kim Ung, and Mu Chong.[82] Under these circumstances, Kim would feel extremely reluctant to tie himself too tightly to the Chinese. Kim's uneasiness in dealing with the Chinese must have been further strengthened by his feelings as an intense Korean nationalist: the historical fact that the Korean peninsula had long been under the shadow of the "Central Kingdom" certainly made Kim aware that he could not give Beijing leaders his full trust. Kim needed Beijing's support, but he would not totally rely on Chinese goodwill.

As discussed in the previous chapter, throughout 1949 and early 1950, Kim Il-sung had been discussing his plans of invading South Korea with the Soviets. In April 1950, he secretly visited the Soviet Union to get Stalin's approval of his plans, and would not travel to Beijing to meet Mao until mid-May.[83]

Why did Kim wait to visit Beijing until this moment? How was Kim's visit to Beijing related to his decision to attack the South in late June? Because of the sensitive nature of this question, no Chinese publication (even publication for "internal circulation only") has touched upon this visit. According to the study by Hao and Zhai, Kim "only informed Mao of his determination to reunify his country by military means during this visit, and released no details of his military plan, let alone the date of the action."[84] Interviews with Beijing's researchers with archival access, especially with Shi Zhe, allow me to draw a general outline about the background and contents of Kim's visit.

This visit was almost certainly Kim's only trip to Beijing before the outbreak of the Korean War. He did not come to Beijing again until early December 1950, when Chinese troops had not only entered the Korean War but had also completed their first two victorious campaigns against UN forces.[85] During Kim's stay in Beijing from May 13 to 16, he told Mao that Stalin had approved his plans to attack the South.[86] Mao solicited Kim's opinions of possible American response if North Korea attacked the South, stressing that as the Syngman Rhee regime had been propped up by the United States and that as Korea was close to Japan the possibility of an American intervention could not be totally excluded. Kim, however, seemed confident that the United States would not commit its troops, or at least, it would have no time to dispatch them, because the North Koreans would be able to finish fighting in two to three weeks. Mao did ask Kim if North Korea needed China's military support, and offered to deploy three Chinese armies along the Chinese-Korean border. Kim responded "arrogantly" (in Mao's own words, according to Shi Zhe) that with the North Koreans' own forces and the cooperation of Communist guerrillas in the South, they could solve the problem by themselves, and China's military involvement was therefore unnecessary.[87]

In short, Kim came to Beijing largely because Stalin wanted him to get Beijing's support for his attack on the South. Although Mao seemed to have some reservations, he never seriously challenged Kim's plans. When Kim left China he thus had every reason to inform Stalin and his comrades in Pyongyang (and we have every reason to believe that he did) that he had the support of his Chinese comrades. In fact, after his visit to Moscow and Beijing Kim accelerated preparations to attack the South. With the help of Soviet military advisers, the North Korean military worked out the operational plans for the attack in late May and early June.[88] Thus Kim's visit to Beijing represented another crucial step toward the coming of the Korean War, and Beijing's Korea policy escalated further the potential confrontation between China and the United States in East Asia.

Washington's New Vision of "Communist Threat" in East Asia

While the CCP's policy toward the United States became increasingly hostile in late 1949 and 1950, Washington's East Asian strategy also underwent important changes. Not accidentally, Indochina, Taiwan, and the Korean Peninsula received special attention from American policymakers. One of the immediate causes of this change was the signing of the Sino-Soviet alliance treaty.

Before late 1949, when Communist forces swept through China, policymakers in Washington based their global strategy on waging "a strategic offensive in the West and a strategic defensive in the East."[89] Accordingly, Secretary of State Acheson tried to drive a wedge between the Chinese Communists and the Soviets by imposing political and economic pressure on the CCP to contain the expansion of Soviet influence in East Asia. The Sino-Soviet alliance came at the time when Chinese-American relations were deteriorating and Senator Joseph McCarthy had started his verbal emasculation of the State Department. It was now clear to many advocates of the "wedge strategy" in Washington that the prospect of a Sino-Soviet split was remote and policymakers in Washington felt threatened by the emergence of the Beijing-Moscow revolutionary axis.[90] The United States had to reexamine its Far Eastern strategy.

In April 1950, the National Security Council approved NSC-68 as a response to Soviet possession of the atomic bomb and the Communist victory in China. Stressing that a "more rapid building up of political, economic, and military strength . . . than is now contemplated is the only course which is consistent with progress toward achieving our fundamental purpose," NSC-68 proposed a sharp increase in American military expenditure and armed forces. It also called for unprecedented American efforts in meeting the Communist threat anywhere it emerged.[91] In accordance with the spirit of NSC-68,

America's Far Eastern strategy in general and China policy in particular evolved in the spring of 1950.

First, America's politico-economic strategy toward China changed subtly along with the making of NSC-68. Since early 1949, the State Department had placed only moderate restrictions on Chinese-Western trade with the hope that the CCP would finally understand that an accommodation with Western countries was more valuable to them than cooperation with the Soviet Union. Now the State Department had second thoughts. Following a new estimation of the Soviet military threat to the United States, the State Department decided in April 1950 to restrict Chinese-Western trade relations severely. The former rule of "presumptive denial" of shipments of critical goods to China was replaced by the rule of "uniform denial," and shipments of important goods to Communist China were now "handled according to the criteria used in approving or denying shipments of such goods to the Eastern Europe."[92] This did not mean that Acheson and others in the State Department had abandoned the long-term goal of splitting the CCP and the Soviet Union; but now they were convinced that "if in taking a chance on the long future of China we affect the security of the U.S. at once, that is a bad bargain."[93]

Changes in U.S. East Asian strategy were also reflected in Washington's policy toward Indochina. The Truman administration made containment of Communist expansion in the region an important goal of American foreign policy. Accordingly, there were signs of an active American involvement in the Indochina area.

Since the outbreak of the First Indochina War between the French and the Vietminh in 1946, the United States had kept a pro-French neutrality. The Chinese and Soviet recognition of Ho Chi Minh's government in January 1950 and the making of the Sino-Soviet alliance in the next month triggered a more aggressive American policy in Indochina. Early in February 1950, the French Parliament, in order to win international support, decided to give more autonomous rights to Vietnam, Laos, and Cambodia. To bolster anti-Communist forces in Southeast Asia, the Truman administration immediately recognized the new governments in the three Indochina countries. At the end of the month, the State Department advised the National Security Council that Indochina was "under [the] immediate threat" of "Communist expansion" and that a program must be established promptly to protect American strategic interests there through "all practical measures," which became the accepted assumption of NSC-64.[94] Military planners in Washington shared this opinion and, in April 1950, the Joint Chiefs of Staff proclaimed that "the mainland states of Southeast Asia also are at present of crucial strategic importance to the United States."[95] On April 24, 1950, Truman approved NSC-64, and instructed the State and Defense Departments to "prepare as a matter of priority a program of all practical measures designed to protect United States security interests in Indochina."[96] Finally, Acheson announced on May 8 in Paris that the United States would provide economic and military aid to the French in Indochina.[97] This was a decisive change which, in retrospect, symbolized the start of America's involvement in the "longest war" in its history.

The new U.S. policy toward Indochina was partly attributable to continuous pressure from the French government for assistance. Nevertheless, strategic and psychological considerations played a more important role in bringing about this new American attitude. The State Department and the JCS agreed that Indochina was strategically significant to the United States, and that its fall to Communism would eliminate those nations which were still friendly to the U.S. from the Asian continent. As a result, policymakers in Washington believed that the United States and Japan would be denied access to the raw materials of this region and American security interests in the Far East would be seriously damaged if Communist forces further expanded in Indochina.[98] Therefore, the new U.S. policy toward Indochina was part of the overall change in American Far Eastern strategy.

The change in U.S. Far Eastern strategy was also reflected by the new stress of Washington's policy toward Taiwan. Having previously excluded Taiwan from the American "defensive perimeter" in the western Pacific region, many policymakers and military planners in Washington were now more inclined to keep Taiwan out of the CCP control.

Many in Washington had long emphasized Taiwan's importance to American security in Asia. As early as November 1948, when the Truman administration reexamined America's China policy, the JCS concluded in a memo entitled "Strategic Importance of Formosa" that the prospect of a Taiwan controlled by "Kremlin-directed Communists" would be "very seriously detrimental to our national security" because this would allow the Communists to dominate sea lanes between Japan and Malaya, thus threatening the Philippines, the Ryukyus, and ultimately Japan itself. The memo suggested the use of "diplomatic and economic steps as may be appropriate to insure a Formosan administration friendly to the United States."[99] A State Department draft report to the National Security Council in January 1949 agreed with the general conclusions of the JCS's memo and further stated that "the basic aim of the U.S. should be to deny Formosa and the Pescadores to the Communists."[100] General Douglas MacArthur, the Far Eastern commander, also shared this view. In a conversation with Max W. Bishop, chief of the State Department's Division of Northeastern Asian Affairs, MacArthur stressed that "if Formosa went to the Chinese Communists our whole defensive position in the Far East [would be] definitely lost."[101]

However, given America's strategic emphasis at the time on the West and the limited military capacity of the United States in East Asia, neither the State Department nor the JCS favored the use of military means to protect Taiwan. In a report to the president in early February 1949, the JCS made it clear that considering "the current disparity between our military strength and our many global obligations," active American military operations in Taiwan would result in "the necessity for relatively major effort there, thus making it impossible then to meet more important emergencies elsewhere."[102] The State Department shared this view and, moreover, believed that American military involvement in Taiwan might arouse Chinese sentiment against "American imperialism," thus undermining the Department's comprehensive politico-economic strategy of detaching Communist China from the Soviet Union.[103] Although pressured by congressional supporters of Jiang, who endorsed the use of military force if necessary to deny Taiwan to the Communists, the general consensus in Washington was not to use military force to protect Taiwan.

After the Chinese Communists won control of the mainland, and after the failure of an attempt to promote a Taiwan autonomy movement to deny the island to both the CCP and the GMD, the State Department further considered the acceptability of giving up Taiwan. On December 29, 1949, Acheson met with General Omar N. Bradley, chairman of the JCS, General J. Lawton Collins, chief of staff of the Army, and General Lauris Norstad, chief of staff of the Air Force. Although the military planners stressed the importance of Taiwan to the security interests of the United States, Acheson still questioned

Taiwan's real strategic significance. He worried that the price of defending Taiwan could be too high, that Washington's direct intervention in Taiwan could "bring upon ourselves the united Chinese hatred of foreigners," and that U.S. prestige would eventually suffer.[104]

In the context of these discussions President Truman stated on January 5, 1950 that "the United States has no desire to obtain special rights or privileges or to establish military bases on Formosa at this time." One week later, Acheson announced in his speech at the National Press Club that the U.S. West Pacific defensive perimeter would cover the Aleutians, to Japan, to the Ryukyus, and ultimately, to the Philippines, excluding Taiwan and South Korea.[105] The continuous deterioration of Sino-American relations and the establishment of the Sino-Soviet Alliance, however, caused the stress of American attitudes toward Taiwan to change.

The driving force behind the change was the Pentagon. On January 25, 1950, General Bradley indicated in off-the-record testimony before the Senate Foreign Relations Committee that the JCS fully understood the danger posed to the American position in the Pacific if a potential enemy were to control Taiwan. The next day, the JCS made it clear that an emergency war plan to prevent Taiwan from Communist control in case of war should remain in effect through the middle of 1951.[106] On February 14, the same day of the signing of the Sino-Soviet alliance, Secretary of Defense Louis A. Johnson wrote to Acheson to discuss the principles of further military aid to Taiwan.[107] With the making of NSC-68, the pressure for committing more American strength to the defense of Taiwan became stronger. On May 6, Secretary Johnson wrote to Acheson to suggest a reexamination of the Taiwan policy and, before such a review was completed, to continue assistance to the GMD.[108]

The Pentagon's initiatives were now echoed by John Foster Dulles, Dean Rusk, and others in the State Department. After a series of discussions, Rusk and Dulles handed a memo (drafted by Dulles for Rusk) to Acheson on May 30, requesting a reconsideration of the implications of the Taiwan problem for U.S. Far Eastern strategy. Dulles and Rusk believed that the United States faced "a new and critical period in its world position" because "the loss of China to Communists" would have "repercussion throughout the world" as well as mark "a shift in the balance of power in favor of Soviet Russia and to the disfavor of the United States." They stressed that if the

U.S. indicated "a continuing disposition to fall back and allow doubtful areas to fall under Soviet Communist control," then American
influence would rapidly deteriorate in other parts of the world and
Communism would be viewed as "the wave of the future." Therefore,
Washington should adopt "a dramatic and strong stand that shows our
confidence and resolution." Dulles and Rusk believed that Taiwan had
"advantages superior to any other [areas]" in taking such a stand. They
suggested a neutrality plan for Taiwan by "not permitting it either to
be taken by Communists or to be used as a base of military operations
against the mainland." They admitted that such a new policy toward
Taiwan had risks, such as "complications with the Nationalist Government" and "spreading our military force"; but they emphasized
that "sometimes such a risk has to be taken in order to preserve peace
in the world and to keep the national prestige required if we are to
play our indispensable part in sustaining a free world."[109]

Meanwhile, General MacArthur conveyed two memorandums on
the Taiwan problem to the Pentagon, stressing the importance of Taiwan for America's strategic interests. In the memorandum dated May
29 MacArthur noted that Soviet jets had been sent to China and that
Sino-Soviet cooperation had developed rapidly in the Shanghai and
Peiping [Beijing] areas. He emphasized that the problem of Taiwan
had become an urgent matter. If Taiwan were captured by Communist forces, the Soviet Union could use Taiwan to cut the Malay-
Philippine-Japan shipping lanes and isolate Japan, thus giving the
Soviets the capability for operating against the central and southern
flanks of the existing American strategic frontier of the littoral island
chain from Hokkaido through to the Philippines. He argued that "in
the event of war between the United States and the USSR, Formosa's
value to the Communists is the equivalent of an unsinkable aircraft
carrier and submarine tender, ideally located to accomplish Soviet
strategy as well as to checkmate the offensive capabilities of the central and southern positions of the FEC [Far East Command] front
line." He believed that in no circumstances should Taiwan be easily
given up.[110]

In another memorandum, dated June 14, MacArthur reemphasized
his main points on Taiwan. He further requested the authorization
from Washington "to initiate without delay a survey of the military,
economic and political requirements to prevent the domination of
Formosa by a Communist power and that the results of such a survey

be analyzed and acted upon as a basis for United States national policy with respect to Formosa."[111]

It is apparent that even before the outbreak of the Korea War there
were strong pressures in Washington for adopting a new Taiwan policy, consistent with the spirit of NSC-68 and the new situation in Asia
created by the formation of the Sino-Soviet alliance. The keynote of
this policy was the use of American military forces to "neutralize" Taiwan to prevent its loss to the Communists. The main driving force for
this policy change came from the military. In terms of its impact on
Sino-American relations, such policy pressures would certainly create
a new "hot-spot" between Communist China and the United States,
thus further complicating the prospect of Sino-American relations.

The influence of the changing American Far Eastern strategy on
Korea was more subtle. In his speech of January 12, 1950, Acheson
excluded South Korea from the American defense perimeter in the
Pacific. His statement was certainly consistent with the general tendency of American policy toward this area at the time. Considering
that American global strategic emphasis lay in the West and that Japan
was the core of American security interests in the Asian-Pacific area,
President Truman, on the NSC's advice, had ordered the withdrawal
of U.S. troops from Korea in March 1949, which was completed in
June the same year.[112]

Even though policymakers in Washington did not see South Korea
as vital to American strategic interests, they widely accepted that
maintaining a pro-Western South Korea enhanced American prestige.
As early as April 1947, the Joint Strategic Security Committee pointed out that Korea was "the one country within which we alone have
for almost two years carried on ideological warfare in direct contact
with our ideological opponents"; and that the American loss in this
battle "would be gravely detrimental to United States prestige, and
therefore security, throughout the world."[113] In March 1949, an NSC
document, approved by President Truman, further stated that "The
overthrow by Soviet-dominated forces of a government established in
South Korea under the aegis of the UN would . . . constitute a severe
blow to the prestige and influence of the latter; in this respect the
interests of the U.S. must be regarded as parallel to, if not identical
with, those of the UN."[114]

Acheson virtually shared this sense of maintaining American prestige in his January 12 speech. While leaving South Korea out of Amer-

ican defense perimeter, he claimed that an invasion of South Korea would invoke "the commitments of the entire civilized world under the Charter of the United Nations."[115] Acheson's reservation provided a clue about future American intervention in the Korean War.

With U.S. Far Eastern strategy placing more emphasis on containing Communist expansion in East Asia, policymakers in Washington wanted to strengthen South Korea as a stronghold against the Communist threat. Because South Korea faced economic difficulties, Acheson worked for a Korean Aid Bill. Originally introduced in 1947, the bill was narrowly defeated by the House of Representatives in January 1950, a week after Acheson's January 12 speech. Acheson immediately wrote to Truman to stress that the bill's defeat would have "the most far-reaching adverse effects upon our foreign policy." With Truman's active support, Acheson worked out a compromise bill slightly reducing the first year aid to Korea. When the House received the revised bill in February, Acheson stressed the importance of supporting a pro-Western South Korea. The Korean Aid Bill was approved by Congress in mid-February and signed immediately by President Truman. Acheson, however, did not stop here. He pushed through additional economic aid to South Korea of $100 million for the 1951 fiscal year, and this became law in early June.[116]

In order to show American concern about South Korea, John Foster Dulles visited Seoul in mid-June. In private talks with Syngman Rhee, the South Korean president, he encouraged the South Koreans to "create a stable economy and a government which deserved the support of its people." In his public rhetoric, he expressed clearly America's determination to stand by South Korea.[117] South Korea, although not included in America's defense perimeter, represented now "major interests," as Russell Buhite defined them, of U.S. strategic interests in Asia.[118]

America's growing emphasis on East Asia, especially its increasing concerns about Indochina, Taiwan, and the Korean peninsula, further strengthened Beijing's sense of insecurity. Not coincidentally, throughout the spring of 1950, Chinese propaganda continuously broadened its accusations against America's "military encirclement and economic blockade" of China, criticizing sternly the "U.S. imperialist ambition of aggression" toward China and East Asia. Zhou Enlai, on one occasion, even openly charged that the final aim of American policy was to control all of Asia, including the liberated

China.[119] Apparently, the interaction of Chinese and American policies resulted in further escalation of hostilities between the two countries.

By mid-1950, Beijing and Washington had firmly perceived each other as a dangerous enemy. Beijing leaders believed that the United States lacked the capacity to involve itself in major military operations in East Asia at the current stage, but that in the long-run, a Chinese-American confrontation, most likely in Taiwan, Indochina, or Korea, was inevitable. This fundamental perception of the "American threat," combined with the buildup of the Sino-Soviet alliance, served as the basis for Beijing leaders' concept "to confront the United States on three fronts," and caused Beijing to adopt a more aggressive strategy vis-à-vis the United Sates. Policymakers in Washington were alarmed by the making of the Sino-Soviet alliance, as well as by the perceived danger of Communist expansion in East Asia. In the wake of the making of NSC-68, they began to reexamine America's Far Eastern strategy in order to increase American commitment to contain the "Communist threat" in Indochina, Taiwan, and, in a more subtle sense, Korea.

All of this was happening when the last group of American diplomats were leaving China and, as a result, Beijing and Washington lost any channel of direct communication. Consequently, even before the outbreak of the Korean War, the fundamental differences in political ideology and perceived national interests had set up a stage for further confrontation between Communist China and the United States: policymakers in Beijing and Washington now gave more weight to the deepening conflict of interests between their countries, making the two's relationship increasingly dangerous—even a small spark could ignite an enormous explosion.

Part Three

The Road to Intervention

June 1950–October 1950

5 | Beijing's Response to the Outbreak of the Korean War

Sunday, June 25, 1950, should have been a relatively quiet day for Chinese leaders. During the first three weeks of June, Beijing had been the scene of an array of important meetings, especially the party Central Committee's third plenary session. After extensive discussions devoted to China's economic reconstruction, defense projects, and issues related to the long-range confrontation with the United States, Beijing leaders must have felt the need of a break. They had scheduled nothing important for that day.[1]

But June 25, 1950 was destined to be unusual. At four in the morning, intensive gunfire shattered a tranquil pre-dawn along the thirty-eighth parallel, which had separated North and South Korea since 1945. The well-trained North Korean troops, fitted out with Soviet weapons and spearheaded by Soviet-made T-34 tanks, rapidly advanced into the territory of the South. After learning of the North Korean invasion, policymakers in Washington responded swiftly and firmly. Within thirty-six hours, they had decided to dispatch military forces to assist South Korea. On June 27, at the request of the United States, the UN Security Council, in the absence of the Soviet Union,[2] passed two emergency resolutions condemning the North Korean invasion and requesting sanctions against it. Meanwhile, President Truman ordered the Seventh Fleet to enter the Taiwan Strait to neutralize this area.[3] The Korean War quickly changed into an international crisis.

The Implications of the Crisis for Beijing

Mao Zedong and others in Beijing should not have been surprised by the North Korean invasion, but they were certainly shocked by the quick and unyielding American reaction. The Korean crisis immediately posed several serious challenges to Mao and the CCP leadership.

Washington's decision to intervene in Korea and Taiwan challenged in the first place a crucial perception that CCP leaders had held since 1946–47: that East Asia represented "the weak point of the international front of imperialism." The CCP leadership, influenced by their own experience during the Chinese civil war, believed correctly that American strategic emphasis at that time lay in Europe. They also perceived, less correctly, that American military strength in the Asian-Pacific area was inadequate, making major American intervention in the internal conflicts or revolutionary changes in an Asian country unlikely.

However, Mao and his fellow CCP leaders overlooked three crucial factors relating to U.S. East Asian policy. First, the United States had intimate ties with the Syngman Rhee government (although many in Washington disliked Rhee as they disliked Jiang). U.S. forces had occupied Korea since the end of World War II and had established the Rhee government. Thus, while the importance of the GMD declined in Washington's policy considerations, South Korea gained weight. A North Korean victory over the Rhee government, in the view of American policymakers, would damage the credibility of American policy in East Asia. South Korea's close connections with Japan made it even less likely that the United States would tolerate its destruction.[4] Second, the failure to maintain a non-Communist China had caused severe criticism of the Truman administration at home. Truman and other policymakers in Washington realized that hesitation or timidity in the face of the North Korean invasion would play into the hands of domestic political enemies who accused the Truman administration of being soft on Communism. To President Truman, an appeasement policy toward the North Korean invasion could mean political suicide.[5] Third, U.S. East Asian strategy had quietly changed in early 1950. The CCP's victory in China, together with Soviet possession of the atomic bomb, changed the world balance of power and forced American policymakers to reassess American strategy in East Asia. Consequently, they believed that the United States should not allow further expansion of Soviet influence in any part of the world, including the Asian-Pacific area. While the American decision to aid South Korea was not a foregone conclusion, it was consistent with the new direction of American foreign policy.[6] With the outbreak of the Korean War, the CCP leadership had to reevaluate American intentions and military capacities. The result of this assessment, together with Beijing leaders' understanding of other immediate and long-range domestic and international needs facing the newly established PRC, would determine Beijing's response to the Korean conflict.

U.S. response to the Korean War also changed the scenario of the CCP-GMD confrontation across the Taiwan Strait. Although President Truman maintained that the task of the Seventh Fleet was a neutral one, the United States had virtually reentered China's civil war on the GMD's behalf. GMD leaders welcomed this U.S. protection against the pending Communist attack.[7] Viewing the military prospect for a Taiwan campaign dramatically changed with the appearance of the Seventh Fleet in the Taiwan Strait, CCP leaders had to reconsider the implications of America's hostility toward the new China and, accordingly, had to readjust their strategy toward Taiwan.

The central challenge, as CCP leaders viewed it, came from U.S. military involvement in Korea. They clearly sensed that as the result of the U.S. military intervention in Korea, the balance of strength between the North and South Koreans had changed enormously. Did the North Korean Communist forces have the ability to crush the resistance of South Korean troops and to defeat reinforcements from the United States? Chinese leaders were uncertain.[8] If the conflict in Korea were prolonged or even reversed because of the involvement of the United States, among other things, the safety of China's northeastern region would be threatened. Beijing leaders could not forget that Japanese imperialists had first annexed Korea, then penetrated and occupied China's Northeast, and then began a war of aggression on China. In this sense, it was not simply for propaganda purposes that Beijing leaders would emphasize that the safety of Korea was closely related to China's security.[9] Furthermore, the American decision to intervene in Korea and to dispatch the Seventh Fleet into the Taiwan Strait convinced CCP leaders that the result of the conflict in Korea was linked with the fate of the entire East. In a conversation on June 30 with Chai Chengwen, recently appointed as China's political counsellor to Korea, Zhou Enlai stressed that the Truman administration's actions in Korea and Taiwan reflected an overall American plan of aggression in Asia.[10] Chai recalled that after the outbreak of the Korean War policymakers in Beijing widely believed that the U.S. intervention in Korea and Taiwan represented a general plot to surround and attack China from three directions—Korea, Taiwan, and Indochina.[11] This perception of American policy caused Mao and his fellow CCP leaders to keep a vigilant eye on the development of the Korean conflict.

America's military intervention in Korea and Taiwan also created tremendous internal pressures on Mao and the CCP leadership. In June 1950, the Chinese Communist regime was only eight months old. The CCP had been busy restoring order and consolidating the rule of the Communist regime. For Mao and the CCP leadership, the most difficult task was neither how to smash the final resistance of GMD remnants on the mainland, nor how to establish the CCP's control over China's political and economic life, but rather to establish the authority and credibility of the CCP as China's ruler by creating a true, extensive, and internalized support on the part of the Chinese people to the Communist regime.[12] The completion of this task was particularly important for Mao in terms of carrying out his great plans of continuing the revolution after the Communist victory in China. Consequently, Mao and his fellow CCP leaders feared that the crisis situation created by the Korean War would stimulate "reactionaries" remaining on the mainland, social classes who were hostile to the Communist revolution, and the GMD regime in Taiwan would try to make trouble.[13] More important, the common people in China, who had experienced domestic turmoil and foreign invasion for almost a century and who had still only limited knowledge of the CCP's internal and external policies, would take the CCP's management of the Korean crisis as a test case of the CCP's ability to rule China and to safeguard China's prestige and national interests.

While the eruption of the Korean crisis imposed serious challenges to CCP leaders, at the same time it offered them a series of potential opportunities. Deeply influenced by the dialectic Chinese strategic culture defining crisis (*weiji*) as a combination of danger (*wei*) and opportunity (*ji*), Mao treated the Korean crisis as an opportunity as well as a challenge from the very beginning.

What needs to be stressed is that in assessing the impact of the

Korean War's outbreak on the Beijing leadership one should not overemphasize the degree to which CCP leaders had been shocked by America's intervention in Korea and Taiwan. CCP leaders had long been aware of Washington's hostility toward the Chinese revolutionaries, and they believed that a direct confrontation between Communist China and the United States would come sooner or later. Since late 1949, they had concluded that such a confrontation would occur in any of the three locations: Taiwan, Indochina, or Korea. In this sense, U.S. intervention in Korea and Taiwan confirmed at the grand strategic level the CCP leaders' fundamental perception of the aggressive nature of U.S. policy in East Asia.

In this context it is not surprising to see that Mao and the CCP leadership believed that by firmly confronting "U.S. imperialist aggression" in Korea and Taiwan, they could turn the tremendous outside pressure to new dynamics for creating the revolutionary momentum of the Chinese people: if they could properly manage the Korean crisis, they would greatly strengthen the CCP's authority and reputation as China's rulers, thus laying the basis for Mao's long-range plans of transforming the old Chinese society into a new socialist country. As Chai Chengwen points out in his memoir, CCP leaders, who had shown a talent for changing "the disfavors to the favors" in their previous experiences, realized immediately that the new American intervention in East Asia was an opportunity to "mobilize the masses as well as to inspire the comrade-in-arms."[14] On June 29, 1950, China's General Information Bureau issued an internal directive to all official propaganda agencies, which reflected the CCP leadership's train of thought in face of the Korean crisis:

> The U.S. president Truman announced on June 27 to intervene in the Korean civil war and to use naval forces to control the Taiwan Strait with the attempt to stop our liberation of Taiwan. Foreign Minister Zhou has issued a statement to solemnly condemn these actions. This is an important event at the present time. The United States has thus exposed its imperialist face, which is not scary at all but is favorable for the further awakening of the Chinese people and the people of the world. All over China, we have to hold this opportunity to echo Foreign Minister Zhou's statement and to start a widespread campaign of propaganda, so that we will be able to educate our people at home and to strike firmly the arrogance of the U.S. imperialist aggressors.[15]

In terms of its international impact, the crisis situation caused by the Korean War had shaken the balance of power in the Asian-Pacific region. For Mao and the CCP leadership, this represented again a threat as well as an opportunity. The new China had never been afraid of challenging the established international order, which, from the CCP's viewpoint, was created and dominated by Western imperialist powers. This approach did not necessarily mean that the CCP, for the purpose of creating a "new world," would intentionally attack the established order in East Asia through violent means. Such an approach, nevertheless, certainly influenced the CCP's response to the Korean War. At least, under the circumstance that the Korean War had already changed into an international crisis, Mao and his fellow CCP leaders realized that by adding their strength to the North Koreans they could contribute to the creation of a new international order in East Asia more favorable to revolutionary China.[16]

From Beijing's perspective, even an expansion of warfare in the Korean peninsula, though not desirable, might not necessarily be intolerable. The relationship between the CCP and the North Korean Communists had been intricate. Kim Il-sung, while endeavoring to maintain cooperation with his Chinese comrades, maintained vigilance against Chinese influence, especially during the time that his leading position was still threatened by the "Chinese section" within the Communist party.[17] To Mao and the CCP leadership, expanding warfare in Korea would inevitably menace China's security interests. At the same time the Korean War could offer the Chinese Communists a possible opportunity to expand the influence of the Chinese revolution into an area at the top of the CCP's Asian revolutionary agenda. From the beginning, Mao and the CCP leadership viewed the Korean War with mixed feelings: failure to eject the Americans from Korea could mean insecurity for China; success would advance China's prestige and influence in the East.

Korea Becomes the Focus

Viewing the Korean crisis both as danger and opportunity, the CCP leadership responded to the new American involvement in Asia with major adjustment in the Chinese strategy vis-à-vis the Untied States. As Beijing leaders perceived from the beginning of the crisis that "the focus of contradictions in the East, or even in the whole world, lay in Korea"[18] and that the American action influenced both Beijing's internal and external policies, their management of the Korean crisis both focused on Korea and went beyond it.

Beijing's first strategic adjustment was to criticize U.S. intervention in Taiwan while at the same time putting on hold its Taiwan campaign plan. Beijing leaders indignantly criticized Truman's new Taiwan policy, and they explicitly linked Truman's policy to a broader American plot of aggression in the East. On June 28, 1950, Mao addressed the eighth session of the Chinese central government council. The chairman pointed out angrily that America's military intervention in Taiwan had proved that Truman's January 5 statement was nothing but "a pack of lies," and that the United States "had torn to shreds all international agreements regarding the nonintervention in China's internal affairs." He stressed that the Chinese people and peoples all over the world "should unite and be fully prepared to crush any provocation by the American imperialists." The same day, Zhou Enlai issued an even stronger statement. He called Truman's June 27 decision "a violent invasion of Chinese territory as well as a thorough violation of the UN charter," which was "an open exposure and putting into practice the long-prepared [American] plan to invade China and to dominate Asia." The premier declared that all of this could only arouse the Chinese people's indignity against the American imperialists.[19]

In reaction to the Seventh Fleet's appearance in the Taiwan Strait, the CCP leadership quickly decided to put preparations for invasion on hold. On June 30, Zhou Enlai met with Xiao Jinguang, commander of the navy, to inform him of the Central Committee's decision to postpone preparations for the Taiwan campaign. While Zhou pointed out that American intervention in the Taiwan Strait had increased difficulties for the CCP to attack Taiwan, he nevertheless believed that the delay was not necessarily a bad thing, especially because the PLA had not completed its preparations for the Taiwan campaign. Beijing's plans to cope with the situation, according to Zhou, would be "to continue the demobilization of our land forces while at the same time strengthening the construction of our naval and air forces. And the Taiwan campaign will be postponed."[20]

The CCP's military forces acted accordingly. In mid-July, Su Yu formally explained to the Third Field Army that "in order to focus on resisting America and assisting Korea" the Taiwan campaign plan would be postponed.[21] Following this new policy, the CCP leadership and the PLA's East China Headquarters redeployed military forces vis-à-vis Taiwan. In the Fujian area, opposite Taiwan, PLA troops had been preparing since late 1949 to launch amphibious assaults against GMD-controlled offshore islands. By early June six armies (the 24th, 25th, 28th, 29th, 31st, and 32nd) had concentrated in the Fujian area preparing for a second attack on Jinmen, the first step toward a final invasion of Taiwan. After the outbreak of the Korean War, the main task of the troops in Fujian changed from military operations against GMD-controlled offshore islands to "suppressing local bandits and stabilizing the rear area."[22] On August 8, Chen Yi , commander of the East China Military Region , suggested that the CCP leadership drop the Taiwan campaign until after 1951.[23] On August 11, the CMC approved Chen's proposal and formally delayed the Taiwan campaign until 1952, and an assault against Jinmen would not be attempted before April 1951.[24] Following this order, the Third Field Army began to consider the "liberation" of Taiwan as a long-range task; and three of its armies would be later transferred from Fujian to the Korean border. The Ninth Army Corps, the reserve force for the Taiwan campaign, would also be transferred to the Northeast. Meanwhile, the strategic emphasis of Chinese naval forces shifted from the Taiwan area to areas closer to the Korean peninsula.[25]

Beijing's policy toward Indochina also changed. Treating the Indochina war as a part of the overall confrontation between the revolutionary forces and reactionary forces in the East, Mao and the CCP leadership accelerated their support for the Viet Minh. On June 27, three days after the outbreak of the Korean War, Mao Zedong, Liu Shaoqi, Zhu De, and other top CCP leaders met with Chinese military advisers preparing to work in Vietnam. Mao told the advisers to help the Vietnamese organize and establish a formal army and to assist them in planning and conducting major operations to defeat French forces. Liu Shaoqi explained that if the Chinese failed to support the Vietnamese revolutionaries and allowed the enemy to remain the Chinese would meet more difficulty and trouble on their southern borders.[26] The Chinese Military Advisory Group, composed of 79 experienced PLA officers, was formally established in late July, with General Wei Guoqing as the head, assisted by General Mei Jiasheng and General Deng Yifan, both army-level commanders from the Third Field Army. To maintain secrecy, they were known publicly as the "Working Group in Southern China."They arrived in Vietnam in early August, and started to serve with the Vietnamese Communist forces.[27]

Meanwhile, the CCP leadership had decided to send General Chen Geng, one of the most talented, high-ranking PLA commanders and a member of the CCP Central Committee, to Vietnam. His task was to help organize a major military campaign along the Chinese-Vietnamese border, so that the Viet Minh would be directly backed by the PRC. This idea was first put forward by Ho Chi Minh during his secret visit to China in early 1950 and was received with much interest by the CCP leadership. Ho himself had suggested Chen Geng, whom he had known since the 1920s.[28] On June 30, the CCP Central Committee formally appointed Chen Geng as the party's representative to Vietnam.[29] General Chen traveled to the Viet Minh's bases in northern Vietnam in mid-July. After a series of meetings with Ho, General Vo Nguyen Giap, and other Viet Minh leaders, Chen worked out the campaign plan in late July.[30] In order to guarantee success, Beijing provided military equipment and other war materials. By September 1950, the Chinese had delivered more than 14,000 guns, 1,700 machine guns, about 150 pieces of artillery, 2,800 tons of grain, and large amounts of ammunition, medicine, uniforms, and communication equipment.[31] With the joint effort of the Viet Minh and Chinese Communists, the Border Campaign turned out to be a great success for the Viet Minh, and changed the balance of power on the Indochina battlefield. With the vast territory of the PRC becoming the Viet Minh's strategic rear, Ho Chi Minh and the Vietnamese Communists were now in an unbeatable position.[32] General Chen believed this battle important for the pressure it added to the "imperialist camp" already engaged in Korea.[33]

The Korean battlefield held the main attention of the CCP leadership. Mao and other Beijing leaders were concerned not only with how to "hold ground" in the face of the new American threat but also with how further to strengthen the CCP's leading position at home and influence abroad through successfully managing the Korean crisis. Beijing's strategy toward the Korean crisis was thus belligerent in nature from the outset.

A crucial question for Beijing leaders was how to judge correctly the prospect of the Korean War, especially after American ground forces began landing in South Korea. In accordance with Mao's long-time philosophy of "striving for the best while preparing for the worst," Beijing leaders believed that the Korea War could have three different outcomes. First, North Korean troops might succeed in sweeping cross the Korean Peninsula and forcing American troops to retreat from Korea. If so, the Korean crisis would be solved in a way favorable to the revolutionaries, making the power and influence of the United States in East Asia suffer. Second, with the continuous arrival of American reinforcements on battlefield, a strategic stalemate could emerge with neither side gaining an upper hand, causing a prolonged crisis and making both the military and political implications of the war more complicated. Third, America's military involvement might succeed and the situation in Korea could be reversed. If so, the reversal would presumably be followed by a UN forces' counteroffensive toward the Yalu, and the reactionary forces at home and abroad, including the GMD government in Taiwan, would take this opportunity to recover "lost ground" in China. If the worst possibilities occurred, China's security interests would be seriously threatened.[34] CCP leaders hoped that North Korea would succeed, but they could not ignore the danger involved in a possible setback.

The sensitive relationship between Beijing and Pyongyang made the situation even trickier for CCP leaders. In preparing his invasion of the South, Kim Il-sung had not informed Mao and the CCP of his specific plan and timing of invasion, and even after the war began, he did not formally inform Beijing leaders until June 27, when his troops had already occupied Seoul.[35] In the initial stage of the war, the well-prepared and equipped North Korean military forces had the upper hand on the battlefield. Kim Il-sung appears to have believed that direct help from Beijing was neither necessary nor desirable, especially if such help would strengthen the position of opposition factions within the North Korean Communist Party. Under these circumstances, Kim acted on his own, and Beijing seemed to have had little influence on Kim's handling of the war. In the first two weeks of conflict, Beijing leaders even lacked first-hand information on the war's development.[36] This perhaps explains why the Beijing leadership did not convene decision-making meetings on new military deployments aimed at Korea until two weeks after the outbreak of the War.

Beijing leaders, however, tried their best to follow the changing situation on the battlefield from the very beginning. After learning that President Truman had announced that the United States would come to the rescue of South Korea, the Chinese General Staff suggested immediately that Beijing send a group of military observers to Pyongyang to "investigate the military situation" as well as to "strengthen the connection with the [North] Koreans."[37] After reviewing this report, Zhou Enlai, obviously with Beijing's intricate relationship with Kim Il-sung in mind, decided to send a group of Chinese military-intelligence officers to Pyongyang, not as "military observers" but as members of the Chinese embassy.[38] On the late evening of June 30, Zhou, together with Zhang Hanfu, vice foreign minister, and Liu Zhijian, first deputy director of the CMC's Intelligence Department, received Chai Chengwen, former director of the Intelligence Department of the PLA's Southwestern Military Region. Zhou named Chai political counsellor of the Chinese embassy in Pyongyang in order to "establish connections with Comrade Kim Il-sung" as well as to collect first-hand information on the fighting. Zhou wanted Chinese diplomats sent to Pyongyang within one week.[39] Less than one week after the outbreak of the war, Korea was becoming the focus of Beijing's strategy vis-à-vis the United States.

The Establishment of the NEBDA

With their attention increasingly centering on Korea, Beijing leaders became more worried about the effect of American intervention. On July 6, an editorial of *Renmin ribao* openly warned that the presence of U.S. military forces in Korea meant that "the Korean people's victory could be a bit slower" and that "the Korean people had to prepare for a prolonged and more arduous warfare."[40] On July 7, the UN Security Council, again in the absence of the Soviet Union, authorized the creation of a unified UN command, which would be directed by an American commander. On the same day, the American 24th Division began to land in Korea. All of this immediately captured the attention of the Beijing leadership. The next day, in a talk with the Chinese diplomats who were leaving for Korea, Zhou pointed out that as American troops had already entered the Korean War and the UN Security Council had authorized the United States to command the UN troops, the conflict in Korea would likely be prolonged.[41] The deep-rooted worries that Pyongyang could lose the initiative in the war precipitated Beijing's new military deployment to cope with the Korean conflict.

On July 7 and 10, Zhou, under Mao's instructions, chaired two conferences focusing on military preparations and other issues related to the Korean conflict. The participants in these conferences were leading members of the CMC, directors of the CMC's different departments, commanders of the PLA's services and arms, as well as the PLA's regional headquarters.[42] At the beginning of the July 7 conference, Zhou conveyed to the participants Mao's analysis of the situation which emphasized that it was necessary to establish a "Northeast Border Defense Army," so that "in case we needed to enter the war we would be prepared."[43] The central decision made at these conferences was that the 38th, 39th, and 40th Armies of the 13th Army Corps under the Fourth Field Army (these were the best units of the PLA which had been used as a general reserve force since late 1949) would be moved into the Northeast immediately. These forces, added to the 42nd Army and the First, Second, and Eighth Artillery Divisions, which had been stationed in the Northeast, would be transformed into the Northeast Border Defense Army (NEBDA). The redeployed troops were to be in position on the Chinese-Korean border by the end of July.[44] The two conferences also decided that Su Yu, then vice commander of the East China Military Region, who had been responsible for planning the Taiwan campaign since the summer of 1949, would be appointed commander and political commissar of the NEBDA. Xiao Jinguang, commander of the navy, would become the NEBDA's vice commander, and Xiao Hua, vice director of the PLA's General Political Department, would take the position as the NEBDA's vice political commissar. In order to guarantee the logistical support for the troops that were moving into the Chinese-Korean border areas, the two conferences decided to appoint Li Jükui, then deputy chief of staff of the PLA's Central-southern Military Region, as the logistics commander of the NEBDA. Considering that the PLA had undergone a demobilization following the principle of cutting off the numbers while improving the quality of the troops since early 1950, the two conferences decided to ask the PLA's General Logistics Department to formulate and implement new plans for recruiting soldiers. The two conferences also decided to start immediately a movement of political mobilization following the slogan of "defending the safety of our country" among PLA soldiers, and they assigned the PLA's General Political Department the responsibility for organizing this political mobilization.[45]

Mao and other members of the CCP Politburo Standing Committee immediately approved the decisions of the two conferences.[46] On July 13 the CMC formally issued the "Orders to Defend the

Northeast Borders." The main contents of the orders were: First, four armies (the 38th, 39th, 40th, and 42nd) and three artillery divisions (the First, Second, and Eighth) would be concentrated on the Chinese-Korean border to establish the NEBDA. Their main tasks were "to defend the borders of the Northeast, and to prepare to support the war operations of the Korean People's Army if necessary." Second, Su Yu was appointed as commander and political commissar of the NEBDA; Xiao Jinguang the vice commander; Xiao Hua the vice political commissar; and Li Jükui the commander of logistic affairs.[47] Third, the headquarters of the 15th Army Corps was to be transformed into the new headquarters of the 13th Army Corps to command the 38th, 39th, and 40th Armies. Deng Hua, the commander of the 15th Army Corps and a talented high-ranking officer of the PLA, was appointed commander of the 13th Army Corps, Xie Fang the chief of staff, and Du Ping the director of the Political Department.[48] In less than three weeks after the outbreak of the Korean War, the Beijing leadership took a crucial step to make China's intervention in Korea possible.

Initial Military and Political Mobilization

Immediately after the issuance of the CMC's July 13 order, large-scale military redeployment started. The 38th Army arrived in the Fengcheng area of Liaoning province on July 24; the 39th Army entered the Liaoyang-Haicheng areas in Liaoning the next day; the 40th Army, which had to travel from Guangdong province in the south to the Northeast, arrived by train at Andong, a border city on the Yalu River, on July 27. Meanwhile, the 42nd Army, which had been previously stationed in the Qiqihaer area of Heilongjiang province in northern Manchuria, moved into the Tonghua-Ji'an area of Jilin province. By the end of July, four armies, three artillery divisions, four air-defense artillery regiments, three truck transport regiments, one tank regiment, one engineer regiment, and one cavalry regiment, with a total of more than 255,000 troops, had taken positions on the Chinese-Korean border.[49] In order to guarantee the transportation lines between China and North Korea, Nie Rongzhen proposed to Mao and Zhou on August 2 that the Northeast Military Region send anti-aircraft artillery units to defend bridges over the Yalu River. Mao approved this proposal immediately.[50]

While military redeployment was under way, military planners in Beijing labored to stockpile war materials, establish rear bases for war operations, and organize a logistical supply network. On July 14, Zhou Enlai telegraphed the Northeast People's Government, the Headquarters of the Northeast Military Region, and the Headquarters of the Central-southern Military Region (the 13th Army Corps belonged to this region before moving into the Northeast), setting up rules to ensure logistical support and military expenditures for the NEBDA. After the 13th Army Corps entered the Northeast, according to Zhou's instructions, the CMC would be in charge of supplying the NEBDA with weapons, ammunition, clothing, medicine and medical equipment, communication equipment, and automobile parts, while the Northeast Region should be responsible for offering the NEBDA food, fuel, daily operating costs, and operation expenditures.[51] When all units of the NEBDA had almost completed their redeployment in the Northeast, the CMC decided on July 26 to reestablish the Logistics Department under the Headquarters of the Northeast Military Region and formally appointed Li Jükui its director, to coordinate logistical preparations for the NEBDA. Then logistics departments were established at both army and division levels for all units of the NEBDA. The Logistics Department of the PLA's Northeast Military Region Headquarters was formally established on August 7, 1950.[52]

Meanwhile, the PLA high command made extensive efforts to establish war material stockpile for troops moving into the Northeast. In mid-July, the General Logistics Department assigned the Northeastern, Northern, Eastern, and Central-southern Military Regions to prepare for the NEBDA 340,000 sets of cotton-padded uniforms, 360,000 pairs of cotton-padded leather shoes, 400,000 cotton-padded hats, cotton-padded waistcoats, and cotton-padded overcoats, 400,000 pairs of sweat pants, 700,000 pairs of cotton-padded gloves and socks, and 5,000 field cauldrons. In late July, the CMC gathered for the NEBDA from different military regions 54 types of ammunition, totalling 1,600 tons. The CMC also tried to establish for the NEBDA field hospitals with a capacity of 100,000 beds and assigned to them 20 surgical operation teams. Assisted by the Northeast Military Region, the CMC allocated more than 1,000 transport trucks, together with drivers and driver assistants, for troops in the Northeast, so that the NEBDA would be able to establish food storage for three months and fuel storage for six months.[53]

The Beijing leadership made these logistical preparations not only for battles on the Chinese-Korean border areas but also for possible military operations in Korea. In early August, on his way to his new post in Shenyang, Li Jükui stopped by Beijing to have a discussion with Nie Rongzhen. Nie told Li that the CCP leadership had decided to assist North Korea in fighting the United States and was prepared to send troops into Korea. To ensure well-coordinated logistics, Mao had approved the establishing of a Logistics Department at the Headquarters of the PLA Northeast Military Region. If Chinese troops entered military operations in Korea, the department would be responsible for all logistical needs of troops in both the Northeast and in Korea.[54] Nie's talks demonstrated clearly that the purpose of China's military preparations had gone beyond the simple defense of the Chinese-Korean border.

While military preparations were under way, the CCP leadership paid special attention to the political mobilization of the entire Chinese nation. At the decision-making conference of July 7 as well as in a series of other discussions by the CCP leadership, an issue of central importance was how to utilize the Korean crisis to precipitate a widespread political mobilization. Mao and the CCP leadership decided to start a political indoctrination movement combining "internationalism and patriotism," following the slogan of "defending the homeland and safeguarding the country" (*baojia weiguo*).[55] All of this turned out to be the prelude of the "Great Movement to Resist America and Assist Korea," one of the "three great movements" (the other two were the land reform movement and the movement to suppress reactionaries) in the early years of the PRC.

In accordance with the considerations of changing outside pressures into the dynamics of internal mobilization, a semi-official organization, "The Chinese People's Committee of the Movement to Fight against U.S. Invasion of Taiwan and Korea," was established on July 10. Directly controlled by the CCP, the committee consisted of all non-Communist "democratic parties" and "people's organizations" (such as the General Chinese Workers' Union, the General Chinese Youth Association, and the General Chinese Women's Association). The main task of the committee was to coordinate and promote a nationwide anti-American imperialism propaganda movement. On July 14, the committee announced that the week from July 17 to 23 would be a "Special Week for the Movement of Opposing the U.S.

Invasion of Taiwan and Korea." The purpose of this particular movement, according to the announcement of the committee, was "to wage a profound propaganda campaign and to educate the people all over the country, so that they would be able to understand thoroughly that U.S. imperialists had committed crimes in their aggression towards Asian countries and destruction of the world peace, and that U.S. imperialists were totally defeatable." The committee called on the entire country to use newspapers, radio broadcasts, magazines, wall posters, movies, dramas, songs, speeches, store windows, and exhibitions to stir the "hatred of the U.S. imperialists" and the "sympathy and support of the Korean people" among the great masses in China.[56]

What should be noted here is the CCP's eagerness to inculcate a new image of the United States into the minds of the Chinese people through political indoctrination and propaganda. They emphasized that the United States had long engaged in both political and economic aggressions against China, that the United States had been hostile to the Chinese revolution, that the United States, as a declining capitalist country, was in reality not as powerful as it seemed to be, and that a confrontation between China and the United States was inevitable. "Beating American arrogance" became a central propaganda theme.[57]

In the meantime, the Beijing leadership decided to further promote a nationwide campaign aimed at suppressing "reactionaries and reactionary activities." CCP leaders regarded this as a long overdue task. In the last stage of China's civil war, while Communist forces marched forward rapidly and the GMD regime and its military forces disintegrated, the Communists would often occupy a region, especially in outlying areas, without properly cleaning up GMD remnants. Furthermore, in order to maintain social order during the initial days of Communist takeover, the CCP adopted a relatively lenient policy toward members of GMD government and military forces who had stopped resisting the Communists. This policy, however, created elements of instability within Communist-controlled territories. After the PLA had conquered the mainland (except for Tibet) by early 1950, the CCP leadership felt the necessity to consolidate its rule through "suppressing reactionary activities." In mid-March 1950, the CCP Central Committee issued a formal directive on "suppressing reactionaries," which symbolized the start of this "great movement" of the early days of the PRC.[58]

Until the outbreak of the Korean War, the movement to suppress reactionary activities had achieved only marginal progress. In addition to such factors as Communist cadres lacking experience and CCP local authorities being busy with other affairs (such as fighting with the runaway inflation left by the GMD regime), another key reason for the slow progress of the movement was the CCP's need for a stronger rationale to convince the great masses in China that the terror created by such a movement was necessary. The crisis situation caused by the Korean War offered the opportunity. On July 23, when the "Special Week for the Movement of Opposing the U.S. Invasion of Taiwan and Korea" had reached its peak, the Beijing leadership, in the name of the State Council and the Supreme People's Court, issued the "Instructions on Suppressing Reactionary Activities." The instructions emphasized that the reactionary activities at home were "directed by imperialists abroad." The Beijing leadership ordered all party organs and government agencies to take it as "one of their utmost tasks" to "lead the people to mop up ruthlessly all open and hidden reactionaries, thus establishing and consolidating the revolutionary order, safeguarding the democratic rights of the people, and guaranteeing that the reconstruction and all necessary social transformations would be carried out smoothly."[59] Following the instructions, a new wave of "suppressing reactionaries" swept across China, reaching its peak after China's entry into the Korean War.[60]

In short, the Beijing leadership's management of the Korean crisis was a comprehensive effort. While Beijing leaders paid special attention to military preparations, they also emphasized the importance of political mobilization in a variety of forms. In the eyes of Mao and the CCP leadership, the new China's security interests would be best served by guaranteeing the safety of the Chinese-Korean border, promoting the CCP's authority and credibility at home, and enhancing the new China's prestige on the international scene. Mao and the CCP leadership were determined to achieve all of these goals.[61]

War Preparations Intensified

In view of the gradual emergence of a stalemate on the Korean battlefield, Beijing leaders' fear about a reversal in the Korean War was justified. After the UN Security Council's call for assisting South Korea, Truman instructed MacArthur on June 29 to use the naval and air resources of the Far East Command to support South Korean forces. The next day Truman approved the use of ground forces stationed in Japan for battles in South Korea. American reinforcements reached Korea in early July, five days before the creation of the UN command. Troops from fifteen other member nations of the UN gradually joined the United States to participate in operations in Korea. The North Korean forces were still able to advance relentlessly during July and early August until they were stopped in the southeastern part of the Korean Peninsula, the last toehold of the UN forces. Then the currents of war began to change. By August 5, the UN command had established a defensive perimeter behind the Naktong River, around the southernmost port of Pusan, through which UN forces were reinforced and supplied. Although Kim Il-sung announced on August 15 that the month of August would become the month of "national liberation," repeated North Korean attacks on the "Pusan perimeter" made no substantial progress, primarily because the North Koreans had too long a supply line and their offensive power had been exhausted. The war had entered a stalemate and the prospect for a North Korean victory was slipping away.

In the meantime, warning signals emerged in Taiwan when General MacArthur made a dramatic, unauthorized trip there for two days at the end of July. During his stay there, MacArthur claimed that "arrangements have been completed for effective coordination between American forces under my command and those of the Chinese Government" to meet any attack.[62] Beijing quickly pointed to MacArthur's activities in Taiwan as strong evidence of "American aggression and invasion of Taiwan," which was part of the overall U.S. imperialist plot to surround and strangle the new China.[63]

Under these circumstances Mao and his fellow Beijing leaders believed that it was necessary to accelerate preparations for sending Chinese troops to Korea. On August 4, 1950, the Politburo met to discuss the Korean situation. Top CCP leaders speculated that the Korean War could either be a short one or a long one, that the war could be further expanded, and even that the atomic bomb might be used. They understood that if the United States were to use the atomic bomb in Korea China had no way to stop it. But they would not be scared by such a prospect and would try to use conventional weapons to fight the Americans. In any case, they believed that China had to prepare for the worst possible scenario. Mao mentioned the necessity of intervention at the meeting: "If the U.S. imperialists won the war, they would become more arrogant and would threaten us. We should not fail to assist the Koreans. We must lend them our hands in the form of sending our military volunteers there. The timing could be further decided, but we have to prepare for this." Zhou Enlai echoed Mao's ideas by stressing that "if the U.S. imperialists defeated North Korea, the cause of peace would suffer and the Americans would become more aggressive." In Zhou's opinion, "in order to win the war, China's strength must be added to the struggle." He believed that "if China's strength were added, the whole international situation could be changed." He asked his comrades to "establish such a broad perspective."[64]

In a move obviously related to the Politburo's August 4 discussion, Mao, in the name of the CCP Central Committee, cabled Gao Gang the following day, ordering him to "take the main responsibility to call a meeting of all the army and division cadres [of the NEBDA] in mid-August and to outline the goals, significance, and general directions of the war operations." The chairman emphasized that "it is required that all the troops must complete their preparations within this month and be ready for orders to carry out war operations. The troops must maintain high morale and be well-prepared. Questions raised by officers and soldiers regarding the war must be answered."[65] The Politburo discussion and Mao's telegram demonstrate unmistakably that the CCP leadership had seriously considered sending troops to assist North Korea in fighting the UN forces in early August, more than one month before the Inchon landing.

Following Mao's August 5 instruction, the 13th Army Corps held a conference attended by army- and division-level commanders on August 13. Gao Gang chaired the meeting. Xiao Hua and Xiao Jinguang traveled to Shenyang to attend it. Gao conveyed the Politburo's instructions, emphasizing that the main task of the Border Defense Army was to prepare to assist the North Korean forces to defeat the Americans if necessary.[66] According to the memoirs of Du Ping, director of the 13th Army Corps' Political Department, the major theme of the meeting was: "Should we allow the Americans to occupy Korea and attack China and then destroy them? Or should it be better if we take the initiative, assisting the Korean People's Army to wipe out the enemy and defend ourselves?" The answer of the majority attending the conference was: "We should take the initiative, cooperate with the Korean People's Army, march forward without reluctance, and break up the enemy's dream of aggression."[67]

Participants at the conference also believed that China possessed several advantages that would guarantee its victory in a military confrontation with the United States. Chinese troops outnumbered the Americans by three to one. While U.S. military commitments in West Europe and North America were preventing Washington from sending any more than half million troops to Korea, China had an army of more than four million to draw on. Moreover, the quality of Chinese soldiers, their morale in particular, was superior to American soldiers. As they were fighting for a just cause, the Chinese would be able to prevail. Third, China, much closer to the battlefield than the United States, held an upper hand in logistics. Finally, the sympathy of the world's people was on the side of China, while the United States was in a morally unfavorable position.[68] These points would be emphasized repeatedly as China further mobilized toward an intervention in Korea.

Obviously influenced by the CCP Politburo's attitudes regarding the possibility that the United States might use nuclear weapons, the conference participants discussed the limits of the atomic bomb as a weapon to be used in Korea. They emphasized that human forces, not one or two atomic bombs, would determine the result of a war. Participants in the conference also believed that in a tactical sense, if the Americans used the bomb in Korea, it would not only hurt the Chinese but also harm the Americans themselves, and that in a strategic sense, policymakers in Washington had to consider the shocking influence on world opinion if they used the bomb.[69] In short, the dominant voice of the conference favored the CCP Politburo's opinion that China should not be scared by the bomb.

The conference also touched upon possible Chinese military strategies and tactics to be used in operations against the Americans on the Korean battlefield. Deng Hua, commander of the 13th Army Corps, reported to the meeting the result of the studies by himself and his staff in this regard. According to him, the strong point of the Americans was that they possessed superior fire power and greater mobility. It would thus be extremely difficult for the Chinese to defeat the Americans by adopting a strategy of waging a frontal offensive. Deng introduced an alternative strategy. He proposed that Chinese troops should seek out weak links in American lines, bravely penetrate into the rear of the enemy, destroy the enemy's transportation and communication networks, and then annihilate enemy forces by separating and surrounding them. These advantages, according to Deng, would make a Chinese victory over the Americans possible.[70]

The conference, however, also concluded that preparations for entering the Korean War were "too onerous to be completed in August." The most conspicuous difficulties existed in equipment supply, medical support, and in establishing a secure communication network. Most participants believed that it would take additional time to carry out the task of political mobilization among the troops that would enter operations in Korea.[71] Gao Gang reported these conclusions to Mao by telegraph on August 15 and suggested that the date for sending Chinese troops to Korea be postponed. Gao's report was further reinforced by Xiao Jinguang, who conveyed the NEBDA's difficulties to Mao in person after returning to Beijing.[72] Mao, having second thoughts, cabled Gao Gang on August 18, again in the name of the CCP Central Committee, approving that "the deadline for the Border Defense Army to complete its training and other preparations can be postponed to the end of September." In the meantime, he ordered Gao to "step up supervision, and make sure that all preparations will be completed by September 30."[73]

Following Mao's instructions, the NEBDA made every effort to push forward military preparations and political mobilization to meet the new deadline for completing war preparations. In mid-August, the 13th Army Corps convened a meeting focusing on the political indoctrination and mobilization of its troops. Participants in the meeting reported that the soldiers of the 13th Army Corps differed on the problem of entering the Korean War. About 50 percent of the soldiers, most of whom were Communist Party or Communist Youth League members, were positive about fighting in Korea. Many of them had even submitted petitions for participating in "resisting Americans and assisting the Korean people." About 40 percent of the soldiers appeared indifferent, neither enthusiastic nor unwilling to fight in Korea. They would obey orders. Around 10 percent of the soldiers, the majority of whom were former GMD soldiers or new recruits from the "newly liberated areas," did not want to be sent to Korea. They were particularly worried about having to fight the Americans, who had the atomic bomb. Some even openly opposed China's entry into the war because this could "draw the fire to China itself."[74]

The 13th Army Corps responded with a political indoctrination and mobilization campaign in late August, focusing on three themes—"if we *must* fight the war" (*bi'da*), "if we *dare to* fight the war" (*gan'da*), and if we *can* win the war" (*neng'da*). In answer to the first question, political cadres of the 13th Army Corps stressed that U.S. imperialists historically had been aggressive toward China and that just as the Japanese imperialists, America's intervention in the Korean War aimed to threaten the security of China. They emphasized that the United States had proved itself to be the most dangerous enemy of the Chinese people, that China's confrontation with the United States was inevitable, and that to aid the North Koreans was also to safeguard China itself. In answering the second and the third questions, CCP cadres made every effort to convince the soldiers that American troops, though equipped with modern weapons, were fighting an unjust war, and thus lacked a high morale, that the Americans were too far away from their own country, making them logistically vulnerable, and that the UN forces would be easily outnumbered by the Chinese and North Koreans. In order to make these points more persuasive, they arranged for some "liberated soldiers" (GMD captives who joined the PLA) who had fought together with American troops in Burma during the Second World War to discuss the weaknesses of American soldiers, to demonstrate that the Americans were beatable.[75]

Meanwhile, the troops in the Chinese-Korean border areas conducted a series of training programs specifically designed for fighting the Americans in Korea. For example, all military and political officers over battalion level were required to study carefully Korea's geographic features and topography, as well as the character of American troops. Many of them were also trained in special anti-aircraft and anti-tank programs. In order to prepare for military operations in Korea, the PLA's Northeast Military Region recruited more than 2,000 Korean nationals in the Northeast to serve as interpreters and liaison personnel for Chinese troops.[76] Du Ping later recalled that he and his colleagues all felt that "the order for operations could soon come, and we have to hurry up."[77]

Concerns for a Reversal

With military preparations for entering the war under way, the PLA's General Staff, together with the Ministry of Foreign Affairs, held a series of meetings in the second half of August to analyze possible changes on the Korean battlefield. PLA military planners noticed that the Americans had concentrated two divisions of troops and many naval vessels in Japan. They worried that General MacArthur might use these forces in a major landing operation behind the North Korean lines.[78]

Members of the Ministry of Foreign Affairs were also alarmed by two statements by Warren Austin, U.S. delegate to the UN, on August 10 and 17, which emphasized that the goal of UN military action in Korea was to unify the entire peninsula.[79] Responding to Austin's statement, Zhou cabled Trygve Lie, UN secretary general, and Jacob Malik (the Soviet delegate who returned to the UN on August 1 to chair the Security Council for the month), on August 20, emphasizing that as Korea was China's neighbor, Beijing was very concerned with the solution of the Korean question.[80]

Following Zhou's instructions, on August 23 the staff of the Operation Bureau of the PLA's General Staff convened a meeting to discuss the situation on the Korean battlefield, chaired by Zhou's military secretary Lei Yingfu (who had then also been appointed as the Bureau's vice director). After debating different options and conducting a simulated scenario on maps, the participants unanimously concluded that the enemy's next step would be a landing operation at one of five possible Korean ports, Wonsan, Nampo, Inchon, Kunsan, and Hungnam. Among these ports, the most likely and threatening one would be Inchon.

According to Lei Yingfu's recollections, which are supported by his personal notes, the meeting summarized six reasons for this conclusion. First, the enemy had concentrated more than ten divisions in a narrow and small area behind the Naktong River and adopted a strategy of neither retreating nor attacking. It was obvious that the purpose of such a strategy was to trap as many KPA troops as possible, thus creating opportunities to strike the KPA's rear. Second, the Americans had held two divisions in Japan, and recently more mobile units had arrived there. These troops, however, were not used to reinforce the Pusan perimeter; nor were they deployed along the coast of Japan for strengthening its defense. Instead, they were conducting intensive training, especially for landing operations. Third, General MacArthur and many other American commanders had fought in the Pacific area during the Second World War and were experienced in amphibious operations. Fourth, many British and American naval vessels, including numerous landing craft, had been moving from other parts of the world to East Asia. This indicated American intentions to land in the North Koreans' rear. Fifth, under the heavy pressure of the KPA's continuous offensives, the enemy troops had been pushed into the small areas behind the Naktong River. They had constructed strong defensive works, making it difficult for the KPA to annihilate them in a short period. The longer the KPA's main forces were bogged down before the Naktong River, the deeper the crisis could be. Sixth, Korea was a narrow and long peninsula and Seoul served as the key linkage for almost all north–south transportation lines. Inchon, located close to Seoul, became the most practical place for the Americans to land. If the enemy landed at Inchon while at the same time starting a counteroffensive from the Naktong area, the KPA would be forced to engage in a two-front war with its main forces being cut off in the South. The entire situation of the Korean War could thus change immediately in the enemy's favor.[81]

Lei personally reported the conclusions of the meeting to Zhou Enlai on the evening of August 23. Zhou took them very seriously and immediately relayed to Mao the conclusions Lei and his staff had reached. Alarmed, Mao instructed Zhou and Lei to come to his office to give a more detailed report. Mao, obviously convinced by the ideas of Lei and his colleagues, then began to ask Lei questions, particularly about General MacArthur's personality. Lei replied that as a military commander MacArthur was famous for his arrogance and stubbornness. Mao, greatly interested in this, commented: "Fine! Fine! The more arrogant and more stubborn he is, the better. An arrogant enemy is easy to defeat."[82]

Mao then had a brief discussion with Zhou and decided to take three measures immediately. First, they decided to reiterate to the NEBDA that no matter what the difficulties, all preparations for operations should be completed by the end of September. Second, they decided to inform the North Koreans and the Soviets immediately that Chinese military planners believed that the Americans might land at Inchon, and to suggest the KPA move some units from the Naktong area to Inchon to strengthen its defense. Third, they decided to order both the Ministry of Foreign Affairs and the PLA's General Staff to pay close attention to the enemy's movement and report any change promptly.[83]

Mao was truly concerned with the danger of the possible reversal of the Korean War. Several days after the meeting with Zhou and Lei, Lee Sang-jo, a representative of the Korean People's Army, came to Beijing to inform the Chinese of the situation on the Korean battlefield. While meeting Lee, Mao stressed that the North Koreans needed to pay sufficient attention to the possibility that UN forces could land at some place on the East or West coasts of the Korean peninsula, thus attacking the North Korean forces from the rear. Mao pointed to a map and mentioned specifically that Inchon was one of the most likely spots for such a landing. Mao suggested that the North Koreans prepare for the contingency.[84] Kim Il-sung, however, ignored Mao's warnings.[85]

In the eyes of the Chinese leaders, the situation was urgent. To speed up the NEBDA's war preparations, Zhou chaired a long-scheduled coordinating meeting late on the evening of August 23 to solve the NEBDA's supply problems. At the meeting it was decided that the Northeastern People's Government would be responsible for the NEBDA's food, forage, and coal supplies and the Fourth Field Army would pay for the NEBDA's budget. All of the NEBDA's operational expenditures beyond budget would be covered by the central government, which would use cotton, yarn, and cloth to support the currency in circulation in the Northeast.[86]

On August, 26 the CMC convened a crucial meeting, chaired by Zhou, to further discuss the nature of the Korean crisis and to define the NEBDA's tasks and strategies.[87] Zhou offered a central report, which reflected clearly top CCP leaders' perception of the Korean situation. Zhou first summarized the international nature of the Korean crisis:

> The U.S. imperialist [intervention in Korea] aims to open a breach in Korea, to change Korea into the base for their actions in the East, and to prepare for starting a new world war. . . . Therefore, Korea is indeed the focus of the struggles in the world. Taking advantage of the Korean War, the U.S. imperialists have succeeded in seizing the banner of the United Nations in their confrontation with the peace front. They have also used the Korean problem to wage domestic mobilization. As the American strategic emphasis lies in Europe, they are also doing everything possible to use the Korean problem to mobilize capitalist countries in Europe, so that these countries will obey the domination of the United States. [The Americans] want also to take this

opportunity to remilitarize Japan and West Germany, with the consent of other capitalist countries. After conquering Korea, the United States will certainly turn to Vietnam and other colonial countries. Therefore the Korean problem is at least the key to the East.

Viewing the Korean crisis from this international perspective, Zhou believed it necessary for Beijing "to use the Korean problem to explore the plots of the U.S. imperialists." He emphasized that the Chinese should "not treat the Korean problem merely as one concerning a brother country [North Korea] or as one related to the interests of the Northeast"; rather, Zhou stressed, the Korean problem "should be regarded as an important international issue."

Zhou continued to analyze possible prospects of the development of the Korean crisis. He stated that with the eruption of the Korean War, Mao, himself, and other top Beijing leaders had expected that the North Koreans would either liberate the entire Korean peninsula in a short time or face a long and difficult confrontation with the Americans and Rhee's troops. "After observing the fighting for two months," Zhou stated, "it is now apparent that the pursuit of the first possibility is almost impossible." Zhou believed that China should get ready to cope with a reversal of the Korean conflict. "Our duty is now much heavier," stressed Zhou, "and we should prepare for the worst and prepare quickly." Zhou emphasized particularly that in no circumstance should the plan to enter the Korean War be released, even to the North Koreans, so that "we could enter the war and give the enemy a sudden blow."[88]

Zhou then entered into a detailed discussion of how the three services of the Chinese military should prepare for a direct confrontation with the United States. He instructed all of the arms of the PLA to make long-range plans for "the coming war [with the United States]." Regarding the tasks and strategies of the NEBDA, Zhou conveyed Mao's instructions that the NEBDA should speed up training and establish a unified command structure, and when the troops began operations in Korea, a commander-in-chief would be appointed to lead them. Zhou mentioned that in order to rotate combat troops in Korea, the Central Committee was considering asking each of the PLA's military region to offer ten armies as reserve forces.

The meeting examined the current status of air force, airborne troops, and tank units, and found that the offensive air force, with a size of only seven regiments, could not begin operations in Korea earlier than December, and that neither the airborne forces nor the tank units were in a position to enter the war. The meeting concluded that it was necessary to purchase more weapons from the Soviet Union, so that ten armies would get proper artillery supply, and by the end of 1950 four air regiments, nine tank regiments, and eighteen anti-aircraft artillery regiments could be used in operations in Korea.[89]

Following the lines of the August 26 meeting, Zhou chaired another meeting on August 31 to further discuss the structure and strategy of the NEBDA.[90] The meeting decided that the NEBDA would be composed of eleven armies (36 divisions) or about 700,000 troops, deployed in three lines: the 13th Army Corps, plus the 42nd Army would become the first line, the Ninth Army Corps the second line, and the 19th Army Corps the third line. The meeting also decided to further strengthen the NEBDA's artillery units by adding seven artillery divisions and twenty-six anti-aircraft artillery regiments. The meeting estimated that casualties of around 200,000 (60,000 deaths and 140,000 wounds) would occur in the first year of the war, and proper medical support should be prepared.[91] Accordingly, the CMC decided on August 31 to establish three branches under the Logistics Department of the Northeast Military Region, so that supplies to combat troops in different areas would be securely guaranteed.[92]

For the purpose of strengthening reinforcements for the NEBDA, in early September, the CMC, following General Nie Rongzhen's suggestion, decided to move the Ninth Army Corps and the 19th Army Corps from the Shanghai area and northwestern China to areas close to Shanhaiguan, which lay close to northeastern China.[93] The Chinese military forces involved in coping with contingencies in Korea had thus reached twelve armies. On August 27, Mao informed Peng Dehuai, military and administrative head of the Northwest Region and later commander of Chinese troops in Korea, that the CCP central leadership would decide how to use the concentrated Chinese troops by the end of September.[94]

These preparations and redeployments were made with the assumption that Chinese troops would begin military operations in Korea sooner or later, which was demonstrated clearly in a report by NEBDA commanders in late August. Viewing that a stalemate had emerged on the Korean battlefield, Xie Fang, Deng Hua, and Hong Xuezhi increasingly worried about a UN counterattack. They believed that it would be foolish for China to wait until an American counteroffensive had placed the Northeast under direct threat; it would be better to enter the war earlier to assist the North Koreans to maintain the initiative on the battlefield.[95] On August 31, 1950, they sent a report, drafted by Xie, to the CMC. The situation in Korea, in their view, was not optimistic:

> The U.S. imperialists are endeavoring to hold the Taegu-Pusan area and to use partial counter-offensive to consolidate their position, so that they could gain time and start a counter-offensive after the arrival of reinforcements. On the other hand, opportunities for the Korean People's Army to break up and destroy the enemy are no longer there. . . . The intentions of the enemy's counter-attack are assumed to be as follows: first, to land part of its troops on some coastal areas in north Korea for harassing and holding operations and advance its main forces northward along main highways and railways gradually; second, to make a large-scale landing of its main forces on our flank rear areas (Pyongyang or Seoul) and at the same time employ a small force to pin down the [North Korean] People's Army in its present position, enabling it to attack from the front and rear simultaneously. In that case the People's Army would be in a very difficult situation.

In order to avoid this scenario, they believed that the North Koreans had to win the war quickly and needed China's help. To assure the success of Chinese intervention, they made three suggestions. First, China should make every effort to secure strong Soviet air support and more Soviet equipment when Chinese troops entered operations in Korea.[96] Second, in addition to the 13th Army Corps, China needed to commit two additional army corps to Korea, with proper artillery and tank support. They also needed more anti-aircraft artillery and anti-tank weapons. Third, logistical support for Chinese troops entering the Korean War needed strengthening. In addition to preparing food and ammunition and establishing field hospitals, Chinese reconnaissance groups should be sent to Korea in advance to get familiar with the war situation as well as the topography. The report suggested that the best timing for entering the war might be when the UN forces had counterattacked back across the 38th parallel, because this would put China in a politically and militarily more favorable position to defeat the enemy.[97]

This report received careful attention in Beijing. On September 7 Chai Chengwen, now the Chinese political counsellor in Pyongyang, was summoned back to Beijing by the Foreign Affairs Ministry. Zhou

Enlai received him the same evening. Chai had prepared an outline for this meeting, which stressed: "Since the American and Rhee troops retreated from Taejon, the Korean People's Army has entered an impasse in its confrontation with the enemy, and can hardly move forward. Without mastery of the sea and control of the air, it will be detrimental [to the North Koreans] if [they] run into a protracted warfare with the enemy in such a long and narrow peninsula surrounded by sea in three directions." Zhou read the report carefully and asked Chai: "If the situation changes suddenly and we decide to send our troops to enter the Korean War, what difficulties do you think we will meet?" Chai believed that the most difficult problems would be transportation and logistics. Zhou circulated Chai's report to all members of the Standing Committee of the Politburo. It was Chai's impression that top CCP leaders had made up their minds and "China would surely send troops to Korea; what remained a problem was when to issue the final order."[98]

As preparations for entering the Korean War continued, concerns about, or even opposition to, involving China in a direct military confrontation with the United States emerged among top CCP leaders. The most conspicuous representative of this position was Lin Biao.[99] According to Chai, two days after his meeting with Zhou he was directed by the CMC to see Lin. To Chai's confusion, he found Lin had strong reservations about sending Chinese troops to Korea. At one point, Lin even asked Chai if the North Koreans had the determination to fight a guerrilla war if the situation reversed.[100] There are strong reasons to believe that others among the CCP leadership shared Lin Biao's view.[101]

Mao, however, seemed confident of the necessity for a Chinese intervention and tried to convince his comrades. On September 5 Mao spoke to the Ninth Session of the Central People's Government Council, stressing that China was superior to the United States in several aspects. The United States, according to Mao, though strong economically, was waging an unjust war of aggression and lacking people's support. In a political sense, the United States, suffering from political divisions at home and divergences with allies, was isolated and vulnerable. In the military field, Mao believed that the United States "had only one advantage, namely having a lot of steel, but three weak points." Mao listed these weak points as: "(1) Their front line is too long, stretching from Berlin to Korea; (2) their supply line is too extensive, separated by two oceans (the Atlantic and the Pacific); and (3) their combat ability is very low . . . not so strong as the troops of Germany and Japan [during World War II]."[102] In discussing possible American responses to Chinese intervention in Korea, the CCP leadership also considered the United States might use nuclear weapons. Mao believed this was unlikely and the Chinese should not fear this prospect. Mao emphasized confidently: "We will not allow you [the Americans] to use the atomic bomb. But if you insist on using it, you may use it. You can follow the way you choose to go, and we will go our own way. You can use the atomic bomb. I will respond with my hand grenade. I will catch the weak point on your part, hold you, and finally defeat you."[103]

These opinions indicate that Mao had considered the potential pros and cons involved in China's entry into the Korean War, and that he favored sending troops to Korea. Mao's arguments had set the basic tone for the CCP leadership's decision-making process on the Korean problem, and Mao would repeat this analysis again and again in the CCP leadership's discussion of sending Chinese troops to Korea. Although the situation would change dramatically between early September and mid-October, when Chinese troops finally crossed the Yalu, Mao would stick to these basic arguments. Mao's problem was how to convince his comrades (and, sometimes, even himself) of the correctness of his judgment.

Intervention Delayed

With the evidence presented above, it is clear that Mao Zedong and the CCP leadership had been inclined to send Chinese troops to Korea in late August and early September. The problem remaining for them was when and under what circumstances. Why then did Beijing fail to act at once, waiting instead until after the Inchon landing? To answer this question, one has to understand that Mao's final decision was constrained by complicating internal and external factors, some of which were beyond his control.

First of all, the Northeast Border Defense Army had been unable to complete preparations to enter the war before the Inchon landing, although it had been pushed continuously by Mao. This gave Mao little choice but to postpone the deadline for the Chinese troops' completion of preparations from the end of August to the end of

September. Furthermore, although Mao and the Chinese high command had anticipated that UN forces would attempt to land in the rear of the North Korean forces, there is no evidence that either the Chinese or the North Koreans had any idea that the landing would come in mid-September. If Beijing leaders had known General MacArthur's schedule, it is likely that Mao would have further pushed Chinese military preparations so that the troops could have been operations ready earlier.

Mao's status as the party leader as well as his desire to win China a glorious victory in the Korean conflict may also have prevented him from acting prematurely. Although in 1950 Mao dominated the CCP's decision-making process both on domestic and foreign affairs, he could not dictate everything as he would during the Cultural Revolution. Mao might not need to yield to the different opinions held by his colleagues, but it would have been foolish for him not to take them into consideration. In fact, unless China's territorial safety were directly threatened by the Americans, Mao would have had difficulty in convincing the party and the Chinese people of the necessity to intervene in Korea. Meanwhile, Mao's underlying calculus for entering the Korean War—to mobilize the party and the nation under the banner of patriotism and nationalism—must be kept in mind. Mao could easily understand that a premature entry into the Korean War could have weakened the appeal of the CCP's stress on nationalism and patriotism, something Mao wanted to use to mobilize the Chinese nation.

Crucial diplomatic factors also hindered China's entrance into the war. In retrospect Beijing's war decision was restricted by its relationships with Moscow and Pyongyang. Before Mao could send his troops to Korea, he needed to get the cooperation of the Soviet Union and, equally important, the consent of Kim Il-sung. Neither, unfortunately for Mao, was easy.

Direct American military intervention in Korea sent a strong warning to Stalin, making him aware that he had underestimated America's intentions and capacity to engage in major military actions in East Asia. Because the promotion of revolutionary movements in the East had been Beijing's domain and because the main strategic interests and attention of the Soviet Union were in Europe, Korea was not Stalin's primary concern. A Communist victory in Korea might still be important to Stalin, but was not crucial for the strategic interests of the Soviet Union. Stalin had strong reasons to avoid a major confrontation with the United States over Korea. Several Chinese sources point out that Stalin did not want to involve the Soviet Union in a showdown with the United States.[104] Although Chinese sources currently available reveal no concrete discussions between top leaders of Beijing and Moscow from late June to mid-September 1950, it is plausible that the CCP leadership would have maintained close contacts with the Soviets. In actuality, we do know, through at least two Chinese sources, that a Soviet air force division, with 122 Mig-15 fighters, "following the agreement of the Chinese and Soviet governments," arrived in the Northeast in August 1950, "to take the responsibility of defending this area."[105] Considering that the Sino-Soviet alliance was now a cornerstone of Beijing's foreign policy, Mao had reason to take Stalin's cautious attitude seriously.

Kim Il-sung's attitude was even more troublesome for Mao. As a Korean nationalist, Kim hoped to win the war with his own forces. Facing the complicated factional divisions within the Korean Communist Party, Kim wanted to avoid strengthening the influence of the "Chinese section," a result that was more than possible if Chinese troops directly entered the war.[106] Kim thus seemed unwilling to request Chinese help as long as he believed the situation was under control.[107] When Beijing inquired if China could send high-ranking military observers to Korea, Kim did not cooperate. For example, in early August, the CCP Central Committee decided to dispatch to Korea Deng Hua, who had just taken the position as the commander of the 13th Army Corps, to learn about the war situation. When he arrived in the border city of Andong on the Chinese side of the Yalu, however, "the situation suddenly changed." The North Koreans made it clear at the last minute that Deng was unwelcome and he had to give up his mission.[108] Indeed, except for a group of Chinese military-intelligence officers sent to Pyongyang in mid-July as Chinese diplomats, Beijing was unable to dispatch high-ranking military observers to Korea.[109] In the days before Inchon, Mao could easily sense that Kim's attitude would influence the moral justification as well as effectiveness of Chinese intervention in Korea. Without Kim's invitation, Chinese leaders preferred not to go ahead. And China's entry into the Korean War had to be delayed.

Two-and-half months after the outbreak of the Korean War, China became an intensively mobilized country. Beijing leaders established the NEBDA by transferring over 300,000 of China's best troops to the Chinese-Korean border area (with another 400,000 serving as reserve forces), took preliminary steps to ensure the troops' logistical supplies, and initiated the domestic political mobilization that would be essential for the country to enter a major military intervention on a foreign land. These accomplishments would prove to be crucial when intervention became urgent in late September and early October. However, even with Mao's repeated pushing, Chinese troops in the Northeast were still some distance away from combat readiness. Moreover, Beijing had difficulties in establishing an effective strategic coordination with Pyongyang and, to a lesser extent, Moscow. Although Mao and many other Chinese leaders and military planners became increasingly worried that a reversal might occur in Korea, they could do little to influence the process of the war. They had to wait.

After Inchon: The Making of
the Decision on Intervention

Beijing's waiting period did not last long. On September 15 the American X Corps succeeded in landing at Inchon. The North Korean forces, forced to turn from the offensive to the defensive, in a few days began to disintegrate. The UN forces started marching northward. Even though Mao and his military planners had anticipated that a reversal in Korea might occur, the Inchon landing still shocked them. Mao had lost much sleep and consumed many cigarettes in the days after Inchon.[1] From the NEBDA's headquarters in Shenyang to Zhongnanhai, the CCP Central Committee's compound in Beijing, people talked about almost nothing but Inchon and Korea: What was happening at Inchon? How would the Americans do the next? Could the Korean People's Army hold in face of American counteroffensive?[2] In Zhongnanhai, Mao and his Politburo colleagues had to answer these questions and thereby make a decision.

Impacts of the Inchon Landing

Beijing viewed Inchon with gravity. First of all, in a military sense, the landing had invalidated one of the basic assumptions under which the Beijing leadership had been acting since early July: that Chinese troops would be used to accelerate a KPA victory or, at least, to prevent a possible reversal. With the dramatic shift of the offensive and defensive positions of the two sides after the Inchon landing, the North Koreans were no longer in a position to play a major role in war operations. If the Chinese entered the war, they would be facing an enemy who held the initiative on the battlefield. Therefore, Chinese troops first needed to try to restore the strategic balance and then to pursue a victory over the enemy. All of this meant that the main burden of waging the war would fall on the shoulders of the Chinese, and that the duration of, and risks involved in, China's military intervention would be substantially increased.

In Beijing's view, the deteriorating situation in Korea after Inchon further endangered China's security interests. Before the Inchon landing, the main battlefield of the war was in South Korea. Even with the U.S. military intervention in Korea and the Seventh Fleet moving into the Taiwan Strait, the safety of the Chinese mainland was not directly threatened. The Inchon landing led to the rapid shift of the primary combat zone from the South to the North, and war flames moved continuously closer to the Chinese-Korean border, threatening the Northeast and China's main source of coal, steel, and water power.[3]

The reversal of the Korean situation, Beijing leaders feared, also darkened the prospect of revolutionary development in the East and the world. Viewing the disintegration of the North Korean Communist forces, they realized that a total victory on the part of the UN forces meant also a fatal strike against the development of the Eastern revolution, in which Beijing wished to play a crucial role. As a result, the worldwide balance of power between the "revolutionary camp" and the "reactionary camp" would take a turn in favor of the latter. On one occasion, Zhou Enlai even expressed a thesis which might be called the Chinese version of the "domino theory": "The Korean question is an international one and it cannot be separated from other international issues. . . . Only if [North] Korea could win the victory, the enemy would not open a breach in the peace camp. If Korea fell down, breaches in other places would also be opened one by one. If the enemy were allowed to break down the gate of the Eastern Front and make his way into our house, how could we devote ourselves to construction?"[4] This prospect was intolerable for Mao and other Chinese Communist leaders, especially because they had been so eager to advance China's international prestige through the promotion of an Eastern revolution following the model of the Chinese revolution.

More important, Beijing leaders could not ignore the profound negative impact that the reversal of the Korean War would have on China's domestic situation. In the minds of Beijing leaders, this would appear at least in two ways. First, the remnants of the GMD forces, together with those who opposed or were dissatisfied with the Communist regime (such as the former landowners and rich peasants who had lost their land and their social status as local elites during the land reform), would echo the UN counteroffensive by rebelling against the Communist government.[5] Second, the GMD government in Taiwan, eager to join the UN forces in the Korean conflict, would either participate directly in the UN march toward the Yalu or try to attack coastal areas in East China if the situation became favorable for them. After the Inchon landing, Mao cabled to commanders of the PLA's East China Military Region, stressing that defense in East China should be put on alert on the assumption that the United States and Jiang Jieshi would try to make landings there.[6] The CCP leadership had to consider either of these contingencies very seriously.

The combination of these factors made China's military intervention in Korea a more urgent yet more complicated matter. In a letter to Gao Gang immediately after the Inchon landing, Mao stated that the Chinese now had no choice but to enter the conflict and that war preparations needed to be further accelerated.[7] The practical course of the Beijing leadership's decision-making process, however, was still constrained by attitudes in Moscow and Pyongyang. Meanwhile, decisions in Washington, especially on the question of whether or not UN forces should cross the 38th parallel, was another factor that Mao and the CCP leadership had to take into account.

Like the policymakers in Beijing, Stalin understood the crucial impact of the Inchon landing on the Korean War as well as on the balance of power in East Asia. Stalin had been shocked by the quick and unyielding American response to North Korea's invasion of the South, and worried that too bold an approach on the part of Moscow and Beijing could result in a direct confrontation between the Soviet Union and the United States. After the Inchon landing, he saw another possibility: if the United States succeeded in occupying the Korean peninsula, the balance of power between the Soviet Union and the United States in Northeast Asia would totally change in Washington's favor. The appearance of U.S. forces on the Korean-Soviet border would create a hot-spot for direct conflict between the Soviet Union and the United States. Either for the purpose of enhancing the reputation of the Soviet Union as a great power in the Far East or for maintaining the strategic structure established after the Second World War in Northeast Asia, the Soviet Union could not allow the United States to become the master of the entire Korean peninsula. Stalin, however, was neither ready nor willing to bring on a direct military confrontation with the United States to save Kim Il-sung's North Korean regime. The fate of Korea, while related to the security concerns of the Soviet Union, did not affect the most vital Soviet interests. If Soviet troops appeared in Korea, the conflict would most probably be expanded, and, in the worst possible situation, the world order established after the Second World War would be overturned. Stalin did not want to take the risk. Furthermore, according to the agreement reached between the Chinese and Soviet Communists during Liu Shaoqi's and Mao Zedong's visits to Moscow, the promotion of revolutionary movements in Asia was primarily Beijing's duty. Under these circumstances, having the Chinese send in their troops became the most reasonable choice for Stalin.[8] On September 16 or 17, Stalin cabled Mao, inquiring about China's military deployment in the Northeast and asking if the Chinese were in a position to send troops to help the North Koreans.[9] It is also reported that Stalin inquired if Beijing leaders would allow Kim to establish an exile government in the Northeast.[10]

Chinese sources now available indicate that Mao did not give a comprehensive response to Stalin until October 2, when the UN forces had crossed the 38th parallel. The Beijing leadership, though, did give positive consideration to the Soviet suggestion. During the second half of September, the Chinese and Soviets discussed, probably through Chinese embassy in Moscow and Soviet embassy in Beijing, possible Chinese-Soviet cooperation in Korea. Following the spirit of the Sino-Soviet alliance treaty, the Soviets agreed in late September that if the Chinese troops entered the Korean War, the Soviet Union would provide the Chinese with an air umbrella. The Soviets also agreed to supply the Chinese with military equipment and war materials.[11]

Facing a dramatic military reversal, the North Koreans had to invite the support of Chinese troops. After the Inchon landing, two high-ranking Korean Communists, Pak Il-yu and Pak Hon-yong came to China to ask the Chinese to send troops to Korea.[12] Hong Xuezhi, then vice commander of the 13th Army Corps and later vice commander of the Chinese People's Volunteers to Korea, recalled that Pak Il-yu came to Andong to explain to the commanders of the NEBDA the deteriorating situation in Korea after the Inchon landing. According to Hong, Pak "could only introduce the situation in the most general sense, and he had no way to go into the detailed development of the war situation, as communications between Pyongyang and the front-line troops were no longer effective." Pak, as Hong recalled, "on the behalf of the Korean Party and Government, sincerely asked China to send troops to Korea." Hong and other NEBDA leaders agreed to convey Pak's request to Beijing and promised that "as soon as we have received the order, we would immediately come to Korea's rescue."[13]

It is important to note that Kim Il-sung did not come to China, and that both Pak Il-yu and Pak Hon-yong belonged respectively to the Chinese section and the southern section within the Korean Workers' Party. Both were later purged by Kim Il-sung.[14] Why did Kim not come to China personally? While it is possible that he was too busy in the disastrous days after Inchon to do so, his absence may also indicate tensions between himself and the Beijing leadership, as well as escalating internal struggles among the Korean Communists. In Hong Xuezhi's and Chai Chengwen's memoirs, they mentioned that Pak Il-yu and Pak Hon-yong came to China under "Kim's instructions"; other Chinese sources, however, suggest something different. Interviews with Beijing's researchers suggest that after the Inchon landing the opposition factions within the Korean Communist Party sent their representatives to China, asking the Chinese to send troops to Korea while at the same time requesting help in getting rid of Kim Il-sung, whom they held responsible for the catastrophic situation after Inchon. After careful deliberations, Mao made it clear that it would be improper for China to interfere with the internal affairs of the Korean leadership, that Kim Il-sung was the "banner" of the Korean Communist revolution, and that if Kim were removed at the time of great difficulties North Korea would fall into disorder and turmoil. Mao concluded that the Chinese would continue to deal with Kim on the matter of sending Chinese troops to Korea.[15] No printed Chinese sources available can prove or disprove this information. If it is correct, the activities of the "opposition factions" must have been related to the visits of Pak Il-yu and/or Pak

Hon-yong. This also explains why the Chinese waited until early October, when Kim personally requested China's assistance, before finally making the decision to enter the war.

To prepare for China's entry into the war, the Beijing leadership sent five additional military attachés to Korea immediately after the Inchon landing, all of whom were PLA officers.[16] Their dispatch was first proposed by NEBDA commanders in a report to the CMC on August 31, which suggested that an advance team, composed of four officers, be sent to Korea to "get familiar with the general situation, make surveys of Korean topography, and prepare for future battles." Zhou Enlai did not respond to this suggestion.[17] Right after the Inchon landing the CMC decided that it was now necessary to send this group of officers to Korea, and the North Koreans also approved this dispatch.[18] Instead of acting as an "advance team," the group went to Korea as Chinese military attachés. On September 17 Zhou received Chai Chengwen and four of the five-member group, instructing them to leave for Pyongyang immediately to prepare for the coming of Chinese troops. The group arrived in Pyongyang around September 20, and all five members received letters of introduction personally signed by Kim Il-sung. They started off immediately for different parts of North Korea to investigate the military situation.[19]

Meanwhile, Zhou Enlai was working on the operational outlines for the Chinese troops to be sent to Korea. On September 20, he laid down the following principles for Communist military actions in Korea: "The war to resist America and assist Korea should be conducted as a protracted war on the basis of self-reliance. In every campaign and battle, we have to gain superiority by concentrating our manpower and firepower in order to break up and destroy the enemy. By weakening the enemy gradually, we will be able to carry out a protracted war." These suggestions were conveyed to Kim Il-sung through Ni Zhiliang, the Chinese ambassador to Korea.[20] Mao approved these principles.

As Mao and the Beijing leadership approached the final decision to send troops to Korea, they issued a series of protests and warnings against the American intention of "expanding the war to the Chinese-Korean border and China itself." On September 24, Zhou Enlai cabled UN headquarters to protest against alleged U.S. air bombardment of Andong. He argued that the United States intended to "extend the war of aggression against Korea, to carry out armed aggression on Taiwan, and to extend further its aggression against China."[21] The next day, General Nie Rongzhen, in a meeting with K. M. Panikkar, Indian ambassador to China, sent another signal which could be understood as a warning against the UN forces' marching northward: China would not "sit back with folded hands and let the Americans come up to the [Sino-Korean] border."[22] Zhou's and Nie's statements indicate again the intentions of the Beijing leadership to further mobilize China's public opinion, as well as to appeal to the international media to support China's entry into a "just war."

Mao and other Beijing leaders still needed to answer another crucial question: Would the UN forces cross the 38th parallel and continue to march toward the Yalu? The answer to this question was important for the timing as well as the nature of China's intervention. As Mao and his fellow Beijing leaders had been following the "worst case assumption" since the start of the Korean War, they tended to believe that the UN advance would not stop at the 38th parallel. However, from a military perspective, stopping, or even delaying, UN forces at the parallel would allow the Chinese more time to make the final decision to enter the war. The answer to this question, however, lay in Washington.

The American "Rollback"

The Inchon landing and the UN troops' successful advance to the 38th parallel posed serious challenges to the wisdom of policymakers in Washington: Should the UN forces cross the 38th parallel and continue to march toward the Korean-Chinese border? How would the Soviet Union and China respond to such a move? What should be the limits of U.S. goals in the Korean War? These questions were crucial to Washington's strategy for resolving the Korean crisis.

As early as July, when North Korean forces held the battlefield initiative, the problem of whether UN forces would cross the 38th parallel became one of Washington's central concerns. This question was first raised by Rhee. He emphasized in a statement on July 13 that "the action of the North Korean forces had obliterated the 38th parallel and that no peace and order could be maintained in Korea as long as the division at the 38th parallel remained."[23] Policymakers in Washington were willing to consider this argument. On July 17, President

Truman instructed the NSC to offer recommendations "covering the policy which should be pursued by the United States after the North Korean forces have been driven back to the 38th parallel."[24]

Disagreements existed among policymakers in Washington as to what to do. Opposition to crossing the 38th parallel came mainly from George Kennan. The Korean War had erupted just when Kennan was preparing to leave the State Department, and he stayed on to offer advice to Acheson and other policymakers in Washington. While favoring the idea that the United States should firmly counter the North Korean invasion for the sake of American prestige as well as the balance of power in East Asia, he opposed viewing events in Korea as the prelude to a well-coordinated Soviet plot to expand in other parts of the world, and he predicted that a shift of the tide in the Korean War to America's favor could lead to a Soviet and/or Chinese intervention. Kennan thus believed the attempt to cross the 38th parallel risky.[25]

Kennan's view was shared, though to a lesser extent, by some members of the Policy Planning Staff, who were still under the strong influence of Kennan's strategic thinking. A PPS memorandum of July 25 argued that crossing the parallel might bring the Soviet Union and/or China into the conflict, as well as lead to the loss of support in the UN. The memorandum suggested that "decisions regarding our course of action when the UN forces approach the 38th parallel should be deferred until military and political development provide the additional information necessary to enable us: (a) to base our decisions on the situation in Korea and in other parts of the world at that time; (b) to consult with other UN members who are supporting the Security Council resolutions in regard to measures which might be necessary or desirable once the aggression had been brought to an end; and (c) to keep our military capabilities and commitments in safe balance." [26]

The voices advocating advancing into North Korea, however, were much louder and more explicit. The Pentagon believed that it did not make military sense to stop at the 38th parallel, which was "a geographical artificiality violating the natural integrity of a singularly homogeneous nation." If the UN forces failed to cross the parallel, the pentagon argued, a renewal of military instability on the Korean Peninsula would follow. In contrast, the Pentagon believed that a decision to cross the parallel and unify Korea would offer "the United

States and the free world the first opportunity to displace part of the Soviet orbit," and therefore became "a step in reversing the dangerous strategic trend in the Far East in the past twelve months." Responding to the PPS's emphasis on the necessity of splitting Beijing and Moscow, the Pentagon argued that as a result of the unification of Korea under UN auspices, "elements in the Chinese Communist regime, and particularly important segments of the Chinese population, might be inclined to question their exclusive dependence on the Kremlin. Skillfully manipulated, the Chinese Communists might prefer different arrangements and a new orientation."[27]

The majority of the State Department also favored crossing the 38th parallel for political, strategic, and psychological reasons. John Foster Dulles, for example, argued that "the 38th parallel was never intended to be, and never ought to be, a political line." The failure to march across the parallel, Dulles warned, would provide an "asylum to the aggressor" and cause great danger to both South Korea and the United States.[28] The opinion of John M. Allison, director of the Office of Northeastern Asian Affairs in the State Department, was more vehement and influential, as he was placed in charge of studies on future Korean policy on July 22.[29] While acknowledging the existence of a "grave danger of conflict with the USSR and the Chinese Communists" if Washington adopted a "rollback" strategy, he still strongly favored actions aimed at unifying the entire Korean peninsula under UN auspices. He stressed that it was the duty of the United States to make it clear "that he who violates the decent opinions of mankind must take the consequences and that he who takes the sword will perish by the sword." Allison asked his colleagues in Washington: "When all the legal and moral right is on our side why should we hesitate?"[30]

General MacArthur was another influential advocate for crossing the 38th parallel. Longing for a total victory over the North Korean Communists, MacArthur made it clear that it was his intention to destroy North Korean forces rather than merely drive them back to the 38th parallel. In a talk on July 13 with Generals J. Lawton Collins and Hoyt Vandenberg, the Army and Air Force chiefs of staff, MacArthur stated that it might be necessary to occupy all of Korea. He stressed that a victory over the Communists on the Korean peninsula "would check Communist expansion everywhere and thus obviate the necessity of our being fully prepared to meet aggression elsewhere." He opposed vigorously "any delay or half-way measures."[31]

The influence of these arguments for marching north of the parallel was further strengthened by America's domestic setting after the outbreak of the Korean War. The intensifying Cold War atmosphere, together with Senator McCarthy's renewed attack on the State Department for giving communism "a green light to grab whatever it could in China, Korea, and Formosa," placed tremendous pressure upon the Truman administration. Outcries for more resolute American action in the face of Communist aggression prevailed among members of both parties and on major newspapers. Overwhelmingly, the view was that now was the time to break the "purely fictitious line" of the 38th parallel and to pursue a unified Korea.[32]

Under these circumstances, Truman and Acheson leaned toward marching across the 38th parallel. What worried Truman most, however, was the possible reaction of the Soviet Union and China. Would Moscow and Beijing interfere directly if the UN forces counterattacked? This was the question policymakers in Washington had to answer if they decided to take the war into North Korea.

Strongly influenced by the general perception that Beijing leaders, at least at the present stage, were following orders from Moscow, Washington's attempt to seek a reliable assessment of Moscow's and Beijing's reactions to an expanded conflict into North Korea focused on the former. In the first several weeks after the outbreak of the Korean War, many in Washington did believe, as Rosemary Foot points out, "that the Korean operation was a feint to lure U.S. forces away from some more vital area where a Soviet attack was planned."[33] Gradually, however, they found that this was not the case. Moscow appeared reluctant to play a significant role in the Korean conflict. The Soviet Union's return to the UN Security Council in early August, as well as the introduction of a Soviet proposal to end the conflict through negotiation, was taken by members of the State Department as evidence of the Soviet unwillingness to act boldly in Korea. The Defense Department found also the Soviet leaders' attitude toward the Korean conflict to be extremely cautious. The USSR did not put forward any harsh protest when in August UN air forces bombed the oil supply depot at Rajin in North Korea, only 17 miles from the Soviet border.[34] Yet both the State and Defense Departments continued to view Soviet interference as likely in August and September, especially if Soviet leaders felt that it "would not involve a substantial risk of global war."[35]

While making its recommendations for U.S. strategy for a counteroffensive in Korea, the NSC postulated that the possibility of Soviet and Chinese intervention could be diminished by allowing only
South Korean troops to march into North Korea while American
ground forces avoided this step. On September 11, President Truman
approved the NSC's report, known as NSC 81/1, authorizing the
invasion and occupation of North Korea provided Soviet or Chinese
intervention did not occur. The UN command was directed to use
only South Korean forces to conduct the final march toward the
Korean-Chinese border with operations restricted to Korean territory. In the event of open or covert Soviet or Chinese intervention, UN
forces would assume the defensive and avoid escalating the conflict
into a general war. Nevertheless, since the NSC, with the approval of
the President, now defined American war aims in Korea as pursuing
Korea's "complete independence and unity," the UN movements
north of the parallel became almost certain.[36]

The success of the Inchon landing turned the question of whether
the UN forces would cross the 38th parallel into an issue of imminent importance. Policymakers in Washington continued to act
according to the contingency plans set up by NSC 81, and their basic
assumption was that if Moscow failed to take action of some kind
before UN forces crossed the parallel, it could well mean that the
Soviets, and also the Chinese, had adopted a hands-off policy. On
September 27, the JCS instructed General MacArthur that UN
forces could now conduct military, air, and naval operations across the
38th parallel to destroy North Korean forces. The general was also
told to make certain that there was no major Soviet and Chinese military involvement in Korea, that UN forces should restrict their operations in Korean territory, and that only South Korean troops were
to be used in Korea's northeastern provinces.[37] Two days later, Secretary of Defense George Marshall informed MacArthur: "We want
you to feel unhampered tactically and strategically to proceed north
of [the] 38th parallel."[38]

General MacArthur had thus been put in a position to act on his
own judgment. As a military leader with a strong personality and eager
to see a complete military victory, MacArthur was determined to
march forward; and he had long believed that the 38th parallel was a
meaningless line that had lost any significance after the North Korean attack. The strategy he tried to carry out was aimed at establishing

"privileged sanctuaries" along the Manchurian border, thus preventing Communist expansion in the future. With the approval of top policymakers in Washington, he declared "all of Korea open for our military operations unless and until the enemy capitulates."[39]

At this juncture, Beijing issued a series of explicit warnings about its intentions if the UN forces crossed the 38th parallel. Policymakers in Washington, however, regarded them as no more than "bluffing." When Zhou Enlai, through the Indian ambassador to Beijing, K. M. Panikkar, warned Washington on October 3 that if UN troops crossed the 38th parallel, China would intervene, Acheson viewed it as "bluff, pending more information." Although he recognized that there was a risk involved in UN forces marching toward the Yalu, he emphasized that "a greater risk would be incurred by showing hesitation and timidity."[40] Policymakers in Washington simply did not believe Beijing's warnings.

Several assumptions supported this approach. First, American policymakers were inclined to believe that after Inchon the best time for China's intervention in Korea had passed. A CIA report of September 28 alleged that the Chinese had missed the opportunity to turn the tide of the war at an early point, and "like the USSR, [China] will not openly intervene in North Korea." Alan Kirk, U.S. ambassador to Moscow, predicted that the threat of Chinese intervention had receded because the most favorable time for China's intervention "was logically when UN forces were desperately defending the small area of Taegu-Pusan, when the influx of overwhelming numbers of Chinese ground forces would have proved the decisive factor." The CIA concluded on October 12 that "from a military standpoint the most favorable time for [Chinese] intervention in Korea has passed."[41]

Second, policymakers in Washington believed that Beijing leaders had to focus on domestic problems, and it would be unlikely for them to send troops to Korea. The CIA observed in its October 12 memo that the Chinese Communists faced tremendous domestic problems. If the CCP led China into a military conflict with the United States, "the regime's entire domestic program and economy would be jeopardized," and "anti-Communist forces would be encouraged and the regime's very existence would be endangered." Acheson was more than ready to accept such a view. He stated that "it would be sheer madness" for Beijing leaders to enter the Korean conflict when they themselves had numerous problems.[42] Third, Washington believed that China's entry into the Korean War would make Beijing regime even more dependent on Soviet support while at the same time minimizing Beijing's opportunity to take China's seat in the United Nations.[43] Indeed, American policymakers simply could not imagine that Beijing could gain anything by involving itself in a major confrontation with the United States.

Underlying these assumptions was a deep-rooted sense of American superiority in face of a backward China, as well as a stubborn contempt of Chinese Communist leaders because they were Chinese. There existed virtually no divergence between hard-liners like Dulles, Allison, and, of course, General MacArthur and moderates like Kennan on the problem of judging China's power potential. In fact, a consistent belief among policymakers in Washington was that even if the Chinese Communists did engage themselves in the Korean War, America's military and technological superiority would guarantee an easy victory over them.[44] Thus, while assessing Moscow's and Beijing's possible reaction to America's "rollback" policy, Washington's eyes fixed on Moscow. Once American policymakers became convinced that direct Soviet intervention in Korean was unlikely, they believed that a Chinese intervention was even less possible. Influenced by this mentality, intelligence analysts and policymakers in Washington easily ignored clues about Beijing's military redeployment and political mobilization for entering the war. And, not surprising at all, the CIA concluded as late as October 12, four days after Mao issued the formal orders to send Chinese troops to Korea: "Despite statements by Chou [Zhou] Enlai, troops movements to Manchuria, and propaganda charges of atrocities and border violations, there are no convincing indications of an actual Chinese Communist intention to resort to full-scale intervention in Korea."[45] It is apparent that what was involved here was more than a simple intelligence failure.

Under these circumstances, we see an interesting yet ironic phenomenon: although Acheson and many others in Washington had been endeavoring to encourage Titoism in China, thus splitting Beijing and Moscow, they persistently emphasized the CCP leaders' subordination to Moscow after the outbreak of the Korean War. Truman believed that the "so-called Communist Chinese Government was nothing but a tool of Moscow." Acheson claimed that Beijing played a major role in serving Kremlin's plot of expansion in East Asia.[46]

These allegations would reach their height when policymakers in

Washington were shocked by Beijing's military intervention in Korea. In a heated debate with Clement Attlee, the British prime minister visiting Washington in early December 1950, both Truman and Acheson insisted that Beijing was not an independent actor in the international arena. Acheson would argue that Beijing's behavior was "based on the Moscow pattern" and that CCP leaders were "better pupils even than the Eastern European satellites," and Truman would stress that the CCP leaders "are satellites of Russia and will be satellites as long as the present Peiping [Beijing] regime is in power."[47] Is this a reflection of Washington's hostility toward revolutionary China? Yes. But mixed with these hostile feelings was also an unwillingness to appreciate the way Beijing leaders defined and defended the new China's security interests. It is clear that policymakers in Washington misperceived Beijing's intentions. This misperception, in the final analysis, was deeply rooted in the mentality that Mao called "American arrogance."

The First Decision: October 1–2

In late September, Beijing leaders could see that the situation in Korea was deteriorating with every passing minute, and that North Korean resistance was collapsing under enormous pressure from superior UN forces. On September 30, the South Korean Third Division crossed the 38th parallel. The next day, General MacArthur issued an ultimatum to Kim Il-sung demanding an unconditional surrender.[48]

Facing the imminent downfall of their regime, the North Korean leaders had no other choice but to seek direct Soviet and Chinese military assistance. On September 29, Kim Il-sung and Pak Hon-yong sent a letter to Stalin, which stated that "at the moment when enemy troops cross the 38th parallel it is very necessary for us to have direct military aid from the Soviet Union." If the Soviet Union was not in a position to provide such aid, Kim and Park asked Stalin to "assist us in the creation of international volunteer units in China and in other people's democracies to render military assistance to our struggle."[49] As Stalin was unwilling to risk a confrontation with the United States, he considered a "more acceptable form of assistance [to North Korea] to be assistance by people's volunteers," which, in his view, was a "question we must consult first of all with the Chinese comrades."[50]

Now Kim Il-sung had to make a personal appeal to Beijing for

China's direct support. On the evening of September 30, the Chinese embassy in Pyongyang held in the embassy's basement a reception for the PRC's first anniversary. Kim showed up and met with Ni Zhiliang and Chai Chengwen, requesting that the Chinese send the 13th Army Corps into Korea. Ni and Chai agreed to convey Kim's request to Beijing in the shortest possible time.[51]

As the situation deteriorated, on October 1, Kim, together with Pak Hon-yong, sent off an emergency letter to Mao, formally asking the Chinese to send troops to Korea. To make sure that the message would reach Mao in time, Pak Hon-yong flew to Beijing on the evening of October 1 to deliver the letter by hand.[52] The letter started with an overall summary of the course of the Korean War from late June to late September. Kim and Pak emphasized that before the American landing at Inchon, the KPA had possessed a highly advantageous position. While the enemies were constricted in a small area in the southernmost part of the Korean peninsula, the KPA had every opportunity to "win the decisive final victory." Then, Kim and Pak stated, the U.S. imperialists, "for the purpose of changing Korea into their colony and military base," gathered almost all of their forces in the Asian-Pacific area to make the landing at Inchon. The KPA had since been forced to change from the offensive to the defensive. Describing the current situation in Korea as "most grave," Kim and Pak confessed that "it is difficult for us to cope with the crisis with our own strength." They ended the letter "urgently soliciting that the Chinese People's Liberation Army directly enter the war to support us."[53]

The North Koreans' request came at the time when the Beijing leadership had reached the final stage of their deliberations over whether or not to send troops to Korea. On September 30, Zhou Enlai declared at a mass conference that "the Chinese people will absolutely not tolerate foreign aggression, nor will they supinely tolerate seeing their neighbors being savagely invaded by imperialists."[54]

Zhou sent off this open warning at the same time when top leaders in Beijing acted to make the decision to intervene in Korea. The first day of October was a long one for Mao and his fellow Beijing leaders. During the day, urgent reports from the Chinese embassy in Korea poured into Zhongnanhai. In the late evening, the emergency message by Kim and Pak reached Mao. Then Mao summoned an urgent meeting attended by members of the Standing Committee of the CCP Politburo.[55] The message from Kim Il-sung and the Korean situation was the main topic of the meeting. Top CCP leaders decided that an enlarged Politburo Standing Committee would meet the next day, attended also by Beijing's top military planners. After this decision was made, Mao did not go to bed. Instead, at 2 a.m., the morning of October 2, he telegraphed to Gao Gang and Deng Hua in Shenyang, ordering Gao to "come to Beijing for a meeting immediately." He also ordered the NEBDA to "complete its preparations ahead of the original schedule and to await the order to carry out operations against new enemies on the basis of the original plan." He instructed Deng to make the party leadership abreast of the NEBDA's status of preparation.[56]

In the early afternoon, Gao Gang flew from Shenyang to Beijing. Around 3 p.m., the enlarged meeting of the Politburo Standing Committee began at Zhongnanhai. Mao Zedong, Liu Shaoqi, Zhu De, and Zhou Enlai (all members of the Standing Committee) attended the meeting; Gao Gang, who had been in charge of the NEBDA since August, and Nie Rongzhen, the PLA's acting chief of staff, also attended.[57]

Mao's opening statement revealed his inclination to enter the war at this moment. Emphasizing the dangerous situation in Korea, Mao made it clear that "the question now is not whether or not but how fast we should send troops to Korea. One day's difference will be crucial to the whole situation. Today we will discuss two urgent questions—when should our troops enter Korea and who should be the commander."[58] Mao's statement is crucial. It virtually dictated the outcome of the meeting. Moreover, as further developments would prove, the ideas Mao expressed also established the basic tone of the Beijing leadership's discussion over China's role in Korea in the days to come. Mao demonstrated that he was the person in control. If at several other meetings CCP leaders would debate the pros and cons of entering the Korean War, they did so for his consideration. When the Beijing leadership wavered on several occasions concerning the problem of when and how Chinese troops should enter Korea, the wavering was largely the reflection of the internal struggle in Mao's own mind.

Following Mao's agenda, the discussion at the meeting first focused on selecting a commander for Chinese troops in Korea. This task would have been easy if Lin Biao, who had long enjoyed the reputation as one of the most talented military commanders of the PLA, had been willing to take the position. Lin had been the commander of the Fourth Field Army, which had fought mostly in the Northeast during the civil war, and was familiar with the situation in Manchuria and in nearby Korea. Furthermore, the four armies (the 38th, 39th, 40th, and 42nd Armies) concentrated in the Chinese-Korean border area were all units of the former Fourth Field Army, which Lin would more naturally command than other top PLA commanders. Lin, however, refused to lead Chinese troops to Korea. In the three months from early July to late September, Mao and other members of the CCP Politburo Standing Committee had inquired several times about Lin's intentions concerning commanding Chinese troops in Korea. Lin stressed consistently that he was unable to accept this duty because of his poor health. During the CCP leadership's previous discussions about the necessity of sending Chinese troops to Korea, Lin expressed strong reservations. He believed that as the PRC faced tremendous challenges at home and abroad and as the United States was technologically superior to China, China should not put itself into a direct military confrontation with the United States. In early October, Lin was preparing to travel to the Soviet Union for medical treatment. The combination of all these factors made Lin an impossible choice.[59]

Mao and top CCP leaders briefly considered Su Yu, vice commander of the Third Field Army, who had been responsible for organizing the Taiwan campaign since mid-1949. In early July, at the two conferences chaired by Zhou Enlai, the CMC even made the decision to appoint Su as the commander of the NEBDA. But Su was later hospitalized for medical treatment, eliminating him from consideration.[60]

Mao's mind now turned to Peng Dehuai. As one of the creators of the Chinese Red Army, Peng had fought alongside Mao from the late 1920s and established a prominent reputation as a military leader with great talent and broad vision. Peng had commanded the First Field Army, fighting in northwestern China, during the civil war. He had also served simultaneously as vice commander-in-chief of the PLA and vice chairman of the CMC, so that his influence extended far beyond the First Field Army. If selected as the commander for Chinese troops to Korea, he would certainly have had no difficulty in dealing with commanders from the Fourth Field Army.[61] Mao, who knew Peng very well, had considered asking him to lead the troops in Korea even before the Inchon landing. In a telegram to Peng on August 27 Mao informed him that "in order to accommodate the current situation," the CCP leadership believed that "it was necessary to concentrate twelve armies for emergencies," and that Peng would "be invited to Beijing for a direct consultation at the end of September."[62] At the October 2 meeting, Mao proposed Peng as the commander of the Chinese army in Korea. The proposal was immediately seconded by Zhu De, commander-in-chief of the PLA and Peng's close personal friend. The decision was made, contingent on the agreement of Peng himself.[63]

When should China enter the war? This was another problem the meeting addressed. The answer depended basically on two factors: how soon might the NEBDA complete final preparations and how much time would be allowed by the development of the Korean situation? The meeting decided that Chinese troops would enter Korea around October 15. In other words, the NEBDA should be ready to begin war operations in less than two weeks.[64]

The meeting also discussed how to establish effective Chinese-Soviet cooperation over China's entry into the Korean War. Mao obviously felt that this was the right time to make a comprehensive response to Stalin's request, which he had received two weeks earlier. Before the end of the meeting, Mao suggested that he should personally cable Stalin to inform him of the decision so that Beijing and Moscow could work out details for wartime Chinese-Soviet military cooperation. The meeting approved this suggestion.[65]

Right after the meeting, Mao sent a lengthy telegram to Stalin, summarizing the Chinese leaders' basic assessment of the risks involved in China's entry into the Korean War, the goals they hoped to achieve by sending troops to Korea, and the means through which these goals could be realized:

(1) We have decided to send a portion of our troops, under the name of [the Chinese] Volunteers, to Korea, assisting the Korean comrades to fight the troops of the United States and its running dog Syngman Rhee. We regarded the mission as necessary. If Korea were completely occupied by the Americans and the Korean revolutionary force were fundamentally destroyed, the American invaders would be more rampant, and such a situation would be very unfavorable to the whole East. (2) We realize that since we have decided to send Chinese troops to Korea to fight the Americans, we must first be able to solve the problem, that is, we are prepared to wipe out the invaders from the United States and from other countries, and [thus] drive them out [of

Korea]; second, since Chinese troops will fight American troops in Korea (although we will use the name of the Chinese Volunteers), we must be prepared for an American declaration of war on China. We must be prepared for the possible bombardments by American air forces of many Chinese cities and industrial bases, and for attacks by American naval forces on China's coastal areas. (3) Of the two questions, the first one is whether the Chinese troops would be able to wipe out American troops in Korea, thus effectively resolving the Korean problem. If our troops could annihilate American troops in Korea, especially the Eighth Army (a competent veteran U.S. army), the whole situation would become favorable to the revolutionary front and China, even though the second question (that the United States declares war on China) would still remain as a serious question. In other words, the Korean problem will end in fact with the defeat of American troops (although the war might not end in name, because the United States would not recognize the victory of Korea for a long period). If so, even though the Untied States declared war on China, the confrontation would not be a large-scale one, nor would it last very long. We consider that the most unfavorable situation would be that the Chinese forces fail to destroy American troops in large numbers in Korea, thus resulting in a stalemate, and that, at the same time, the United States openly declares war on China, which would be detrimental to China's economic reconstruction already under way and would cause dissatisfaction among the national bourgeoisie and some other sectors of the people (who are absolutely afraid of war). (4) Under the current situation, we have decided, starting on October 15, to move the twelve divisions, which have been earlier transferred to southern Manchuria, into suitable areas in North Korea (not necessarily close to the 38th parallel); these troops will only fight the enemy that venture to attack areas north of the 38th parallel; our troops will maintain a defensive warfare, while fighting with small groups of enemies and learning about the situation in every respect. Meanwhile, our troops will be awaiting the arrival of Soviet weapons and to be equipped with those weapons. Only then will our troops, in cooperation with the Korean comrades, launch a counter-offensive to destroy the invading American forces. (5) According to our information, every U.S. army (two infantry divisions and one mechanized division) is armed with 1500 pieces of artillery of various calibers ranging from 70mm to 240mm, including tank guns and anti-aircraft guns, while each of our armies (three divisions) is equipped with only 36 pieces of such artillery. The enemy would control the air while our air force, which has just started its training, will not be able to enter the war with some 300 planes until February 1951. Therefore, at present, we are not assured that our troops are able to wipe out an entire U. S. army once and for all. But since we have decided to go into the war against the Americans, we should be prepared so that, when the U.S. high command musters up one complete army to fight us in one campaign, we should be able to concentrate our forces four times larger than the enemy (that is, to use four of our armies to fight against one enemy army) and to use a firing power one and a half to two times stronger than that of the enemy (that is, to use 2200 to 3000 pieces of artillery of 70mm caliber and upward to deal with the enemy's 1500 pieces of artillery of the same calibers), so that we can guarantee a complete and thorough destruction of one enemy army. (6) In addition to the above-mentioned twelve divisions, we are transferring another twenty-four divisions, as the second and third echelons to assist Korea, from the south of the Yangzi River and the Shannxi-Ganshu areas to the Long-hai, Tianjin-Pukou, and Beijing-Southern Manchuria railways; we expect to gradually apply these divisions next spring and summer in accordance with the situation of the time.[66]

Interviews with Shi Zhe and Beijing's military researchers with access to Mao's manuscripts suggest that the original text of Mao's telegram to Stalin is longer than the published version. Mao also asked Stalin to deliver to the Chinese large amounts of military equipment, including tanks, heavy artillery, other heavy and light weapons, and thousands of trucks, as well as to confirm that the Soviet Union would provide the Chinese with air support when Chinese troops entered operations in Korea.[67] This telegram, and other available materials, places us in a position to answer several crucial questions:

First, what sort of a war did Chinese leaders anticipate they would be fighting in Korea? As Mao indicated, he understood that once Chinese troops entered a direct military confrontation with the United States the possibility existed that the United States might formally declare war on China and that American naval and air forces might attack China's coastal areas. Mao did not fear this prospect. He believed that even if the United States were to declare war on China, the focus of the war would still be in the Korean peninsula. If Chinese forces were able to eliminate American troops on the Korean battlefield, it would be unlikely that the confrontation between China and the United States would change into a total war. As far as the duration of China's intervention was concerned, Mao stressed that after focusing on the defensive in the initial stage of the confrontation, Chinese troops, if properly equipped by the Soviets, would begin an offensive to "annihilate the enemy." In other words, Mao did not anticipate that China would be involved in a long war.[68] It is also noticeable that Mao's analysis of America's military power focused on the conventional strength of the traditional three services. Nowhere did Mao mention America's nuclear power. This indicates again that Mao did not believe that the atomic bomb would be used on the Korean battlefield. All this demonstrates that when Mao and top CCP leaders made the decision to send Chinese troops to Korea, they were looking forward to a regional war, a conventional war, a short war, and a limited war. They did not anticipate that China's intervention would either lead to a world war involving the two superpowers or evolve into a nuclear slaughter.

Second, what goals did Chinese leaders hope to achieve by sending troops to Korea? In this telegram Mao assigned the Chinese troops the task of "solving the Korean problem." According to Mao's own explanation, this meant that the Chinese troops should be able to "eliminate the invaders from the United States and from other countries, and drive them out [of Korea]." Mao mentioned in the telegram that if the Chinese failed to "eliminate American troops in large numbers in Korea," a stalemate could emerge on the battlefield, putting China under serious domestic and international pressure. However, he treated this as no more than the worst possibility. The emphasis of his perceived war aims was clearly on a total victory over the United States and its "lackeys."[69] Against this background, when Mao talked about "the settlement of the Korean problem," his vision went far beyond the Korean peninsula and China. He linked the "settlement of the Korean problem" with its influence on the "whole East." When Mao considered the negative impact if Beijing failed to send troops to Korea, he emphasized that this could result in an unfavorable situation in the overall confrontation between the "reactionary forces" and the "revolutionary forces" in the East. And when he stressed the necessity of China's entry into the war, he made it clear that this would serve to promote the Eastern revolution.

Third, what were the basic conditions underlying Mao's pursuit of a victorious war in Korea? Mao acknowledged in this telegram that the United States possessed technological superiority as well as the domination of the air. But Mao believed that this could be handled by Chinese troops if properly equipped by the Soviets and supported by the Soviet air force. Furthermore, Mao relied on China's superior manpower and his belief in the higher morale of Chinese soldiers. He was confident that the Chinese Communists would be able to adopt the strategy that they had so successfully used in China's civil war, that is, "to concentrate our own forces four times larger than the enemy" to separate and annihilate the enemy. Mao even perceived that by using this strategy the Chinese would be able to annihilate an entire American army on the Korean battlefield. It is apparent that Mao's confidence in a Chinese victory over the United States was largely based on the reliability of the Chinese-Soviet strategic alliance, as well as on the CCP's own military experience.

In retrospect, Mao's perceptions proved to be only partially correct. As Mao predicted here, the direct Chinese-American military confrontation in Korea remained a regional, conventional, and limited war, although it lasted longer than Mao expected. During the practical course of China's military intervention in Korea, however, Mao and other Chinese leaders discovered that the United States was a resourceful enemy and the Soviet Union an uncertain ally. The CCP's long-established military and political strategies, including "separating and annihilating the enemy by concentrating our own forces," "fighting at close quarters and fighting in the dark," and "strengthening the military quality of the troops through widespread and profound political mobilization," would not be enough to bring about a Chinese victory in Korea. Mao and his fellow CCP leaders would gradually realize that they had underestimated both the determination of the Americans to fight in Korea and the effects of modern technology and military equipment in modern warfare. The Chinese-North Korean forces, although outnumbering the UN forces, could not overcome inadequate military equipment, vulnerable supply lines, and lack of air support. This made Mao's plan of "driving Americans out of the Korean peninsula" unfeasible. Moreover, Mao and his fellow Chinese leaders would find Stalin to be much less trustworthy than they initially believed. Mao would get far less support from Moscow than he had hoped to receive. As a result, Mao would be forced to redefine China's aims during the course of the Korean War and, in the long run, to redefine China's security strategy and foreign policy.[70]

Mao, of course, could not have foreseen these problems on October 2, 1950. Although under huge psychological pressure, Mao did not lack self-confidence. For him, the problem now was how to get the

Politburo's backing for the decision, and how to implement it. He was a soldier willing to face one of the most difficult challenges in his life.

Several hours after Mao sent off this crucial telegram to Stalin, Beijing issued another warning to the United States. Early on the next morning, Zhou Enlai arranged an emergency meeting with the Indian ambassador Panikkar. Zhou asked Panikkar to convey a message to the Americans: "The American forces are trying to cross the 38th parallel and to expand the war. If they really want to do this, we will not sit still without doing anything. We will be forced to intervene [*women yao guan*]."[71]

Why did Zhou send off this message after top CCP leaders had made the primary decision to enter the Korean War? In the past, without an understanding of the relationship between Beijing's decision to enter the war and Zhou's issuance of this warning, many scholars of the Korean War took this as evidence that Beijing did not want a direct military confrontation with the United States. This warning served as the last chance to avoid direct Chinese-American confrontation, scholars argue, and if Washington had responded seriously to this warning and ordered the UN forces not to cross the 38th parallel, China's military intervention could have been averted. Zhou's warning has thus been taken by many scholars both in the West and in China as the single most important piece of evidence supporting the argument that the Beijing leadership sent Chinese troops to Korea only to protect the safety of the Sino-Korean border.[72]

We now know that top Chinese leaders had made the primary decision to enter the war before Zhou's warning, not after it. A question thus emerges: What was the real meaning of Zhou's warning? To answer this question is obviously not an easy task, especially because we have no way to creep into the minds of Mao, Zhou, and other CCP leaders. While one cannot exclude the possibility that Chinese leaders sent off the warning for the purpose of avoiding China's military involvement at the final moment,[73] one should not merely rely on the apparent meaning of Zhou's statement. Combining the clues available now, two hypothetical alternative interpretations are offered here. First, Zhou's statement could have been designed to serve China's last-minute military preparations. In a military sense, as the Chinese were then still not fully ready to enter the war and as UN forces were advancing northward rapidly, top Beijing leaders must have realized that the UN forces could reach the Chinese-Korean borders before they could act. If so, they would lose the grounds on which to send in Chinese troops. By giving the Americans a clear warning, they may have hoped to delay the advance of UN forces, winning valuable time to complete final preparations.

Second, Zhou's statement could have been made for political considerations. Eager to use "The Great Movement to Resist America and Assist Korea" as a means to mobilize the Chinese nation as well to promote China's prestige and influence in the world, Mao and Beijing leaders may have concluded that a warning would further justify China's interference in the Korean War at home and abroad. If the United States failed to heed the warning (Beijing leaders obviously believed that the United States would continue the march), Mao and the CCP leadership would be in a stronger position to tell their own people and peoples in other parts of the world that they had tried everything before resorting to force. The Beijing leaders' considerations behind Zhou's warning could well offer another strong case for the political scientist Richard Ned Lebow's argument that "justifications of hostility crises serve to mobilize domestic and foreign support for an impending war and deprive an adversary of such support."[74]

The Politburo Backs Mao

At 10 a.m., October 4, a Russian-made Iliushin-14 plane landed on the airport of Xian, the largest city in Northwestern China. Within an hour, Peng Dehuai, then chairman of the Military and Administrative Committee of the Northwest and commander of the PLA's Northwest Military Region, boarded the plane. Mao and Zhou had ordered Peng to come to Beijing without any delay, so Peng did not have time to say goodbye to his colleagues before boarding the plane, which took off immediately, heading for Beijing via Taiyuan.[75]

While Peng was on his way to Beijing, an emergency meeting of the CCP Central Committee Politburo began around 3 p.m. in Zhongnanhai. The central topic of the meeting was the Politburo Standing Committee's decision to send Chinese troops to Korea. Those at the meeting included almost all members of the CCP Politburo and other key leaders: Mao Zedong, Zhu De, Liu Shaoqi, Zhou Enlai, Ren Bishi, Chen Yun, Kang Sheng, Gao Gang, Peng Zhen, Dong Biwu, Lin Boqü, Deng Xiaoping, Zhang Wentian and Li Fuchun. Peng Dehuai arrived at the meeting at about 5 p.m. Yang

Shangkun, director of the Office of the CCP Central Committee, and Hu Qiaomu, director of the Central Information Agency, also attended.[76]

Mao announced at the beginning of the meeting that the Politburo Standing Committee had made the decision to send troops to Korea. Because of the importance of the decision, Mao asked "those attending the meeting to list the possible disadvantages involved in dispatching [Chinese] troops to Korea."[77] Following Mao's call, most people attending the meeting expressed their reservations about the decision to enter the war; and, surprisingly, their views prevailed during the first day's meeting.[78] Their opinions can be summarized as three main arguments. First, having experienced decades of wars, China faced tremendous economic and financial problems. To achieve economic recovery and reconstruction, China needed a period of peaceful recuperation. To send troops into Korea might cause discontent at home. Second, China faced difficult political problems. The country had not been finally unified, and Taiwan and some offshore islands were still controlled by remnants of the GMD. Furthermore, land reform was just beginning in many "recently liberated areas." To participate in the Korean War would weaken the efforts to solve these problems. Third, the Chinese army would meet in Korea a geographic situation completely different from that of China, and would have to conduct warfare without control of the air or guarantees of logistic supply. They could therefore suffer in face of superior American weapons and equipment.[79] Mao did not directly rebut these opinions, but before the adjournment of the October 4 meeting he revealed his disagreement to them: "All you have said is not without ground. But when other people are in a crisis, how can we stand aside with our arms folded. This will make me feel sad."[80] The meeting was to resume the next day.

Mao's determination to enter the war, obviously, had not been weakened by the reservations of his comrades. Indeed, these arguments proved only that the difficulties involved in sending Chinese troops to Korea did not go beyond what he had contemplated. And he may also have felt that some of the problems listed by his comrades, such as the necessity of further consolidation of the new Communist regime, would be better solved if China could win a major confrontation with the United States. As the paramount leader of the party who had established his leading authority during the long course of the Chinese Communist revolution, Mao remained confident of his own judgment and of his ability to convince his comrades of the correctness of his determination.

The key person, in Mao's view, was Peng Dehuai. Peng came to the meeting with no preparation for discussions about sending Chinese troops to Korea. He arrived late and did not speak at the meeting.[81] But as the Politburo Standing Committee meeting of October 2 had already decided to ask Peng to command Chinese troops to Korea, his attitude toward intervention would have decisive influence on other people.

On the morning of October 5 Mao asked Deng Xiaoping to meet Peng at his hotel room and then accompany him to Mao's quarters for an exchange of opinions. As soon as Peng arrived at Mao's office, Mao told him that the situation in Korea was extremely urgent, that the UN forces had crossed the 38th parallel, and that China had an obligation to send troops to Korea. The difficulties involved in sending troops to Korea were obvious, Mao asserted, but there were advantages that favored the decision to enter the war. Mao asked Peng to state his opinions frankly. Peng, who had spent most of the night carefully considering Mao's decision to dispatch troops to Korea, had concluded that the decision was correct because it "not only combined the ideal of internationalism with considerations of patriotism, but was also crucial to the safety of China's Northeastern borders." The chairman, excited by Peng's response, asked him if he was willing to command Chinese troops in Korea. He explained that Lin Biao had been the first choice but had refused the appointment, claiming that he was physically unfit. The chairman stressed again that the situation in Korea was extremely urgent, that the UN forces were marching toward Pyongyang, and that it would be too late to send troops to Korea if the enemy forces reached the Yalu River. He argued that "we have to move forward immediately." After a brief moment, Peng agreed to take command of Chinese troops in Korea. A relieved Mao asked Peng to express his opinions when the Politburo meeting resumed the same afternoon. Peng's acceptance of the duty to command Chinese troops played a key role in enhancing Mao's control of the decision-making process.[82]

The Politburo meeting resumed in the afternoon. Peng, following Mao's instructions, spoke firmly in support of sending troops to Korea. He stressed that if U.S. forces reached the Yalu River, they could easily find an excuse to invade China; if China failed to enter the war until after the U.S. had occupied the entire Korean Peninsula, the situation would become more complicated. Disagreeing that sending troops to Korea would slow political consolidation at home, Peng emphasized that by entering the Korean War, the CCP would have an opportunity to beat both the arrogance of the United States and the bluster of reactionaries at home. Peng concluded that it was absolutely necessary to send troops to Korea.[83]

Peng's speech transformed the mood of the meeting, and the discussion now centered on the advantages of sending troops to Korea. The participants finally reached a series of consensuses: First, the Korean problem was not an isolated one. It had become the focus of the confrontation between the socialist camp and the imperialist camp in the East, perhaps even in the world. The purpose of sending troops to Korea was not only to rescue Korea, but also, and more important, to defend and promote an Asian and world revolution. Second, the safety of Korea was closely linked to the security of China. If the Americans reached the Yalu River, China would lose an important strategic buffer zone and face a heavy burden in defending its Northeast border. Third, comparing China's situation with that of the United States, China was superior in terms of manpower, moral strength, and support from the people, which would balance China's inferiority in terms of weapons and equipment.[84] The meeting formally confirmed Peng Dehuai's appointment. Mao concluded the meeting, stressing the necessity to enter the Korean War: "We have now only one choice, that is, no matter how many difficulties or dangers we may encounter, we have to send troops to Korea immediately, before Pyongyang is occupied by the enemy."[85]

The Politburo's meeting on October 4 and 5 was not a decision-making one in a strict sense, because the key decision had been made by the Politburo Standing Committee on October 2. Mao's purpose was to secure acceptance of his decision to enter the Korean War. To achieve this objective, Mao adopted the tactics that he had used with such sophistication since having become the paramount leader of the CCP: he first encouraged all members of the Politburo to express their opinions, especially the opinions that were different from his own, and then he used his wisdom and authority to persuade his comrades to yield to his ideas. Mao himself called this process "democratic centralism," a reflection of the combination of Leninist principles with an enlightened emperor's "way of dealing with different opinions" in traditional Chinese political culture (*na jian zhi dao*). Mao proved himself a master at dominating the party's decision-making apparatus.

After the meeting, Mao invited Zhou Enlai, Gao Gang, and Peng Dehuai to dine with him. They further discussed the concrete problems involved in implementing the decision to send troops to Korea. Mao stressed again that Chinese troops needed to enter Korea quickly, and he worried that any delay could result in fatal consequences. He directed Peng and Gao to travel to Shenyang as soon as possible to convey the decision to commanders above the division level of the NEBDA. The troops of the Border Defense Army, Mao emphasized, should enter Korea by October 15. At the same time, Zhou Enlai would fly to the Soviet Union to finalize details of Soviet air support for Chinese land forces and supply of military equipment.[86]

The next morning, Zhou Enlai chaired an enlarged meeting of the CMC, the focus of which was supposedly on how to guarantee logistical support for Chinese troops in Korea and how Peng would form his headquarters. Lin Biao, however, again expressed his reservations. He stressed that fighting the Americans was a very different matter from the CCP's previous experience of fighting the GMD. As the United States possessed modernized military forces and the atomic bomb, argued Lin, Chinese troops engaged in direct confrontation with the Americans would suffer severe losses. Zhou immediately criticized Lin in stern terms, emphasizing that the decision to send troops to Korea had been made by Mao and the Central Committee and that the remaining problem was how to carry out the decision. The meeting decided that Nie Rongzhen would take charge of general logistical matters and that Peng's headquarters would be established on the basis of that of the 13th Army Corps. This meeting also confirmed that Zhou Enlai would visit the Soviet Union to expedite the delivery of Soviet military supplies to China.[87]

Mao met again with Peng and Gao on October 7 to discuss a few details concerning the command and logistical systems for Chinese troops going to Korea. Mao suggested to Peng that he establish his headquarters in a hidden location north of the Yalu River to guarantee his safety. Peng believed it better for him to be with Kim Il-sung to coordinate the operations of Chinese troops with those of the North Korean forces. Peng also stressed the need to maintain secrecy before Chinese troops entered operations. He recommended that even after the fighting started, the Xinhua New Agency should be restricted in reporting the activities of Chinese troops. Mao agreed.[88]

The Issuance of the Order

The time for action had arrived. The Americans further justified Mao's decision to enter the Korean War at this moment. On October 7, the UN General Assembly, at the urging of the United States, approved the establishment of a UN Commission of the Unification and Rehabilitation of Korea. The same day, the American First Cavalry Division crossed the 38th parallel. Zhou's warning made through Ambassador Pannikar had been totally ignored. Mao now had every reason to tell his comrades that to enter the war was the only choice. On October 8, in the name of the chairman of the Chinese People's Revolutionary Military Commission, Mao issued the order to send Chinese troops to Korea:

> (1) In order to assist the Korean people's war of liberation, repel the invasion launched by the American imperialists and their running dogs, and to defend the interests of the Korean people, the Chinese people and the people of all Eastern countries, it has been ordered that the Northeast Border Defense Army be turned into the Chinese People's Volunteers and that the Chinese People's Volunteers move immediately into the territory of Korea to assist the Korean comrades in their struggle against the invaders and to strive for a glorious victory. (2) The Chinese People's Volunteers comprises the 13th Army Corps and its constituents including the 38th, 39th, 40th, and 42nd Armies, and the Border Defense Artillery Headquarters and its First, Second, and Eighth Artillery Divisions. All the above-mentioned units are required to complete preparations immediately and get ready for the order to begin operations. (3) Comrade Peng Dehuai is appointed as the Commander and Political Commissar of the Chinese People's Volunteers. (4) The Chinese People's Volunteers will take the Northeast Administrative Region as its general logistical base. Comrade Gao Gang, commander and political commissar of the Northeast Military Region, will take full charge of coordinating and guaranteeing all requisitions for supplies from the

rear base, as well as for the assistance provided to Korean comrades. (5) When moving into Korean territory, the Chinese People's Volunteers must demonstrate friendship and respect for the Korean people, for the Korean People's Army, for the Democratic Government of Korea, for the Workers' Party of Korea (the Korean Communist Party) and other democratic parties, and for Kim Il-sung, the leader of the Korean people. They must strictly comply with military and political discipline. This is a very important political precondition through which the fulfillment of the military operations is ensured. (6) [The Chinese People's Volunteers] must fully anticipate all kinds of difficult situations that they may, and will, encounter and must be prepared to exercise a high degree of enthusiasm, courage, caution, and a spirit of perseverance in overcoming these difficulties. At the present moment, the general international and domestic situations are favorable to us, but unfavorable to the aggressors; if only our comrades are resolute, brave, good at working with the local people and good at fighting against the aggressors, the final victory will be ours.[89]

Why did Mao call the Chinese troops going to Korea "Chinese People's Volunteers"? Before the Inchon landing, as Mao and the CCP leadership contemplated sending troops to Korea, they discussed what to call these troops. To minimize risk of a formal war with the United States and to follow the original assumption that Chinese troops would play only a supplementary role in the fighting, Mao and the CCP leadership were inclined to call Chinese troops in Korea "Chinese People's Supporters." After Inchon, the implications of China's intervention changed dramatically. In further discussions on how to describe Chinese troops in Korea, Huang Yanpei, a pro-Communist "democratic figure," then China's vice premier, suggested that it would be better to call Chinese troops in Korea "volunteers." Mao and other CCP leaders immediately saw the merits of this suggestion. By calling Chinese troops in Korea volunteers, they would be able to better convince the Chinese people of the moral justification of the intervention, while at the same time alleging that Chinese troops were organized on an unofficial basis, thus reducing the risk of a formal war with the United States and other Western countries.[90]

Mao's emphasis that the CPV should demonstrate "friendship and respect" to Kim Il-sung, the Korean party, and the Korean people was not just propaganda. For the chairman, Kim's cooperation concerned both the effectiveness and significance of China's intervention in Korea: While the wholehearted cooperation of Kim and his comrades would better guarantee the success of China's war effort, the new China's influence and prestige would be significantly enhanced if the Chinese could prove that their intervention in the war did not aim to extend China's political control over Korea but to fulfill true "internationalist obligations."

Mao was now ready to give Kim's and Pak's formal request an affirmative response. He sent a telegram to Kim Il-sung via the Chinese embassy in Korea on the evening of October 8, formally informing him that China had decided to "dispatch the Volunteers to Korea to assist you in fighting against the aggressors." Mao asked Kim to send Pak Il-yu immediately to Shenyang to meet Peng Dehuai and Gao Gang to "discuss a series of concrete problems concerning the CPV's entering fighting in Korea."[91] Late that evening Ni Zhiliang and Chai Chengwen arrived at Kim's underground headquarters in Pyongyang and delivered Mao's telegram.[92] The Chinese war machine was now in motion.

The process leading to the decision to intervene was not straightforward. Under the shadow of the grave impacts of the Inchon landing, Beijing leaders had to consider the implications of the northward movement of UN forces, to coordinate with both Moscow and Pyongyang, and, most important of all, to unify party leaders. Mao played a crucial role in leading the CCP leadership toward intervention. His opening statement at the October 2 Political Bureau Standing Committee meeting, which was apparently the result of his extensive considerations during those sleepless days and nights after Inchon, set up the basic tones for the decision-making process. The following debates among top Beijing leaders about the necessity of sending troops to Korea were substantial, but had never got out of Mao's control. In fact, the opposition opinions from other Beijing leaders strengthened, rather than weakened, Mao's determination. Consequently, twenty-three days after the Inchon landing, eight days after the South Korean troops crossed the 38th parallel, and one day after American forces entered North Korean territory, Mao ordered "Chinese People's Volunteers" to enter the war. To turn the order into action, though, Mao and the Beijing leadership still had things to do: to further mobilize the country, to consolidate the consensus of the party leadership, to push the troops to complete the final preparations, and, not least of all, to make sure that when Chinese troops were engaged in operations Soviet air forces would be with them. The issuance of the October 8 order, therefore, did not conclude Beijing's path to intervention.

7 | The Decision Stands the Test: China Crosses the Yalu

Peng Dehuai and Gao Gang flew from Beijing to Shenyang early in the morning of October 8. They had about one week's time to solve any remaining problems before Chinese troops had to cross the Yalu. A few hours later, another plane flew Zhou Enlai to the Soviet Union. His task was to meet Stalin to finalize the Chinese-Soviet cooperation in Korea. In the meantime, Mao and his colleagues in Beijing wasted no time in considering how to accelerate military preparations, to further mobilize the country, as well as to make certain that when China was in a war its domestic situation would remain stable. The road leading to China's intervention in Korea had now reached the final stage, but the test for the Beijing leadership's war decision, as we shall see, was not yet over.

Domestic Mobilization Expanded

Mao had always been a believer that military actions should serve the party's political needs, and that intensive mass mobilization would best guarantee successful military operations. When he ordered Chinese troops to enter the Korean War, he endeavored to push the "Great Movement to Resist America and Assist Korea" to a new high peak. Following Mao's instructions, cadres of the CCP Central Committee's

Propaganda Department began in early October to work on a document offering guidelines for the movement. Mao supervised the drafting of the document, personally revising its contents and polishing its wording. A draft of this inner-party document was ready around the time when Mao issued the order to enter the war. After several revisions, including the revision by Mao himself, the document was finally issued to all party organs on October 26, entitled "The CCP Central Committee's Directives on the Current Situation." On November 5, the Xinhua News Agency, on the basis of this document, issued another more detailed, openly circulated document, entitled "How to Regard the United States (Outlines for Propaganda)." These important documents not only reveal the series of considerations underlying the CCP leadership's decision to enter the Korean War but also offer clues crucial for an understanding of why Mao was willing to risk a major confrontation with the United States.[1]

A central task of the "Great Movement to Resist America and Assist Korea," according to these documents, was "how to regard the United States correctly." Historically, they argued, many Chinese had been either deceived by the "outward appearance of American democracy" or psychologically overwhelmed by the strength of the United States. These Chinese thus believed that China should "learn from the United States," that China's modernization needed America's support, and that China could not afford to offend Americans. The Beijing leadership emphasized that "it was reactionary to be pro-America" and that "it was wrong to either adore or to be afraid of the Untied States."

Beijing leaders therefore established the goals for a nation-wide propaganda movement aimed at "exposing the real nature of U.S. imperialism," placing emphasis on three points. First, both from historical and current perspectives the United States was China's enemy: historically the United States had persistently pursued extraterritoriality and privileges through unequal treaties with China; currently the United States had invaded Korea and Taiwan, threatening China's security. Second, it was a myth that the United States was a "democratic and peace-loving" country. In reality, the "reactionary ruling classes" in the United States were exploiting and oppressing the working masses at home and making the United States "the bastion of international wars of aggression" abroad. Third, the United States was by nature a "paper tiger." It was politically isolated in the world as the result of its reactionary policies and militarily weak because of the contradictions between America's limited resources and Washington's unlimited aims of expansion. As a result, China's confrontation with the United States was both necessary and reasonable—because the United States was China's enemy and because China could defeat the United States.

Beijing leaders offered four arguments to bolster their claim that the United States was militarily vulnerable. First of all, since Washington had committed itself to Europe, Asia, and almost everywhere in the world, it could not possibly hold all fronts. Second, the United States, as a country located in the western hemisphere, was almost halfway across the earth from East Asia. American troops and war materials needed to travel across the Pacific Ocean for operations in Korea. This would greatly restrict "the American capacity for logistical supply and military reinforcement." Third, the United States had limited human resources to spend in the Korean War and American soldiers did not like to fight in a remote foreign land. The Beijing leadership estimated that the United States had around 1.45 million men serving in the armed forces, two thirds of whom were either inexperienced or non-combat personnel. In comparison, the Chinese and Korean forces easily outnumbered the Americans and their allies. Moreover, Chinese and Korean soldiers, fighting to defend their own homeland, would have a much higher morale than the Americans. Finally, the United States could not rely on the support of strong allies, since West Germany and Japan had not been rearmed, and Britain, France, and Italy were no longer great military powers.

Beijing leaders gave three reasons to persuade the Chinese people not to fear the prospect of atomic warfare. First, while it was true that the atomic bomb was a weapon of massive destruction, its power should not be exaggerated. In fact, they argued, "the atomic bomb would produce only the effect equal to the accumulation of thousands of regular bombs," which might "influence the process of a war but could not decide the fate of a war." Second, considering the nature of the atomic bomb, it could not be used everywhere. "As the bomb had such capacity for destruction, it could not be used in a battle engaging the troops of the two sides; otherwise, the users' troops would also be destroyed." Furthermore, as the bomb had such a concentrated, massive power of destruction, it would be less threatening to a vast country like China than to the United States and other Western industrial countries which were heavily dependent on a few big industrial centers. Third, the United Stated had to consider the fact that it was no longer in a position to monopolize the bomb. "If the United States dared to use it, it would naturally face retaliation, and this would be most horrible for the United States, which had a concentrated industry."

In order to "combine patriotism and nationalism with internationalism," Beijing leaders adopted "resist America and assist Korea, and defend our home and our country" as the central slogan for the "Great Movement to Resist America and Assist Korea." They stressed the importance of establishing a close relationship between "the deeprooted patriotic and nationalist feeling" of every common Chinese and the great task of "beating American imperialists in Korea." They called on the Chinese people to "hate the U.S. imperialists," to "disdain the U.S. imperialists," and to "look down on the U.S. imperialists." In short, the Chinese people, as Mao repeatedly emphasized, had to "beat American arrogance."

These instructions illustrated again the Beijing leadership's intention to change the external pressure caused by the Korean crisis into a driving force for promoting the continuation of the great Chinese revolution. Mao believed that nothing could be more appealing to the Chinese people's profound nationalist feelings than the prospect of defeating a powerful enemy like the United States in a major military confrontation. The new China's successful confrontation with the United States, even at a heavy price, would inculcate into the Chinese people a new mentality combining the inner acceptance of Communist ideals with the regenerating sense of China as a great nation in the world. As a result, the CCP would be in a much stronger position to carry out its plans to transform totally Chinese society, as well as to expand China's international influence through the promotion of the Eastern revolution. Even if China could not defeat the Americans in the Korean War, it would not represent an intolerable blow to the Beijing leadership. One of Peng Dehuai's statements, with which Mao fully agreed, made clear the Beijing leadership's view of this problem: "It is necessary to send troops to assist Korea. Even if we were to be defeated in Korea, this would be no worse than that our victory in the War of Liberation would come several years later."[2]

Mao and the CCP leadership understood what they needed to do and what they were in a position to do at that moment. On October 10, two days after Mao formally issued the order to send Chinese troops to Korea, the CCP Central Committee issued "The Directive for Correcting the Rightist Tendency in Suppressing Reactionary Activities." Criticizing "the failure on the part of many party members and cadres" to take "resolute measures to suppress reactionary activities" in the past several months, the directive stressed that the entire party should be determined to destroy "all reactionaries and reactionary activities." The directive emphasized that the ruthless suppression of reactionary activities was crucial "for guaranteeing the smooth progress of land reform and economic reconstruction, as well as for the consolidation and further development of the Chinese people's revolution." The directive called for "striking the imperialist plot of sabotage and thoroughly destroying the remnants of Jiang Jieshi bandits."[3]

This directive was certainly an indication of the Beijing leadership's concern about creating a stable rear while Chinese troops were engaged in a major military confrontation with the United States.[4] It reflected also the CCP's need to achieve an absolute control over Chinese society. The CCP leaders understood that "the most ruthless suppression of the counter-revolutionaries, spies, saboteurs, and landlord-tyrants who were the most reactionary under the premise of resisting and assisting Korea would not only be fully supported by the labouring people but would also be favored by members of the upper bourgeoisie class and upper intellectuals."[5] As a matter of fact, although most violent, anti-Communist activities existed in outlying provinces and regions, the emphasis of the "suppression of reactionary activities" lay in urban areas.[6] With the introduction of the October 10 directive, a nationwide mass movement aimed at "suppressing reactionary activities" quickly emerged together with the "Great Movement of Resisting America and Assisting Korea." By May 1951, more than 2.5 million "reactionaries" had been arrested and 710,000 were executed.[7] CCP leaders justified such widespread terror on the grounds that otherwise the newly established Republic would be in danger.[8] The movement thus became one of the most important domestic campaigns in the first years of the PRC.[9]

Military Preparations further Accelerated

The issuance of the order to enter the Korean War made military preparations a more urgent task than ever before. On the morning of

October 8, immediately after their arrival in Shenyang, Peng and Gao met with leading commanders of the 13th Army Corps, including Deng Hua, Hong Xuezhi, Xie Fang, and Du Ping. Peng conveyed to them the party leadership's decision to send troops to Korea and asked them to try their best to fulfill the tasks assigned by the party.[10] That afternoon, Peng and Gao had a meeting with the leading figures of the CCP Northeast Bureau and the PLA's Northeast Military Region, informing them of the Politburo's decision to enter the Korean War. Peng stressed that it was crucial to "send troops to Korea as soon as possible to fight against the enemy; otherwise, the consequences could be disastrous." Following the decision of the Politburo, Peng also asked the Northeast Region to guarantee logistical support for Chinese troops fighting in Korea.[11] In the evening, Peng met with Pak Il-yu, who had just rushed from Korea to Shenyang. Pak explained battlefield situation to Peng, asking Chinese troops to enter Korea in the shortest possible time and, as the first step, to guarantee the control of Sinuiju and Hamhung.[12]

On October 9, Peng Dehuai summoned a conference in Shenyang, attended by all army-level commanders in the CPV. The purpose of the conference was "to introduce the current situation and the intentions of the Central Committee, as well as to learn about the real moral status of the troops."[13] Peng emphasized at the conference that because enemy forces were moving rapidly toward the Yalu, "we have to compete with the enemy." Following the instructions of the CCP leadership, he also made it clear that China "sent troops to Korea for winning the war while at the same time being prepared to be defeated." He asked his subordinates to "strengthen political mobilization of the troops, helping the cadres and soldiers to establish the determination to win the war." He ordered all armies to complete preparations for battle within ten days, and some units to enter Korea even earlier.[14] Considering that UN forces still controlled the air, Xie Fang, now the CPV's chief of staff, suggested that Chinese troops should cross the river under darkness to maintain secrecy. Peng agreed.[15]

The same evening, Peng took a train to Andong, so that he could be in a more direct position to monitor the movement of UN troops and to discover any problem still existing in Chinese military preparations. Informed that UN forces had about 400,000 soldiers, including around 10 divisions or 130,00 front-line troops, Peng concluded that he needed reinforcements to enable his troops to overwhelm UN forces in the initial confrontation. He cabled to Mao on the evening of October 9: "Originally we planned to send out two armies and two artillery divisions. . . . Now we have decided to change our original plan and to assemble all of our forces [four armies, three artillery divisions, and three antiaircraft artillery regiments] at the south bank of the Yalu River." Mao approved this change immediately.[16] Peng also reported to Mao that the largest problem facing the CPV was the lack of means of transportation. He estimated that the CPV needed at least 700 more trucks and 600 more drivers.[17] At 8 p.m. on October 10, Peng cabled to Mao again, informing him that he would meet Kim Il-sung in Korea the next day to discuss coordination between Chinese and North Korean troops.[18] At this stage, the Chinese troops were like an arrow on a bowstring—they could enter Korea at any time.

Moscow's Renege

The situation, however, changed suddenly at this juncture. At 8:00 p.m. on October 12, Mao sent an urgent telegram to Peng Dehuai, Gao Gang and other leading figures in the Northeast, ordering them to stop implementing the war order immediately. Mao directed that all units of the 13th Army Corps should "stay where they were to undertake more training, not to begin operations," and that Peng and Gao should come back to Beijing for further discussion about the war decision.[19] On the same day, Mao sent another telegram to Rao Shushi and Chen Yi, respectively political commissar and commander of the PLA's East China Military Region, ordering the units under their command that had served as the NEBDA's reserve forces to stop all actions and "stay in their current positions for rectification." Mao stressed also that they should "not give any new explanations to our cadres and the democratic figures [from other parties]" for such a dramatic change.[20] Worrying that Mao's telegram would not reach Peng in time (it would take a few hours to translate the telegram from confidential codes to texts), Nie Rongzhen hurried to the General Staff's operation department to make a long-distance call to Peng, informing him that he was to return to Beijing immediately to attend a Politburo meeting which would "reconsider the decision to dispatch troops to Korea."[21]

Mao and the CCP leadership had stopped the movement of Chinese troops at this late stage because of Stalin. Since late September, the CCP Politburo had based its decision to enter the war on the understanding that China would provide the land forces and the Soviet Union the air cover. Mao in his October 2 telegram to Stalin therefore requested that the Soviet air force enter Korea to cover Chinese troops. On October 8, at the same time Mao issued the orders to send Chinese troops into Korea, Zhou Enlai, together with Shi Zhe, the interpreter, and Kang Yimin, the confidential secretary, flew to the Soviet Union to finalize details of Chinese-Soviet military cooperation in Korea, arriving in Moscow on October 10.[22] Accompanied by Bulganin and joined by Lin Biao, now in Russia to receive his medical treatment,[23] and Wang Jiaxiang, Chinese ambassador to the Soviet Union, Zhou flew to southern Russia to meet Stalin at his villa on the Black Sea on the same afternoon.[24]

The meeting was a long one—lasting from 7 p.m. until 5:00 the next morning. Chinese participants at the meeting were Zhou Enlai, Lin Biao, Wang Jiaxiang and Shi Zhe, and the Soviet participants included Stalin, Malenkov, Beria, Kaganovich, Bulganin, Mikoyan, Molotov, and N. T. Fedorenko (the Russian interpreter).[25]

Shi Zhe offers a detailed account of the meeting. The atmosphere was tense at first because neither side knew the exact stand of the other. Stalin initiated the conversation by discussing the general situation in Korea, emphasizing that the North Koreans faced serious difficulties and that the situation was most urgent. He wanted to know the view of his Chinese comrades on the situation. Zhou responded, stressing that China also faced serious difficulties resulting from years of warfare, and he made it clear that China's stand was that "it would be better for us not to enter the Korean War." Stalin seemed disappointed. He stated that without outside assistance, the North Koreans could survive for no more than one week. Instead of pressing the Chinese too hard, however, Stalin asked Zhou to consider the tremendous American menace to China's security, to the Northeast in particular, if UN forces reached the Yalu. He commented that American occupation of the entire Korean peninsula would cause a very difficult situation for both the Soviet Union and China in East Asia. Stalin also warned the Chinese that even the task of absorbing Korean refugees could place a heavy burden on the Chinese and they should plan for this immediately.

Then Stalin made it clear that the Soviet Union was not in a position to send troops to Korea because the Russian border with Korea was too small and the Soviet Union had already announced a complete withdrawal from Korea. If the Soviet Union sent troops there, Stalin emphasized, a direct confrontation between the Soviet Union and the United States could follow. He then suggested that China send troops to Korea. In order to encourage the Chinese to enter the war on Kim Il-sung's behalf, Stalin promised that the Soviet Union would provide sufficient military equipment and war material for the Chinese. He mentioned that the Soviet Union had large amounts of weapons and ammunition left over from the Second World War to supply the Chinese, and stated that the Soviet air force would defend China's Northeast and coastal areas and also cover the Chinese troops along the Korean side of the Yalu. The discussion then focused on if and when Soviet air forces would enter Korea. Stalin insisted that Soviet air force needed more preparations and was therefore unable to cover Chinese troops in Korea, at least not at first. Zhou told Stalin that he was not in a position to make the decision on when to enter the war and that he needed to contact the CCP leadership in Beijing. Therefore, the meeting was unable to reach any conclusion on whether or under what conditions China would enter the war.[26]

Shi Zhe's account, which outlines the Zhou-Stalin meeting, also raises a series of questions. The Beijing leadership had made the decision to enter the Korean War and conveyed the decision to the North Koreans, and the Chinese troops gathering on the Chinese-Korean border were ready to cross the Yalu. Why then did Zhou inform Stalin that the Beijing leadership preferred not to enter the war? Is Shi Zhe's account reliable? If not, what really occurred during the Stalin-Zhou meeting? If yes, why did Zhou fail to inform Stalin of the true intention of the Beijing leadership? In fact, Shi Zhe's account is not the only version of the story offered by Chinese sources, and Shi himself has been challenged for telling such a seemingly dubious and contradictory story.[27] Kang Yimin, the confidential secretary who also accompanied Zhou to Moscow, for example, claimed that "Shi Zhe could have been misled by his memory" and offered another version of the story. He emphasized that the purpose of Zhou's visit was "to inform Soviet leaders that China had decided to send troops to resist America and assist Korea, as well as to ask the Soviet Union to provide China with military support and send [Soviet] air forces to the Northeast and such coastal cities as Beijing, Tianjin, and Shanghai."[28]

A brief discussion about the purpose(s) and contents of Zhou's visit is therefore in order. Shi Zhe insists that Zhou was to inform the Soviets that China would not enter the Korean War. After discussing the matter with Shi Zhe and other researchers in Beijing and checking all available documentary sources, I believe that Shi Zhe may have confused the *contents* of Zhou's statement to Stalin and the *purpose* of his visit. In both Shi's published memoirs and my extensive interviews with him in August 1992, he also recalled consistently that the central topic of the Zhou-Stalin meeting was to determine whether the Soviet Union would offer the Chinese troops an air umbrella over Korean territory and, to a lesser degree, if the Soviets could satisfy the military needs of Chinese troops fighting in Korea. Several other Chinese sources have confirmed that Zhou's visit to the Soviet Union was to work out the details of Soviet military support to China, especially securing the Soviet air umbrella.[29] One of Mao's own recollections helps to clarify the question. In a conversation with Kim Il-sung in 1970, Mao recalled the situation in October 1950:

> Although we have placed five armies along the Yalu River, it was difficult for our Politburo to make the final decision. . . . Stalin was tired and disappointed and said: "Let it go at that. [*suan le ba*]." Then did you [pointing to Zhou Enlai] visit the Soviet Union? Did you tell him [Stalin] that we would not send troops to Korea? (Zhou replies: No. I gave him two options and asked him to make the decision). Oh, yes. When we were to send troops to Korea, we desperately needed to make sure that they [the Soviets] would send their air forces to cover us. At first Molotov agreed, but then Stalin telephoned us saying that their air forces could not go beyond the Yalu River. Finally we made the decision and telephoned him that whether the Soviets would dispatch its [air] forces to Korea or not, we would go ahead.[30]

Mao's statement confirms the main purpose of Zhou's visit—Zhou went to the Soviet Union not to call off Beijing's involvement in the Korean War but to pursue the best possible deal from Stalin. It also offers important clues to clarify why Zhou informed Stalin that Beijing preferred not to send troops to Korea—this was possibly a trick designed by Mao to place more pressure on Stalin. Shi Zhe agrees with this view, and in our discussions about the Zhou-Stalin meeting he repeatedly emphasized that by Zhou's informing Stalin that China would not enter the Korean War "Mao was intentionally playing with [*wan*] Stalin."[31] Considering that during Mao's visit to the Soviet

Union he chose not to reveal his true intentions to Stalin, it is fully reasonable to believe that Mao would repeat the same pattern in other dealings with him.

Stalin, however, was certainly familiar with this kind of game. He would not be easily pressed by the Chinese, especially because he must have learned from the North Koreans that the Chinese had made the decision to enter the war. He was thus able to carefully design and stick to his basic stand. He strongly encouraged the Chinese to enter the war, but he would not allow the Soviet air force to cross the Yalu River at too early a time. Zhou had no way to further "play with" Stalin. From a Chinese point of view, however, Stalin's attitude violated the Soviet promise in the treaty signed with China eight months earlier which stated that the Soviets would offer "all-out" support for the Chinese if the latter entered a military confrontation with the imperialist countries. It is easy to understand why Stalin's decision was viewed by Chinese leaders as nothing less than a betrayal at a time of real crisis.

Now let us return to the Zhou-Stalin meeting. Probably because the meeting could not overcome the barrier of air support and, finally, failed to reach a deal acceptable to both sides, Stalin and Zhou decided to send a telegram jointly to the CCP Central Committee. The telegram made it clear to Mao and other Beijing leaders that "the Soviet Union will fully satisfy China's need for the supply of artillery, tanks, airplanes, and other military equipment," but "it will take at least two or two-and-half months for the Soviet air force to be ready to support the CPVs' operations in Korea."[32] Zhou then flew back to Moscow to wait for Beijing's response.[33]

The Second Decision: October 13, 1950

Stalin's sudden change angered Mao and CCP leaders while at the same time it created tremendous pressures for them. After receiving the telegram from Zhou and Stalin, Mao put the CPV's movement on hold.[34] He and other CCP leaders in Beijing now had to decide if they would intervene without direct Soviet air support—a very difficult question. Since early October, after the decision to enter the Korean War, the chairman and his colleagues had been acting on the assumption that Chinese troops would have sufficient support from their Soviet comrades. According to the understanding of Mao and the CCP leadership, the Soviet Union would supply the Chinese with military equipment and war materials, take the responsibility of protecting important industrial centers in China's coastal area, and provide air cover for Chinese ground troops in Korea. When Chinese troops were about to enter the Korean War, the last issue drew increasing attention from Chinese military planners. For example, at the October 9 conference attended by army-level commanders in Shenyang, the officers questioned Peng Dehuai about whether their troops would be well protected from the air after entering operations in Korea. Unable to answer this question, Peng and Gao jointly cabled Mao at 11 a.m., when the meeting was still underway, asking: "How many bombers and fighters can the CMC send to Korea after our troops are engaged in operations there? When will [the air force] be dispatched and who will be in charge?"[35]

Lack of air cover was also a widespread concern among the low-level officers and soldiers who were preparing to enter operations in Korea. According to the memoirs of Jiang Yonghui, then associate commander of the 38th Army, one of the CPV's best units, while responding to soldiers' inquiries about air support, many platoon and company commanders responded that with the backing of the powerful motherland as well as the support from the brotherly Soviet Union, they would get "as many cannons and planes as they wanted."[36] The Soviet air umbrella in Korea thus became an issue that influenced the morale of the Chinese troops.

Gao and Peng quickly returned to Beijing. The CCP politburo held an emergency meeting on the afternoon of October 13 to discuss whether China should intervene without Soviet air support.[37] Peng Dehuai reported on his talks with Pak Il-yu, the movements of UN forces, and the status of CPV preparations, making it clear to the participants that the CPV troops were ready to cross the Yalu. The discussion then focused on whether China should send troops to Korea without direct Soviet air support. Reportedly, Peng became angry when he learned that the Soviet Union would not send its air force to Korea to cover the Chinese troops, and threatened to resign as the CPV's commander.[38] Mao again dominated the discussion. He emphasized to Peng and other participants that although Soviet air force would not enter Korea in the initial stage of the war, Stalin had promised air defense over Chinese territory as well as the supply of large amounts of military equipment to Chinese troops. He asked

Peng not to resign from his position.[39] After weighing the pros and cons, especially having evaluated the serious consequences of China's failure to send troops to Korea, participants reached a consensus that even without direct Soviet air support in Korea, the Chinese were still in a position to fight the Americans there. They would now depend more on Mao's principles of self-reliance, emphasizing that an army with higher morale could beat an enemy with superior equipment. They also believed that if the United States occupied the entire Korean peninsula, China's immediate security as well as the fate of the revolution in the East would be in severe danger. As a result, the meeting reaffirmed that, as Mao recalled to Kim Il-sung, "whether or not the Soviets would dispatch its air forces to Korea, we would go ahead."[40] Peng immediately called his secretary, instructing him to send a most-urgent telegram to Deng Hua, Xie Fang, and other CPV commanders, ordering CPV units to "accelerate preparations for entering operations in Korea."[41]

After the meeting, Mao telegraphed to Zhou to respond to Zhou's and Stalin's October 11 telegram by summarizing the reasoning and conclusions of the Politburo meeting:[42]

(1) As a result of my discussion with the comrades of the Politburo, we are still convinced that dispatching our troops to Korea would be beneficial to us. In the first phase of the war, we may concentrate on fighting the [South Korean] puppet army, which our troops are quite capable of coping with. We may open up some bases in the mountainous areas north of Wonsan and Pyongyang. This will surely raise the spirits of the Korean people. If we can eliminate several divisions of the [South Korean] puppet army in the first phase, the Korean situation would take a turn in our favor. (2) The adoption of the above-mentioned active policy will be very important to the interests of China, Korea, the East, and the whole world. If on the other hand we sent none of our troops and allowed the enemy to reach the banks of the Yalu River, the international and domestic reactionary bluster would surely become louder; such a situation would be very unfavorable to us and it would be even worse for the Northeast. The whole Northeast Border Defense Army would be tied down there, and the electric power in south Manchuria would be subject to the control [of the enemy]. In short, we believe that we should enter the war and that we must enter the war. Entering the war can be most rewarding; failing to do so may cause great harm.[43]

While making it clear that China would enter the Korean War, Mao continued to bargain with Stalin. He instructed Zhou Enlai in the same telegram to clarify whether the Soviets would ask China to lease or to purchase the military equipment that Stalin agreed to provide. "If the equipment could be provided through leasing, and we would therefore be able to devote 200 million dollars of our budget to economic and cultural reconstructions, as well as to other general military and administrative expenses, our troops would then enter Korea without much worry. And we would be able to wage a prolonged war while at the same time maintaining the unity of the majority of our people at home." Furthermore, the chairman wanted to make sure that the Soviet air force would enter operations in Korea later. He stressed in the telegram: "If the Soviet air force could, in addition to sending volunteer pilots to support our military operations in Korea in two to two-and-a-half months, dispatch units to Beijing, Tianjin, Shenyang, Shanghai, Nanjing, and Qingdao, we then would not need to fear the [American] air attack, although we still have to endure some losses if the American air attack occurred during the coming two to two-and-a-half months." Mao Zedong instructed Zhou Enlai to "stay in Moscow for a few more days, further consult with the Soviet comrades, and solve the above-mentioned questions."[44]

At first glimpse, it is surprising that the CCP leadership reaffirmed its decision to intervene after Stalin reneged on air protection in Korea. Considering Mao's understanding of the relationship between the Korean crisis and the CCP's revolutionary commitment and the new China's security needs, however, the decision was a natural, or even inevitable, development. Mao believed that Korea's fate concerned both the vital security interests of China and the destiny of an Eastern and world revolution, of which the Chinese Communist revolution was an important part. Moreover, the CCP leadership's management of the Korean crisis had been strongly influenced by Mao's desire to use the crisis to mobilize the party and the entire Chinese nation. Given Mao's frame of reference, he had to enter the Korean War. This is why even a dramatic shift (such as Stalin's breaking his promise to provide air support) did not alter Mao's resolve. His decision to send Chinese troops into Korea was not an easy one; however, it was a decision consistent with the CCP's specific revolutionary commitments and security concerns.

New Problems and Challenges to the War Decision

After receiving Mao's telegram, Zhou telephoned Molotov to inform him of the CCP Politburo's decision.[45] The next day Zhou cabled Stalin from Moscow. Following Mao's instructions, Zhou continued to try to persuade Stalin to send the Soviet air force to Korea. He put a series of questions before Stalin: "In addition to the dispatch of the 16 Soviet volunteer air regiments [to China], can [the Soviet Union] continue to send bombers to Korea to support the operations of the Chinese troops? . . . Besides sending volunteers to join operations in Korea, can the Soviet government send more air units to station in big cities in China's coastal area?"[46]

Stalin continued to refuse to use Soviet air units in operations in Korea when Chinese ground forces began operations, no matter how much this might disappoint his comrades in Beijing. He did confirm, though, that the Soviets would take the responsibility of safeguarding China's territory, that the Soviet air force might enter Korea later (but no deadline was given), and that the Soviet Union would guarantee China's military supply.[47] This ambiguous approach left a stamp on the long-range development of Sino-Soviet relations. Stalin's incomplete commitment made clear to Mao and the CCP leadership the limitations of the Sino-Soviet alliance. Yet the Chinese desperately needed Soviet support in any form at this moment, and Mao had no other choice but to swallow the fruit of the Soviet "betrayal." Mao, however, would never forgive it. A seed of the future Sino-Soviet split had thus been sowed in the process of China's intervention in the Korean War.

After the CCP Politburo reaffirmed that Chinese troops would go to Korea without direct Soviet air protection, Gao Gang left Beijing during the early morning of October 14 for Shenyang to convey the decision to top CPV commanders, leading members of the CCP Northeast Bureau, and the PLA's Northeast Military Region.[48] Meanwhile, Mao and Peng spent the day formulating new strategy and redeploying the CPV in light of the changing situation on the Korean battlefield as well as the changing attitude of the Soviet Union. In two telegrams to Zhou Enlai, still in Moscow, Mao informed him of a series of adjustments in the CPV's operation plans and war aims, based on his discussions with Peng. Intelligence reports on recent developments in Korea suggested to Mao that after occupying Pyongyang and Wonsan, the UN forces would either stay where they were or continue to march northward. While "it would take some time" for the American units, most of which at the moment "remained at the 38th parallel," to reach and capture Pyongyang, "they would need more time to take Tokchon from Pyongyang." Meanwhile, Mao judged that "if the Americans did not attack Tokchon, it would be quite difficult for the puppet forces at Wonsan to attack [Tokchon] alone." Mao believed that "our troops would gain time to advance [into planned positions], prepare defense and complete deployment."[49]

Following these judgments and facing the cruel fact that Chinese troops in Korea would not be protected from air attack, Mao decided to restrict the CPV's operational goals in the initial stage of the war. Mao summarized the CPV's new strategy for the initial fighting: The CPV troops were to take a defensive position after entering Korea; they would establish a defensive perimeter, composed of two or three defense lines, north of Pyongyang and Wonsan in order to hold bases as the starting point for future offensive operations. If UN troops attacked the perimeter in six months, they planned to wipe out the enemy before the perimeter; if UN troops did not initiate an offensive, the Chinese would not either. Only after all preparations were completed would a counteroffensive be launched toward Pyongyang and Wonsan.[50]

However, Mao did not give up the hope that Chinese troops could gain the initiative on the battlefield through a few victories over the UN forces, especially over the South Korean "puppet" units, in the initial contacts. Mao mentioned in his telegram to Zhou that both Peng and he believed that "once we destroyed one to two, or two to three, entire divisions of the puppet army, the situation would become more flexible for us."[51] To regain the initiative, Mao decided that all four armies and three artillery divisions of the CPV would start entering Korea on October 19. He also ordered the Ninth Army Corps to continue to move into areas with easy railway access to the Northeast.[52]

The rapidly changing situation in Korea placed new pressures on Mao and the CCP leadership in the next twelve hours. Early in the morning of October 15, Mao learned that UN forces, including the Americans, were preparing to seize Pyongyang. Confronted with the accelerating northward march of UN forces, Mao cabled Gao Gang and Peng Dehuai, who had just left Beijing for the Northeast by plane, instructing them to "have our advanced troops start off on the 17th so that they would reach Tokchon on the 23rd, rest for a day and then start the construction of defensive works on the 25th to achieve a superior position against the enemy."[53]

Peng arrived in Shenyang shortly after the arrival of this telegram. He found that besides Gao Gang and top CPV commanders, Pak Hon-yong was there. Pak told Peng that the enemy troops had approached Pyongyang, that the North Korean Communists needed their Chinese comrades to assist them at the earliest time, and that Kim Il-sung wished to meet Peng as soon as possible. Peng told Pak that top CCP leaders had decided to send troops across the Yalu on the 18th or the 19th. He invited Pak to join Gao Gang and himself to travel to Andong the next day.[54]

On October 16, Peng chaired a conference attended by division-level commanders from the CPV at Andong. He first conveyed the final decision of the Politburo to send troops to Korea. Obviously having sensed that reservations existed among the participants, Peng particularly explained the reasons for the decision to enter the Korean War. He emphasized that if China "failed to support positively the revolutionary government and people in Korea by sending its troops there, the reactionaries at home and abroad would be increasingly rampant, and those pro-Americans would become much more active." He warned his future subordinates that the American occupation of the entire Korean peninsula "would present a direct threat to our country, causing an extremely unfavorable situation for our national defense and border defense." As a result, Peng anticipated, the Chinese troops would have to fight the Americans in Chinese territory. So, Peng concluded, "to support Korea is also to consolidate our own national defense."[55]

Peng stressed also that all units needed to prepare for a difficult and protracted war. He ordered that all CPV units should enter Korea in the shortest possible time.[56] When recalling this meeting, Du Ping commented that "if the August 13 conference was one designed for mobilization, the October 16 conference was one to pledge resolution before going into operations."[57] After the meeting, a regiment of the 42nd Army entered Korea in the night of October 16.[58] The next morning, Peng instructed Xie Fang to cross the Yalu to Sinuiju to prepare for the coming of the CPV's main forces.[59]

The influence of the Soviet withdrawal of direct air support, however, was demonstrated again at this final moment. When Peng traveled back from Andong to Shenyang to solve the remaining logistical problems for the CPV on October 17, he and Gao Gang received a surprising telegram from Deng Hua, Hong Xuezhi, and other top CPV commanders, which expressed strong reservation for entering the Korean War at that moment:

> After yesterday's conference for the deployment of crossing the [Yalu] River, many comrades have expressed the opinion through discussions that our troops have only a few anti-aircraft artillery pieces and have no air support at this moment, and that the enemy could concentrate large numbers of planes, artillery, and tanks to wage heavy attacks against us without any worries. And as the Korean terrain is mostly composed of mountainous areas and water rice fields, it will be difficult to construct defensive works in the chilly weather and out of frozen soil. If the enemy started an all-out offensive, it would be less than possible for us to hold our ground. The opinion of the majority is that as we have not been fully prepared and as political mobilization is far from complete, it would be better if we send off our troops not this winter but next spring.[60]

Peng and Gao understood the seriousness involved in the suggestion of the telegram: some leading CPV commanders had not yet been convinced of the necessity for China to send troops to Korea. They reported these generals' opinions immediately to Mao.

The continuous existence of reservations to entering the Korean War, together with the fact that Zhou Enlai would return to Beijing on the 18th, made Mao reluctant to issue the final order. He decided to postpone again the CPV's entry into Korea until he and the Politburo could meet with Zhou and receive a first-hand report on Stalin's stand. In a telegram to Peng and Gao on October 17, he ordered the advanced units of the CPV to continue "preparing to" enter Korea and wait for a "formal order" which would be issued the next day. He also asked Peng and Gao to return to Beijing again for discussions.[61]

The Final Decision: October 18

Peng and Gao flew to Beijing on the early morning of October 18 and top CCP leaders met again that day. Peng reported on the reservations expressed by CPV commanders, especially their worries about the consequences of the lack of proper Soviet air support in Korea. Zhou made it clear that although Stalin would not send Soviet air forces directly into Korea, he did promise to supply the Chinese with as much military equipment and ammunition as they needed in the Korean conflict, and that Soviet air forces would provide the Chinese with an umbrella over China's territory, especially important industrial centers in coastal areas. It was also possible that the Soviet air force would enter operations in Korea later. Listening to Peng's and Zhou's reports, Mao's mind was dominated by the worries that "the enemy troops were now attacking Pyongyang and in a few days they could reach the Yalu River." He told his comrades that "no matter how many difficulties were there, we should not change the decision to send our Volunteers to cross the [Yalu] River to assist Korea, and we should not delay the time of action." Following Mao's suggestions, the meeting finally established the evening of October 19 as the deadline for the CPV to cross the Yalu.[62]

At 9 p.m. on October 18, Mao personally cabled Deng Hua and other CPV commanders (Peng and Gao were then still in Beijing) to order CPV troops to cross the Yalu:

> It has been decided that the four armies and three artillery divisions will follow our original plan to enter northern Korea for war operations. These troops will start to cross the [Yalu] River from the Andong-Ji'an section tomorrow (the 19th) evening. In order to maintain strict secrecy, the troops should start to cross the river after dusk every day and stop [crossing] at four o'clock the next morning; by five all troops should be completely under cover, which should be carefully checked. In order to gain experience, only two to three divisions will cross the river on the first night (the night of the 19th), and the number can be increased or decreased on the second night according to the situation. Details will be conveyed to you in person by Gao Gang and Peng Dehuai.[63]

In the early morning of October 19, Peng and Gao flew back to Andong. They immediately convened a meeting of top CPV commanders to guarantee that Mao's decision would be implemented. Peng stressed that he would not tolerate any further opposition and reservation to the war decision. Peng met also with Pak Il-yu, who learned with excitement that the main forces of Chinese troops would enter Korea "today, after dark."[64]

In order not to reveal prematurely the CPV's movement into

Korea, Mao ordered the entire country, especially the public media, to adopt a policy of "only act and not talk." He made it clear that "no open propaganda about what we are doing should appear in our newspapers" and that "only high-ranking cadres of the party will be notified of the actions undertaken."[65] Mao also ordered CPV soldiers to dress in the uniforms of the Korean People's Army in the initial stage of their operations, so that they would be in a position to take the UN forces by surprise when the first encounter occurred. In accordance with Mao's instructions, CPV solders were not allowed to send personal letters to families or friends before their departure for Korea.[66] Chinese troops were now ready to cross the Yalu.

The week between October 12 and 19 witnessed the final stage of Beijing's path to the Korean War. The decision to enter it was challenged from both within (especially by the doubt cast by several CPV commanders) and, more seriously, without (Stalin refused to give operations in Korea an air umbrella); and the challenges continued until the moment the Chinese troops were to cross the Yalu. Mao's determination to enter the war, however, proved to be much firmer and deeper than these challenges. He again played a central role in convincing his fellow CCP leaders in Beijing that for the sake of China's security interests as well as the promotion of the Eastern revolution, China had no choice but to enter the war. Consequently, the war decision stood the test.

After dark on the evening of October 19, massive numbers of CPV troops began to cross the Yalu River.[67] Around midnight, General Nie Rongzhen reported to Mao that Chinese troops were smoothly entering Korea. For the first time in many days, Mao had a sound sleep.[68]

Conclusions

The Chinese Experience During the War

China's entry into the war immediately altered the balance of power on the Korean battlefield. With Mao's approval, Peng adopted a strategy of inducing the enemy troops to march forward and then eliminating them by superior forces striking from their rear and on their flanks. On October 25, the CPV initiated its first campaign in Korea, suddenly attacking South Korean troops in the Unsan area. In twelve days, South Korean troops were forced to retreat from areas close to the Yalu to the Chongchun River. According to Chinese statistics, about 15,000 South Korean soldiers were killed in this campaign.[1]

This setback should have sent a strong warning to UN forces, but General MacArthur was too arrogant to heed it. He, like many policymakers in Washington, underestimated the size and determination of his Chinese adversaries. In mid-November, he decided to initiate a new "end the war" offensive. Considering MacArthur's aggressiveness and the fact that the CPV's heavy equipment remained on the north bank of the Yalu River, Peng adopted a strategy of "purposely showing ourselves to be weak, increasing the arrogance of the enemies, letting them run amuck, and luring them deep into our areas." He ordered all CPV units to retreat for about 30 kilometers, to occupy favorable positions, and to wait for the best opportunity to strike.[2] In late November, advancing UN forces entered areas where CPV troops had laid their trap. Starting on November 25, Chinese troops began a vigorous counteroffensive. Under tremendous pressure, UN troops had to undertake what the political scientist Jonathan Pollack has called "the most infamous retreat in American military history."[3] By mid-December, the CPV and the reorganized KPA troops had regained control of nearly all North Korean territory.

In light of the achievements of the CPV's first two campaigns in Korea, Mao reemphasized the original goal of "eliminating the enemy troops and forcing the Americans out of the Korean peninsula." He refused to consider any proposal about ending the Korean conflict through negotiations, and was determined to solve the Korean problem by winning a clear military victory. On December 21, he ordered Peng "to fight another campaign" and "to cross the 38th parallel."[4]

On the last day of 1950, the Chinese troops started the third campaign, and UN forces again retreated. Seoul fell to Chinese and North Korean troops on January 4, 1951. Concluding that Beijing's war effort was progressing smoothly, the Soviet air force entered the Korean War on a limited scale in early January.[5] Both North Korean leaders and Soviet advisers in Korea pushed Peng to develop the offensive into one "to end the war by a total victory."[6] With their supply lines extended and casualties increased, however, the Chinese offensive gradually bogged down. Peng then ordered the Chinese-North Korean forces to halt offensive operations and consolidate their gains.[7] This decision angered Kim Il-sung, who had hoped to drive the Americans out of the Korean peninsula.[8]

Before the Chinese and North Koreans had the opportunity to coordinate their strategies, the UN forces began a counteroffensive in mid-January. On January 27, Peng, with his troops exhausted and short of ammunition and food, proposed a tactical retreat to Mao. The chairman, however, was not willing to consider anything short of a total victory. The next day he ordered Peng back on the offensive.[9] Peng, again, had to obey Mao's order; but the Chinese counteroffensive, as Peng had predicted, was quickly repulsed by the UN forces. In late February, Peng returned to Beijing to convey to Mao in person the real situation on the battlefield. Peng believed that the CPV should shift to the defensive, that new troops should be sent to Korea to replace those units that had suffered heavy casualties, and that preparations should be made for a counteroffensive in the spring. In the light of Peng's report, Mao's ideas on Chinese strategy in Korea began to change subtly. He now acknowledged that the war would be prolonged and that the best strategy was to rotate Chinese troops in and out of Korea. Still, Mao believed that the Chinese could force the UN forces out of Korea in a war of attrition: he believed that the Americans lacked the heart to sustain heavy losses.[10]

After two months of readjustment and preparations, the Chinese-North Korean high command gathered twelve armies to start an overall offensive in late April, planning to destroy the bulk of UN forces and to establish clear Communist superiority on the battlefield. Without adequate air cover and reliable logistical supply, this offensive failed too. In the last stage of the campaign, several Chinese units that had penetrated too deeply into the UN front were surrounded by counterattacking UN forces. One Chinese division, the 180th Division, was totally lost.[11]

The cruel reality forced Beijing leaders to reconsider China's war aims. Becoming willing to accept a ceasefire, Mao and the Beijing leadership began to place tight controls on the scale of the CPV's war operations. On July 10, 1951 Chinese and North Korean representatives and U.S./UN delegates met for the first time at Kaesong to discuss conditions for an armistice. Neither the Chinese nor the Americans, though, would trust the value of negotiations unless they themselves could be in a position of strength. It would take two long years for the two sides to reach an agreement. Fighting ended on July 27, 1953, with each side holding approximately the same positions as they had three years before.

Revolution Versus Containment:
Origins of the Confrontation

The pursuit of an overall explanation of the origins of the Sino-American confrontation in Korea requires an understanding of the environment in which Beijing and Washington found themselves. One encounters two sides interacting with little understanding of each other's rationales.

As suggested by this study, three fundamental and interrelated rationales had dominated Beijing's formulation of foreign policy and security strategy: the party's revolutionary nationalism, its sense of responsibility toward an Asian-wide or worldwide revolution, and its determination to maintain the inner dynamics of the Chinese revolution. Beijing's management of the Korean crisis cannot be properly comprehended without an understanding of these rationales and the mentality related to them.

Mao and his fellow CCP leaders grew up in an age when China had lost the status as the "Central Kingdom" and the very survival of the Chinese nation was at stake. Their conception of China's national interests was deeply influenced by the unequal exchanges between China and the foreign powers; and their commitment to Communist revolution in China grew out of the belief that the revolution would revitalize the Chinese nation and lead to the destruction of the "old world," and that China's position as a "Central Kingdom" would be resumed in the emergence of the "new world." Mao's concept of revolution reflected his generation's emotional commitment to China's national liberation as well as of its longing for China to take a central position in world politics. Not surprisingly, with the Communist seizure of power in China the CCP's revolutionary nationalism became a persistent driving force for changing China's weak power status and pursuing a prominent position in the world. All of this played a crucial role in defining Beijing's sense of security (or insecurity), strongly influencing the PRC's foreign policy in general and Beijing leaders' management of the Korean crisis in particular.

Closely related to the CCP's revolutionary nationalism was the Beijing leaders' lofty aspiration to promote an Eastern revolution or even a world revolution following the Chinese model. With the victory of the Chinese revolution, Mao and the CCP leadership were more confident than ever before that the Chinese revolution had established for other "oppressed peoples" in the world a brilliant example of national liberation. Mao believed that it was the duty of Chinese Communists to support Communist revolutions and national liberation movements in other countries. Communist China's foreign policy was in essence revolutionary: Mao and the other CCP leaders made it clear that the "new China" would not tolerate any of the diplomatic legacies of the "old China," that Communist China would lean to the side of the Soviet Union and other "world revolutionary forces," and that, in the final analysis, Communist China would not be bound by any existing norms and codes of behavior in international relations. Again, Mao's perception of the significance of the Chinese revolution was interwoven with Chinese ethnocentrism and universalism. He believed that the rejuvenation of China's position as a central world power would be realized through the promotion of Asian and world revolutions following the Chinese model. The Korean crisis presented a test case for this rationale.

In a deeper sense, the CCP's foreign policy in general and its attitude toward the Korean crisis in particular were shaped by the determination on the part of Mao and the CCP leadership to maintain the inner dynamics of the Chinese Communist revolution. When the Chinese Communists achieved nation wide victory in 1949, Mao and his comrades were worried that their revolution, which had merely accomplished the "first step in its long march," might lose its momentum. How to maintain and enhance the inner dynamics of the great Chinese revolution thus became Mao's central concern. When Mao first encountered this problem as the ruler of the new China in 1949, among other things, his train of thought developed in terms of emphasizing the continuous existence of outside threats to the revolution. While identifying the United States as the PRC's primary enemy, Mao and the CCP leadership did not necessarily perceive Washington as an immediate threat to China's physical security (in fact, after the summer and fall of 1949, they concluded that the United States lacked the capability to engage in major military conflicts in East Asia in the near future); but they did continue to emphasize the seriousness of the "American threat" and prepared for a long-range confrontation with the United States. After the outbreak of the Korean War, Mao and the CCP leadership found that the Korean crisis challenged China's national security while at the same time offering them a possible means to mobilize the Chinese nation under the CCP's terms. That the CCP's understanding of China's security interests was defined by the perceived necessity of maintaining and promoting the momentum of the Chinese revolution explains to a large extent the uncompromising character of Beijing's management of the Korean crisis. In this sense, it is legitimate to believe that China's road to the Korean War started long before the outbreak of the war itself.

Indeed, Communist China was a new type of international actor. As a revolutionary country it intended to break with the existing principles and codes of behavior in international relations, which, in the minds of Beijing leaders, were the product of Western domination of international relations. Communist China's foreign policy had its own language and theory, and behaved according to its own values and logic. Accordingly, the CCP leadership consistently treated the Untied States as China's primary enemy and prepared throughout 1949–1950 for the coming of an inevitable confrontation.

The Chinese Communists encountered an America that was not in a position to understand either the rationale or the mentality galvanizing Mao and the CCP leadership. Profound divergences in political ideology and perceived national interests did exist between Beijing and Washington; and suspicion and hostility between the CCP and the United States were further crystallized as the result of Washington's continuing support for the GMD regime and the CCP's determination to "make a fresh start" in the new China's foreign policy. But what made the situation more complicated was American policymakers' superpower mentality. President Truman, Secretary of State Acheson, and other American policymakers of their generation came to the political scene in an age when the United States had emerged as a prominent world power and American interests abroad were expanding continuously. This fact, combined with a long-existing belief in America's special destiny in the world as well as traditional American hostility toward revolutionary changes, made it easier for this generation of American policymakers to assume that American values held universal significance.[12] In the case of China, this assumption took on greater importance because of a long-held notion of America's "special relationship" with China based on the "Open Door" ideology.[13] American policymakers, who had fundamental problems adjusting to the realities created by the Chinese revolution, were also unwilling to understand the environment in which Beijing leaders made decisions. As a result, there was little possibility that Washington might correctly perceive the foreign policy behavior of the Chinese Communists; nor would Washington's China policy easily serve its perceived aims. (For example, Washington's "wedge strategy," designed to force Beijing's detachment from the Soviet orbit, led only to Beijing's increasing hostility toward the United States.) Consequently, when Communist China first faced the United States in the international arena, no common language or common codes of behavior existed to bind the two sides.[14] It was easy for each side to misperceive the intentions of the other; and it was difficult for both sides to avoid sharp collision in a crisis situation. It is therefore hardly surprising that a confrontation between Communist China and the United States finally occurred.

These observations, however, are not meant to deny the extremely complicated circumstances involved in the Beijing leadership's adoption of a decision to go to war against an international coalition composed of almost all the industrial powers; nor is it the conclusion of this study that Beijing's response to the Korean crisis had been predetermined or crystallized at its beginning. Rather, the decision to send Chinese troops to Korea was certainly the most difficult one that Mao and his fellow CCP leaders had to make in the early years of the PRC. Top Beijing leaders were under intense pressure caused by cruel domestic and international conditions while making the decision. In fact, as revealed by this study, the opinion of the party leadership was far from unanimous on the necessity of entering the Korean War. Lin Biao and many others were worried that Beijing's intervention in Korea might hurt the newly established PRC. At the Politburo meeting of October 4–5, the majority of CCP leaders, with Mao's encouragement, expressed reservations about sending troops to Korea. Even after Mao had issued the formal order to enter the war on October 8, he twice postponed the deadline in the wake of the Soviet renege on the promised air support. The historian Michael Hunt is certainly right when he argues that "any effort to pin down the exact motive behind Mao's decision to intervene must enter a mind as complicated as the crisis it wrestled with."[15]

Nevertheless, with the support of the insight gained from new Chinese sources, it is still possible for historians to sketch out the main considerations underlying Beijing's decision to enter the Korean War, thus identifying the basic tendency of this decision-making process. For Mao and his colleagues, the Korean crisis had multiple implications from the beginning. It is apparent that American military intervention in Korea and the Seventh Fleet's movement into the Taiwan Strait after the eruption of the Korean conflict endangered the PRC's security interests. It is also true that when the UN forces crossed the 38th parallel and marched toward the Yalu in early October 1950 the PRC's physical security, especially the safety of the strategically and economically important Manchuria, was under immediate threat. Mao and the other Beijing leaders could not allow American forces to reach the Yalu River; nor would they be willing to see a friendly neighboring Communist regime destroyed by a hostile imperialist power. The motive of defending China's territorial safety, as well as safeguarding a neighboring country belonging to China's traditional sphere of influence, certainly played an important role in bringing the Beijing leadership to the decision to enter the Korean War. And, with hindsight, it can also be seen that Washington's decision to cross the 38th parallel provided a justification for Beijing's entrance into the Korean War.

To safeguard China's physical security, however, was only one element of Beijing's policy. Beijing's management of the Korean crisis has to be understood in the context of the escalating confrontation between the PRC and the United States in East Asia in 1949 and 1950: by the summer of 1950, each country had firmly perceived the other as a dangerous rival. We should also take into our account the CCP's need to consolidate its rule in China while at the same time mobilizing the Chinese population for a total transformation of Chinese society. Moreover, we should not forget that Mao and his fellow Beijing leaders were eager to revitalize China's great power status through the promotion of revolutions following the Chinese model in East Asia and in the world. These complicated motives explained why the magnitude of Beijing's preparations for intervention had reached such a degree even before the Inchon landing, and why the Beijing leadership was so eager to win a total victory over the United States on the Korean battlefield.

Mao played a central role at every crucial juncture in the formulation of Beijing's war decision. In early July 1950, only two weeks after the outbreak of the Korean War, the CMC followed Mao's instructions to establish the Northeast Border Defense Army, which proved to be a pivotal step toward China's entry into the war. In mid-July, in accordance with Mao's ideas of crisis management, the CCP leadership initiated the "Great Movement to Resist America and Assist Korea," starting to fit the entire country to a war orbit. When the North Koreans' position began to deteriorate continuously in August, Mao came to the fore of Beijing's decision-making. His speech to the August 4 Politburo meeting and his August 5 and 18 telegrams to the NEBDA established the deadlines for completion of China's preparations for beginning military operations in Korea and revealed his inclination to intervene. Facing doubts among top party leaders about the wisdom of engaging China in a major military confrontation with the United States, Mao's address to the September 5 People's Government Council meeting clarified that his ideas about confronting the United States and his belief that China did not need to fear America's nuclear power. Consequently, even before the Inchon landing, Mao used his credibility and authority within the party leadership to establish the pattern for Beijing's management of the Korean crisis, which was based on the assumption that China would eventually enter the war. During the first three weeks of October, when the Beijing leadership made the final war decision, the chairman's role became even more important. At the October 2 Politburo Standing Committee meeting, he argued that China had to enter the war, and pushed top CCP leaders to make the primary decision to send troops to Korea. At the October 4–5 Politburo meeting, he applied both his authority and political wisdom to securing the war decision's confirmation and implementation. Finally, when Beijing leaders faced a severe challenge posed by Moscow's withdrawal of its promise to provide air support in Korea, he again convinced his comrades that China had to enter the conflict. Considering the above, it is clear that without Mao's leadership role, Beijing's response to the Korean crisis could have been dramatically different.

To understand Mao's handling of the Korean crisis, one has to refer to his challenge-oriented personality. The chairman regarded the Korean crisis as both a challenge and an opportunity for the new China to achieve greater domestic and international aims: if the PRC could successfully meet the challenge posed by the United States, the world's number one power, it would not only greatly enhance the CCP's ruling position at home and push forward Mao's perceived revolutionary transformation of Chinese society; but it would also signal revolutionary China's reemergence as a prominent world power. Mao surely understood the tremendous difficulties involved in sending Chinese troops to Korea, but it was his deep-rooted eagerness to change the challenge into the dynamics of the continuous progress of the Chinese revolution that dominated his handling of the Korean crisis.

The CCP's foreign policy structure, in retrospect, gave Mao the freedom to manipulate the party's policy-making process. By the late 1940s, Mao had become the CCP's paramount leader and key decisionmaker. As the result of Mao's repeating efforts to place the CCP's external activities under the tight and direct control of the party's central leadership, the new China's external policies became a domain reserved exclusively for the party's top leadership and, particularly, Mao himself. During the discussion on whether or not China should enter the Korean War, different opinions and reservations for the decision to intervene did emerge among top leaders. But none of this went beyond the framework of "democratic centralism," and there is no evidence of factional opposition to Mao's leadership or the decision to enter the war.

American policymakers fail to understand the fundamental assumptions underlying the CCP's policies toward the Korean crisis. From the early stage of the crisis, Washington fixed its eyes on possible reactions from Moscow and paid little attention to the implications and logic of Beijing's behavior. Members of the Truman administration consistently underestimated the political-military capacities of Communist China. In retrospect, it is ironic that American policymakers, while publicly warning about the danger of Communist expansion in East Asia, misjudged Communist China's determination and capacity to act in Korea. In the final analysis, all of this was a natural result of Washington's mentality: if all important clues of China's intervention had been ignored, this was simply because policymakers in Washington did not view the Chinese Communists as a qualified challenger to the strategic interests of the United States.

Revolution Enhanced: The Aftermath of the War

A superficial glance would suggest that the effect of the Korean War on China was largely adverse. China's participation in the war caused the loss of tens of thousands of its soldiers on the battlefield, forced the expenditure of billions of dollars on military purposes at the expense of China's economic reconstruction, prevented Beijing from recovering Taiwan, made Beijing, at least in the short-run, more dependent upon Moscow than before, and excluded Beijing from the UN until the early 1970s.

But from Mao's perspective, China's gain was considerable. China's involvement in the Korean War stimulated a series of political and social revolutions in China that would have been otherwise inconceivable during the early stage of the new republic. In the wake of China's entrance into the Korean War, as Mao had anticipated, the Communist regime found itself in a powerful position to penetrate into almost every cell of Chinese society through intense mass mobilization. During the three years of the war, along with the "Great Movement to Resist America and Assist Korea," three other nationwide campaigns swept across China's countryside and cities: the movement to suppress counter-revolutionaries, the land reform movement, and the "Three Antis" and "Five Antis" movements.[16] When the war ended in July 1953, China's society had been different: the reactionary resistance to the new regime had been destroyed; land had been redistributed and the landlord class had disappeared; the Communist cadres who were believed to have lost their revolutionary momentum had been either "reeducated" or removed from leading positions; the national bourgeoisie was under the tight control of the Communist state, and the "petty-bourgeoisie" intellectuals had experienced the first round of Communist reeducation. Consequently, the CCP had effectively strengthened its organizational control of Chinese society and dramatically increased its authority in the minds of the Chinese people. Never before in modern Chinese history had a regime accomplished so much in so short a period. Mao was therefore more confident and enthusiastic than ever before to take a series of new steps to transform China, including the collectivization of agriculture, the nationalization of industry, the anti–rightist campaign, and the Great Leap Forward. Mao and the CCP would have undertaken these tasks even without the "Great War to Resist America and Assist Korea." However, the Korean War experience made the timing, magnitude, and depth of the CCP's designs to transform Chinese society more ambitious than they would have been otherwise.

The Korean War also symbolized China's rise to prominence in the international arena. The simple fact that Chinese troops forced the UN forces to retreat from the Chinese-Korean border areas to the 38th parallel allowed the Beijing leadership to call its involvement in the Korean War a great victory. For the first time in its modern history China had succeeded in confronting a coalition of Western powers and emerging undefeated. At the Geneva Conference of 1954, which was designed to solve both the Korea and Indo-China problems, and attended by such big powers as the United States, the Soviet Union, Britain, and France, China played a crucial role.[17] Mao and his fellow Beijing leaders then had powerful grounds on which to claim that international society—friends and foes alike—had accepted China as a real world power. Moreover, China's performance in Korea enhanced the image of Beijing as a leader in the revolutionary struggle against Western domination in Asia and other parts of the world, and Beijing would play a central role at the Bandung Conference of

1955. This remarkable change in China's international status further stimulated the Chinese people's patriotism, revolutionary nationalism and, in turn, gave Mao and the CCP leadership more freedom in escalating the transformation of China's state and society.

Mao lost his eldest son, Anying, during the Korean War.[18] But this personal pain was mitigated by the fact that the war further strengthened his leading position in the CCP and in China, leaving him unchallengeable. If Mao's comrades in the CCP Politburo previously had doubts about Mao's determination to involve China in the conflict in Korea, they had to recognize at the conclusion of the war that Mao had a much greater vision than they had. Mao's decision to enter the Korean War was widely praised as a "brilliant decision" [*yingming juece*], and Mao's name became tightly linked with "truth" and "correctness." A pattern thus emerged: the new China's state building became increasingly entangled with the development of Mao's personal cult. Enjoying political power with fewer checks and balances, Mao was in a freer position to carry out his utopian plans to transform Chinese society, so that it would turn into a land of universal equality and justice. A Mao with unlimited power would finally lead the country toward such disastrous experiments as the "Great Leap Forward" and the "Great Proletarian Cultural Revolution."

In retrospect, the Korean War experience offered the Beijing leadership invaluable opportunities to test and redefine China's security strategy with three particularly important consequences. First, Mao and his fellow CCP leaders would feel a strong need to reexamine China's alliance with the Soviet Union and, in a broader sense, the relationship of maintaining self-reliance and seeking alliance as a principle dominating the PRC's foreign policy. They could not forget that as the result of Stalin's "betrayal" at a crucial juncture, China had to begin military operations in Korea without Soviet air support, thus making China vulnerable in pursuing its initial goals of "driving the Americans out of Korea." They could also see that even with a shared ideology, Beijing's security interests frequently contradicted with those of Moscow's. The reliability of the "lean-to-one-side" approach, the cornerstone of Communist China's early foreign policy, was called into question. As a result, Mao and the other Beijing leaders would put more emphasis on "self-reliance" as the fundamental principle in maintaining China's security interests. China's experience during the

Korean War thus turned into the prelude of the future Sino-Soviet split.

Second, the Korean War experience further convinced Mao that mass mobilization was an effective way to maintain and enhance China's security status. During the Korean War, the successful mobilization of the Chinese population on the home front, as Mao and the other CCP leaders viewed it, strengthened the ruling basis of the Chinese Communist regime, thus making the Communist power more consolidated than before. On the Korean battlefield, the Chinese had pushed the Americans back to the 38th parallel from the Chinese-Korean border by outnumbering the UN forces and possessing, in Mao's belief, a higher morale as the result of successful political mobilization. Mao would thereafter take political mobilization as one of the most important means in pursuing China's national security interests.

Third, in contemplating the lessons of the Korean War, Mao could not ignore the role played by modern technology and equipment in a modern war. The American technological superiority cost hundreds of thousands of Chinese lives on the battlefield, and consequently, the Chinese did not achieve the total victory that Mao had so eagerly pursued largely because of their technological backwardness. In the years to come, Mao would still emphasize the importance of the "human factor" in modern warfare, but he would also call for the development of China's own atomic bomb and other advanced armaments, so that China's "spiritual atomic bomb" would be reinforced by the real bomb. The Korean War, seen here in fresh historical perspective, deserves credit for leaving an indelible stamp on China's foreign policy and security strategy.

Notes

INTRODUCTION

1. Except for a few books written by journalists, such as Isidor F. Stone's *The Hidden History of the Korean War* (New York: Monthly Review Press, 1952), this approach dominated the study of the origins of the Koreans War in the 1950s and part of the 1960s. See, for example, Robert T. Oliver, *Why War Came in Korea* (New York: Fordham University Press, 1950); Philip E. Mosley, "Soviet Policy and the War," *Journal of International Affairs*, 6 (Spring 1952): 107–114; Alexander L. George, "American Policy Making and the North Korean Aggression," *World Politics* 7, no. 2 (January 1955): 209–232; and Tang Tsou, *America's Failure in China, 1941–1950* (Chicago: The University of Chicago Press, 1963), pp. 555–556. In his classic study of the Korean War, *Korea: The Limited War* (New York: St. Martin's Press, 1964), pp. 18–20, David Rees continued to draw a picture reflecting a well-coordinated Communist plot to start the war. For summaries of various scholarly interpretations of the origins of the Korean War based on the assumption that the North Korean invasion obeyed Moscow's grand strategic design, see Denna F. Fleming, *The Cold War and Its Origins, 1917–1960*, 2 vols. (Garden City, NY: Doubleday, 1961), 2: 605; and Kim Hak-joon, "Approaches and Perspectives to the Origins of War," in War Memorial Service-Korea, comp., *The Historical Reillumination of the Korean War* (Seoul: Korean War Research Conference Committee, 1990), pp. 1–9. For general historiographical discussions of the origins of the Korean War, see John Merrill, *Korea: The Peninsula Origins of the War* (Newark: University of Delaware

Press, 1989), chapter 1; Philip West, "Interpreting the Korean War," *American Historical Review*, 94, no. 1 (February 1989): 80–96; Rosemary Foot, "Make the Unknown War Known: Policy Analysis of the Korean Conflict in the Last Decade," *Diplomatic History*, 15, no. 3 (Summer 1991): 411–431.

2. Truman's statement, June 27, 1950, *Foreign Relations of the United States* (hereafter *FRUS*), 1950, 7: 202–203.

3. Allen S. Whiting, *China Crosses the Yalu, The Decision to Enter the Korean War* (New York: Macmillan, 1960).

4. These interpretations are evident in Robert R. Simmons, *The Strained Alliance: Peking, Pyongyang, Moscow and the Politics of the Korean Civil War* (New York: The Free Press, 1975); Melvin Gurtov and Byong-Moo Hwang, *China Under Threat: The Politics of Strategy and Diplomacy* (Baltimore: Johns Hopkins University Press, 1980), pp. 25–62; Peter Lowe, *The Origins of the Korean War* (London and New York: Longman, 1986), pp. ix, 189–201; Ronald Keith, *The Diplomacy of Zhou Enlai* (New York: St. Martin's, 1989), pp. 45–47; Richard Whelan, *Drawing the Line: The Korean War, 1950–1953* (Boston: Little, Brown, 1990), pp. 236–238.

5. This approach can be found in a wide range of Chinese publications, such as Shen Zonghong and Meng Zhaohui et al., *Zhongguo renmin zhiyuanjun kangmei yuanchao zhanshi* (History of the War to Resist America and Assist Korea by the Chinese People's Volunteers, Beijing: Military Science Press, 1988), chapter 1; Han Nianlong et al., *Dangdai zhongguo waijiao* (Contemporary Chinese Diplomacy, Chinese Social Sciences Press, 1987), pp. 37–38; Hao Yufan and Zhai Zhihai, in "China's Decision to Enter the Korean War: History Revisited," *The China Quarterly*, 121 (March 1990), attempt to offer an alternative to Whiting's thesis but generally follows Whiting's stress on Beijing's concerns for the safety of the Chinese-Korean Border.

6. In a series of recent studies, scholars in the U.S. have begun to use the new Chinese sources. Russell Spurr's *Enter the Dragon: China's Undeclared War against the U.S. in Korea* (New York: Newmarket, 1988) was the first one in this regard. Allegedly supported by "information from extensive interviews," this book is virtually based on hearsays and fiction-style imagination. Harrison Salisbury devotes a whole chapter to China's decision to enter the Korean War in his new book, *The New Emperors: China in the Era of Mao and Deng* (Boston: Little, Brown, 1992), which is based on a few interviews and a random reading of secondary Chinese sources. Lacking support of corroborating documentary sources, this book contains a lot of errors. The studies by Michael Hunt and Thomas Christensen represent the best efforts in reinterpreting China's entrance into the Korean War with the support of new Chinese sources. Hunt, in "Beijing and the Korean Crisis, June 1950–June 1951" (*Political Science Quarterly*, 107, no. 3 [Fall 1992]:

453–478), offers enlightening analyses of Beijing's management of the Korean Crisis and Mao's direction of the CPV's first-year operations in Korea. Christensen, in "Threats, Assurances, and the Last Chance for Peace: The Lessons of Mao's Korean War Telegrams" (*International Security*, 17, no. 1 [Summer 1992]: 122–154), uses Beijing's response to the Korean crisis to challenge the traditional view based on deterrence theory. Also of note is Sergei N. Goncharov, John W. Lewis, and Xue Litai, *Uncertain Partners: Stalin, Mao, and the Korean War* (Stanford: Stanford University Press, 1993), which offers interesting, though sometimes highly speculative, interpretations of the Sino-Soviet alliance and its relations with the origins of the Korean War.

7. The most important ones include Chai Chengwen and Zhao Yongtian, *Banmendian tanpan* (The Panmunjom Negotiations, Beijing: People's Liberation Army Press, 1989; second edition, 1992); Du Ping, *Zai zhiyuanjun zongbu: Du Ping huiyilu* (My Days at the Headquarters of the Chinese People's Volunteers: Du Ping's Memoirs, Beijing: People's Liberation Army Press, 1988); Hong Xuezhi, *Kangmei yuanchao zhanzheng huiyi* (Recollections of the War to Resist America and Assist Korea, Beijing: People's Liberation Army Literature Press, 1990); Nie Rongzhen, *Nie Rongzhen huiyilu* (Nie Rongzhen's Memoirs, Beijing: People's Liberation Army Press, 1986); and Shi Zhe, *Zai lishi jüren shenbian: Shi Zhe huiyilu* (Together with Historical Giants: Shi Zhe's Memoirs, Beijing: The Central Press of Historical Documents, 1991).

8. For example, Qi Dexue, *Chaoxian zhanzheng juece neimu* (The Inside Story of the Decision-making during the Korean War, Liaoning: Liaoning University Press, 1991); Xu Yan, *Diyici jiaoliang: kangmei yuanchao zhanzheng de lishi huigu yu fansi* (The First Test of Strength: A Historical Review and Evaluation of the War to Resist America and Assist Korea, Beijing: Chinese Broadcasting and Television Press, 1990); Yao Xu, *Cong yalujiang dao banmendian* (From the Yalu River to Panmunjom, Beijing: People's Press, 1985); and Zhang Xi, "Before and After Peng Dehuai's Appointment to Command Troops in Korea," (hereafter cited as "Peng's Appointment") *Zhonggong dangshi ziliao* (Materials of the CCP History), no. 31 (1989): 111–159.

9. Good examples in this category include Tan Jingqiao et al., *Kangmei yuanchao zhanzheng* (The War to Resist America and Assist Korea, Beijing: Chinese Social Sciences Press, 1990); and Han Huaizhi and Tan Jingqiao et al., *Dangdai zhongguo jundui de junshi gongzuo* (The Military Affairs of Contemporary Chinese Army, Beijing: Chinese Social Sciences Press, 1989), 2 vols. Both volumes are part of the "Contemporary China" series.

10. The most useful ones include *Zhonggong dangshi jiaoxue cankao ziliao* (Reference Materials for Teaching CCP History, Beijing: National Defense

University Press, 1986), vols. 18–19 (1945–1953); *Zhonggong zhongyang wenjian xuanji* (Selected Documents of the CCP Central Committee, hereafter cited as *ZYWJXJ*, first edition, Beijing: CCP Central Academy Press, 1983–1987), 14 vols. Both collections were published for "internal circulation" only. An open and generally enlarged version of the second collection has been published in 1989–1992, but a few important documents are not included.

11. *Mao Zedong junshi wenxuan* (Selected Military Works of Mao Zedong, Beijing: Soldiers' Press, 1981, hereafter cited as *MJWX*); and *Jianguo yilai Mao Zedong wengao* (Mao Zedong's Manuscripts Since the Founding of the People's Republic, Beijing: The Central Press of Historical Documents, 1987, 1989, hereafter cited as *MWG*), vol. 1, September 1949–December 1950, and vol. 2, January 1951–December 1951. Both collections are "for internal circulation" only. Also useful are the openly published *Mao Zedong junshi wenji* (A Collection of Mao Zedong's Military Papers, 6 volumes, Beijing: Military Science Press and the Central Press of Historical Documents, 1993, hereafter cited as *MJWJ*), and Pang Xianzhi et al., *Mao Zedong nianpu, 1893–1949* (A Chronology of Mao Zedog, 1893–1949, 3 volumes, Beijing: People's Press and the Central Press of Historical Documents, 1993, hereafter cited as *MNP*).

1. REVOLUTIONARY COMMITMENTS AND SECURITY CONCERNS: NEW CHINA FACES THE WORLD

1. The GMD neared financial and economic collapse by the end of 1948. From August 1948 to March 1949, the price index in Shanghai increased 83,000 times, and Jinyuanjuan, the paper currency issued after the end of the Second World War, became little more than scraps of paper. Meanwhile, GMD military forces lost 173 divisions and 1.54 million men in three major campaigns (Liaoshen, Huaihai, and Pingjin), and, for the first time in China's civil war, the Communist forces established a numerical superiority. See Mo Yang and Yao Jie et al., *Zhongguo renmin jiefangjun zhanshi* (The War History of the Chinese People's Liberation Army), 3 vols. (Beijing: Military Science Press, 1987), 3: 305–6, 313; Mao Zedong, "The Momentous Change in China's Military Situation," *Mao Zedong xuanji*, 5 vols. (Selected Works of Mao Zedong, hereafter cited as *MXJ*, Beijing: People's Press, 1960, 1977), 4: 1363–64.

2. Mao Zedong, "Carry the Revolution through to the End," *MXJ*, 4: 1377; "The Current Situation and the Party's Tasks in 1949," *MJWX*, p. 328.

3. Mao Zedong, "Report and Conclusion at the CCP Central Commit-

tee Politburo Meeting," September 8 and 13, 1948, *Dangde wenxian* (Party Historical Documents), no. 5 (1989): 3–7; Chen Enhui, "An Important Conference of Strategic Decision Making: The Politburo's Meeting of September 1948," ibid., pp. 12–15.

4. Mao Zedong, "The Current Situation and the Party's Tasks in 1949," *MJWX*, pp. 326–332; Mao Zedong, "Report to the Second Plenary Session of the Seventh Central Committee," *MXJ*, 4: 1425–1440.

5. Zhou Enlai, "The Principles and Tasks of Our Diplomacy," *Zhou Enlai xuanji*, 2 vols.(Selected Works of Zhou Enlai, hereafter cited as *ZXJ*, Beijing: People's Press, 1984), 2: 85–87; for the CCP leadership's design of principles in the building of Communist China's foreign policy, see Han Nianlong et al., *Dangdai zhongguo waijiao*, pp. 3–6.

6. Mao Zedong, "Basic Problems of the Chinese Revolution," *MXJ*, 1: 281.

7. Scholars should not be confused or misled by the term "people's democracy" here. CCP leaders widely used the term "democracy" in the 1940s, especially in denouncing Jiang Jieshi's "dictatorship." As Mao made it clear in "On New Democracy," the CCP defined "democracy" as "the other side of the proletarian dictatorship," which had nothing to do with establishing a political institution with checks and balances. See Mao Zedong, "On New Democracy," *MXJ*, 2: 655–704, especially pp. 659–664, 672–676; "On People's Democratic Dictatorship,"*ibid.*, 3: 1473–1486, especially pp. 1481–1485; and Liu Shaoqi, "On the Nature of the Government and State of China's New Democracy," in Liu Wusheng et al., *Gongheguo zouguo de lu: jianguo yilai zhongyao wenjian xuanbian, 1949–1952* (The Paths the Republic Has Walked through: A Selected Collection of Important Historical Documents, 1949–1952, Beijing: The Central Press of Historical Documents, 1991), pp. 56–59.

8. Mao Zedong, "Carry the Revolution through to the End," *MXJ*, 4: 1380, 1382–1383; "Comments on the War Criminal's Suing for Peace," ibid., pp. 1387–90; and "The Current Situation and the Party's Tasks in 1949," *MJWX*, p. 327; *MJWJ*, 5: 472..

9. Liu Guoguang et al., *Zhonghua renmin gongheguo jingji dangan ziliao xuanbian: zhonghejuan* (A Selected Collection of Economic Archival Materials of the People's Republic of China: The Comprehensive Volume, 1949–1952, Beijing: Chinese Urban Economic Society Press, 1990), pp. 36–135; Guo Bingwei and Tan Zongji, *Zhonghua renmin gongheguo jianshi* (A Brief History of the People's Republic of China, Changchun: Jilin Literature and History Press, 1988), pp. 6–7; Chen Yun, "Check the Skyrocketing Prices," *Chen Yun wengao xuanbian*, 1949–1956 (Selected Manuscripts of Chen Yun, 1949–1956, Beijing: People' Press, 1984), pp. 29–32.

10. Mao Zedong, "The Current Situation and the Party's Tasks in 1949,"

MJWX, pp. 329, 332; "Report to the Second Plenary Session of the Seventh Central Committee," *MXJ*, 4: 1429; and Mao's conclusion at the Second Plenary Session of the Seventh Central Committee, minute. The original of this document is maintained in Chinese Central Archives in Beijing (hereafter cited as CCA).

11. Mao Zedong, "Report to the Second Plenary Session of the Seventh Central Committee"; and "On the People's Democratic Dictatorship," *MXJ*, 4: 1432–34, 1479–1480.

12. Mao Zedong, "Report to the Second Plenary Session of the Seventh Central Committee," Ibid., p. 1434.

13. Mao Zedong, "On the People's Democratic Dictatorship," Ibid., pp. 1432–34; " Chen Yun, "To Overcome Serious Difficulties in Financial and Economic Affairs," *Chen Yun wengao xuanbian*, p. 2.

14. Mao Zedong, "Problems of Strategy in Guerilla War Against Japan"; "On Protracted War," *MXJ*, 2: 395–504; see also Mao Zedong, "The Chinese Revolution and the Chinese Communist Party," ibid., pp. 615–626. For a discussion of the development of Mao's view on self-reliance, see Stuart Schram, *The Though of Mao Tse-tung* (Cambridge: Cambridge University Press, 1989), pp. 92–93; for a discussion of the CCP's self-reliance strategy during the Yanan era, see Mark Selden, *The Yenan Way in Revolutionary China* (Cambridge: Harvard University Press, 1971), pp. 249–259.

15. The CCP Central Committee, "Instructions on Problems Concerning Foreign Trade Policy," February 16, 1949, *ZYWJXJ*, 18: 136.

16. Mao Zedong, "Report to the Second Plenary Session of the Seventh Central Committee," *MXJ*, 4: 1434, 1436.

17. Zhou Enlai, "The Present Financial and Economic Situation and Relations Between Different Aspects of the Economy of the New China," *ZXJ*, 2: 10–11.

18. Zhou Enlai, "Report on Problems Concerning the Peace Talks," *ZXJ*, 1: 318.

19. Mao Zedong, "Report to the Second Plenary Session of the Seventh Central Committee," *MXJ*, 4: 1439–40.

20. Mao Zedong, "The Chinese Revolution and the Chinese Communist Party," and "On New Democracy," *MXJ*, 2: 626–47, 656–72. For a discussion of Mao's definition of "New Democracy" in a historical context related to Marxist-Leninist analysis, see Schram, *The Thought of Mao Zedong*, pp. 75–79; on the political implication of Mao's introduction of the "New Democracy" thesis in 1939–1940, see John Garver, *Chinese-Soviet Relations, 1937–1945* (New York: Oxford University Press, 1988), pp. 126–128.

21. Mao Zedong, "On People's Democratic Dictatorship," *MXJ*, 4: 1473–86.

22. See Zhou Enlai to the CCP Central Committee and Mao Zedong,

August 10, 1946, and Zhou Enlai to the CCP Central Committee, August 31, 1946, in Tong Xiaopeng et al., *Zhonggong zhongyang nanjing jü* (The CCP Central Committee's Nanjing Bureau: Selected Documents, Beijing: CCP History Press, 1990), pp. 117–118, 138–139; The CCP Central Committee to Dong Biwu and others, January 30, 1947, ibid., pp. 222–223; Mao Zedong's talks with Liu Shaoqi and Zhou Enlai, November 21, 1946, minute, CCA, and *MNP*, 3: 150–51; and Liu Shaoqi, "Speech to A Party Cadres Meeting, July 1, 1948," *Dangshi yanjiu* (Party History Studies), no. 3, 1980): 14.

23. Mao Zedong, "The Current Situation and the Party's Tasks in 1949," *MJWX*, p. 328; the CCP Central Military Commission's instructions, 28 February 1949, *ZYWJXJ*, 18: 157; Jin Chongji et al., *Zhou Enlai zhuan* (A Biography of Zhou Enlai, 1898–1949, Beijing: The Press of Party Historical Materials, 1987), p. 751; and Li Ping and Fang Ming et al., *Zhou Enlai nianpu, 1898–1949* (A Chronicle of Zhou Enlai, 1898–1949, Beijing: The Central Press of Historical Documents and People's Press, 1989), p. 808.

24. The Resolution of the CCP's Front-line Committee of the Third Field Army, January 25, 1949, Ba Zhongtan et al., *Shanghai zhanyi* (The Shanghai Campaign, Shanghai: Xuelin Press, 1989), pp. 290–291; Zhang Zhen, "In Reminiscence of the Shanghai Campaign," ibid., pp. 87–88; and Yao Xu, *Cong Yalujiang dao banmendian*, p. 2.

25. Mao Zedong, "The Current Situation and the Party's Tasks in 1949," *MJWX*, p. 328 and *MJWJ*, 5: 473.

26. Mao Zedong, "Report to the Second Plenary Session of the Seventh Central Committee," *MXJ*, 4: 1425–26, 1428; see also *MNP*, 3: 410–411.

27. Mao Zedong, "Plans to March to the Whole Country," May 23, 1949, *MJWX*, p. 338; and *MJWJ*, 5: 591. Mao pointed out here that "if Shanghai, Fuzhou and Qingdao were quickly and smoothly occupied, the possibility of American military intervention would disappear." See also Liu Shaoqi's memo on the CCP's domestic and international policies, July 4, 1949, in Shi Zhe, *Zai lishi jüren shenbian*, p. 399.

28. Mao Zedong, "Address to the Preparatory Committee of the New Political Consultative Conference," *MXJ*, 4: 1469.

29. For a discussion of the emergence of revolutionary movements and revolutionary states in East Asia and its challenge to the West in general and the United States in particular, see Michael Hunt and Steven Levine, "The Revolutionary Challenge to Early U.S. Cold War Policy in Asia," In Warren I. Cohen and Akira Iriye eds., *The Great Powers in East Asia, 1953–1960* (New York: Columbia University Press, 1990), pp. 13–34; see also Odd Arne Westad, "Rethinking Revolution: The Cold War in the Third World," *Journal of Peace Research*, 29, no. 4 (November 1992): 455–464.

30. "Main contradiction" was a term Mao frequently used. He believed

that the natural world and human society were full of contradictions, and that among all contradictions there was a decisive one, the "main contradiction," which would determine the changing course of all contradictions. It was therefore important for the Chinese revolutionaries to distinguish the "main contradiction" from the others in making their strategies and policies. See Mao Zedong, "On Contradiction," *MXJ*, 1: 308–314.

31. Niu Jun, *Cong Yanan zouxiang shijie: zhongguo gongchandang duiwai guanxi de qiyuan* (From Yanan to the World: The Origins of the CCP's External Relations, Fuzhou: Fujian People's Press, 1992), chapter 9.

32. Ibid.; Yang Kuisong, "The Soviet Factor and the CCP's Policy toward the United States in the 1940s," *Chinese Historians*, 5, no. 1 (Spring 1992): 23.

33. Mao Zedong, "Talks with the American Correspondent Anna Louise Strong," *MXJ*, 4: 1191–1192.

34. Mao Zedong's conversations with Liu Shaoqi and Zhou Enlai, November 21, 1946, minutes, CCA; see also *MNP*, 3: 150–151.

35. For an official confirmation of Mao's personal revision of the article, see *ZWJWX*, p. 554, n. 343; and *MNP*, 3: 158.

36. See *Renmin ribao* (People's Daily), January 4 and 5, 1947.

37. In his influential study, *The World and China, 1922–1972* (London: Eyre Methuen, 1974), p. 124, John Gittings argues that Mao's theory of intermediate zone represented an effort on the part of the CCP to pursue an independent status from both Washington and Moscow. Such a view neglects the CCP's strong anti-American stand as well as its persistent desire to attach the Chinese Communist revolution to the Soviet-headed international proletariat movement.

38. Mao Zedong, "The Present Situation and Our Tasks," *MXJ*, 4: 1258–1259.

39. Liu Shaoqi, "On Internationalism and Nationalism," *Renmin ribao*, November 7, 1948.

40. This approach is most explicitly expressed by Liu Shaoqi in his speech to the Trade Union Meeting of the Asian and Australian Countries: "The path taken by the Chinese people in winning their victories over imperialism and its lackeys and in founding the People's Republic of China is the road that people of various colonial and semi-colonial countries should traverse in their struggle for national independence and people's democracy." *Xinhua yuebao* (New China Monthly), 1, no. 2 (1949): 440; see also Liu Shaoqi, "On Internationalism and Nationalism"; Si Mu, "The International Significance of the Victory of the Chinese People's Revolutionary War," *Shijie zhishi* (World Knowledge), 21, no. 1 (December 1949): 19–21; Lu Dingyi, "The Worldwide Significance of the Chinese Revolution," *Lu*

Dingyi wenji (A Collection of Lu Dingyi's Works, Beijing: People's Press, 1992), pp. 432–439.

41. For discussions of the traditional Chinese view of the world and China's position in it, see Samuel S. Kim, *China, the United Nations, and the World Order* (Princeton: Princeton University Press, 1979), pp. 19–23; Mark Mancall, *China at the Center: 300 Years of Foreign Policy* (New York: The Free Press, 1984), pp. xii–xiii; John K. Fairbank, "A Preliminary Framework," in J. K. Fairbank, ed., *The Chinese World Order: Traditional China's Foreign Relations* (Cambridge: Harvard University Press, 1968), pp. 1–2; Immanuel Hsü, *China's Entrance into the Family of Nations* (Cambridge: Harvard University Press, 1960), pp. 6–16; and Charles P. Fitzgerald, *The Chinese View of Their Place in the World* (London: Oxford University Press, 1964).

42. See Edgar Snow, *Red Star Over China* (New York, 1938), pp. 118–119. For a good discussion of Mao's adoption of the restoration of China's historic status as one of the top goals of his revolution, see Mancall, *China at the Center*, chapter 9,

43. Scholars in the West have been divided on assessing the impact of the traditional Chinese world view on Chinese Communist foreign policy. While some scholars emphasize "continuity," i.e., that the Maoist image of the world had not been altered in its fundamentals compared with the traditional one, others allege a "complete break," that is, there existed a sharp gap between the CCP's view of the world and the traditional image. For a summary of the two schools, see Kim, *China, the Untied Nations, and the World Order*, pp. 90–93. My argument here, as the reader can see, is more toward the continuity school.

44. Fairbank, ed., *The Chinese World Order*, pp. 1–4.

45. See, for example, Mao Zedong's conversations with Liu Shaoqi and Zhou Enlai, November 21, 1946, minute, CCA; Mao Zedong, "Talks with the American Correspondent Anna Louise Strong," *MXJ*, 4: 1192–1193; see also John Lewis and Xue Litai, *China Builds the Bomb* (Stanford: Stanford University Press, 1988), p. 7.

46. Frederick C. Teiwes, "Establishment and Consolidation of the New Regime," in Roderick MacFarquhar and John K. Fairbank, eds., *The Cambridge History of China* (Cambridge: Cambridge University Press, 1987), 14: 51.

47. For a useful analysis of the security policies of China as a *weak* state, see Michael Mandelbaum, *The Fate of Nations: The Search for National Security in the 19th and 20th Centuries* (Cambridge: Cambridge University Press, 1988), pp. 193–253. There is one major problem, though, existing in Mandelbaum's analysis. Throughout the chapter about China's security policies, he suggests that the maintenance of China's independence be the single most

important goal in Mao's security strategy. The goals of Mao and the CCP leadership, in my opinion, were much more ambitious.

48. Whiting, *China Crosses the Yalu*, p. 10.

49. For more extensive discussions on this problem, see Chen Jian, "The Making of a Revolutionary Diplomacy: A Critical Study of Communist China's Policy toward the United States, 1949–1950," *Chinese Historians*, 3, no. 1 (January 1990): 36–38; see also discussions in chapters 4 and 5.

50. For the CCP leadership's interests in East Asia around the formation of the PRC, see Du Ruo, "China's Liberation and the Southeast Asia," *Shijie zhishi*, 20, no. 1 (June 1949): 13; Shi Xiaochong, "The Crisis in India," ibid., 20, no. 4 (July 1949): 20–21; Hu Jin, "India and the British-American Imperialism," ibid., 20, no. 14 (October 1949): 12–13; Huang Caoliang, *Zhanhou shijie xinxingshi* (New Situations of the Postwar World, Shanghai, 1950); and Mao Zedong to Hu Qiaomu, January 14, 1950, *MWG*, 1: 237.

51. For the CCP leadership's understanding of the relationship of the changing world situation and the prospect of the Chinese revolution, see, for example, Mao Zedong, "Report to the CCP Politburo Meeting," September 8, 1948, in Liu Wusheng et al., *Gongheguo zouguo de lu*, pp. 10–11.

52. Mao Zedong, "The Chinese People Have Stood Up," *MWG*, 1: 6–7; "Long Live the Grand Unity of the Chinese People," ibid., pp. 10–12; and *MNP*, 3: 575, 580.

53. For an excellent discussion about Mao's relationship with his father and the making of his rebellious character, see Chen Jin, *Mao Zedong de wenhua xingge* (The Cultural Character of Mao Zedong, Beijing: The Press of Chinese Youth, 1991), pp. 316–317; see also Snow, *Red Star Over China*, pp. 129–139; Stuart Schram, *Mao Tse-tung* (London: Penguin Books, 1975), pp. 19–21. For a discussion of the rebellious-oriented Hunan regional cultural and its influence upon the making of Mao's rebellious character, see Schram, *Mao Tse-tung*, pp. 29–30.

54. See Chen Jin, *Mao Zedong de wenhua xingge*, pp. 233–259; and Li Rui, *Mao Zedong de zaonian yu wannian* (Mao Zedong's Early and Late Ages, Guiyang: Guizhou People's Press, 1992), pp. 7–8.

55. Hu Sheng et al., *Zhongguo gongchandang de qishinian* (A Seventy-year History of the Chinese Communist Party, Beijing: CCP History Press, 1991), p. 231; and Li and Fang et al., *Zhou Enlai nianpu*, p. 551.

56. See, for example, the CCP Central Committee to the CCP Northeast Bureau, November 10, 1948, cited from Jin Chongji et al., *Zhou Enlai zhuan*, p. 739; Mao Zedong to the CCP Tianjin Municipal Committee, January 20, 1949, telegram, CCA.

57. For a good discussion, see Zhang Shuguang, "In the Shadow of Mao: Zhou Enlai and New China's Diplomacy," in Gordon A. Craig and Francis

L. Loewenheim eds., *The Diplomats, 1939–1979* (Princeton: Princeton University Press, forthcoming).

58. See Gong Yuzhi, Pang Xianzhi, and Shi Zhongquan, *Mao Zedong de dushu shenghuo* (The Reading Experiences of Mao Zedong, Beijing: The Sanlian Bookstore, 1986); and Zhang Yijiu, *Mao Zedong dushi* (Mao Zedong's Reading of History, Beijing: The Chinese Friendship Press, 1992).

2. THE RECOGNITION CONTROVERSY:
THE ORIGINS OF SINO-AMERICAN CONFRONTATION

1. The State Department dictated a series of principles to Ward in a telegram on November 2, instructing him to restrict his contacts with local Chinese Communist authorities to an "informal and personal basis." Ward could "choose [the] suitable time to call upon appropriate local officials for [the] purpose [of] informing them he and his staff had remained in city in consular capacity only and for [the] purpose of assisting and protecting American citizens and protecting American property." In no circumstance, the State Department stressed, should the retention of American Consulate be interpreted as a "formal acknowledgement" of the Communist regime. Lovett to Ward, November 2, 1948, *FRUS* (1948), 7: 826.

2. Ward to Marshall, November 5, November 9, 1948, ibid., pp. 829–831; see also Angus Ward, "The Mukden Affair," *American Foreign Service Journal* (February 1950): 15.

3. The CCP Central Committee to the CCP Northeast Bureau, November 1, 1948, cited from Li and Fang et al., *Zhou Enlai nianpu*, p. 794.

4. Chen Yun later took the responsibility for "the mistake committed in diplomatic affairs" after Shenyang's liberation. See *Chen Yun wenxuan, 1926–1949* (Selected Works of Chen Yun, 1926–1949, Beijing: People's Press, 1984), p. 273. See also the CCP Central Committee to Chen Yun and the Northeast Bureau, December 15, 1949, *ZYWJXJ*, 17: 573–574.

5. Ward, "The Mukden Affair," p. 15.

6. Ward to Marshall, November 15, 1948, *FRUS* (1948), 7: 834–35; see also William Stoke, "The Future between America and China," *Foreign Service Journal* (January 1968): 15.

7. See Bernard Gwertzman, "The Hostage Crisis: Three Decades Ago," *The New York Times Magazine* (May 4, 1980): 42.

8. The CCP Central Committee to the CCP Northeast Bureau, Lin Biao, Luo Ronghuan and Chen Yun, November 10, 1948, cited in Jin Chongji et al., *Zhou Enlai zhuan*, p. 739.

9. Sergei Goncharov, "Stalin's Dialogue with Mao Zedong: I. V.

Kovalev, Stalin's Representative, Answers Questions of Sinologist S. N. Goncharov," *Journal of Northeast Asian Studies*, 10, no. 4 (Winter 1991–92): 65–66; Goncharov et al., *Uncertain Partners*, p. 34. See also Gao Gang to the CCP Central Committee, November 16, 1948, telegram, CCA. It is also interesting to note that Ward noticed that when he and other Western consuls were received by Zhu Qiwen, the Soviet trade representative in Shenyang arrived earlier and left later. Ward to Marshall, November 5, 1948, *FRUS* (1948), 7: 829.

10. Li Rui, "An Account on the Takeover of the Shenyang City," *Zhonggong dangshi ziliao* (Materials of the CCP History) no. 40 (February 1992): 58–59. Li Rui was then Chen Yun's political secretary. This account is based on his personal notes from September 1948 to January 1949.

11. See Yang Kuisong, "The Soviet Factor and the CCP's Policy toward the United States in the 1940s," pp. 31–32. After the end of the Second World War, U.S. Office of Strategic Services set up "Operation Cardinal" in Manchuria, which was intended to "establish [an] agent network to secure information on Russian and Chinese actions" there. Throughout Chinese civil war, this network "continued to supply Washington with massive, if not always accurate, information on Soviet and CCP intentions." (See Odd Arne Westad, *Cold War and Revolution: Soviet-American Rivalry and the Origins of the Chinese Civil War, 1944–1946* [New York: Columbia University Press, 1992], pp. 204–205.) It is possible that Shenyang Communist authorities had some knowledge of "Operation Cardinal," although I have no hard evidence.

12. Yang Kuisong, "The Soviet Factor and the CCP's Policy toward the United States in the 1940s," p. 31. Why did the Northeast Bureau take action again before requesting approval from the CCP central leadership? One explanation is that Gao Gang, with the support of the Soviets, hoped to create a *fait accompli* for the CCP leadership so that the party would pursue a harsher policy line toward the Ward case.

13. Mao Zedong to Gao Gang, November 17, 1948, telegram, CCA.

14. Lovett to Stuart, November 15, 1948, *FRUS* (1948), 7: 836; and Gwertzman, "The Hostage Crisis," p. 42.

15. Mao Zedong to the CCP Northeast Bureau, November 18, 1948, telegram, CCA.

16. Cabot to Marshall, November 18, 1948, *FRUS* (1948), 7: 837; Stuart to Marshall, November 21, 1948, ibid., pp. 838–39; Clubb to Marshall, November 26, 1948, ibid., p. 840.

17. See Gwertzman, "The Hostage Crisis," p. 42.

18. Mao Zedong to the CCP Tianjin Municipal Committee, January 20, 1949; Mao Zedong to Su Yu, April 27 and 29, 1949, telegrams, CCA; see also the CCP Central Military Commission's instructions on diplomatic affairs, April 26, 1949, *ZYWJXJ*, 18: 246–247.

19. The CCP Central Committee, "Instructions on Diplomatic Affairs," January 19, 1949, *ZYWJXJ*, 18: 49.

20. The CCP Central Committee to the CCP Northeast Bureau, November 23, 1948, cited from Jin Chongji et al., *Zhou Enlai zhuan*, p. 740.

21. Mao Zedong's remarks on the CCP Central Committee's "Instructions on Diplomatic Affairs," *Dangde wenxian*, no. 1 (1992): 27; see also the CCP Central Committee, "Instructions on Diplomatic Affairs," *ZYWJXJ*, 18: 44.

22. Mao, "Report to the Second Plenary Session of the Seventh Central Committee," *MXJ*, 4: 1436; see also Han Nianlong et al., *Dangdai zhongguo waijiao*, p. 4.

23. Mao Zedong's conclusion at the Second Plenary Session of the Seventh Central Committee, March 13, 1949, minute, CCA; Zhou Enlai, "Report on Problems Concerning the Peace Talks," *ZXJ*, 1: 323; "New China's Diplomacy," *Zhou Enlai waijiao wenxuan* (Selected Diplomatic Works of Zhou Enlai, Beijing: The Central Press of Historical Documents, 1990, hereafter cited as *ZWJWX*), pp. 4–5.

24. Ke Bainian, "How the Soviet Union Struggled with Imperialism Right after the October Revolution," *Xuexi* (Study), 1, no. 3 (1949): 12–14; Hu Sheng, *Diguo zhuyi yu zhongguo zhengzhi* (Imperialism and Chinese Politics, Beijing: People's Press, 1949); and Mao Zedong, "Cast Away Illusions, Prepare for Struggle," *MXJ*, 4: 1487–1488.

25. The CCP Central Committee, "Instructions on Diplomatic Affairs," *ZYWJXJ*, 18: 44–45; see also Jin Chongji et al., *Zhou Enlai zhuan*, p. 742; Li and Fang et al., *Zhou Enlai nianpu*, p. 809.

26. Han Nianlong et al., *Dangdai zhongguo waijiao*, p. 4; Mao Zedong's conclusion at the Second Plenary Session of the Seventh Central Committee, March 13, 1949, minute, CCA; Mao Zedong, "Report to the Second Plenary Session of the Seventh Central Committee of the CCP," *MXJ*, 4: 1435–36, and *MNP*, 3: 410–411.

27. Mao Zedong, "Chinese People Stand Up," *MWG*, 1: 6–7; "On the People's Democratic Dictatorship," *MXJ*, 4: 1477–80.

28. Mao Zedong, "Report to the Second Plenary Session of the Seventh Central Committee," *MXJ*, 4: 1436.

29. Ibid., pp. 1435–1436; the CCP Central Committee, "Instructions on Diplomatic Affairs," *ZYWJXJ*, 18: 44.

30. Jin Chongji et al., *Zhou Enlai zhuan*, p. 742.

31. The CCP Central Committee, "Instructions on Diplomatic Affairs," *ZYWJXJ*, 18: 44; see also Jin Chongji et al., *Zhou Enlai zhuan*, p. 742; Li Ping and Fang Ming et al., *Zhou Enlai nianpu*, p. 809.

32. Mao Zedong to the CCP East China Bureau, July 17, 1949, telegram, CCA.

33. James Reardon-Anderson, in *Yenan and the Great Powers: The Origins of Chinese Communist Foreign Policy, 1944–1946* (New York: Columbia University Press, 1980), p. 1, for example, asserts that "circumstances rather ideas have been the principal force shaping Chinese Communist behavior in international affairs." For argument of similar nature, see Donald Zagoria, "Containment and China," in C. Gati, ed., *Caging the Bear* (Indianapolis: Bobbs-Merrill, 1974), pp. 109–127.

34. Jin Chongji et al., *Zhou Enlai zhuan*, p. 742; and Li and Fang et al., *Zhou Enlai nianpu*, pp. 805–806.

35. Mao Zedong to the CCP East China Bureau, July 17, 1949, telegram, CCA.

36. Gwertzman, "The Hostage Crisis," p. 44.

37. Hopper to Marshall, December, 6, 15, 21, 1948, *FRUS* (1948), 7: 842–43, 845, 847; Stuart to Marshall, January 5, 1949, ibid., (1949), 8: 933–34.

38. Acheson to Clubb, March 2, 1949, *FRUS* (1949), 8: 943–944. Clubb to Acheson, February 24, 1949, March 8, 1949, March 9, 1949, March 18, 1949, March 26, 1949, May 9, 1949, ibid., pp. 940, 944–946, 949–50, 956; Acheson to Clubb, April 15, 1949, April 26, 1949, ibid., pp. 952, 955.

39. Acheson to Clubb, February 3, 1949, *FRUS* (1949), 9: 11.

40. Acheson to Stuart, May 13, 1949, ibid., p. 22.

41. Dean Acheson, *Present at the Creation: My Years in the State Department* (New York: Norton, 1969), p. 340.

42. For discussions of U.S. policy toward China during the Chinese civil war and its relations with the emerging Cold War, see Robert L. Messer, "American Perspectives on the Origins of the Cold War in East Asia," in Akira Iriye and Warren I. Cohen, eds., *American, Chinese, and Japanese Perspectives on Wartime Asia, 1931–1949* (Wilmington: Scholarly Resources, 1990), especially pp. 254–261; Warren I. Cohen, *America's Response to China: A History of Sino-American Relations* (3rd edition), (New York: Columbia University Press, 1990), pp. 150–158; John Lewis Gaddis, *The Long Peace: Inquiries into the History of the Cold War* (New York: Oxford University Press, 1987), pp. 75–80; and Westad, *Cold War and Revolution*.

43. Memorandum by the Policy Planning Staff, "The Problems to Review and Define United States Policy toward China," September 7, 1949, *FRUS* (1948), 8: 146–55; see also PPS 39/1, November 23, 1949, ibid., pp. 208–211.

44. Ibid., p. 147

45. For an excellent discussion of Acheson's intention of using trade and recognition as lever for winning a favorable position for the United States in its dealing with the CCP, see Warren I. Cohen, "Acheson, His Advisors, and China, 1949–1950," in Dorothy Borg and Waldo Heinrichs, eds.,

Uncertain Years: Chinese-American Relations, 1947–1950 (New York: Columbia University Press, 1980), pp. 13–52, especially pp. 32–33.

46. NSC 34/2, "U.S. Policy toward China," February 28, 1949, *FRUS* (1949), 9: 494.

47. NSC 41, "Draft Report by the National Security Council on United States Policy Regarding Trade with China," February 28, 1949, ibid., pp. 826–34.

48. Cohen emphasizes that Acheson made substantial efforts to work toward accommodation with the CCP in 1949, with the hope that tensions would develop between Beijing and Moscow (Cohen, "Acheson, His Advisors, and China"). Acheson's strategy, however, was self-contradictory in the first place. As he had limited knowledge of the logic underlying the CCP's policy, his approach toward such crucial issues as the recognition of the CCP regime contributed only to making Beijing and Moscow closer. For a good discussion of the self-contradictory nature of the Truman administration's "wedge-driving" strategy toward China, see Gordon H. Chang, *Friends and Enemies: The United States, China, and the Soviet Union, 1948–1972* (Stanford: Stanford University Press, 1990), p. 19.

49. Acheson to Certain Diplomatic and Consular Officers, May 6, 1949, *FRUS* (1949), 9: 17; see also ibid., pp. 18, 25, 26, 28–29, 34, 37, 40–42, 61–62, 76–78, 81–85, 88–91.

50. For the activities and influence of the "China bloc," see Nancy Bernkopf Tucker, *Patterns in the Dust: Chinese-American Relations and the Recognition Controversy, 1949–1950* (New York: Columbia University Press, 1983), chapters 5 and 8; Ross Koen, *The China Lobby in American Politics* (New York: Harper, 1974); Lewis Purifoy, *Harry Truman's China Policy: McCarthyism and the Diplomacy of Hysteria, 1947–1951* (New York, 1976).

51. Chang, *Friends and Enemies*, pp. 24–25.

52. See, for example, Acheson memorandum, April 28, 1949, and Acheson memorandum of conversation with Senator H. Alexander Smith, July 14, 1949, RG 59, 893.00/4–2849/ 7–1449, National Archives (hereafter NA).

53. Gaddis Smith, *Dean Acheson* (New York: Cooper Square, 1972), pp. 423–424.

54. For an excellent study emphasizing the role played by concerns for "American prestige" and "American credibility" in the making of Sino-American confrontation, see William W. Stueck, *The Road to Confrontation: American Policy toward China and Korea, 1947–1950*, (Chapel Hill: University of North Carolina Press, 1981).

55. The decision to stay largely resulted from the initiative of Stuart himself. At the end of 1948, he suggested to the State Department that when the GMD government moved its capital to the South, the principal

staff of the American embassy should "remain in Nanking [Nanjing]." In early 1949, when Stuart learned that the GMD government (not Jiang himself) would move to Canton, he further suggested that the "Ambassador and his principal advisors remain Nanking." In late January, Stuart's suggestion was approved, and he remained in Nanjing after the GMD government moved to Guangzhou (Canton) in early February. After the Communists occupied Nanjing, at Stuart's insistence, however, Acheson agreed not to ask Stuart to "make precipitous departure from China following Commie takeover." See Stuart to the Secretary of State, November 7, 1948, November 29, 1948, November 30, 1948, December 3, 1948, *FRUS* (1948), 7: 851–53, 854, 855, 857–58; Stuart to the Secretary of State, January 26, 1949, February 4, 1949, April 23, 1949; Acheson to Stuart, April 22, 1949, April 23, 1949, *FRUS* (1949), 8: 667–68, 673, 682–84.

56. Stuart to the Secretary of State, March 10, 1949, *FRUS* (1949), 8: 173–77.

57. Acheson to Stuart, April 9, 1949, ibid., pp. 230–231.

58. Cohen, *America's Response to China*, p. 164.

59. Mao Zedong to the CCP's General Front-line Committee, April 28, 1949, *Dangde wenxian*, no. 4 (1989): 43.

60. Mao Zedong, "Statement by the Spokesman of the General Headquarters of the Chinese People's Liberation Army," April 30, 1949, *MXJ*, 4: 1464.

61. Mao Zedong to Su Yu, April 27, 1949, telegram, CCA; see also the CCP Central Military Commission to the CCP General Front-line Committee, April 26, 1949, *ZYWJXJ*, 18: 246–247; Huang Hua, "My Contacts with Stuart after the Liberation of Nanjing," in Pei Jianzhang, et al., *Xinzhongguo waijiao fengyun* (The Experiences of New China's Diplomacy, Beijing: World Affairs Press, 1990), p. 25; and Song Renqiong, "Before and After Nanjing's Liberation," *Zhonggong dangshi ziliao*, no.38 (1991): 82–83.

62. The CCP Central Committee, "Instructions on Diplomatic Affairs," *ZYWJXJ*, 18: 234; and *FRUS* (1949), 8: 104–5, 391, 1062.

63. The CCP Central Committee, "Instructions on Diplomatic Affairs," *ZYWJXJ*, 18: 234.

64. Huang Hua, "My Contacts with Stuart," p. 24.

65. Zhang Zhen, "In Reminiscence of the Shanghai Campaign," p. 87; Chen Guangxiang, "Why the PLA Did Not Liberate Shanghai Immediately after Crossing the Yangzi," *Dangshi yanjiu ziliao* (Party History Research Materials), no. 178 (May 1992): 21.

66. Goncharov, "Stalin's Dialogue with Mao Zedong," p. 50; and Goncharov, et al., *Uncertain Partners*, p. 43.

67. Mao Zedong to the CCP Nanjing Municipal Committee, May 10,

1949, *MNP*, 3:499; see also Huang Hua, "My Contacts with Stuart," pp. 26–27.

68. The CCP's General Front-line Committee to Su Yu and Zhang Zhen, May 21, 1949, telegram, CCA; see also Chen Xiaolu, "China's Policy toward the United States, 1949–1955," in Harry Harding and Yuan Ming, eds., *Sino-American Relations, 1945–1955: A Joint Reassessment of a Critical Decade* (Wilmington, DE: Scholarly Resources, 1989), p. 186.

69. Mao Zedong to the CCP Nanjing Municipal Committee, May 10, 1949, *MNP*, 3: 499–500.

70. For details of Stuart-Huang contact and Stuart's plan to visit Beiping, see *FRUS* (1949), 8: 741–67; for a Chinese version of the story, see Huang Hua, "My Contacts with Stuart," especially pp. 26–28.

71. Huang Hua, "My Contacts with Stuart," p. 30; Stuart to Acheson, June 30, 1949, *FRUS* (1949), 8: 766–67.

72. The CCP Central Committee to the CCP Nanjing Municipal Committee (drafted by Zhou), June 30, 1949, telegram, CCA.

73. Mao Zedong, "Address to the Preparatory Meeting of the New Political Consultative Conference," *MXJ*, 4: 1470.

74. For examples of this argument, see Shi Yinhong, "From Confrontation to War: The Truman Administration's Policy toward the New China" (Ph. D. dissertation, Nanjing University, 1987), p. 49; Stueck, *The Road to Confrontation*, pp. 124–25; and Mineo Nakajima, "Foreign Relations: from the Korean War to the Bandung Line," in MacFarquhar and Fairbank eds. *The Cambridge History of China*, 14: 263.

75. *MXJ*, 4: 1470; see also Zhou Enlai, "Report on Problems Concerning the Peace Talks," *ZXJ*, 1: 322–23.

76. *Renmin ribao*, June 19, 1949; Clubb to Acheson, June 19, 1949, *FRUS* (1949), 8: 965.

77. Mao Zedong to the CCP Northeast Bureau, June 22, 1949, telegram, CCA.

78. Mao Zedong's instruction to Hu Qiaomu, June 24, 1949, *Mao Zedong shuxin xuanji* (Selected Correspondences of Mao Zedong, Beijing: People's Press, 1983), pp. 327–328.

79. Shi Yinhong, "From Confrontation to War," pp. 62–63, 72–74.

80. *Dongbei ribao* (Northeast Daily), June 20, 1949; Clubb to Acheson, June 19, 1949, *FRUS* (1949), 8: 965.

81. Clubb to Acheson, June 1, 1949, *FRUS* (1949), 9: 357–60.

82. All of Zhou's aides denied that Zhou had sent this "desperate message" to the United States. Huang Hua even called it "total nonsense." (Warren I. Cohen, "Conversations with Chinese Friends: Zhou Enlai's Associates Reflect on Chinese-American Relations in the 1940s and the Korean War," *Diplomatic History* [Summer 1987], pp. 284–85; Chang,

Friends and Enemies, p. 304, n. 60) My investigations in Beijing in May 1991, August 1992, and August 1993 confirm that no documentary evidence has ever been found to prove the existence of the alleged Zhou *demarche*.

83. Clubb to Acheson, June 2, June 24, 1949, *FRUS* (1949), 9: 363–64, 397–98.

84. Memorandum by John P. Davis of the Policy Planning Staff to the Director of the Staff [Kennan], June 30, 1949, *FRUS* (1949), 8: 768–69; Acheson to Stuart, July 1, 1949, ibid., p. 769.

85. For a detailed discussion of Liu's visit to the Soviet Union in July and August 1948, see Zhu Yuanshi, "Liu Shaoqi's Secret Visit to the Soviet Union in 1949," *Dangde wenxian*, no. 3 (1991): 74–80; and Shi Zhe, *Zai lishi jüren shenbian*, pp. 396–426; see also discussions in chapter 3.

86. Mao Zedong, "Cast Away Illusions, Prepare for Struggle," "Farewell, John Leighton Stuart," "Why It Is Necessary to Discuss the White Paper," "'Friendship' or Aggression?" "The Bankruptcy of the Idealist Conception of History," *MXJ*, 4: 1486–1520.

87. Memorandum of Conversation with Ernest Bevin by Acheson, Septeber 13, 1949, *FRUS* (1949), 9: 81–82.

88. Clark to Acheson, June 23, 1949, ibid., pp. 1103–4; Memorandum of Conversation by Webb, October 1, 1949, ibid., p. 1141.

89. *Zhonghua renmin gongheguo duiwai guanxi wenjianji, 1949–1950* (Documents of Foreign Relations of the People's Republic of China, 1949–1950, Beijing: World Affairs Press, 1957), pp. 4–5; see also Clubb to Acheson, October 2, 1949, *FRUS* (1949), 9: 93–94.

90. Mao Zedong to Liu Shaoqi and Zhou Enlai, December 19, 1949, *MWG*, 1: 193; Han Nianlong et al., *Dangdai zhongguo waijiao*, pp. 7–9. Beijing's policy of distinguishing Communist countries from non-Communist countries on recognition problem greatly disappointed such countries like Burma and Great Britain. For a discussion, see Edwin W. Martin, *Divided Counsel: the Anglo-American Response to Communist Victory in China* (Lexington: The University Press of Kentucky, 1986), pp. 101–102.

91. Memorandum by Freeman [Acting Deputy Director of the Office of Chinese Affairs], October 3, 1949, *FRUS* (1949), 9: 96–97.

92. *New York Times*, October 3, 1949, p. 1.

93. *FRUS, 1949*: 9: 156–58; see also Stueck, *The Road to Confrontation*, pp. 131–132.

94. U.S. Congress, Senate Foreign Relations Committee, *Reviews of the World Situation*, 81st Congress, first and second sessions, May 19, 1949–December 11, 1950, Historical Series, 1974, pp. 94–94; Acheson to Certain Diplomatic and Consular Officers, October 12, 1949, *FRUS* (1949), 9: 122–23.

95. The Research Department of the Xinhua News Agency, eds., *Xin-*

huashe wenjian ziliao xuanbian (A Selected Collection of Documents of the Xinhua News Agency, Beijing: date of publication unclear), p. 18.

96. Zhou Enlai, "The New China's Diplomacy," *ZWJWX*, pp. 1–3.

97. According to Ward, Ji was fired by the Consulate in late September and was found hiding in the Consulate compound by Ward on October 1. Ward tried to escort him out of the area. When "Ji lay down on stairway and refused to move," Ward endeavored to "expel him with intention handing him over as trespasser to armed sentry guarding office building." This prompted a scuffle with Ji's brother, who was also in the compound. Ji was then sent to hospital although Ward believed "neither he nor [his] brother was injured by me or any member of my staff." Ward to Acheson, December 11, 1949, *FRUS* (1949), 8: 1047–48.

98. *Dongbei ribao*, October 25, 1949; for related Chinese reports on the case, see *Dongbei ribao*, October 28, November 2, 1949.

99. Tucker, *Patterns in the Dust*, p. 150.

100. Acheson to Clubb, October 28, 1949; and Clubb to Acheson, October 29, 1949, *FRUS* (1949), 8: 988–989.

101. "Meeting with the President," memorandum by James E. Webb, November 14, 1949, OCA, Box 14, RG 59, NA; see also *FRUS* (1949), 8: 1008; *FRUS* (1949), 9: 1355.

102. Memorandum by Bradley, chairman of the Joint Chiefs of Staff, to Johnson, the Secretary of Defense, November 18, 1949, ibid., (1949): 8: 1011–13.

103. Acheson to Certain Diplomatic Representatives, November 18, 1949, ibid., pp. 1009–10.

104. *Department of State Bulletin* (November 28, 1949): 799–800.

105. *Dongbei ribao*, November 27, 1949; *Xinhua yuebao*, 1, no. 3 (1949): 620–23; Ward to Acheson, December 11, 1949, *FRUS* (1949), 8: 1049–50.

106. Memorandum by Acting Secretary of State James Webb to the President, January 10, 1950, *FRUS* (1950), 6: 270–72.

107. *Renmin ribao*, January 19, 1950; Han Nianlong et al., *Dangdai zhongguo waijiao*, pp. 18–19.

108. What is noticeable here is the CCP's choice of timing to take this action. It had been a well-established principle for the CCP leadership not to recognize the official status of Western diplomats in China; nor would they treat the assets of Western consulates in China as official. Why then did the CCP choose early January 1950, not earlier, to announce the requisition of former American military barracks? One answer might be found in Mao's experiences in the Soviet Union. Mao started his visit to the Soviet Union on December 16, 1949, with the hope of establishing a substantial Chinese-Soviet strategic alliance. Not until early January 1950, however, did Mao receive a positive response from Stalin. On January 3, Mao had a discussion

with Molotov in Moscow, which established the principles for the forthcoming Sino-Soviet alliance. As a result, Mao cabled to the CCP Central Committee on January 5, formally informing Zhou Enlai to come to Moscow to complete details of the alliance treaty. (Mao Zedong to the CCP Central Committee, January 2, 3, and 5 1950, *MWG*, 1: 211–213, 215) The next day, the Beijing Military Control Commission ordered the requisition. We have no "hard evidence" at this stage to prove that the requisition order came directly from Mao in Moscow. However, it should not be too off the mark to say that the dramatic progress of Mao's contacts with Stalin strengthened the CCP's confidence in confronting the United States, thus resulting in the requisition order at this moment. For more details of Mao's visit to the Soviet Union, see discussions in chapter 3.

109. *Department of State Bulletin* (January 23, 1950): 119.

110. Mao Zedong to Liu Shaoqi, January 13 and 17, 1950, *MWG*, 1: 235, 241.

111. *Renmin ribao*, January 19, 1950.

112. Acheson to Clubb, March 22, 1950, *FRUS* (1950), 6: 321–322.

113. Clubb to Acheson, April 11, 1950, ibid., p. 329.

114. Cited from Michael Schaller, *American Occupation of Japan: The Origins of Cold War in Asia* (New York: Oxford University Press, 1985), p. 253.

3. "LEANING TO ONE SIDE": THE FORMATION OF THE SINO-SOVIET ALLIANCE

1. Mao Zedong, "On the People's Democratic Dictatorship," *MXJ*, 4: 1477.

2. Han Nianlong et al., *Dangdai zhongguo waijiao*, p. 4.

3. Mao Zedong, "Cast Away Illusion, Prepare for Struggle," *MXJ*, 4: 1487–94; and Bo Yibo, *Ruogan zhongda juece yu shijian de huigu* (Recollections of Several Important Decisions and Events, Beijing: CCP Central Academy Press, 1991), p. 38. Bo was a member of the Central Committee of the CCP at that time

4. *Zhonggong dangshi tongxun* (The Newsletter of CCP History), no. 24 (December 25, 1989): 4.

5. The date for Liu's departure for the Soviet Union follows the memoirs of Shi Zhe, who was Liu's interpreter and accompanied Liu to the Soviet Union. See Shi Zhe, "I accompanied Chairman Mao to the Soviet Union," *Renwu* (Biographical Journal), no. 5 (1988): 6; and Shi Zhe, *Zai lishi jüren shenbian*, p. 396.

6. Yang Yunruo and Yang Kuisong, *Gongchan guoji yu zhongguo geming* (The Comintern and the Chinese Revolution, Shanghai: Shanghai People's

Press, 1988), chapter 5; Liao Gailong, "The Relations between the Soviet Union and the Chinese Revolution," *Zhonggong dangshi yanjiu* (CCP History Studies), supplementary issue (1991): 2–4; and Shi Zhe, *Zai lishi jüren shenbian*, pp. 213–215. For a discussion representing recent Western scholarship on this issue, see Garver, *Chinese-Soviet Relations*, chapter 5.

7. Liao Gailong, "The Relations between the Soviet Union and the Chinese Revolution," p. 4; Yang and Yang, *Gongchan guoji yu zhongguo geming*, chapter 5.

8. Liao Gailong, "The Relations between the Soviet Union and the Chinese Revolution," pp. 5–6.

9. Ibid., p. 7; Westad, *Cold War and Revolution,* chapter 1; see also Wang Tingke, "The Impact of the Yalta System upon the Relationship between Stalin and the Soviet Union and the Chinese Revolution," *Zhonggong dangshi yanjiu*, supplementary issue (1991): 12–21, especially pp. 15–16. Salisbury records that in his interview with Yang Shangkun, secretary general of the CCP's Central Military Commission in the late 1940s, he was told that "Moscow never briefed China on the Yalta agreement." Harrison E. Salibury, *The New Emperors: China in the Era of Mao and Deng* (Boston: Little, Brown, 1992), pp. 491–492, n. 15.

10. Li and Fang et al., *Zhou Enlai nianpu*, 616. Shi Zhe recalled that Mao complained after receiving Stalin's message: "How can a nation be completely destroyed simply because its people want to struggle for liberation? I will never believe in this." Shi Zhe, *Zai lishi jüren shenbian*, pp. 307–308.

11. For a recent plausible discussion, see Westad, *Cold War and Revolution,* especially chapter 4.

12. Chang, *Friends and Enemies*, p. 28.

13. It was Mao who first released in a speech on April 11, 1957 that Stalin had advised the CCP before the PLA's crossing of the Yangzi River that the Chinese Communists should not try to cross the Yangzi, "otherwise the Americans would interfere." (See *Dangshi ziliao tongxun*, no. 22 [1982]: 13.) Zhou Enlai, according to the memoirs of Liu Xiao, Chinese ambassador to the Soviet Union (1955–1962), also confirmed that Stalin advised the CCP not to cross the Yangzi (see Liu Xiao, *Chushi sulian banian* [Eight Years as Ambassador in the Soviet Union, Beijing: The Press of Party Historical Materials, 1986], p. 4). In recent years, whether or not Stalin had advised Mao and the CCP leadership is a question that has been widely debated by Chinese researchers. While Yu Zhan and Zhang Guangyou, two former Chinese diplomats, allege that they found no reliable evidence to prove that Stalin had ever offered such advice, the opinion of most Chinese researchers, including that of Xiang Qing's, a widely recognized authority in the field of Chinese Communist party history, is that Stalin did advise Mao and the CCP leadership not to cross the Yangzi River. For Yu Zhan and Zhang

Guangyou's opinion, see their article "An Exploration of Whether Stalin Advised Our Party Not to Cross the Yangzi River," *Dangde wenxian*, no. 1 (1989): 56–58. For the opinion of Xiang Qing and others, see Xiang Qing, "My Opinion on the Question Whether Stalin Had Advised Our Party Not to Cross the Yangzi River," *Dangde wenxian*, no. 6 (1989): 64–66; Liao, "The Relations between the Soviet Union and the Chinese Revolution," p. 7; Chen Guangxiang, "An Exploration of Stalin's Interference with the PLA's Crossing the Yangzi River," *Zhonggong dangshi yanjiu*, supplementary issue (1990): 98–100, 11. For a Russian perspective of this problem, see Goncharov, "Stalin's Dialogue with Mao Zedong," pp. 49–50.

14. Mao and other CCP leaders were unhappy with the Soviet attitude toward China's civil war. Mao stressed on several occasions that "the Chinese revolution achieved its victory against the will of Stalin." Zhou Enlai also observed: "The Soviet policy [toward China's civil war] was largely the result of their erroneous assessment of the international relations at that time. The Soviets were worried that the civil war in China might overturn the established sphere of influence set up by the Yalta conference, thus leading to an American intervention and making the Soviet Union suffer. Stalin was also scared by the prospect of a Third World War. The point of departure of Stalin's policy was to appease the United States [in China] so that the Soviet Union would be guaranteed time necessary for their peaceful reconstruction. The Soviet Union had a strong reservation upon our ability to liberate the whole China. . . . There existed fundamental divergences between us and the Soviet leaders regarding the international situation as well as our ability to liberate the whole China." Mao Zedong, "On the Ten Major Relationships," *MXJ*, 5: 286; Liu Xiao, *Chushi sulian banian*, pp. 4–5; see also Wu Xiuquan, *Wangshi cangsang: Wu Xiuquan huiyilu* (The Vicissitude of My Life: Wu Xiuquan's Memoirs, Shanghai: Shanghai Literature Press, 1986), p. 181.

15. After the Long March, the CCP Central Committee reestablished telegraphic communication with the Comintern in 1936. In November 1940, the CCP started to use a new set of confidential codes offered by the Comintern to communicate with Moscow, and the telegraphic communication between Yanan and Moscow became very reliable. Mao personally controlled communications with the Comintern and the Soviet Union. He frequently sent long reports to the Comintern and, after the dissolution of the Comintern, to Stalin and the Soviet party, which kept the Soviets well informed of the CCP's strategies and policies. See Shi Zhe, *Zai lishi jüren shenbian*, pp. 200–217, 307–320, 347–348; Yang and Yang, *Gongchan guoji yu zhongguo geming*, pp. 367–368.

16. For plausible discussions, see Yang Kuisong, "The Soviet Factor and the CCP's Policy toward the United States," p. 30; and Niu Jun, *Cong Yanan zouxiang shijie*, pp. 272–274.

17. Shi Zhe, *Zai lishi jüren shenbian*, pp. 365–366; Goncharov, "Stalin's Dialogue with Mao Zedong," pp. 46–47.

18. The CCP Central Committee, "Resolution on the Problem Concerning the Yugoslavian Communist Party," July 1, 1949, CCA; The CCP Central Committee, "Instructions on Circulating the Northeast Bureau's Resolution on Learning Lessons from the Problems Concerning the Yugoslavian Communist Party," August 4, 1948, the United Front Department of the CCP Central Committee, comp., *Minzu wenti wenjian ji* (A Collection of Documents on National Problems, Beijing: CCP Central Academy Press, 1991), pp. 1155–1157. The quote is from the second document, p. 1155.

19. Shi Zhe, *Zai lishi jüren shenbian*, pp. 365–367.

20. Cited from Bo Yibo, *Ruogan zhongda juece yu shijian de huigu*, p. 36.

21. Stalin to Mao Zedong, January 14, 1949, and Mao Zedong to Stalin, January 17, 1949 cited from *MNP*, 3: 438–439; see also Shi Zhe, "I Accompanied Chairman Mao to the Soviet Union," p. 6; Jin Chongji et al., *Zhou Enlai zhuan*, p. 718.

22. This account of Mao's talks with Mikoyan is based on my interviews with Shi Zhe in May 1991 and August 1992, and Shi Zhe, "With Mao and Stalin: the Reminiscences of a Chinese Interpreter," (translated by Chen Jian), *Chinese Historians*, 5, no. 1 (Spring 1992): 35–44. This part of Shi's memoirs is written with the assistance of Li Haiwen, a senior researcher of the CCP history who has archival access. For a Russian version of Mikoyan's meetings with Mao offered by Kovalev, see Goncharov, "Stalin's Dialogue with Mao Zedong," pp. 48–49. According to Kovalev, Mao cited the opinion of a "female leader of the revolutionary wing of the Kuomintang" to put forward the question of Soviet Union returning to China the China-Changchun railroad, as well as allowing China to restore sovereignty over Outer Mongolia, and that Mikoyan responded that he was not authorized to discuss such matters (Goncharov, "Stalin's Dialogue with Mao Zedong," p. 49). Shi Zhe denies that Mao had ever touched upon a topic like this in his conversations with Mikoyan. See Li Haiwen, "A Distortion of History: An Interview with Shi Zhe about Kovalev's Recollections," *Chinese Historians*, 5, no. 2 (Fall 1992): 61–62.

23. Shi Zhe, "I Accompanied Chairman Mao to the Soviet Union," p. 6; Jin Chongji, *Zhou Enlai zhuan*, pp. 742–43; Yan Changlin, *Zai dajuezhan de rizi li* (In the Days of Decisive Campaigns, Beijing: Chinese Youth Press), 1986, p. 222; Zhu Yuanshi, "Liu Shaoqi's Secret Visit to the Soviet Union in 1949," p. 75.

24. Shi Zhe, "I Accompanied Chairman Mao to the Soviet Union," p. 7.

25. Ibid, p. 7; Zhu Yuanshi, "Liu Shaoqi's Secret Visit to the Soviet Union in 1949," p. 76.

26. For a detailed summary of the memo, see Shi Zhe, *Zai lishi jüren shenbian*, pp. 398–404; for the complete text of the domestic part of the memo, see Liu Wusheng et al., *Gongheguo zouguo de lu, 1949–1952*, pp. 56–59.

27. Shi Zhe, *Zai lishi jüren shenbian*, pp. 396–397; Zhu Yuanshi, "Liu Shaoqi's Secret Visit to the Soviet Union in 1949," p. 76; and Ge Baoquan, "In Commemoration of Wang Jiaxiang, China's First Ambassador to the Soviet Union," The Editorial Group of "Selected Works of Wang Jiaxiang," ed., *Huiyi Wang Jiaxiang* (In Commemoration of Wang Jiaxiang, Beijing: People's Press, 1985), p. 151.

28. Shi Zhe, "I Accompanied Chairman Mao to the Soviet Union," p. 8.

29. According to Shi Zhe, when Liu reported to the CCP Politburo that Stalin made the apology for the mistakes he committed to the Chinese revolution, CCP leaders were "greatly moved and encouraged." Shi Zhe, *Zai lishi jüren shenbian*, p. 426.

30. See Wu Xiuquan, *Zai waijiaobu banian de jingli* (My Eight Years' Experience in the Ministry of Foreign Affairs, Beijing: New World Press, 1984), pp. 4–5; Han Nianlong et al., *Dangdai zhongguo waijiao*, pp. 21–22.

31. Shi Zhe, *Zai lishi jüren shenbian*, pp. 404–405.

32. Ibid., pp. 405, 418–419; Shi Zhe, "I Accompanied Chairman Mao to the Soviet Union," pp. 9–10.

33. Zhu Peimin, "The Process of the Peaceful Liberation of Xinjiang," *Kashi shiyuan xuebao* (The Journal of Kashi Normal College), no. 4 (1989): 14–15; Deng Liqun, "Before and After Xinjiang's Peaceful Liberation: A Page of Sino-Soviet Relations," *Jindaishi yanjiu* (Studies of Modern History), no. 5 (1989): 143–144; and Shi Zhe, *Zai lishi jüren shenbian*, pp. 407–408. Kovalev confirms that Stalin promised Liu Shaoqi that the Soviets "were prepared to give direct assistance in the [CCP's] liberation of Xinjiang." See Goncharov, "Stalin's Dialogue with Mao Zedong," p. 69.

34. Zhu Peimin, "The Process of the Peaceful Liberation of Xinjiang," pp. 16–17; Deng Liqun, "Before and After Xinjiang's Peaceful Liberation," p. 144.

35. Shi Zhe, "Random Reflections of Comrade Liu Shaoqi," *Geming huiyilu* (Revolutionary Memoirs), supplementary issue, no. 1 (October 1983): 110–111; Shi Zhe, "I Accompanied Chairman Mao to the Soviet Union," p. 10.

36. Shi Zhe, *Zai lishi jüren shenbian*, pp. 406–407; Kovalev recalls that Liu asked Stalin if the Soviet Union could use air force and submarines to support the PLA's attack on Taiwan. Stalin refused because he feared a direct military conflict between the Soviet Union and the United States (Goncharov, "Stalin's Dialogue with Mao Zedong," pp. 52–53; Goncharov et al., *Uncertain Partners*, p. 69). Shi Zhe denies that Liu had ever put forward such

request (See Li Haiwen, "A Distortion of History," p. 62). No other Chinese sources can confirm this part of Kovalev's recollections.

37. The Soviet Union exploded its first atomic bomb on August 29, 1949, and Liu Shaoqi left the Soviet Union in mid-August, so this film-showing must have depicted something else. But Shi Zhe insisted that they were told that the film recorded a successful bomb test. Interviews with Shi Zhe, August 1992.

38. Shi Zhe, *Zai lishi jüren shenbian,* p. 410. According to Kovalev, Stalin told Liu at one meeting: "The Soviet Union is sufficiently strong now not to fear nuclear blackmail by the United States." Goncharov, "Stalin's Dialogue with Mao Zedong," p. 52.

39. Shi Zhe could not recall if Liu had discussed with Stalin the Korean problem during his stay in the Soviet Union. Interviews with Shi Zhe, August 1992.

40. For a more detailed discussion, see chapter 4.

41. According to Shi Zhe, Liu Shaoqi and his delegation maintained frequent communications with the CCP Center. Liu reported to the CCP Central Committee and Mao himself immediately after each of his meetings with Stalin. Shi Zhe's recollections are supported by documents kept in Beijing's Central Archives. For example, Liu 's long report about his first meeting with Stalin on July 11 was sent to the CCP Center the next day. Interviews with Shi Zhe and Li Haiwen, August 1992.

42. The CCP Central Committee to Liu Shaoqi, July 26, 1949, cited from Lü Liping, *Tongtian zhilu* (The Path to the Sky, Beijing: People's Liberation Army Press, 1989), p. 137. Lü was himself a member of the Chinese air force delegation to the Soviet Union in August 1949; see also *MNP,* 3:529.

43. Lü Liping, *Tongtian zhilu,* pp. 137, 155–156; Bo Yibo, *Ruogan zhongda juece yu shijian de huigu,* p. 37; Han and Tan et al., *Dangdai zhongguo jundui,* 2: 109; and Yang Wanqing, "Liu Yalou: The First Commander of the People's Air Force," *Zhonggong dangshi ziliao,* no. 42 (June 1992): 220.

44. Lü Liping, *Tongtian zhilu,* p. 138; Yang Wanqing, "Liu Yalou," p. 220.

45. Lü Liping, *Tongtian zhilu,* pp. 144–146; Yang Wanqing, "Liu Yalou," pp. 220–224; and *MNP,* 3:529.

46. Lü Liping, *Tongtian zhilu,* pp. 155–156.

47. Han and Tan et al., *Dangdai zhongguo jundui,* 2: 11; Bo Yibo, *Ruogan zhongda juece yu shijian de huigu,* p. 38; Li Yueran (Zhou Enlai's Russian interpreter), *Waijiao wutai shang de xinzhongguo lingxiu* (The Leaders of New China on the Diplomatic Scene, Beijing: People's Liberation Army Press, 1989), pp. 3–4; Nie Rongzhen, *Nie Rongzhen huiyilu,* p. 730. Zhou Enlai informed the CCP's Northeast Bureau on August 10 that Liu would be back around August 14 and with more than 200 Soviet experts, and that most of

these experts would stay in the Northeast to assist the works there. See the CCP Central Committee (drafted by Zhou) to Gao Gang and Li Fuchun, August 10, 1949, telegram, CCA. See also Goncharov, "Stalin's Dialogue with Mao Zedong," p. 48.

48. Mao Zedong to Liu Shaoqui, Gao Gang, and Wang Jiaxing, August 4, 1949, *MNP*, 3: 541; see also Zhu Yuanshi, "Liu Shaoqi's Secret Visit to the Soviet Union in 1949," p. 79; Shi Zhe, *Zai lishi jüren shenbian*, p. 406. During Liu Shaoqi's stay in Moscow, Gao Gang, representing the Northeast People's Government, signed a trade agreement with the Soviets. The historian Mineo Nakajima believed that Gao Gang did this "apparently without consulting the Peking leadership." (Nakajima, "Foreign Relations: from the Korean War to the Bandung Line," p. 265). As Gao Gang was a member of Liu's delegation, it is highly unlikely that the CCP leadership did not have knowledge of this trade agreement between the Soviet Union and the Northeast.

49. Lü Liping, *Tongtian zhilu*, pp. 156–169; Yang Wanqing, "Liu Yalou," p. 224; Lin Fu, et al., *Kongjun shi* (A History of the PLA's Air Force, Beijing: People's Liberation Army Press, 1989), p. 38; Han and Tan et al., *Dangdai zhongguo jundui* , 2: 160–161.

50. Lü Liping, *Tongtian zhilu*, pp. 168–169.

51. Han and Tan et al., *Dangdai zhongguo jundui*, 2: 161; and Yang Wanqing, "Liu Yalou," p. 228.

52. Lü Liping, *Tongtian zhilu*, p. 165; Yang Guoyu et al., *Dangdai zhongguo haijun* (Contemporary Chinese Navy, Beijing: Chinese Social Sciences Press, 1987), p. 48.

53. Liu Shaoqi, "On the Unity between China and the Soviet Union," September 3, 1949, minute, CCA; see also Zhu Yuanshi, "Liu Shaoqi's Secret Visit to the Soviet Union in 1949," p. 80.

54. *Zhonghua renmin gongheguo duiwai guanxi wenjianji, 1949–1950*, pp. 5–6.

55. *Renmin ribao*, October 4, 1949; see also *MWG*, 1: 17–18.

56. Han Nianlong et al., *Dangdai zhongguo waijiao*, pp. 5–6, 8–9.

57. Mao Zedong to Stalin, October 20, 1949, *MWG*, 1: 81.

58. In a meeting with Roschin, Soviet ambassador to China, in early November 1949, Zhou Enlai made it clear that the purpose of Mao's visit was to discuss and sign a new Sino-Soviet treaty. See the Institute of Diplomatic History under the PRC's Foreign Ministry, ed., *Zhou Enlai waijiao huodong dashiji* (A Chronicle of Zhou Enlai's Diplomatic Activities, Beijing: World Affairs Press, 1993), p. 14.

59. Mao Zedong to the CCP Central Committee, January 3, 1950, *MWG*, 1: 213; Han Nianlong et al., *Dangdai zhongguo waijiao*, pp. 24–25.

60. The CCP Central Committee to Wang Jiaxiang, November 9, 1949, *MWG*, 1: 131; Mao Zedong to Stalin, November 12, 1949, *MWG*, 1: 135.

61. Bo Yibo, *Ruogan zhongda juece yu shijian de huigu*, p. 40; Shi Zhe, *Zai lishi jüren shenbian*, p. 432; see also Goncharov, "Stalin's Dialogue with Mao Zedong," p. 56.

62. Shi Zhe recalls that the Russians meticulously arranged it so that Mao's train arrived at the station exactly at noon so that Mao was welcomed by the ringing clock of the station. Mao's reception by so many high-ranking Soviet officials revealed that the Russians wanted to please him. See Shi Zhe, "I Accompanied Chairman Mao to the Soviet Union," p. 12; and Wang Dongxing's diary entry for December 16, 1949, in Wang Dongxing, *Wang Dongxing riji* (Wang Dongxing's Diaries, Beijing: Chinese Social Sciences Press, 1993), pp. 156–157. For a Russian version of Mao's visit to Moscow, see Nikola Fedorenko, "The Stalin-Mao Summit in Moscow," *Far Eastern Affairs* (Moscow), no. 2, 1989.

63. Shi Zhe, "I Accompanied Chairman Mao to the Soviet Union," p. 13; see also Wang Dongxing, *Wang Dongxing riji*, pp. 157–158.

64. Wu Xiuquan, *Wangshi cangsang*, p. 182; Shi Zhe, "I Accompanied Chairman Mao to the Soviet Union," pp. 13–14.

65. After Stalin's death, Mao would often complain about his experience in the Soviet Union. On one occasion Mao summarized Stalin's "erroneous attitude" toward the Chinese Communist revolution in history: "Stalin did a number of wrong things in connection with China. . . . When we won the [civil] war, Stalin suspected that ours was a victory of the Tito type. He placed great pressure on us in 1949 and 1950." Mao Zedong, "On the Ten Major Relationships," *MXJ*, 5: 286.

66. Again, as discussed in chapter 2, we should not forget that Mao defined "equality" basically as a historical-cultural issue.

67. Interviews with Shi Zhe, August 1992.

68. In Shi Zhe's memoirs, he recalls that Mao had been trying to have a profound discussion with Stalin on the history of the relationship between the Chinese and Soviet parties, but he never got such an opportunity. See Shi Zhe, *Zai lishi jüren shenbian*, pp. 438, 451–452.

69. During his visit to the Soviet Union, Mao expressed such feelings on several occasions. See Shi Zhe, *Zai lishi jüren shenbian*, pp. 443, 456–457, 463.

70. Bo Yibo, *Ruogan zhongda juece yu shijian de huigu*, p. 41; Shi Zhe, *Zai lishi jüren shenbian*, p. 438; Goncharov, Lewis and Xue state that Stalin did not send Kovalev's report to Mao until late January 1950 (*Uncertain Partners*, p. 97). However, according to Wang Dongxing's diary entry of December 28, 1949, Mao had by this day received a copy of Kovalev's report from Stalin (Wang Dongxing, *Wang Dongxing riji*, p. 168).

71. Shi Zhe, *Zai lishi jüren shenbian*, p. 437; and Wu Xiuquan, *Wangshi cangsang*, p. 182.

72. Shi Zhe, "I Accompanied Chairman Mao to the Soviet Union," p.

17; Wu Xiuquan, *Wangshi cangsang*, pp. 182–83; Mao Zedong to the CCP Central Committee, January 2, 1950, *MWG*, 1: 211.

73. *Renmin ribao*, January 3, 1950; see also *MWG*, 1: 206. For Mao's description of the background of this speech, see Mao Zedong to the CCP Central Committee, January 2, 1950, *MWG*, 1: 211.

74. Mao Zedong to the CCP Central Committee, January 2, 1950, *MWG*, 1: 211–12; and Shi Zhe, *Zai lishi jüren shenbian*, pp. 439–440; Wu Xiuquan, *Wangshi cangsang*, pp. 179–180.

75. Among members of Zhou's delegation were Li Fuchun, vice chairman of the Northeast People's Government, Ye Jizhuang, minister of foreign trade, Wu Xiuquan, director of the Soviet-Eastern Europe Section of the Ministry of Foreign Affairs, Lai Yali, deputy director of the administrative office of the Ministry of Foreign Affairs, Lü Dong, vice minister of the Industry Department of the Northeast, Zhang Huadong, vice minister of the Trade Department of the Northeast, and Ouyang Qing, mayor of the Lüda city (Wu Xiuquan, *Wangshi cangsang*, p. 180; Shi Zhe, *Zai lishi jüren shenbian*, p. 444). An air force delegation headed, again, by Liu Yalou also followed Zhou to Moscow. Their main tasks this time were to negotiate details about Soviet assistance to establish China's airborne units, ordering more planes from the Soviet Union, and asking the Soviet air force to take on air-defense responsibility in the Shanghai area. See Wang Dinglie, et al., *Dangdai zhongguo kongjun* (Contemporary Chinese Air Force, Beijing: Chinese Social Sciences Press, 1989), p. 78.

76. Mao Zedong to Liu Shaoqi, January 25, 1950, *MWG*, 1: 252; Shi Zhe, *Zai lishi jüren shenbian*, pp. 445–446.

77. Mao Zedong to Liu Shaoqi, January 25, 1950, *MWG*, 1: 252; Wu Xiuquan, *Wangshi cangsang*, pp. 184–85; and Shi Zhe, *Zai lishi jüren shenbian*, p. 448.

78. Mao Zedong to the CCP Central Committee, January 3, 1950, *MWG*, 1: 213; see also Wu Xiuquan, *Wangshi cangsang*, pp. 186–88. According to Shi Zhe's memoirs, during one meeting between Mao, Zhou and Stalin, Zhou mentioned that the Chinese believed it necessary to issue a statement about the status of Outer Mongolia. Stalin immediately became nervous, saying that the status of Mongolia was a settled matter. Zhou then made it clear that he meant that the Chinese government needed to issue a statement to recognize Mongolia's independence. Stalin was greatly relived with Zhou's suggestion. See Shi Zhe, *Zai lishi jüren shenbian*, p. 450.

79. *Zhonghua renmin gongheguo duiwai guanxi wenjianji, 1949–1950*, pp. 75–76. The English translation here is from Grant Rhode and Reid Whitlock, *Treaties of the People's Republic of China, 1949–1978* (Boulder, CO: Westview Press, 1980), 15b.

80. Simmons has suggested that the Chinese were disappointed with the

amount and condition of the Soviet loan (Simmons, *The Strained Alliance*, pp. 72–73). New Chinese sources, however, point to something different. According to Shi Zhe, for example, the Chinese actually did not ask for a larger loan from the Soviets because Mao believed that it was not good for China to borrow too much money from abroad, even from a friendly country. Interviews with Shi Zhe, August 1992.

81. Wang Dinglie et al., *Dangdai zhongguo kongjun*, pp. 79–80; Han and Tan et al., *Dangdai zhongguo jundui*, 2: 155.

82. Han and Tan et al., *Dangdai zhongguo jundui*, 2: 161; Wang Dinglie, *Dangdai zhongguo kongjun*, pp. 78–79, 110; Lin Fu et al., *Kongjun shi*, pp. 53–54; see also Mao Zedong to Liu Shaoqi, Feburary 17, 1950, *MJWJ*, 6: 76.

83. According to Shi Zhe's recollections, on his way back to Beijing, Mao mentioned several times that he now felt much stronger in the face of the threat from imperialist countries. Interviews with Shi Zhe, August 1992.

84. *Renmin ribao*, February 20, 1950; see also *MWG*, 1: 266–67.

85. *Zhonghua renmin gongheguo duiwai guanxi wenjianji, 1949–1950*, p. 81.

86. Zhou Enlai, "International Situation and Diplomatic Tasks after the Signing of the Sino-Soviet Treaty," *ZWJWX*, pp. 11–17.

87. Mao Zedong's address to the Sixth Session of the Central People's Government Council, April 11, 1950, *MWG*, 1: 291.

88. Nikita Khrushchev, *Khrushchev Remembers*, trans. by Strobe Talbott (Boston: Little, Brown, 1970); Khruschchev, *Khrushchev Remembers: The Glasnost Tapes,* trans. and ed. by Jerrold L. Schecter with Vyacheslav V. Luchkov (Boston: Little, Brown, 1990); and Khruschchev, "Truth about the Korean War: Memoirs," *Far Eastern Affairs*, no. 1 (1991): 63–69.

89. The quotation is from a new version of Khrushchev's recollections of the Korean War, which was first published in Russian and then published in English in *Far Eastern Affairs*. As Merrill has shown in his *Korea: The Peninsula Origins of the War*, the part related to the Korean War in *Khrushchev Remembers* had serious omissions compared with the original Russian tapes. The new version of Khrushchev's recollections of the Korean War contains much more information than *Khrushchev Remembers*. I will use the transcript of this version in my discussion and will compare it with Merrill's findings.

90. See *Khrushchev Remembers*, pp. 371–772, and the discussion about Zhou's visit to the Soviet Union in October 1950 in chapter 7. See also Chen Jian, "The Sino-Soviet Alliance and China's Entry into the Korean War," working paper no. 1 published by the Woodrow Wilson Center's Cold War History Project, Washington, D.C., 1991, p. 21.

91. For brief discussions of this visit, see Bruce Cumings, *The Origins of the Korean War*, 2 vols.(Princeton: Princeton University Press, 1981, 1990), 2: 344–345; Merrill, *Korea: the Peninsular Origins of the War*, pp. 143–144, and Goncharov, et al., *Uncertain Partners*, p. 137. Using South Korean intel-

ligence reports, Merrill points out that the North Koreans and the Soviets signed a secret military agreement during Kim's visit, according to which Moscow made significant commitment to the expansion of the North Korean military machine.

92. The Staff of Soviet Foreign Ministry, "Background Report on the Korean War," trans. by Kathryn Weathersby, *The Journal of American-East Asian Relations*, 2, no. 4 (Fall 1993): 441; Sergei Goncharov, "Origins and the Outbreak of the Korean War: New Archival Material on the Still Uncertain Period, Beginning of 1949-June 1950" (a paper presented to a Norwegian Nobel Institute Seminar on "The Sino-Soviet Alliance and the War in Korea," March 15–16, 1993), pp. 2–4.

93. In his testimony, Yu Song-chol recalled that when "in China the People's Liberation Army had just finished driving the Kuomintang [Guomindang] from the mainland, unifying the country. . . . there was an envy among the KPA's hierarchy over this fact." This, together with other factors, made the North Korean Communists believe that "the time [was] ripe for war." Yu Song-chol, "My Testimony," *Foreign Broadcast Information Service*, December 27, 1990, p. 25. See also Cumings, *The Origins of the Korean War*, 2: 370.

94. For plausible discussions on guerrilla activities in South Korea during this period, see Merrill, *Korea: The Peninsula Origins of the War*, chapters 5 and 6; Cumings, *The Origins of the Korean War*, vol. 2, chapters 7, 8, and 12.

95. Goncharov, "Origins and the Outbreak of the Korean War," pp. 3–28. Goncharov's investigation of Russian archival sources shows that Kim Il-sung did not visit Moscow in November or December 1949 as alleged by Khrushchev, but he did constantly try to get Stalin's support for his plans to unify Korea by military means. One Chinese source, though, citing the "Russian archival materials that were handed to China in late 1993," indicates that Kim Il-sung was in Moscow from mid-December 1949 to, probably, late January 1950, and that it was during this visit that he convinced Stalin of the feasibility of his plans to invade the South. Author's correspondence with a Chinese researcher with access to archival sources, November 1993.

96. Khrushchev, "The Truth of Korean War," p. 162. Merrill points out that in the original tape of Khrushchev's memoirs, his description of Mao's response to Stalin's inquiries about the possibility of American intervention was "much more hesitant and tenuous." The transcript of this part of the tape reads: "He (Stalin) asked him (Mao) what he thought about the essence behind such an action. In my opinion, to both issues Mao answered with approval—that is he approved Kim Il-sung's proposal, and also expressed the opinion that the United States wouldn't interfere in an internal matter which the Korean people would decide for themselves." (Merrill, *Korea: The Peninsula Origins of the War*, pp. 26–27)

97. Chen Boda became China's number four figure during the Cultural

Revolution in the late 1960s. But he lost Mao's trust in 1970 and was then arrested. In 1980 he was sentenced to twenty-year imprisonment but was quickly paroled because of illness. Before his death in 1989, he had several interviews with researchers, and he offered this version of the story. See Zhu Jianrong, *Mao Zedong's Korean War: China Crosses the Yalu* (in Japanese), (Tokyo: Iwanami Book Store, 1991), pp. 25–26. I wish to thank Ms. Tokiko Sakuragawa for helping translate portions of Zhu's book.

98. Hao and Zhai, "China's Decision to Enter the Korean War," p. 100.

99. Interviews with Shi Zhe, August 1992. This part of Shi Zhe's recollections is not included in his *Zai lishi jüren shenbian*—it was omitted because of the sensitivity of the problem. A careful reader of Shi's published memoirs will find that in the name glossary following the chapter covering Mao's visit to the Soviet Union there is a listing for "Kim Il-sung," but nowhere in the chapter can the reader find any discussion about Kim.

100. Kim Kwang-hyop was then commander of the KPA's Second Division, who would later play a key role in the KPA's southbound march. For his career, see Robert Scalapino and Lee Chong-sik, *Communism in Korea*, 2 vols. (Berkeley and Los Angeles: University of California Press, 1972), 2: 997–998.

101. Nie Rongzhen, *Nie Rongzhen huiyilu*, pp. 743–744.

102. Ibid., p. 744. Interviews with Beijing's military researchers suggest that 23,000 Korean-nationality soldiers returned to Korea in spring 1950, much higher than the figure offered by Nie Rongzhen. These soldiers came from the 156th division and other units of the PLA's Fourth Field Army and were later organized as the Korean People's Army's 7th Division. This number is also much closer to figures given by Cumings in *The Origins of the Korean War*, 2: 363, which is based on South Korean and American intelligence sources.

103. Su Yu, "Report on the Problem of Liberating Taiwan," January 5, 1950, and "Report on Liberating Taiwan and Establishing Military Forces," January 27, 1950, CCA. see also Zhou Enlai, "International situation and Diplomatic Tasks after the Signing of the Sino-Soviet Treaty," *ZWJWX*, pp. 12–14.

104. Goncharov, "Origins and the Outbreak of the Korean War," p. 33; Weathersby, "The Soviet Role in the Early Phase of the Korean War," p. 432.

4. TAIWAN, INDO-CHINA, AND KOREA: BEIJING'S
CONFRONTATION WITH THE U.S. ESCALATES

1. Su Yu, "Instructions on East China Military Region's Political Affairs in 1950," cited in Xu Yan, *Jinmen zhizhan* (The battles of Jinmen, Beijing: Chinese Broadcasting and Television Press, 1992), p. 117; Su Yu, "Report on the Problem of Liberating Taiwan," January 5, 1950, and "Report on

Liberating Taiwan and Establishing Military Forces," January 27, 1950, CCA; Zhou Enlai, "International situation and Diplomatic Tasks after the Signing of the Sino-Soviet Treaty," *ZWJWX*, pp. 12–14.

2. Yao Xu, *Cong yalujiang dao banmendian*, p. 21; He Long, "Speech at Battalion-level Officers of the 60th Army," *He Long junshi wenxuan* (Selected Military Papers of He Long, Beijing: People's Liberation Army Press, 1989), p. 473; and Zhou Enlai, "International Situation and Diplomatic Tasks after the Signing of the Sino-Soviet Treaty," *ZWJWX*, pp. 14, 16.

3. See, for examples, Du Ruo, "China's Liberation and the Southeast Asia"; "China's Revolution and the Struggle against Colonialism," *People's China*, February 16, 1950, pp. 4–5; Huang Caoliang, *Zhanhou shijie xinxingshi* (New Situation of the Postwar World, Shanghai, 1950); and Lu Dingyi, "The Worldwide significance of the Chinese Revolution," *Lu Dingyi wenji*, pp. 432–439.

4. For a good discussion, see He Di, "The Last Campaign to Unify China: The CCP's Unmaterialized Plan to Liberate Taiwan, 1949–1950," *Chinese Historians*, 5, no. 1 (Spring 1992): 1–2.

5. See Yao Xu, *Cong yalujiang dao banmendian*, pp. 21–22.

6. Deng Lifeng, *Xin Zhongguo junshi huodong jishi, 1949–1959* (A Factual Record of the New China's Military Affairs, Beijing: CCP Historical Materials Press, 1989), p. 97; The CCP Central Committee's instructions on the demobilization of military forces, April 21, 1950, *MWG*, 1: 310–311; Nie Rongzhen, "Report on Military Affairs to the Second Session of the First People's Consultative Council," June 1950, *Zhonggong dangshi jiaoxue cankao ziliao*, 19: 163; see also discussions in Whiting, *China Crosses the Yalu*, pp. 17–18.

7. See, for example, Qi Dexue, *Chaoxian zhanzheng juece neimu*, p. 21; and Xu Yan, *Diyici jiaoliang*, pp. 12–13; and Goncharov et al., *Uncertain Patners*, pp. 148–149..

8. Nie Rongzhen, "Report on the Restructuring and Demobilization of the Military forces," *Nie Rongzhen junshi wenxuan* (Selected Military Works of Nie Rongzhen, Beijing: People's Liberation Army Press, 1992), p. 340; see also Xu Yan, *Diyici jiaoliang*, p. 13.

9. Nie Rongzhen, "Report on the Restructuring and Demobilization of the Military forces," *Nie Rongzhen junshi wenxuan*, p. 340.

10. Ibid., pp. 340–341; see also Deng Lifeng, *Xin Zhongguo junshi huodong jishi*, p. 101.

11. Zhu De's speech at the PLA's staff conference, May 16, 1950, Wang Xianli and Li Ping, et al, *Zhu De nianpu* (A Chronology of Zhu De, Beijing: People's Press, 1986), p. 344; see also Deng Lifeng, *Xin Zhongguo junshi huodong jishi*, p. 101.

12. In fact, in the winter and spring of 1949–1950, the CCP leadership

made great efforts to develop the PRC's newly established air force and navy. See, for examples, Wang Dinglie et al., *Dangdai zhongguo kongjun*, pp. 78–79; and Yang Guoyu, *Dangdai zhongguo haijun*, chapter 2.

13. Nie Rongzhen, "Report on the Restructuring and Demobilization of the Military forces," *Nie Rongzhen junshi wenxuan*, p. 341; see also Zhu De's speech at the PLA's staff conference on May 16, 1950, *Zhu De nianpu*, p. 344.

14. Du Ping, *Zai zhiyuanjun zongbu*, pp. 7, 11–12; Jiang Yonghui, *38jun zai chaoxian* (The 38th Army in Korea, Shenyang: Liaoning People's Press, 1989), p. 1; Chen Xiaolu, "China's Policy toward the United States, 1949–1955," p. 186; and Yao Xu, "The Brilliant Decision to Resist America and Assist Korea," *Dangshi yanjiu*, no. 5, 1980, p. 7.

15. See He Di, "The Last Campaign to Unify China, " p. 2; and Whiting, *China Crosses the Yalu*, p. 21.

16. "Chinese People are Determined to Liberate Taiwan," *Renmin ribao*, March 15, 1949.

17. Xu Yan, *Jinmen zhizhan*, pp. 91–92; Yang Dezhi, *Weile heping*, pp. 5–6.

18. Mao Zedong to Su Yu, Zhang Zhen, Zhou Jingming, and the CCP East China Bureau, June 14, 1949, *Dangde wenxian*, no. 2 (1990): 48–49.

19. Mao Zedong to Su Yu, Zhang Zhen, Zhou Jingming, and the CCP East China Bureau, June 21, 1949, cited from He Di, "The Last Campaign to Unify China," pp. 1–2; see also *MNP*, 3: 519..

20. Mao Zedong to Zhou Enlai, July 10, 1949, cited from Wang Dinglie et al., *Dangdai zhongguo kongjun*, p. 35. See also Li and Fang et al., *Zhou Enlai nianpu*, p. 833

21. Lü Liping, *Tongtian zhilu*, p. 143; Wang Dinglie et al., *Dangdai zhongguo kongjun*, p. 35.

22. Lü Liping, *Tongtian zhilu*, pp. 156–159; Han and Tan et al., *Dangdai zhongguo jundui*, 2: 160–161; Yang Guoyu et al., *Dangdai zhongguo haijun*, p. 48.

23. Xu Yan, *Jinmen zhizhan*, pp. 39–40, 42; Ye Fei, *Ye Fei huiyilu* (Ye Fei's Memoirs, Beijing: People's Liberation Army Press, 1988), pp. 588–589.

24. Mao Zedong and the CMC to all Field Armies, May 23, 1949, *MJWX*, pp. 337–338; and *MJWJ, 5:591*; see also Ye Fei, *Ye Fei huiyilu*, pp. 571–572; Xu Yan, *Jinmen zhizhan*, pp. 20–23.

25. For the CCP's accounts of the PLA's Jinmen defeat, see Ye Fei, *Ye Fei huiyilu*, pp. 597–609; Han and Tan et al., *Dangdai zhongguo jundui de junshi gongzuo*, 1: 233–237; Mo and Yao et al., *Zhongguo renmin jiefangjun zhanshi*, 3: 340–341; Deng Lifeng, *Xin zhongguo junshi huodong jishi*, p. 10; for a Nationalist account of the Jinmen battle, see Di Zongheng, *Toushi taihai zhanshi* (Battles in the Taiwan Strait, Taipei: Lianfeng Book Store, 1985), pp. 41–80.

26. For the CCP's accounts of the Dengbu battle, see Han and Tan et al., *Dangdai zhongguo jundui*, 1: 249–251; Mo and Yao et al., *Zhongguo renmin jiefangjun zhanshi*, 3: 341; for a Nationalist account of the Dengbu battle, see Di Zongheng, *Toushi taihai zhanshi*, pp. 81–100.

27. Mao Zedong, "A Circular by the CMC about the Lessons of the Jinmen Defeat," October 29, 1949, *MWG*, 1: 100–101.

28. Mao Zedong to Su Yu, Tang Liang, Zhang Zhen, Zhou Jingming and others, November 3, 1949, ibid., p. 118.

29. Mao Zedong to Su Yu, November 14, 1949, ibid., p. 137.

30. Xiao Jinguang, *Xiao Jinguang huiyilu*, 2 vols. (The Memoirs of Xiao Jinguang, Beijing: People's Liberation Army Press, 1988 and 1989), 2: 2–3.

31. Mao Zedong to Lin Biao, December 18 and December 31, 1949, *MWG*, 1: 190–191, 203.

32. Zhou Jun, "A Preliminary Exploration of Reasons for the People's Liberation Army's Abortive Plan to Attack Taiwan after the Formation of the People's Republic," *Zhonggong dangshi yanjiu*, no. 1 (1991): 68.

33. Ibid., p. 68; see also He Di, "The Last Campaign to Unify China," p. 7.

34. Mao Zedong to Su Yu, December 5, 1949, *MWG*, 1: 179.

35. For detailed discussions of the CCP's changing attitudes toward setting up a deadline for the Taiwan campaign in the winter and spring of 1950, see He Di, "The Last Campaign to Unify China," pp. 7–12; and Xu Yan, *Jinmen zhizhan*, pp. 117–128.

36. Mao Zedong to Zhang Zhizhong, March 11, 1950, *MWG*, 1: 271.

37. Xu Yan, *Jinmen zhizhan*, pp. 135–136; Yang Dezhi, *Weile heping*, pp. 5–6

38. Xiao Jinguang, *Xiao Jinguang huiyilu*, 2: 8–9, 26–27.

39. Su Yu, "Report on the Problem of Liberating Taiwan," January 5, 1950, CCA; see also He Di, "The Last Campaign to Unify China," pp. 7–8.

40. Su Yu, "Report on the Problem of Liberating Taiwan and Establishing Military Forces," January 27, 1950, CCA; see also He Di, "The Last Campaign to Unify China," p. 8.

41. For a Chinese account of Ho Chi Minh's connection with the Chinese Communist revolution from the 1920s to early 1940s, see Huang Zheng, *Hu Zhiming he zhongguo* (Ho Chi Minh and China, Beijing: People's Liberation Army Press, 1987), chapters 1–4; see also Hoang Van Hoan, *Canghai yisu: Hoang Van Hoan geming huiyilu* (A Drop in the Ocean: Hoang Van Hoan's Revolutionary Reminiscences, Beijing: People's Liberation Army Press, 1987), chapters 3 and 4.

42. The Indochina Communist Party was established in 1930 but after February 1951 its name was changed to Vietnamese Workers' Party.

43. Hoang, *Canghai yisu*, pp. 247–253. Hoang later became the first DRV

ambassador to the PRC, defected to China in the late 1970s and died there in 1991.

44. Luo Guibo, "Comrade Liu Shaoqi Sent Me to Vietnam," in He Jingxiu and others, eds., *Mianhuai Liu Shaoqi* (In Commemoration of Liu Shaoqi, Beijing: The Central Press of Historical Documents, 1988), pp. 233–234; interview with Luo Guibo, August 22, 1992.

45. Mao Zedong to Liu Shaoqi, January 17 and 18, 1950, *MWG*, 1: 238–239; see also Zhou Enlai's statement of recognizing the Democratic Republic of Vietnam, January 18, 1950, *Xinhua yuebao*, 2, no. 2 (1950): 847; Hoang, *Canghai yisu*, pp. 255–256; *Renmin ribao*, February 7, 1950.

46. According to Luo Guibo, the Vietnamese Communists were unable to maintain regular telegraphic communication with the CCP Central Committee before Luo's arrival in Vietnam in March 1950 because their radio transmitter was too weak. Interview with Luo Guibo, August 22, 1992.

47. Luo Guibo, "Comrade Liu Shaoqi Sent Me to Vietnam," pp. 234–235; Qian Jiang, *Zai Shenmi de zhanzheng zhong: Zhongguo junshi guwentuan fu yuenan zhengzhan ji* (In the Course of a Mysterious War: Chinese Military Advisory Group in Vietnam, Zhengzhou: Henan People's Press, 1992), pp. 14–16; see also Hoang, *Canghai yisu*, pp. 254–256 (In his memoir, Hoang recalls that Mao held a banquet in Ho's honor after Ho reached Beijing. As Mao was then in Moscow, it was impossible for Mao to do this. Hoang's memory is confusing here); the Editorial Group of the History of the Chinese Military Advisory Group, *Zhongguo guwentuan yuanyue kangmei douzheng shishi* (A Factual History of the Chinese Military Advisory Group in the Struggle of Assisting Vietnam and Resisting France, Beijing: People's Liberation Army Press, 1990), pp. 1–2; Han Nianlong et al., *Dangdai zhongguo waijiao*, p. 55.

48. Hoang, *Canghai yisu*, pp. 254–255; Huang Zheng, *Ho Chi Minh and China*, p. 125.

49. Luo Guibo, "Comrade Liu Shaoqi Sent Me to Vietnam," p. 235; Hoang, *Canghai yisu*, pp. 254–255.

50. For a summarized analysis of Stalin's attitude toward Ho Chi Minh and the Viet Minh in the early period of the First Indochina War, see Gary Hess, *Vietnam and the United States: Origins and Legacy of War* (Boston: Twayne Publishers, 1990), p. 37. For Stalin's attitude toward Ho during Ho's visit to Moscow, see Li Ke, "Chinese Military Advisors in the War to Assist Vietnam and Resist France," *Junshi lishi* (Military History), no. 3, 1989, p. 27; Qian Jiang, *Zai Shenmi de zhanzheng zhong*, pp. 16–18; Wu Xiuquan, *Huiyi yu huainian* (Recollections and Commemorations, Beijing: CCP Central Academy Press, 1991), pp. 242–243; and Xu Yan, "An Outstanding History of Extinguishing the War Flame in Indochina," *Dangde wenxian*, no. 5, (1992): 20.

51. Huang Zheng, *Ho Chi Minh and China*, pp. 125–126; Hoang, *Canghai yisu*, pp. 254–255; Han and Tan et al., *Dangdai zhongguo jundui*, 1: 520, 576.

52. From late 1949 to early 1951, Mao and Chinese military planners paid close attention to the annihilation of remnant Nationalist troops in areas adjacent to the Vietnamese border. See Mo and Yao et al., *Zhongguo renmin jiefangjun zhanshi*, 3: 394–398.

53. Luo Guibo, "Comrade Liu Shaoqi Sent Me to Vietnam," p. 238; interview with Luo Guibo, August 22, 1992.

54. Han and Tan et al., *Dangdai zhongguo jundui*, 1: 518–519; the Editorial Group, *Zhongguo guwentuan yuanyue kangmei douzheng shishi*, p. 3.

55. The Editorial Group, *Zhongguo guwentuan yuanyue kangmei douzheng shishi*, p. 3.

56. The CCP's earlier interests in Korea were demonstrated by an order issued by Zhu De, commander-in-chief of CCP military forces, at the end of the Second World War. On August 11, 1945, Zhu De ordered "the Korean Volunteer Army, which were now fighting against the Japanese in Northern China, to follow the Eighth Route Army and units of former Northeast Army to march toward the Northeast." See "The Sixth Order of the Yanan Headquarters," August 11, 1945, *ZYWJXJ*, 13: 121.

57. For a recent Chinese account of Korean Communists in China in the 1920s, see Yang Zhaoquan, *Zhongchao guanxi lunwenji* (Essays on Sino-Korean Relations, Beijing: World Affairs Press, 1988), pp. 220–231.

58. For a Chinese account of Kim Il-sung's connection with the Chinese Anti-Japanese United Army in the 1930s and early 1940s, see Ibid., pp. 392–428; see also Cumings, *The Origins of the Korean War*, 2: 351–352.

59. Zhao Nanqi and Wen Zhengyi, "The Korean Nationality People's Contribution to the War of Liberation in the Northeast," in Wu Xiuquan et al., *Liaoshen zhanyi*, 2 vols. (The Liaoshen Campaign, Beijing: People's Press, 1992), 2: 384–405; Xu Yan, *Diyici jiaoliang*, p. 21; see also Cumings, *The Origins of the Korean War*, 2: 358–359, 363.

60. The CCP Central Committee's order on "Maintaining Defensive in the South and Waging Offensive in the North," September 19, 1945, *ZYWJXJ* (internal version), 13: 147–148. This document is not included in *ZYWJXJ*'s 18-volume open version.

61. The CMC to the CCP Northeast Bureau, September 28, 1945; The CCP Central Committee to the CCP Northeast Bureau, October 2, 1945, CCA; see also Ding Xuesong et al., "Recalling the Northeast Bureau's Special Office in North Korea During the War of Liberation in the Northeast," *Zhonggong dangshi ziliao*, no. 17 (March 1986): 198.

62. Mo and Yao et al., *Zhongguo renmin jiefangjun zhanshi*, 3: 92–93; Liu Wenxin and Li Yueqing, *Zhou Baozhong zhuan* (The Biography of Zhou Baozhong, Harbin: Helongjiang People's Press, 1987), pp. 282–283.

63. Ding Xuesong et al., "Recalling the Northeast Bureau's Special Office in North Korea," pp. 198, 201.

64. Ibid., p. 198; and Chen Mu and Zhang Wenjia, "Zhu Lizhi," in Hu Hua, et al., *Zhonggong dangshi renwu zhuan*, 50 vols. (A Collection of Biographies of CCP Historical Figures, Xian: Shaanxi People's Press, 1991), 48: 235–236.

65. Cumings, *The Origins of the Korean War*, 2: 358.

66. Ding Xuesong et al., "Recalling the Northeast Bureau's Special Office in North Korea," p. 201.

67. Ibid., pp. 202–203; and Chen and Zhang, "Zhu Lizhi," p. 236.

68. Cumings, *The Origins of the Korean War*, 2: 358.

69. Interviews with Hu Guangzheng, a researcher at Beijing's Academy of Military Science, May 1991.

70. Ding Xuesong, "Recalling the Northeast Bureau's Special Office in North Korea," p. 204; and Chen and Zhang, "Zhu Lizhi," pp. 236–237. Cumings's study, which is largely based on American intelligence reports, points out that North Korean rail network was devoted to the movement of CCP troops and that "most of the output of the big Hungnam explosive plant was shipped to China." See Cumings, *The Origins of the Korean War*, 2: 358–359.

71. In Chai Chengwen's memoirs, he mentions that when he was sent by Zhou Enlai to North Korea in July 1950, Zhou specifically emphasized that the North Korean Communists offered tremendous support to the Chinese Communist forces in the Northeast during China's civil war, so that the CCP "would do our best to support the Korean comrades if they so ask." See Chai and Zhao, *Banmendian tanpan*, p. 40.

72. Cumings, *The Origins of the Korean War*, 2: 350.

73. The Editorial Committee of the War History under the Ministry of Defense of Korea, comp., *History of the Korean War* (in Korean), 1: 689; Piou Doufu (Pak Tu-bok), *Zhonggong canjia chaozhan yuanying zhi yanjiu* (A Study of the CCP's Participation in the Korean War, Taipei, publisher unclear, 1975), pp. 65–66; for a brief biographical note of Pang Ho-san, see Cumings, *The Origins of the Korean War*, 2: 361.

74. *Zhongyang ribao* (The Central Daily, official newspaper of the GMD government), May 5, 1949; Pak Tu-bok, *Zhonggong canjia chaozhan yuanying zhi yanjiu*, pp. 60–61. See also Simmons, *The Strained Alliance*, p. 32; Cumings, *The Origins of the Korean War*, 2: 359.

75. Yao Xu, a former intelligence officer of the Chinese Volunteers in the Korean War, is the author of *Cong yalujiang dao banmendian*, the first Chinese monograph on China's participation in the Korean War, and several other articles about the Korean War. In my telephone interview with him on May 27, 1991, he stated that he had never heard of the existence of this

agreement; he also claimed that Zhou Baozhong, one alleged participant of the discussion leading to the agreement according to GMD sources, was then not in the Northwest but in the South. However, other sources indicate that Zhou did not leave the Northeast until September 1949.

76. Interviews with Hu Guangzheng and Xu Yan, May 1991.

77. South Korean and American intelligence sources have long maintained that between 30,000 and 40,000 Korean PLA soldiers were sent back to Korea from July to October 1949 (for a good summary of South Korean and American sources covering this movement, see Cumings, *The Origins of the Korean War*, 2: 363, 838, n. 33). The account about the two PLA divisions' return follows the Military Library of the Academy of Military Science, eds., *Zhongguo renmin jiefangjun zuzhi he geji lingdao chengyuan minglu* (A List of the Historical Evolution of Organizations and Leading Members of the People's Liberation Army, Beijing: Military Science Press, 1990), p. 878.

78. The number here follows interviews with Hu Guangzheng and Xu Yan in May 1991, which, interestingly, is compatible with Cumings's account based on studies of American intelligence reports. See *The Origins of the Korean War*, 2: 363.

79. For a detailed account of Kim Kwang-hyop's visit, see Nie Rongzhen, *Nie Rongzhen huiyilu*, p. 748; see also Yao Xu, *Cong yalujiang dao banmendian*, p. 10. In my interviews with Hu Guangzheng and Xu Yan in May 1991, and with Qi Dexue in August 1993, they all pointed out that the total number of Korean soldiers returned to Korea in spring 1950 was around 23,000, much higher than the number (14,000) offered by Nie Rongzhen. Their number is also much closer to that offered by Bruce Cumings in *The Origins of the Korean War* (see Cumings, *The Origins of the Korean War*, 2: 363). For reorganization of these troops in Korea, see Whiting, *China Crosses the Yalu*, p. 44.

80. Cumings, *The Origins of the Korean War*, vol. 2, chapters 11 and 12.

81. Roger Dingman, "Korea at Forty-Plus: The Origins of the Korean War Reconsidered," *The Journal of American-East Asian Relations*, 1, no. 1 (Spring 1992): 142.

82. For discussions of the factionalism within the Korean Communists, see Simmons, *The Strained Alliance*, chapter 2; Lim Un, *The Founding of a Dynasty in North Korea: An Authentic Biography of Kim Il-sung* (Tokyo, 1982), chapters 2 and 4; and Merrill, *Korea: The Peninsular Origins of the War*, pp. 44–48. Lim Un (pseud.) was a well-informed North Korean dissident living in Moscow.

83. Reportedly, in March 1950, Pak Chong-ae, a member of the Central Standing Committee of the Korean Labor Party and one of the Central Committee's secretaries, secretly visited Beijing and informed CCP leaders that the North Koreans were about to attack the South. See Zhu, *Mao*

Zedong's Korean War, pp. 30–31. No other Chinese source, though, can confirm this report.

84. Hao and Zhai, "China's Decision to Enter the Korean War," p. 100.

85. For Kim's visit to Beijing in early December 1950, see Chen Jian, "China's Changing Aims during the Korean War," *The Journal of American-East Asian Relations*, 1, no. 1 (Spring 1992): 29. Cumings, following U.S. intelligence sources, mentions that Kim visited Beijing in late October 1950 (Cumings, *The Origins of the Korean War*, 2: 740–741). No available Chinese source confirms this.

86. In my interviews with Shi Zhe in August 1992, he particularly emphasized that Mao did not know what Stalin had discussed with Kim and that Kim gave Mao the impression that he had Stalin's full support. According to Russian sources, Mao even cabled to Stalin to confirm if Stalin had given approval to Kim's plans, and Stalin's response was affirmative. Interviews with Russian historian Sergei Goncharov, March 15–17, 1993.

87. These accounts are based on my interviews with Shi Zhe and several other well-informed Chinese researchers in May 1991 and August 1992. Russian sources available now are generally compatible with these accounts. See Goncharov, "Origins and the Outbreak of the Korean War," pp. 38–41; The Staff of Soviet Foreign Ministry, "Background Report on the Korean War," *The Journal of American-East Asian Relations*, 2, no. 4 (Fall 1993): 442.

88. According to the recently released testimony by Yu Song-Chol, the North Koreans, with the direct assistance of the Soviets, completed the detailed operational plan to attack the South in May and June 1950, or in other words, after Kim's visit to Beijing. Yu makes it clear, though, that Kim might not have informed Beijing leaders of this final plan. Yu, "My Testimony," *FBIS*, December 27, 1990, p. 26; see also the Staff of Soviet Foreign Ministry, "Background Report on the Korean War," p. 442.

89. NSC 48/1, "The Position of the United States with Respect to Asia," December 23, 1949, U.S. Department of Defense, *United States-Vietnam Relations, 1945–1967* (Washington, 1971), 8: 257–258.

90. See, for examples, Editorial Note, *FRUS* (1950), 6: 21–22;

91. For the text of NSC-68, see *FRUS* (1950) 1: 237–292; for the making of NSC-68, see Warner Schilling, Paul Hammond and Glenn Snyder, *Strategy, Politics, and Defense Budgets* (New York: Columbia University Press, 1962), pp. 287–344; and Gaddis, *Strategy of Containment*, chapter 4.

92. Memo, "Summary of Discussion on China Trade Control," April 10, 1950, CA, Box 20, NA; Dean Rusk to Acheson, April 20, 1950, CA, Box 20, NA. For a plausible discussion of the subtle change of American trade policy toward China in the spring of 1950, see Qing Simei, "America's Economic Strategy toward China before the Korean War: Its Formation, Implementation, and Chinese Communists' Response" (a paper delivered at a

conference on Sino-American relations, 1945–1959, Ohio University, September 1989), especially pp. 17–18.

93. Acheson to Lewis Johnson, April 28, 1950, Acheson Papers, Box 66, HST.

94. NSC 64, "The Position of the United States with Respect to Indochina," February 27, 1950, *FRUS* (1950) 6: 745–747.

95. Johnson [Secretary of Defense] to Acheson, April 14, 1950, ibid., p. 781.

96. Gaddis, *The Long Peace*, p. 90.

97. *New York Times*, May 9, 1950, p. 1.

98. NSC 64, "The Position of the United States with Respect to Indochina," *FRUS* (1950) 6: 744–747.

99. NSC 37, "The Strategic Importance of Formosa," November 24, 1948, *FRUS* (1949) 9: 261–262.

100. State Department draft report, NSC 37/1, "The Position of the United States with Respect to Formosa," January 19, 1949, ibid., pp. 271–275.

101. Bishop memorandum, conversation with MacArthur, February 16, 1949, *FRUS* (1949) 7: 656–657.

102. NSC 37/3, "The Strategic Importance of Formosa," February 10, 1949, *FRUS* (1949) 9: 284–286.

103. Livingston Merchant to Acheson, March 23, 1949; Acheson's statement at National Security Council meeting, March 1, 1949, ibid., pp. 302–303, 294–296.

104. Memorandum of Conversation by the Secretary of State, December 19, 1949, ibid., pp. 463–467.

105. It is important to note that Truman used the phrase "at this time." Acheson explained that this "is a recognition of the fact that, in the unlikely and unhappy event that our forces might be attacked in the Far East, the United States must be completely free to take whatever action in whatever area is necessary for its own security." Acheson press conference, January 5, 1950, *Department of State Bulletin*, January 16, 1950, p. 81.

106. Gaddis, *The Long Peace*, p. 84.

107. Johnson to Acheson, February 14, 1950, Records of the Army Staff, Plans and Operations, RG 319, NA.

108. Johnson to Acheson, May 6, 1950, *FRUS* (1950) 6: 339.

109. A draft memorandum by Rusk to the Secretary of State, May 30, 1950, *FRUS* (1950) 6: 349–351.

110. MacArthur to Department of Army, May 29, 1950, cited in Peter Lowe, *The Origins of the Korean War* (Londong: Longman, 1986), p. 152.

111. Memorandum on Formosa by MacArthur, June 14, 1950, *FRUS* (1950) 7: 161–165.

112. *FRUS* (1949), 7: 969.

113. JCS 1769/1, April 29, 1947, ibid. (1947) 6: 744.

114. NSC 8/2, "The Position of the United States with Respect to Korea," March 23, 1949, ibid. (1949), 7: 975.

115. *Department of State Bulletin*, January 23, 1950, p. 116.

116. Ronald McGlothlen, "Acheson, Economics, and the American Commitment in Korea, 1947–1950," *Pacific Historical Review* 58, no. 1 (February 1989): 45–46.

117. Lowe, *The Origins of the Korean War*, pp. 158–159.

118. Russell Buhite, "Major Interests: American Policy toward China, Taiwan, and Korea, 1945–1950," *Pacific Historical Review* 47, no. 3 (August 1978).

119. Zhou Enlai, "Asia's Affairs Should be Controlled by Asian Peoples Themselves," *Renmin ribao*, March 19, 1950; see also *People's China*, 1, no. 7 (1950): 5.

5. BEIJING'S RESPONSE TO THE OUTBREAK OF THE KOREAN WAR

1. The account about Beijing leaders' schedule for June 25, 1950 is based on interviews with Shi Zhe, August 1992. It is also supported by other Chinese sources, such as Chai and Zhao, *Banmendian tanpan*, pp. 25–26.

2. The Soviet Union walked out the UN Security Council in mid-January 1950, allegedly to protest the UN's refusal to seat Communist China. Numerous Western studies, especially Simmons in *Strained Alliance*, have long argued that the real purpose of the Soviet boycott of the Security Council meetings was to prevent Beijing from taking its place in the UN. Recently released Chinese sources revealed that the Soviets discussed the decision to walk out the Security Council with Mao during his stay in Moscow. See Mao Zedong to Zhou Enlai and the CCP Central Committee, January 7, 1950, *MWG*, 1: 219–220.

3. For details of the Truman administration's response to the outbreak of the Korean conflict, see Glenn D. Paige, *The Korean Decision, June 24–30, 1950* (New York: The Free Press, 1968); Rosemary Foot, *The Wrong War: American Policy and the Dimensions of the Korean Conflict, 1950–1953*, (Ithaca: Cornell University Press, 1985), pp. 58–59; Acheson, *Present at the Creation*, pp. 248–249. For considerations underlying the decision to interfere in Korea and Taiwan, see Estimates Group, Office of Intelligence Research, Department of State, "Korea," June 25, 1950, *FRUS* (1950), 7: 148–154. For Truman's statement, see ibid., p. 203. For UN resolutions, see ibid., pp. 155–156, 211. For a different interpretation arguing that the Truman administration reluctantly adopted a policy of direct military intervention in

Korea, see James Irving Matray, *The Reluctant Crusade: American Foreign Policy in Korea, 1941–1950* (Honolulu: University of Hawaii Press, 1985).

4. For a plausible discussion about U.S. policy toward Korea in the late 1940s and its position in U.S. Far Eastern strategy, see Stueck, *The Road to Confrontation*, chapters 1, 3, and 5; and Gaddis, *The Long Peace*, pp. 94–101; see also discussions in chapter 4.

5. Stueck, *The Road to Confrontation*, pp. 196–98; and Schaller, *The American Occupation of Japan*, pp. 76, 273–274.

6. For plausible discussions of the subtle change in U.S. Far Eastern strategy from late 1949 to early 1950, see Gaddis, *Strategies of Containment*, chapter 4; and Chang, *Friends and Enemies*, pp. 69–76.

7. For the GMD's response to Truman's decision to neutralize the Taiwan Strait, see Gu Weijun (Wellington Koo), *Gu Weijun huiyilu*, 13 vols. (Wellington Koo's Memoirs, Beijing: Zhonghua Book Store, 1989) 8: 3–12; Liang Jintun (Chin-tang Liang), "Chinese-American Relations during the Korean War," *Zhongmei guanxi lunwenji* (Essays on Chinese-American Relations, Taipei: The United Publishing House, 1982), pp. 210–216.

8. According to Shi Zhe, in late June Mao was very much worried about if the North Koreans would be able to handle the situation in the face of direct American military intervention. Interviews with Shi Zhe, August 1992.

9. For typical Beijing "propaganda" about the connection between the U.S. invasion of Korea and the threat to China's security based on the analysis of Japan's aggression against China's Northeast in history, see Hu Sheng, "How Did the United States Invade China in History," *Shishi shouce* (Current Affairs Handbook), no. 3 (1950). See also Zhou Enlai, "Resisting U. S. Aggression, Assisting Korea and Defending Peace," *ZWJWX*, p. 31.

10. Chai and Zhao, *Banmendian tanpan*, pp. 35–36. Zhou's view expressed here was widely shared by CCP cadres and PLA commanders, who believed that the United States had a broad plan of aggression against China. See Jiang Yonghui, *38jun zai chaoxian*, pp. 8–9; Yang Dezhi, *Weile heping*, pp. 7–8; Du Ping, *Zai zhiyuanjun zongbu*, pp. 12–13. Zhou himself would repeat the same argument on many other occasions, see, for example, Zhou Enlai, "Resisting U. S. Aggression, Assisting Korea and Defending Peace," *ZWJWX*, p. 29.

11. See Zhu Jianrong, *Mao Zedong's Korean War*, pp. 64–65.

12. Hu Sheng et al., *Zhongguo gongchandang de qishinian*, pp. 313–314.

13. Ibid., p. 328.

14. Chai and Zhao, *Banmendian tanpan*, p. 31.

15. The General Information Agency, "Instructions on the Propaganda of the U. S. Imperialists' Open Interference with the Internal Affairs of China, Korea, Vietnam and other Countries," June 29, 1950, the Research Department of the Xinhua News Agency, eds., *Xinhuashe wenjian ziliao huibian*, 2: 50.

16. In fact, Zhou Enlai clearly expressed this idea at a CCP Politburo meeting in early August 1950. See Bo Yibo, *Ruogan zhongda juece*, p. 43.

17. For a discussion of the intricate cooperation between Kim Il-sung's North Korean Communists and the CCP, see Cumings, *The Origins of the Korean War*, vol.2, chapter 11; see also discussions in chapter 4.

18. Shen and Meng et al., *Zhongguo renmin zhiyuanjun kangmei yuanchao zhanshi*, p. 7.

19. For Mao Zedong's address, see *Zhonghua renmin gongheguo duiwai guanxi wenjianji, 1949–1950*, p. 130; for Zhou Enlai's, see *ZWJWX*, pp. 18–19.

20. Xiao Jinguang, *Xiao Jinguang huiyilu*, 2: 8, 26. What is noticeable is that Zhou Enlai mentioned here that the demobilization plan would continue. This was probably because top Beijing leaders, impressed by the rapid progress of the North Koreans during the first days of the conflict, were uncertain to what extent the United States would be militarily involved in Korea and thus did not consider at this moment sending Chinese troops to Korea. As we will see, however, this approach will quickly change along with the gradual American military involvement in Korea.

21. Yang Guoyu et al., *Dangdai zhongguo haijun*, p. 41.

22. Han and Tan et al., *Dangdai zhongguo jundui*, 1: 384–385; Ye Fei, *Ye Fei huiyilu*, pp. 613–614;

23. Zhou Jun, "The Party Central Committee's Decision on the Strategic Transition from the War of Liberation to the War to Resist America and Assist Korea," *Dangshi yanjiu ziliao*, no.4, (1992): 15; and He Di, "The Last Campaign to Unify China," p. 15.

24. The CMC to Chen Yi, August 11, 1950, cited from He Di, "The Last Campaign to Unify China," p. 15; see also Zhou Jun, "The Strategic Change from the War of Liberation to the War to Resist America and Assist Korea," p. 15.

25. Zhou Jun, "The Strategic Change from the War of Liberation to the War to Resist America and Assist Korea," p. 15; He Di, "The Last Campaign to Unify China," p. 15; Ye Fei, *Ye Fei huiyilu*, p. 614; Shen and Meng et al., *Zhongguo renmin zhiyuanjun kangmei yuanchao zhanshi*, p. 8; and Deng Lifeng, *Xin zhongguo junshi huodong jishi*, p. 123.

26. Han and Tan et al., *Dangdai zhongguo jundui*, 1: 519–520; The Editorial Group, *Zhongguo guwentuan yuanyue kangmei douzheng shishi*, pp. 5–6; Qian Jiang, *Zai shenmi de zhanzheng zhong*, pp. 50–61.

27. Han and Tan et al., *Dangdai zhongguo jundui*, 1: 520; the Editorial Group, *Zhongguo guwentuan yuanyue kangmei douzheng shishi*, p. 4. For a more detailed discussion of the CMAG's activities in Vietnam, see Chen Jian, "China and the First Indo-China War," *The China Quarterly*, no.133 (March 1993): 85–110.

28. Xu Peilan and Zheng Pengfei, *Chen Geng jiangjun zhuan* (A Biogra-

phy of General Chen Geng, Beijing: People's Liberation Army Press, 1988), pp. 580–581; Mu Xin, *Chen Geng dajiang* (General Chen Geng, Beijing: People's Liberation Army Press, 1988), pp. 581–599.

29. Qian Jiang, *Zai shenmi de zhanzheng zhong*, p. 63.

30. Han and Tan et al., *Dangdai zhongguo jundui*, 1: 522–523; the Editorial Group, *Zhongguo guwentuan yuanyue kangmei douzheng shishi*, pp. 15–16; Deng Lifeng, *Xin zhongguo junshi huodong jishi*, pp. 115–116.

31. The Editorial Group, *Zhongguo guwentuan yuanyue kangmei douzheng shishi*, pp. 44–46; Mu Xin, *Chen Geng dajiang*, pp. 590–93.

32. For a more detailed discussion of China's connection with the Border Campaign, see Chen Jian, "China and the First Indo-China War," pp. 93–95; see also Han and Tan et al., *Dangdai zhongguo jundui*, 1: 521–527; the Editorial Gruop, *Zhongguo guwentuan yuanyue kangmei douzheng shishi*, pp. 13–25.

33. Chen Geng, *Chen Geng riji*, 2: 6–7.

34. Shen and Meng et al., *Zhongguo renmin zhiyuanjun kangmei yuanchao zhanshi*, p. 7; Chen Yun, "Policies toward Financial Affairs with the Movement to Resist America and Assist Korea," *Chen Yun wengao xuanbian*, p. 99. See also "Minutes of the Conference to Examine and Discuss the Preparations of the Northeast Border Defense Army, 5:00 PM, August 26, 1950," CCA.

35. In my interviews with Shi Zhe in August 1992, he recalled that not until three days after the outbreak of the Korean War did Kim Il-Sung send a field grade officer to Beijing to inform Mao and other Beijing leaders that the North Koreans were taking military actions "to fulfill the tasks of the Korean revolution and to unify the entire country." According to Shi, Mao was told that it was the South Koreans who first started the attack and that only then did the North Koreans decide to make an overall counterattack. Mao, however, was not convinced by such a story. Shi recalled that in one talk between himself and Mao in late June or early July, Mao commented that Kim was really "too smart a person," and that the North Koreans might meet big trouble in the future.

36. The Chinese did not establish their embassy in Pyongyang until mid-July 1950, although the PRC and the North Korean Communist regime had established diplomatic relations as early as October 1949.

37. Chai and Zhao, *Banmendian tanpan*, p. 36.

38. Ibid., p. 35.

39. Ibid., pp. 35–36. According to Chai's account, seven former Chinese military intelligence officers completed preparations for going to Pyongyang as Chinese diplomats by July 7. They arrived in Pyongyang on July 10, and Chinese embassy was then formally opened.

40. "The Victorious Future of the Korean People's War of Liberation, *"Renmin ribao*, July 6, 1950.

41. Cited in Chai and Zhao, *Banmendian tanpan*, p. 39.

42. Participants in the two conferences included Zhu De, commander-in-chief of the PLA; Nie Rongzhen, acting general chief of staff; Li Tao, director of the Department of Military Operations under the General Staff; Luo Ronghuan, director of the PLA General Political Bureau; Yang Lisan, director of the PLA's General Logistics Department; Xiao Jinguang, commander of the navy; Liu Yalou, commander of the air force; Xu Guangda, commander of the armored force; Su Jin, vice commander of the artillery force; Teng Daiyuan, commander of the PLA railway engineering corps; Lin Biao, commander of the PLA's Central-South Military Region; He Jinnian, vice commander of the PLA's Northeast Military Region; and Wan Yi, commander of the artillery force under the Fourth Field Army. See Han and Tan et al., *Dangdai zhongguo jundui*, 1: 449–50. According to the recollections of Lei Yingfu, Zhou Enlai's secretary for military affairs at that time, among the participants of the July 7 conference were also Xiao Hua, deputy director of the PLA's General Political Department, Li Kenong, director of the CMC's Military Intelligence Department and vice minister of foreign affairs, Lai Chuanzhu, political commissar of the 15th Army Corps, Li Jükui, vice chief of staff of the Forth Field Army, Xiao Ke, director of the CMC's Military Training Department, Zhang Jingwu, director of the CMC's People's Armed Forces Department, Fu Qiutao, secretary general of the Central Demobilization Committee, Zhang Chinghua, vice director of the Cartography Bureau under the PLA's General Staff, and Lei himself. Lei Yingfu, "Random Recollections of the War to Resist America and Assist Korea" (unpublished manuscript); see also Xu Yan, "China's Decision on the Military Intervention in the Korean War" (unpublished paper), p. 3.

43. Zhu Jianrong, *Mao Zedong's Korean War*, p. 81. Zhu's account cited here is based on the testimony by Lei Yingfu.

44. Han and Tan et al., *Dangdai zhongguo jundui*, 1: 449–450; Yao Xu, *Cong yalujiang dao banmendian*, p. 14.

45. Ma Qibing and Chen Wenping et al., *Zhongguo gongchandang zhizheng sishinian* (The Chinese Communist Party as the Ruling Party for Forty Years, Beijing: CCP Historical Materials Press, 1989), p. 19; Han and Tan et al., *Dangdai zhongguo jundui*, 1: 450; Yao Xu, *Cong yalujiang dao banmendian*, p. 14; Qi Dexue, *Chaoxian zhanzheng juece neimu*, pp. 29–30.

46. Mao Zedong to Nie Rongzhen, July 7, 1950, *MWG*, 1: 428; Han and Tan et al., *Dangdai zhongguo jundui*, 1: 450.

47. Later only Li Jükui assumed the position. Su Yu was on sick leave and then hospitalized. Xiao Jinguang needed to focus on the busy affairs of China's newly established navy. Xiao Hua was then in charge of the PLA's General Political Department (as Luo Ronghuan, the director of the department, was in bad health), and he could not assume his position in the NEBDA either. The headquarters of the NEBDA had never been formerly

established. On July 22, Zhou Enlai and Nie Rongzhen reported to Mao that "it seemed difficult at the present stage" to form the headquarters for the NEBDA. They suggested that all units of the NEBDA be commanded by Gao Gang, commander and political commissar of the Northeast Military Region. They also suggested that a single logistics department should be established under the headquarters of the Northeast Military Region to make logistical preparations well coordinated and that Li Jükui be appointed as the director of the department. Mao approved these proposals the next day. See Du Ping, *Du Ping huiyilu*, pp. 14–15; Deng Lifeng, *Xin zhongguo junshi huodong jishi*, p. 113; Huang Yi, "Zhou Enlai: the Leader and Organizer of Strategic Logistic Affairs during the War to Resist America and Assist Korea," *Junshi shiling* (Military History Circles), no. 5 (1989): 10.

48. Du Ping, *Du Ping huiyilu*, p. 14; Qi Dexue, *Chaoxian zhanzheng juece neimu*, p. 18; Han and Tan et al., *Dangdai zhongguo jundui*, 1: 449–50; Yao Xu, *Cong yalujiang dao banmendian*, p. 14; Chai and Zhao, *Banmendian tanpan*, p. 33. Later, Hong Xuezhi and Han Xianchu were both appointed as vice commanders of the Thirteenth Army Corps.

49. Shen and Meng et al., *Zhongguo renmin zhiyuanjun kangmei yuanchao zhanshi*, pp. 7–8; Han and Tan et al., *Dangdai zhongguo jundui*, 1: 450; Chai and Zhao, *Banmendian tanpan*, p. 33; Deng Lifeng, *Xin zhongguo junshi huodong jishi*, p. 113; Huang Yi, "Zhou Enlai: The Leader and Organizer of the Strategic Affairs during the War to Resist America and Assist Korea," p. 9.

50. Deng Lifeng, *Xin zhongguo junshi huodong jishi*, p. 120.

51. With large numbers of troops moving from southern and central China into the Northeast, the PLA's logistic support system immediately faced a serious challenge. In the early days of the PRC, the PLA organized its military regions basically on the basis of former field armies, which had their own budgets. The CMC distributed funds and material supply to them at the beginning of the calendar year. In the case of the 13th Army Corps, the Southern-central Military Region had been responsible for its supplies before it moved into the Northeast. Which military region, the Southern-central or the Northeastern, should supply the 13th Army Corps after the Corps entered the Northeast became a practical problem. Furthermore, in 1950, the Northeast Region had its own currency, which was independent from *Renminbi*, the money used in other parts of China. Zhou Enlai therefore set up rules before troops moved into the Northeast. See Huang Yi, "Zhou Enlai: The Leader and Organizer of the Strategic Affairs during the War to Resist America and Assist Korea," pp. 10–11.

52. Xu Guangyi et al., *Dangdai zhongguo jundui de houqin gongzuo* (The Logistical Affairs of Contemporary Chinese Army, Beijing: Chinese Social Sciences Press, 1990), p. 137; Xie Fang et al., *Kangmei yuanchao zhanzheng houqin jingyan zongjie* (Summaries of the Logistical Experience during the

War to Resist America and Assist Korea, Beijing: The Golden Shield Press, 1987), pp. 10–11; Deng Lifeng, *Xin zhongguo junshi huodong jishi*, p. 115; Li • Jükui, *Li Jükui huiyilu* (Li Jükui's Memoirs, Beijing: People's Liberation Army Press, 1986), p. 264.

53. Xie Fang et al., *Kangmei yuanchao zhanzheng houqin jingyan zongjie*, pp. 11–12; Huang Yi, "Zhou Enlai: The Leader and Organizer of the Strategic Affairs during the War to Resist America and Assist Korea," p. 12.

54. Li Jükui, *Li Jükui huiyilu*, pp. 263–264.

55. See *MWG*, 1: 428, n. 2.

56. *Weida de kangmei yuanchao yundong* (The Great Movement to Resist America and Assist Korea, Beijing: People's Press, 1954), pp. 7–8; and "The Great Political Significance of the 'Special Week of Opposing the U.S. Invasion of Taiwan and Korea," *Shijie zhishi*, 22, no. 3 (July 21, 1950): 2.

57. In Mao's telegrams dealing with the Korean crisis, Mao paid special attention to "American arrogance" (*xiaozhang qiyan* or *aoman*), and he often referred to "beating American arrogance" as an important reason for China to enter the Korean War. See *MWG*, 1: 539, 556; see also discussions in chapters 6 and 7.

58. For the background of the movement to suppress reactionary activities, see Hu Sheng et al., *Zhongguo gongchandang de qishinian*, pp. 328–329; Zhang Min, "A Survey of the Struggle to Suppress Reactionaries in the Early Years of the PRC," *Dangde wenxian*, no. 2, (1988): 38–41; Lin Yunhui et al., *Kaige xingjing de shiqi* (China from 1949 to 1989: The Period of Triumphant March, Zhengzhou: Henan People's Press, 1989), pp. 137–141. For the CCP Central Committee's directive on suppressing reactionary activities issued on March 18, 1950, see Liu Wusheng et al., *Gongheguo zouguo de lu*, pp. 233–235.

59. The State Council and Supreme People's Court, "Instructions on Suppressing Reactionary Activities," July 23, 1950, in Central Institute of Historical Documents, ed., *Jianguo yilai zhongyao wenxian xuanbian, 1949–1950*, (Selected Important Documents since the Founding of the PRC, Beijing: The Central Press of Historical Documents, 1991), pp. 358–360.

60. Lin Yunhui et al., *Kaige xingjing de shiqi*, pp. 137–144; see also discussions in chapter 7.

61. Allen Whiting presented a plausible analysis of Beijing's "Resist American Invasion of Taiwan and Korea" campaign in July and August, pointing out that the real purposes of this campaign were to break down pro-American feeling, to suppress anti-Communist opposition within China, to spur reconstruction and land reform, and, in the final analysis, to mobilize the mass hostility toward the Americans. Whiting, however, argued that the campaign should not be cited "as evidence of preparation for

military intervention in the war" (Whiting, *China Crosses the Yalu*, pp. 82–84). With the insight gained from new Chinese source materials, it is evident that the anti-American campaign served both the need for long-range mobilization and the short-run possibility that China would enter the Korean War. And, as I will further discuss in the next chapter, the two aims were virtually interwoven in Mao's management of the Korean crisis.

62. Michael Schaller, *Douglas MacArthur: The Far Eastern General* (New York: Oxford University Press), p. 194.

63. *Renmin ribao*, August 5, 1950; see also Whiting, *China Crosses the Yalu*, pp. 81–82.

64. Cited in Bo Yibo, *Ruogan zhongda juece yu shijian de huigu*, p. 43; see also Qi Dexue, *Chaoxian zhanzheng juece neimu*, p. 30.

65. Mao Zedong and the CCP Central Committee to Gao Gang, August 5, 1950, *MWG*, 1: 454. According to the reminiscence of Nie Rongzhen, following the decision of the CMC on the same day, he ordered the NEBDA to "finish every preparation by the end of this month and wait for the directive to enter the war." Nie, *Nie Rongzhen huiyilu*, p. 734.

66. Du Ping, *Zai zhiyuanjun zongbu*, p. 18; Hong Xuezhi, *Kangmei yuanchao zhanzheng huiyi*, p. 7.

67. Du Ping, *Zai zhiyuanjun zongbu*, p. 18.

68. Du Ping, *Zai zhiyuanjun zongbu*, pp. 18–20; Xu Yan,*Diyici jiaoliang*, p. 18. Zhang Xi, "Peng's appointment," p. 119. Zhang, an army-level officer himself, served on the PLA's General Staff for more than forty years, and was once on Zhu De's military staff. Since 1983, he has been a member of the editorial group of Peng Dehuai's official biography and was granted special access to Party history and military archives as well as the opportunities to interview a wide range of people from top leaders to secretaries and associates of policymakers. His article provides the most detailed coverage of Beijing's decision-making process in October 1950.

69. Du Ping, *Zai zhiyuanjun zongbu*, pp. 19–20.

70. Ibid., p. 53. It should be noted that the PLA's experiences in China's civil war strongly influenced Deng's strategic design, and that Chinese experiences in the Korean War would prove that Deng and his fellow CCP military planners had underestimated the role played by modern technology and equipment in a modern warfare. See Deng Hua, *Lun Kangmei yuanchao de zuozhan zhidao* (On the Operation Direction of the War to Resist America and Assist Korea, Beijing: Military Science Press, 1989); see also Chen Jian, "China's Changing Aims during the Korean War, 1950–1951."

71. Du Ping, *Zai zhiyuanjun zongbu*, pp. 20–21; Zhou Jun, "The Strategic Change from the War of Liberation to the War to Resist America and Assist Korea," p. 15; Zhang Xi, "Peng's appointment," p. 119.

72. Du Ping, *Zai zhiyuanjun zongbu*, pp. 20–21; Zhang Xi, "Peng's appointment," p.119.

73. Mao Zedong to Gao Gang, August 18, 1950, *MWG*, 1: 469. Nie Rongzhen recalled in his memoirs that he send the same order to the NEBDA, see Nie, *Nie Rongzhen huiyilu*, pp. 734–735.

74. Du Ping, *Zai zhiyuanjun zongbu*, pp. 23–24. Interviews with Beijing's military researchers in May 1991 and August 1992 suggest that while the percentages described by Du could be an exaggeration of the "positive factors," Du's descriptions are generally reliable.

75. Du Ping, *Zai zhiyuanjun zongbu*, pp. 24–25.

76. Ibid., p. 29; Sun Yaoshen and Cui Jingshan, "Winning Victory Not Just on the Battlefield: General Xie Fang in Korea," *Renwu* (Biographical Journal), no. 1, 1991, p. 8.

77. Du Ping, *Zai zhiyuanjun zongbu*, p. 21.

78. Lei Yingfu, "Remember Him and His Teachings for Ever," in Cheng Hua, et al., *Zhou Enlai he ta de mishumen* (Zhou Enlai and His Secretaries, Beijing: Chinese Broadcasting and Television Press, 1991), p. 114.

79. For a discussion of Austin's address, see Whiting, *China Crosses the Yalu*, pp. 78–79.

80. *Renmin ribao*, August 21, 1950.

81. Lei Yingfu, "Remember Him and His Teachings for Ever," pp. 114–116; and Xu Yan,"How Did the CCP Central Committee Decide to Send Troops to Korea," p. 5.

82. Lei Yingfu, "Remember Him and His Teachings for Ever," pp. 115–116; see also Xu Yan,"China's Decision on the Military Intervention in the Korean War," p. 7; Zhu Jianrong, *Mao Zedong's Korean War*, pp. 132–134.

83. Lei Yingfu, "Remember Him and His Teachings for Ever," p. 116; Zhu Jianrong, *Mao Zedong's Korean War*, p. 134.

84. Lyoko Sakuyi, "The First Exposure of the Truth of the Korean War: Interview with Lee Sang-jo," *Spring and Autumn of Literature and Arts* (in Japanese), (April 1990): 171; see also Sun Baoshen, "Mao Zedong Had Predicted that the Americans Could Land at Inchon," *Junshi shiling*, no.10 (1990): 13; Shi Zhe, *Zai lishi jüren shenbian*, p. 492; Lim Un, *The Founding of a Dynasty in Korea*, pp. 187–188. I wish to thank Mr. Zhang Chiping and Ms. Yao Ping for translating portions of Sakuyi's article.

85. According to Lim Un, a well-informed Korean dissident living in Moscow, "Kim Il-sung, with our troops advancing toward what Kim thought was decisive victory, disregarded [Mao's] warnings as matters unworthy of consideration, and ordered his men to keep it secret." Lim Un, *The Founding of a Dynasty in Korea*, p. 188.

86. Zhou Enlai to Mao Zedong, August 24, 1950, *Zhou Enlai shuxin*

xuanji (Selected Correspondences of Zhou Enlai, Beijing: The Central Press of Historical Documents, 1988), p. 433.

87. Participants at this meeting included Zhou Enlai, Zhu De, Lin Biao, Nie Rongzhen, Ruo Ronghuan, Xiao Jinguang, Xiao Hua, Yang Lisan, Zhang Libing, He Cheng, Wang Bingzhang, Xu Guangda, Zhang Jingwu, Li Kenong, Xiao Ke, Wang Jing, Teng Daiyuan, Li Jükui, Fu Qiutao, Li Tao, Lai Chuanzhu, and Su Jing. Zhang Chinghua and Lei Yingfu were assigned to take notes at the meeting. See "Minutes of the Conference to Examine and Discuss the Preparations of the Northeast Border Defense Army, 5:00 PM, August 26, 1950," CCA.

88. Zhou mentioned here that the French had learned of and broadcast China's support to Ho Chi Minh because the Viet Minh had failed to maintain secrecy. Zhou stressed that everyone should keep this lesson in mind.

89. "Minutes of the Conference to Examine and Discuss the Preparations of the Northeast Border Defense Army, 5:00 PM, August 26, 1950," CCA; see also Deng Lifeng, *Xin zhongguo junshi huodong jishi*, p. 122.

90. Besides Zhou, participants at this meeting included Nie Rongzhen, Li Tao, Yang Lishan, Xu Guangda, Su Jing, Xiao Ke, and Wang Bingzhang. Lei Yingfu was again assigned to take notes at the meeting. "Minute of the Meeting on Planning the Construction of the NEBDA," August 31, 1950, CMA.

91. Ibid.; see also Xu Yan, *Diyici jiaoliang*, p. 19.

92. Deng Lifeng, *Xin zhongguo junshi huodong jishi*, p. 123;

93. Shen and Meng et al., *zhongguo renmin zhiyuanjun kangmei yuanchao zhanshi*, p. 8; Deng Lifeng, *Xin zhongguo junshi huodong jishi*, p. 123.

94. Mao Zedong to Peng Dehuai, August 27, 1950, *MWG*, 1: 485.

95. Sun and Cui, "Winning Victory Not Just on the Battlefield," p. 7.

96. The report also suggested that if air support by the Soviets could not be guaranteed, China should delay sending land forces into Korea. See Du Ping, *Zai zhiyuanjun zongbu*, p. 22.

97. Du Ping, *Zai zhiyuanjun zongbu*, pp. 21–22; Luo Yinwen, "Realistically Bringing Forth New Ideas: Stories about General Deng Hua," *Renwu*, no. 5 (1985): 63; Sun and Cui, "Winning Victory Not Just on the Battlefield," pp. 7–8; Xu Yan, *Diyici jiaoliang*, p. 20; Yao Xu, "Comrade Deng Hua in the War to Resist America and Assist Korea," Part I, *Hunan dangshi tongxun* (Newsletter of Party History Studies in Hunan), no. 3 (1985); and "Deng Hua," in the Editorial Department of *Xinghuo liaoyuan*, et al., *Jiefangjun jiangling zhuan*, 12 vols. (Biographies of PLA Commanders, Beijing: People's Liberation Army Press, 1988), 7: 30–31.

98. Chai and Zhao, *Banmendian tanpan*, p. 78.

99. Although Lin was not the only one who felt reluctant to send Chinese troops to Korea, he is the most prominent person mentioned by Chinese

sources whenever the opposition opinion is discussed. This is surely because Lin's downfall in the early 1970s made him an easy target of criticism.

100. Chai and Zhao, *Banmendian tanpan*, pp. 78–79.

101. See, for example, Nie Rongzhen, *Nie Rongzhen huiyilu*, p. 735.

102. Cited from Meng Zhaohui, "The Application and Development of Mao Zedong's Military Thought in the War to Resist America and Assist Korea," *Junshi lishi*, no. 1 (1991): 3.

103. Cited from Shen and Meng et al., *Zhongguo renmin zhiyuanjun kangmei yuanchao zhanshi*, p. 7.

104. For a good discussion of Stalin's attitude after the outbreak of the Korean War, especially his unwillingness to involve the Soviet Union in a direct confrontation with the United States, see Weathersby, "The Soviet Role in the Early Stage of the Korean War," pp. 433–434.

105. Wang Dinglie et al., *Dangdai zhongguo kongjun*, p. 78; Deng Lifeng, *Xin zhongguo junshi huodong jishi*, p. 121.

106. Kim Il-sung had also been skeptical of the combat power of the Chinese troops. See, for example, Lim Un, *The Founding of a Dynasty in North Korea*, p. 182.

107. In Lee Sang-jo's recollections, he particularly stresses that his visit to Beijing before the Inchon landing was "not for the purpose of asking China's military assistance," Lyoko Sakuyi, "The First Exposure of the Truth of the Korean War," p. 171; in my interviews with Shi Zhe in August 1992, he confirmed that Kim did not ask for Chinese assistance until after the Inchon landing.

108. Hong Xuezhi, *Kangmei yuanchao zhanzheng huiyi*, pp. 4, 8. Hong did not clearly point out that it was because of North Korean opposition that Deng gave up his mission. In my interviews with Chinese researchers in May 1991 and August 1992, they all agreed that a last-minute negative signal from the North Koreans is the most reasonable explanation for Deng's giving up the mission at the bank of the Yalu.

109. See Chai and Zhao, *Banmendian tanpan*, p. 77; Hong Xuezhi, *Kangmei yuanchao zhanzheng huiyi*, pp. 8–9. See also discussions in chapter 7.

6. AFTER INCHON: THE MAKING OF THE
DECISION ON INTERVENTION

1. See Li Yingqiao, *Zai Maozhuxi shenbian shiwunian* (With Chairman Mao for Fifteen Years, Shijiazhuang: Hebei People's Press, 1991), p. 159.

2. For personal recollections of the mood in Shenyang and Beijing after the Inchon landing, see Du Ping, *Zai zhiyuanjun zongbu*, p. 22; Hong

Xuezhi, *Kangmei yuanchao zhanzheng huiyi*, pp. 8–9; and Shi Zhe, *Zai lishi jüren shenbian*, pp. 492–493.

3. Although the Beijing leadership had alleged frequently that the real American intention behind invading Korea was to threaten China's Northeast, they did not treat this seriously until after the Inchon landing. In Zhou Enlai's speech to the Chinese People's Consultative Conference on October 24, 1950, he stressed that U.S. subjugation of North Korea would create real problems for the security of Northeast China. "Half of our heavy industry is in the Northeast, and half of the heavy industry in the Northeast is in the southern part, within range of enemy bombers. . . . If the U.S. imperialists get close to the Yalu River, how can we have the peace of mind to go about production?" Zhou Enlai, "Resisting U.S. Aggression, Assisting Korea and Defending Peace," *ZWJWX*, pp. 28–29.

4. Ibid., p. 29.

5. See Zhang Min, "A Survey of the Struggle to Suppress Reactionaries in the Early Years of the PRC," p. 254; Lin Yunhui et al., *Kaige xingjing de shiqi*, pp. 139–140; and Yang Dezhi, *Weile heping*, p. 4.

6. Hu Shiyan et al., *Chen Yi zhuan* (A Biography of Chen Yi, Beijing: Contemporary China Press, 1991), p. 487.

7. Cited from Chai and Zhao, *Banmendian tanpan*, p. 79.

8. This paragraph about Stalin's attitude change after Inchon is largely based on my discussions with Russian historian Goncharov in November 1991 and March 1993. The following Chinese sources offer a similar general account of Stalin's attitude after Inchon: Hong Xuezhi, *Kangmei yuanchao zhanzheng huiyi*, p. 24; and Xu Yan, *Diyici jiaoliang*, p. 22.

9. Shi Zhe, *Zai lishi jüren shenbian*, pp. 492–493. In my interviews with Shi Zhe in August 1992, he recalled that this telegram reached Beijing "one or two days" after the Inchon landing.

10. This was released by Chen Yi, China's foreign minister, in a speech on April 16, 1964, see Yao Xu, *Cong yalujiang dao banmendian*, p. 22; see also Xu Yan, *Diyici jiaoliang*, p. 22.

11. Several Chinese sources mention that before China made the final decision to enter the Korean War, the Soviets agreed to provide air cover if China sent troops to Korea. Few of these sources, however, reveal when and how the agreement was made. Nor do these sources reveal the contents of this agreement. This paragraph follows Hong Xuezhi, *Kangmei yuanchao zhanzheng huiyi*, pp. 24–25, and Zhang Xi, "Peng's Appointment," pp. 142, 147.

12. Hong Xuezhi, *Kangmei yuanchao zhanzheng huiyi*, 8–9; Chai and Zhao, *Banmendian tanpan*, p. 77.

13. Hong Xuezhi, *Kangmei yuanchao zhanzheng huiyi*, p. 9.

14. For a recent study of Kim Il-sung's suppression of his opponents within the Korean Labor Party, including Pak Il-yu and Pak Hon-yong, see

Sin Sam-Soon, "The Repressions of Kim Il-sung: A Historical Memoir," *Korea and World Affairs*, 15 (1991): 279–301; for Kim's purge of Pak Hon-yong, see Scalapino and Lee, *Communism in Korea*, 1: 436–452.

15. Interviews with Chinese party history researchers in May 1991. Shi Zhe confirmed in my interviews with him in August 1992 that after Inchon Kim's opponents within the Korean Labor Party asked Mao to support their efforts to get rid of Kim, but Mao did not agree. According to one Chinese source, the CCP Central Committee cabled Kim Il-sung on September 20, advising him to prepare for a protracted war, to carefully maintain the main formation of North Korean forces, and to avoid staking everything on a single effort in fighting the Americans. See Zhou Jun, "The Strategic Change from the War of Liberation to the War to Resist America and Assist Korea," p. 16. The cable is a clear indication that Mao and the CCP leadership continued to accept Kim Il-sung as the leader of North Korean Communists.

16. These five people were: Zhang Mingyuan, deputy head of the Logistics Department of the PLA's Northeast Headquarters; Cui Xingnong, head of the intelligence Department of the Headquarters of the 13th Army Corps; He Lingdeng, staff officer at the Headquarters of the 39th Army; Tang Jingzhong, chief of staff of the 118th Division under the 41st Army; and Li Fei, deputy head of the Intelligence Department of the Headquarters of the Artillery Force under the CMC. Chai and Zhao, *Banmendian tanpan*, p. 79; see also Xie Fang, *Kangmei yuanchao zhanzheng houqin jingyan zongjie*, p. 12.

17. Zhou worried that sending Chinese military observers could give the Koreans a wrong signal that Beijing was about to send troops to Korea, as well as reveal prematurely China's intentions to the Americans. See "Minutes of the Conference to Examine and Discuss the Preparations of the Northeast Border Defense Army, 5:00 PM, August 26, 1950," CCA.

18. Xie Fang, *Kangmei yuanchao zhanzheng houqin jingyan zongjie*, p. 12.

19. Chai and Zhao, *Banmendian tanpan*, p. 79.

20. Ibid., p. 80.

21. *Renmin ribao*, September 25, 1950.

22. K. M. Panikkar, *In Two Chinas* (London: Allen and Unwin, 1955), p. 108; Chai and Zhao, *Banmendian tanpan*, p. 74; Qi Dexue, *Chaoxian zhanzheng juece neimu*, p. 41.

23. Memorandum by Allison, July 13, 1950, *FRUS*, 1950: 7, p. 373.

24. Memorandum by Lay, July 17, 1950, ibid., p. 410.

25. Kennan, "Possible Further Danger Points in Light of the Korean Situation," June 30, 1950, Box 24, Kennan Papers; Kennan to Acheson, August 8, 1950, PPS papers, Box 8, RG 59, NA; see also Kennan, *Memoirs, 1925–1950* (Boston: Little, Brown, 1967), p. 488.

26. Draft Memorandum Prepared by the PPS, July 25, 1950, *FRUS* (1950), 7: 469–473.

27. Draft Memorandum Prepared by the Department of Defense, "U.S. Course of Action in Korea," July 31, 1950, ibid., pp. 502–10.

28. Memorandum by Dulles, July 14, 1950, ibid., pp. 386–87.

29. Foot, *The Wrong War*, p. 72.

30. Memorandum by Allison to Nitze, July 24, 1950, *FRUS* (1950), 7: 460–61.

31. J. Lawton Collins, *War in Peacetime: The History and Lessons of Korea* (Boston: Houghton Mittin, 1969), pp. 81- 83.

32. Foot, *The Wrong War*, pp. 69–70.

33. Ibid., p. 74.

34. Ibid., pp. 75–76.

35. Draft Memorandum Prepared in the Department of State, August 31, 1950, *FRUS* (1950), 7: 672.

36. NSC 81/1, Report by the National Security Council to the President, September 9, 1950, ibid., pp. 712–721; see also Barton J. Bernstein, "The Policy of Risk: Crossing the 38th Parallel and Marching to the Yalu," *Foreign Service Journal* (March 1977): 18–19.

37. Webb to the U.S. Mission at the United Nations, September 26, 1950, *FRUS* (1950), 7: 781.

38. Marshall to MacArthur, September 29, 1950, ibid., p. 826.

39. Schaller, *Douglas MacArthur*, p. 201.

40. Memorandum of conversation by Allison, October 4, 1950, *FRUS* (1950), 7: 868–869.

41. Cumings, *The Origins of the Korean War*, 2: 734–735; Foot, *The Wrong War*, p. 80; and Memorandum by the CIA, October 12, 1950, *FRUS* (1950), 7: 934.

42. Memorandum by the CIA, October 12, 1950, *FRUS* (1950), 7: 934; Smith, *Dean Acheson*, p. 201.

43. Memorandum by the CIA, October 12, 1950, *FRUS* (1950), 7: 934.

44. Foot, *The Wrong War*, pp. 82–84; Stueck, *The Road to Confrontation*, pp. 230–231.

45. Memorandum by the CIA, October 12, 1950, *FRUS* (1950), 7: 933–934

46. Bernstein, "The Policy of Risk," p. 17; Acheson to Bevin, July 10, 1950, *FRUS* (1950), 7: 348–350.

47. Minutes of Truman-Attlee Discussions, December 4, 1950, *FRUS* (1950), 3: 1706–1709.

48. According to Nie Rongzhen's memoir, the Chinese general staff received the information that the UN forces had crossed the 38th parallel on

the early morning of October 2. See Nie Rongzhen, *Nie Rongzhen huiyilu*, p. 736.

49. Kim Il-sung and Pak Hon-yong to Stalin, September 29, 1950, cited from Weathersby, "The Soviet Role in the Early Phase of the Korean War: New Documentary Evidence," pp. 452–456.

50. Stalin to Matveev, September 30, 1950, and Stalin to Shtykov and Matveev, October 1, 1950, ibid., pp. 455–456. A. I. Matveev was then Stalin's personal military representative in Korea, and Shtykov was then Soviet ambassador to North Korea.

51. Chai and Zhao, *Banmendian tanpan*, p. 80; Zhang Xi, "Peng's Appointment," p. 123.

52. Zhang Xi, "Peng Dehuai and China's Entry into the Korean War" (trans. by Chen Jian), *Chinese Historians*, 6, no. 1 (Spring 1993): 5–6.

53. Cited from Ye Yumeng, *Chubing chaoxian: kangmei yuanchao lishi jishi* (Entering the Korean War: The True Story of the History of Resisting America and Assisting Korea, Beijing: The Press of October Literature, 1990), pp. 39–40; see also Zhang Xi, "Peng's appointment," pp. 123–124; Qi Dexue, *Chaoxian zhanzheng juece neimu*, pp. 46–47. The fact that the letter uses a long paragraph summarizing the situation of the Korean War from late June to late September indicates that it could be the first direct request for China's military intervention by Kim himself. It is also noticeable that this letter was sent off under the name of Kim and Pak Hon-yon, despite the serious problems that had long existed and that had recently got worse between them.

54. Zhou Enlai's speech at the convention celebrating the first anniversary of the establishment of the PRC, September 30, 1950, *Renmin ribao*, October 1, 1950.

55. The Standing Committee of the CCP Politburo was then composed of Mao Zedong, Liu Shaoqi, Zhou Enlai, Zhu De, and Ren Bishi. But as Ren was very sick at that time, he probably did not attend the meeting.

56. Mao Zedong to Gao Gang and Deng Hua, October 2, 1950, *MWG*, 1: 538.

57. Zhang Xi, "Peng's appointment," p. 125; Xu Yan, "The Final Decision to Enter the Korean War," p. 10.

58. Zhang Xi, "Peng's appointment," pp. 125–126.

59. Ibid., pp. 125–126.

60. See Mao Zedong to Su Yu, August 8, 1950, *MWG*, 1: 464.

61. Zhang Xi, "Peng's appointment," pp. 126–127; Qi Dexue, *Chaoxian zhanzheng juece neimu*, p. 54.

62. Mao Zedong to Peng Dehuai, August 27, 1950, *MWG*, 1: 485.

63. Zhang Xi, "Peng's appointment," p. 127. In interviews with Zhang

Xi on August 22 and 26, 1992, I learned that his description was based on his July 1984 interview with Yang Shangkun, director of the CCP Central Committee's administrative office in 1950, and from 1988 to 1993 the PRC's president.

64. Ibid., p. 127.

65. Ibid., p. 127.

66. Mao Zedong to Stalin, October 2, 1950, *MWG*, 1: 539–540.

67. Interviews with Beijing's military researchers and Shi Zhe, August 1992.

68. According to several of Mao's other telegrams after China's entry into the war, Mao believed that Chinese intervention would last no longer than one year. Not until February and March of 1951, when the Chinese offensive had been halted by the UN forces, did Mao begin to mention that the war would probably last for more than two years. For a more detailed discussion of Mao's changing assessment of the duration of China's intervention in Korea, see Chen Jian, "China's Changing Aims during the Korean War."

69. Mao's optimistic mood in defining China's war aims lasted until mid-1951. Only after Chinese troops suffered a major setback in their long-planned offensive aimed at "giving the Americans a decisive strike" in April and May of 1951 did Mao and the CCP leadership begin to give up the unrealistic goal of pursuing a total victory over the United States in Korea. For a discussion, see Chen Jian, "China's Changing Aims," pp. 38–39.

70. For a more detailed discussion on how Mao's perceptions of the power potential of the Americans' and their own had been challenged during the process of the Korean War, see Chen Jian, "China's Changing Aims."

71. Zhou Enlai's talks with Pannikkar, *ZWJWX*, pp. 25–27; *Weida de kang-mei yuanchao yundong*, p. 27; Chai and Zhao, *Banmendian tanpan*, p. 81; Pannikar, *In Two Chinas*, pp. 108–110. According to the recollections of Pu Shouchang, Zhou's English language interpreter, Zhou carefully discussed with him about how to find an accurate English term for "*yao guan*," which in other contexts could be translated as "to be concerned" or "to take care of." Zhou, however, believed that "intervene" was a more proper term to express what he meant. See Pei Jianzhang et al., *Xinzhongguo waijiao fengyun*, p. 97.

72. The literature related to this argument is too vast to be all listed here. For a recent example of this approach, see Hao and Zhai, "China's Decision to Enter the Korean War."

73. In fact, both Mao and Zhou later stated that if the United States had listened to Zhou's warning and stopped at the 38th parallel, China would not have sent troops to Korea. These statements, though, are open to question.

74. Richard Ned Lebow, *Between Peace and War: The Nature of International Crisis* (Baltimore: The Johns Hopkins University Press, 1981), p. 29.

75. Zhang Xi, "Peng's appointment," pp. 128–129; Hu Guangzheng and Bao Mingrong, "Several Factual Corrections of Yao Xu's 'The Brilliant Decision to Resist America and Assist Korea,'" *Dangshi yanjiu*, no. 3 (1981): 60; Wang Yan et al., *Peng Dehuai zhuan* (A Biography of Peng Dehuai, Beijing: Contemporary China Press, 1993), pp. 400–401.

76. The list of the participants follows Qi Dexue's *Chaoxian zhanzheng juece neimu*, p. 49. It is noticeable that Lin Biao's name is not on the list. Nie Rongzhen, in his discussion of Lin Biao's opposition to sending troops to Korea, leaves the impression that Lin attended the meeting, see Nie Rongzhen, *Nie Rongzhen huiyilu*, p. 736.

77. Peng Dehuai, *Peng Dehuai zishu* (The Autobiographical Notes of Peng Dehuai, Beijing: People's Press, 1981), p. 257.

78. We may never be able to identify those who opposed or expressed doubts about the decision to enter the war and those who favored it. The Politburo meetings of October 4–5, according to my interviews with experts on CCP history in May 1991 and August 1992, left no written records behind them. The memoirs of those who participated in the meeting, understandably, are often self-serving. In a generally plausible study of China's participation in the Korean War, Zhu Jianrong offers a concise summary of the division within the Politburo on the problem of sending troops to Korea. According to him, at the October 4 meeting, Mao Zedong and Zhou Enlai were the only two who wanted to send troops to Korea. Among the potential supporters of Mao and Zhou were Zhu De, Deng Xiaoping, and Peng Dehuai. Gao Gang and Lin Biao firmly opposed Mao and Zhou. And Liu Shaoqi, Chen Yun, Zhang Wentian, and Li Fuchun demonstrated a "negative" attitude toward sending troops. The division changed the next day. Mao and Zhou were supported by Zhu, Peng, Deng, and Liu, while the attitude of Chen and Li was still "negative," and Gao and Lin continued to oppose sending troops to Korea—they probably did not attend this day's meeting. (Zhu Jianrong, *Mao's Korean War*, pp. 201–201). Zhu does not document his account. In my interviews with Beijing's experts in August 1992, I discussed Zhu's account with them, and they all believed that Zhu's summary was too absolute to be convincing. For example, it is doubtful that Zhou had been such a firm supporter of Mao's ideas. According to Shi Zhe, Zhou had real reservations about sending troops to Korea. In fact, my interviews suggest that it would be safe to say that almost all members of the Politburo, except for Mao, expressed reservations in different degrees about sending troops to Korea.

79. Nie Rongzhen, *Nie Rongzhen huiyilu*, p. 737; Xu Yan, "How Did the CCP Central Committee Make the Decision to Dispatch Troops to Resist America and Assist Korea", p. 6.

80. Peng Dehuai, *Peng Dehuai zishu*, pp. 257–258.

81. Zhang Xi, "Peng's appointment," pp. 131–132; Peng Dehuai, *Peng Dehuai zishu*, p. 257.

82. Zhang Xi, "Peng's appointment," pp. 133–134. In my interviews with Zhang Xi, he confirmed that his account of Mao's talks with Peng was based on Peng's own recollections later given to his staff.

83. Zhang Xi, "Peng's appointment," p. 136; Nie Rongzhen, *Nie Rongzhen huiyilu*, p. 736.

84. Nie Rongzhen, *Nie Rongzhen huiyilu*, p. 737; Yao Xu, *Cong yalujiang dao banmendian*, pp. 23-24; Shen and Meng et al., *Zhongguo renmin zhiyuanjun kangmei yuanchao zhanshi*, pp. 13–14. See also CCP Central Committee, "The Guideline for Interpretations of the Current Situation," October 26, 1950, *Zhonggong dangshi jiaoxue cankao ziliao*, 19: 211–213.

85. Zhang Xi, "Peng's appointment," p. 136. According to Zhang, his descriptions of the meeting of October 4 and 5 were based on his interview with Yang Shangkun in July 1984, the diaries of Zhang Yangwu, Peng Dehuai's secretary, and the recollections of Cheng Pu, Peng's military associate, about Peng's own depiction of the meetings.

86. Ibid., pp. 137–138.

87. Ibid., p. 139; Xu Yan, "China's Decision on the Military Intervention," p. 11; Xu Yan, *Diyici jiaoliang*, p. 24; in my interviews with Zhang Xi in August 1992, he stressed that both his and Xu's accounts of the conference were based on available documentary sources.

88. Zhang Xi, "Peng's appointment," p. 39.

89. Mao Zedong's order to form the Chinese People's Volunteers, October 8, 1950, *MWG*, 1: 543–544.

90. Xu Yan, *Diyici jiaoliang*, pp. 26–28; Hong Xuezhi, *Kangmei yuanchao zhanzheng huiyi*, p. 27; see also *Peng Dehuai junshi wenxuan* (Selected Military Works of Peng Dehuai, Beijing: The Central Press of Historical Documents, 1988), p. 322

91. Mao Zedong to Kim Il-sung, October 8, 1950, *MWG*, 1: 545. It is interesting to note that Mao did not inform Kim of China's decision to dispatch troops to Korea until the last minute, although Kim must have been anxiously waiting for a Chinese response.

92. The North Korean leadership had severe internal divisions in the wake of North Korea's military defeats. Chai Chengwen recorded in his memoirs that when he and Ambassador Ni arrived at Kim's headquarters, Kim was involved in an emotional quarrel with Pak Hon-yong. After Pak left, Kim explained to the Chinese: " He [Pak] has no determination to start a guerrilla struggle in the mountainous area." North Korean leaders had begun to prepare for the worst. See Chai and Zhao, *Banmendian tanpan*, p. 84.

7. THE DECISION STANDS THE TEST:
CHINA CROSSES THE YALU

1. Mao and the CCP leadership did not want to prematurely reveal their decision to send troops to Korea, so the first document was not issued until late October, and the second not until early November. For the text of the first document, which was an inner-party one, see *Zhonggong dangshi jiaoxue cankao ziliao*, 19: 211–213; for Mao's revision of the document, see *MWG*, 1: 616; and for the text of the second document, see *Weida de Kangmei yuanchao yundong*, pp. 674–684. The citations of the Beijing leadership's argument in the following paragraphs are all from these sources.

2. Peng Dehuai, *Peng Dehuai zishu*, p. 258.

3. The CCP Central Committee, "The Directive of Correcting the Rightist Tendency in Suppressing Reactionary Activities," October 10, 1950, *Zhonggong dangshi jiaoxue cankao ziliao*, 19: 205–206.

4. Zhang Xi, "The Sudden Cancellation of the CPV's Movement on the Eve of Its Entry into Korea," *Dangshi yanjiu ziliao*, no. 186 (January 1993): 254; Li Jianwei et al., *Zhongguo gongchandang lishi* (A History of the Chinese Communist Party, 3 vols., Beijing: People's Press, 1990), 3: 75–76; Hu Sheng et al., *Zhongguo gongchandang qishinian*, p. 329.

5. Zhou Enlai's speech at a meeting of the CCP United Front Department, January 20, 1951, *Zhou Enlai tongyi zhanxian wenxuan* (Selected United Front Works of Zhou Enlai, Beijing: People's Press, 1984), p. 200.

6. See the CCP Central Committee, "Instructions on Suppressing Reactionary Activities in Big Cities" (drafted by Mao), *MWG*, 2: 139.

7. Liu Shaoqi, "The Politburo's Report to the Fourth Plenary Session of the Seventh Central Committee," February 6, 1954, *Zhonggong dangshi jiaoxue cankao ziliao*, 20: 253; see also Li Jianwei et al., *Zhongguo gongchandang lishi*, 3: 77–78.

8. The CCP Central Committee to CCP Regional Bureaus and PLA Regional Headquarters, February 28, 1951 (drafted by Mao), *MWG*, 2: 147; see also "Why Should We Ruthlessly Suppress Reactionary Activities," editorial, *Renmin ribao*, February 22, 1951.

9. Zhang Min, "A Survey of the Struggle to Suppress Reactionaries in the Early Years of the PRC," p. 250.

10. Zhang Xi, "Peng's appointment," p. 143; and Du Ping, *Zai zhiyuanjun zongbu*, p. 10.

11. Zhang Xi, "Peng's appointment," p. 143.

12. Ibid., pp. 143–144; Wang Yan et al., *Peng Dehuai zhuan*, p. 404; Hu and Bao, "Several Factual Corrections of Yao Xu's 'The Brilliant Decision to Resist America and Assist Korea,' " p. 60.

13. Peng Dehuai to Mao Zedong, October 9, 1950, cited from Zhang Xi, "Peng's appointment," p. 144.

14. Shen and Meng et al., *Zhongguo renmin zhiyuanjun kangmei yuanchao zhanshi*, p. 15; Zhang Xi, "Peng's appointment," p. 144; Hong Xuezhi, *Kangmei yuanchao zhanzheng huiyi*, pp. 17–21.

15. Sun and Cui, "Winning Victory Not Just on Battlefields," p. 8.

16. Nie Rongzhen, *Nie Rongzhen huiyilu*, p. 737; Zhang Xi, "Peng's appointment," pp. 142–145; Chai and Zhao, *Banmendian tanpan*, pp. 84–85; Mao Zedong to Peng Dehuai, October 11, 1950, *MWG*, 1: 548.

17. See Huang Yi, "Peng Dehuai's Great Contribution to the Logistic Affairs during the War to Resist America and Assist Korea," *Junshi shilin*, no.1 (1989): 34.

18. Wang Yan et al., *Peng Dehuai zhuan*, p. 405; Zhang Xi, "Peng's appointment," p. 147.

19. Mao Zedong to Peng Dehuai, Gao Gang and others, October 12, 1950, *MWG*, 1: 552.

20. Mao Zedong to Rao Shushi and Chen Yi, October 12, 1950, Ibid., p. 553.

21. Zhang Xi, "The Sudden Cancellation of the CPV's Movement on the Eve of Its Entry into Korea," p. 5.

22. Chai and Zhao, *Banmendian tanpan*, p. 83; Zhang Xi, "The Sudden Cancellation of the CPV's Movement on the Eve of Its Entry into Korea," p. 3. In my interviews with Shi Zhe in May 1991, he was still uncertain about the date of Zhou's departure, and he believed that it could be either October 6 or 7. Li Haiwen, the CCP history researcher who assisted the writing of Shi Zhe's memoirs, later found that Zhou signed a document in Beijing on the early morning of October 8, so Zhou could not have left Beijing until sometime on October 8. Shi Zhe, *Zai lishi jüren shenbian*, p. 495; interviews with Shi Zhe and Li Haiwen, August 1992.

23. According to Kang Yimin's recollections, Lin Biao flew to the Soviet Union together with Zhou Enlai, but Shi Zhe recalled that Lin Biao went to the Soviet Union separately. See Qi Dexue, *Chaoxian zhanzheng juece neimu*, pp. 62–63; and Shi Zhe, *Zai lishi jüren shenbian*, p. 495, n.3.

24. The date of the meeting has been controversial in Chinese sources. Zhang Xi originally dated Zhou's meeting with Stalin for October 9 in his influential article, "Peng's Appointment," p. 147. Shi Zhe asserted that Zhou arrived in Moscow on October 9, flew to southern Russia and met Stalin on the 10th, and came back to Moscow on the 11th or 12th. (Shi Zhe, *Zai lishi jüren shenbian*, pp. 495, 498) Kang Yimin did not offer an exact date of the meeting, but he mentioned in his recollections that Zhou left Beijing on October 8, and it took Zhou four days to get to Stalin's villa on the Black sea. So Zhou could not meet Stalin until late on October 12. ("Kang

Yimin's Recollections on Zhou Enlai's Secret Visit to the Soviet Union in October 1950," minutes, CCA) Shi Zhe, Zhang Xi, and I concluded on August 22, 1992 after comparing carefully materials available to us that Zhou could not have reached Stalin's villa before the afternoon of October 10. Because Zhou and Stalin sent a telegram to Mao on October 11 to report on the meeting between them, the meeting must have occurred from the evening of 10th to the morning of the next day.

25. The list of the participants of the meeting was offered by Shi Zhe. Zhang Xi in "Peng 's appointment," p. 147, offers a list very close to this one (only Wang Jiaxiang was not included). In my interview with Zhang in August 1992, he confirmed that his information was based on interviews with Shi Zhe. In "Kang Yimin's Recollections on Zhou Enlai's Secret Visit to the Soviet Union in October 1950," p. 2, Kang stated that he stayed in Moscow and Zhou and Shi flew to the Black Sea to meet Stalin.

26. This paragraph is based on Shi Zhe's memoirs, *Zai lishi jüren shenbian*, pp. 495–499, and interviews with Shi Zhe in May 1991 and August 1992. In the next several paragraphs I will discuss those points of the meeting that are unclear in the published version of his memoirs and that I have clarified during my interviews with him in August 1992.

27. I myself, for example, was not convinced by Shi Zhe's account and expressed my doubts in my article, "The Sino-Soviet Alliance and China's Entry into the Korean War," p. 29. Michael Hunt also questions the reliability of Shi Zhe's recollections. See Hunt, "Beijing and the Korean Crisis, June 1950-June 1951," p. 460, n. 26.

28. Qi Dexue, *Chaoxian zhanzheng juece neimu*, pp. 62–63; Kang Yimin, "Kang Yimin's Recollections on Zhou Enlai's Secret Visit to the Soviet Union in October 1950," especially pp. 2–3.

29. See, for examples, Chai and Zhao, *Banmendian tanpan*, p. 83; Hong Xuezhi, *Kangmei yuanchao zhanzheng huiyi*, pp. 25–26.

30. "Mao Zedong's Conversations with Kim Il-sung," October 10, 1970, minute, CCA. The two sentences, "At first Molotov agreed and then Stalin telephoned us that their air force could not go beyond the Yalu River," are ambiguous. No documentary evidence would confirm this concrete process as described by Mao.

31. Interviews with Shi Zhe, August 1992.

32. The original text of this key telegram has not been located in the archives of the CCP Central Secretariat or the CCP's Central Archives. The citation here is from Shi Zhe's *Zai lishi jüren shenbian*, p. 498, n.1, and Zhang Xi's "The Sudden Cancellation of the CPV's Movement on the Eve of Its Entry to Korea," p. 3. In my interviews with Shi Zhe and Zhang Xi in August 1992, they confirmed that this citation was not based on the original of the telegram but on Mao's summary of this telegram in the starting para-

graph of Mao's telegram to Zhou Enlai on October 13, 1950 (part of it has been published in *MWG*, but this part has been omitted).

33. Kang Yimin claims that at the Zhou-Stalin meeting (although he did not attend the meeting), Stalin agreed to offer equipment for ten Chinese divisions and to send Soviet air forces to the Northeast and coastal cities. Shortly after Zhou flew back to Moscow, however, Molotov informed him that the Soviets had changed their mind and would not provide the Chinese with military equipment. Zhou angrily argued with Molotov. Finally "the Soviet side agreed to support China's decision to send troops to Korea and to provide China with military assistance." See "Kang Yimin's Recollections on Zhou Enlai's Secret Visit to the Soviet Union in October 1950," p. 4; and Qi Dexue, *Chaoxian zhanzheng juece neimu*, pp. 62–63.

34. According to Zhang Xi, the text of the telegram was translated from Russian into confidential codes, and then sent from Moscow to the Soviet embassy in Beijing. It was then translated into Chinese, which did not reach Mao's hand until late afternoon, October 12. See Zhang Xi, "The Sudden Cancellation of the CPV's Movement on the Eve of Its Entry to Korea," p. 4.

35. Cited from Zhang Xi, "Peng's appointment," pp. 144–145.

36. Jiang Yonghui, *38 jun zai chaoxian*, pp. 28–29.

37. The time of this meeting follows the account of Zhang Xi (Zhang Xi, "Peng's appointment," p. 150). Zhu Jianrong, based on information offered by Lei Yingfu, claims that the meeting was possibly held from the late evening of October 12 to the early morning of October 13 (Zhu Jianrong, *Mao's Korean War*, pp. 288–289). In my discussions with Zhang Xi in August 1992, he pointed out that if the meeting were held earlier than the morning of October 13, it would have been impossible for Peng to attend the meeting. But there is strong documentary evidence to prove that Peng not only attended the meeting but also presented important opinions about Soviet air coverage to it. So the meeting could not have been held earlier than the afternoon of October 13. The description of the meeting in this paragraph, unless otherwise cited, is based on Zhang Xi, "Peng's appointment," p. 150, and Wang Yan et al., *Peng Dehuai zhuan*, p. 405–406.

38. Zhu Jianrong, *Mao's Korean War*, pp. 288–289; see also Hong Xuezhi, *Kangmei yuanchao zhanzheng huiyi*, p. 26.

39. Zhu Jianrong, *Mao's Korean War*, p. 289. In my interviews with Zhang Xi and Xu Yan in August 1992, they confirmed that the information offered by Zhu here is reliable.

40. "Mao Zedong's Conversations with Kim Il-sung," October 10, 1970, minute, CCA.

41. Zhang Xi, "The Sudden Cancellation of the CPV's Movement on the Eve of Its Entry to Korea," p. 6; and interviews with Zhang Xi, August 1992.

42. The very first sentence of Mao's telegram stated that "the October 11

telegram by Stalin and you received." Then, as discussed before, Mao stated that he had learned that "the Soviet Union was by all means in a position to satisfy China's need for artillery, tanks, airplanes, and other ammunition," and that "it will take at least two or two-and-half months for the Soviet air force to be ready to support Chinese Volunteers' operations in Korea." This, however, is not included in the published text of the telegram in *MWG*.

43. Mao Zedong to Zhou Enlai, October 13, 1950, *MWG*, 1: 556.

44. This part is not included in the published text of Mao's telegram. The summary of this part of the telegram here is based on the original text of the telegram kept in CCA.

45. See Shi Zhe, *Zai lishi jüren shenbian*, pp. 499–500. According to Shi Zhe, even Zhou was surprised when he received Mao's telegram.

46. Zhou Enlai to Stalin, October 14, 1950. Part of the telegram is cited by Shi Zhe in his *Zai lishi jüren shenbian*, p. 502. The original of the telegram is kept in CCA.

47. Interviews with Shi Zhe, August 1992.

48. Zhang Xi, "Peng's appointment," p. 151.

49. Mao Zedong to Zhou Enlai, 3:00 p.m. and 9 p.m., October 14, 1950 *MWG*, 1: 558–559, 560. *MWG* does not give the hour time for the second telegram. The hour cited here is based on Chai and Zhao, *Kangmei yuanchao jishi*, p. 60, and Zhang Xi, "Peng's appointment," pp. 151–152.

50. Mao Zedong to Zhou Enlai, 9:00 p.m., October 14, 1950, *MWG*: 558–559.

51. Mao Zedong to Zhou Enlai, 3:00 p.m., October 14, 1950, ibid., p. 559.

52. Mao Zedong to Zhou Enlai, 3:00 p.m., October 14, 1950; Mao Zedong to Chen Yi, October 14, 1950, ibid., pp. 559, 557.

53. Mao Zedong to Gao Gang and Peng Dehuai, 5 a.m. October 15, 1950, ibid., p. 564.

54. Zhang Xi, "Peng's appointment," pp. 152–153; Wang Yan et al., *Peng Dehuai zhuan*, p. 406; see also Hong Xuezhi, *Kangmei yuanchao zhanzheng huiyi*, p. 27.

55. Peng Dehuai, "Address at the CPV's Division Level Cadres Conference," October 14(?), 1950, *Peng Dehuai junshi wenxuan* (Selected Military Works of Peng Dehuai), (Beijing: The Central Press of Historical Documents, 1988), pp. 320–327. (According to other sources, Peng's address should be given on October 16, but *Peng Dehuai junshi wenxuan* mistakenly dates it for October 14.)

56. Zhang Xi, "Peng 's appointment," pp. 153–154; Shen and Meng et al., *Zhongguo renmin zhiyuanjun kangmei yuanchao zhanshi*, p. 15; Hu Guangzheng, "Brilliant Decisions and Great Achievements: On the Decision to Dispatch Troops to Korea," *Dangshi yanjiu*, no. 1 (1983): 37.

57. Du Ping, *Zai Zhiyuanjun zongbu*, pp. 35–36.

58. Xu Yan, "The Final Decision to Enter the Korean War," p. 11.

59. Zhang Xi, "Peng's appointment," p. 157.

60. Xu Yan, *Diyici jiaoliang*, p. 25; Zhang Xi, "Peng's Appointment," p. 157.

61. Mao Zedong to Peng Dehuai and Gao Gang, October 17, 1950, *MWG*, 1: 567. According to Zhang Xi, Mao also informed Peng and Gao that "it would be better to decide the time for sending off our troops after Zhou comes back to Beijing to report to the Central Committee on the 18th." Zhang Xi, "Peng's Appointment," p. 157; see also Wang Yan et al., *Peng Dehuai zhuan*, p. 407.

62. Xu Yan, "The Final Decision to Enter the Korean War," pp. 11–12; Wang Yan et al., *Peng Dehuai zhuan*, p. 407; Zhang Xi, "Peng's Appointment," p. 158. The quote of Mao's statement is from Zhang's article, which, according to my interviews with him in August 1992, is based on the minute of the meeting.

63. Mao Zedong to Deng Hua, Hong Xuezhi, Han Xianchu, and Xie Fang, October 18, 1950, *MWG*, 1: 568.

64. Hong Xuezhi, *Kangmei yuanchao zhanzheng huiyi*, p. 31; Zhang Xi, "Peng's Appointment," p. 159.

65. Mao Zedong to Deng Zihui, Tan Zheng and others, October 19, 1950, *MWG*, 1: 571; see also Mao Zedong to Hu Qiaomu, October 21, 1950, ibid., p. 580.

66. Zhang Xi, "Peng's Appointment," p. 155; Jiang Yonghui, *38 jun zai chaoxian*, pp. 33–34.

67. Starting on the evening of October 19, four Chinese armies (the 38th, 39th, 40th, and 42nd) and three artillery divisions crossed the Yalu River from three directions. By October 22, all these troops, with a total number of 260,000, had entered Korean territory. see Xu Yan, *Diyici jiaoliang*, pp. 39–40; Shen and Meng et al., *Zhongguo renmin zhiyuanjun kangmei yuanchao zhanshi*, p. 20; and Chai and Zhao, *Kangmei yuanchao jishi*, pp. 61–62.

68. Li Yinqiao (Li was the head of Mao's bodyguards at that time), *Zouxia shentan de Mao Zedong* (The Mao Zedong Who Was No Longer a God, Beijing: Chinese and Foreign Culture Press, 1989), pp. 122–123; and Xu Yan, *Diyici jiaoliang*, p. 25.

CONCLUSIONS

1. Peng Dehuai, *Peng Dehuai zishu*, p. 59; Chai and Zhao, *Banmendian tanpan*, p. 100; Shen and Meng et al., *Zhongguo renmin zhiyuanjun kangmei yuanchao zhanshi*, pp. 37–38.

2. Peng Dehuai, *Peng Dehuai zishu*, pp. 259–60. There exists no evidence to support the hypothesis held by some Western scholars that Beijing's temporary retreat after the first campaign was designed to give the UN forces an opportunity to retreat to areas south of the 38th parallel.

3. Jonathan D. Pollack, "The Korean War and Sino-American Relations," in Harding and Yuan eds., *Sino-American Relations, 1945–1955*, p. 224.

4. Mao Zedong to Peng Dehuai, December 21, 1950, *MWG*, 1: 731–732. Peng, as the commander at the front, had reservations about Mao's plan, but he obeyed Mao. For a more extended discussion, see Chen Jian, "China's Changing Aims during the Korean War," pp. 26–28.

5. According to Soviet sources, the Soviet air force entered operations in Korea as early as November 1950. (see G. Lobov, "In the Sky of North Korea," *Aviatsiia i Kosmonavtika*, no. 10 (1990): 33–34, and Jon Halliday, "Soviet Air Operations in Korea," a paper for the 15th Military History Symposium on "A Revolutionary War: Korea and the Transformation of the Postwar World," Air Force Academy, October 1992, p. 10). According to Chinese sources, however, the Soviet air force did not enter operations in North Korea until January 10, 1951 (see Tan, *Kangmei yuanchao zhanzheng*, p. 201; and Zhang Xi, "The Sudden Cancellation of the CPV's Movement on the Eve of its' Entry into Korea," p. 4.)

6. Hong Xuezhi, *Kangmei yuanchao zhanzheng huiyi*, pp. 110–111; and Shi Zhe, *Zai lishi jüren shenbian*, pp. 503–504.

7. Hong Xuezhi, *Kangmei yuanchao zhanzheng huiyi*, pp. 109–110; Tan Jingqiao et al., *Kangmei yuanchao zhanzheng*, p. 100; and Shen and Meng et al., *Zhongguo renmin zhiyuanjun kangmei yuanchao zhanshi*, p. 87.

8. Peng Dehuai to Mao Zedong and the CMC, January 10, 1951, telegram, CMA. Peng reported in this telegram that the North Koreans were very unhappy with his decision to stop the offensive; and they put forward their complaints through Soviet advisers in North Korea. See also Li, Rui, *Lushan huiyi shilu (An Factual Account of the Lushan Conference*, Beijing: Chunqiu Press, 1989), p. 224.

9. For a detailed discussion of the exchanges between Mao and Peng, see Chen Jian, "China's Changing Aims during the Korean War," pp. 31–33; see also Qi Dexue, *Chaoxian zhanzheng juece neimu*, pp. 116–119.

10. Mao Zedong to Stalin, March 1, 1951, *MWG*, 2: 151–153; see also Chen Jian, "China's Changing Aims during the Korean War," pp. 34–36.

11. For a more extended discussion, see Chen Jian, "China's Changing Aims," pp. 37–38.

12. Michael Hunt emphasizes that American foreign policy was shaped by an ideology based on a conception of national mission, on the racial classification of other countries, and on suspicion and even hostility toward

social revolution (Michael Hunt, *Ideology and U.S. Foreign Policy* [New Haven: Yale University Press, 1987]). I find Hunt's analysis offers an extremely enlightening background for understanding U.S. policy toward revolutionary China in the late 1940s.

13. For an excellent discussion of the American notion of a special relationship with China, see Michael Hunt, *The Making of a Special Relationship: The United States and China to 1914* (New York: Columbia University Press, 1983); For a discussion emphasizing the sense of a special American destiny as the main cause underlying Washington's hostility toward Communist China, see David McLean, "American Nationalism, the China Myth, and the Truman Doctrine: The Question of Accommodation with Peking, 1949–50," *Diplomatic History*, 10, no. 1 (Winter 1986): 25–42.

14. A comparison between Washington's perceptions of the Soviet Union and of China will make this point clearer. Despite the sharp differences between the United States and the Soviet Union in the deepening Cold War confrontation, as pointed out by Rosemary Foot, policymakers in Washington found that at least there existed between themselves and Soviet leaders "certain interests in common" in avoiding a direct military confrontation between them. In contrast, American policymakers found that Beijing's behavior, which was "fundamentalist, violent, and revolutionary," could not be understood by any of their own rationales. They would thus distinguish between the Soviet Union as their "reasonable adversary" and China as their "irrational foe." See Foot, *The Wrong War*, pp. 27–28.

15. Hunt, "Beijing and the Korean Crisis," p. 463.

16. The "Three Antis" movement was designed to oppose corrupt Communist cadres; the "Five-Antis" movement was aimed at the national bourgeoisie class "who should not be destroyed at this stage but who needed to be tightly controlled by the power of the people's state." For discussions of these movements, see Lin Yunhui et al., *Kaige xingjing de shiqi*, chapter 7; and Frederick C. Teiwes, "Establishment and Consolidation of the New Regime," in MacFarquhar and Fairbank, eds., *The Cambridge History of China*, 14: 88–91.

17. See Zhai Qiang, "China and the Geneva Conference of 1954," *The China Quarterly*, no.129 (March 1992): 103–122; and Chen Jian, "China and the First Indo-China War," pp. 104–109.

18. When CPV entered Korea, Mao Anying was appointed as Peng Dehuai's confidential secretary. He died on November 25, 1950 during an American air assault on CPV headquarters.

Selected Bibliography

Chinese Language Sources

Chinese romanizations are not provided for titles of newspaper or journal articles. English names are provided in brackets for periodicals cited. They are as follows:

Dangde wenxian [Party Historical Documents]
Dangshi wenhui [Collection of Party History Studies]
Dangshi yanjiu [Party History Studies]
Dangshi yanjiu ziliao [Party History Research Materials]
Dongbei ribao [Northeast Daily]
Geming huiyilu [Revolutionary Memoirs]
Guoshi yanjiu ziliao [Research Materials of PRC History]
Hunan dangshi tongxun [Newsletter of Party History Studies in Hunan]
Jiefang ribao [Liberation Daily]
Jindaishi yanjiu [Studies of Modern History]
Junshi shilin [Military History Circles]
Junshi lishi [Military History]
Junshi ziliao [Materials of Military History]
Lishi yanjiu [Historical Studies]
Meiguo yanjiu [Journal of American Study]
Mingren zhuanji [The Biographical Journal of Big Names]
Renmin ribao [People's Daily]
Renwu [Biographical Journal]

Shijie zhishi [World Knowledge, also translated as "World Culture" by some scholars]
Shishi shouce [Current Affairs Handbook))
Wenxian yu yanjiu [Documents and Study]
Xinghuo liaoyuan [A Single Spark Starting a Prairie Fire]
Xinhua yuebao [New China Monthly]
Xuexi [Study]
Yanhuang chunqiu [Spring and Autumn of the Chinese People]
Zhonggong dangshi tongxun [Newsletter of CCP History Studies]
Zhonggong dangshi yanjiu [CCP History Studies]
Zhonggong dangshi ziliao [Materials of the CCP History]

Ba, Zhongtan et al. *Shanghai zhanyi* [The Shanghai Campaign]. Shanghai: Xuelin Press, 1989.

Bao, Mingrong and Hu Guangzheng. "Several Problems Concerning the Application and Development of Mao Zedong's Military Thought During the War to Resist America and Assist Korea." *Dangshi yanjiu* (1983), no. 6.

Bo, Yibo. *Ruogan zhongda juece yu shijian de huigu* [Recollections of Several Important Decisions and Events]. Beijing: CCP Central Academy Press, 1991.

Central Institute of Historical Documents, ed. *Jianguo yilai zhongyao wenxian xuanbian, 1949-1950* [Selected Important Documents since the Founding of the PRC]. Beijing: The Central Press of Historical Documents, 1991.

Chai, Chengwen and Zhao Yongtian. *Banmendian tanpan* [The Panmunjom Negotiations]. Beijing: People's Liberation Army Press, 1989; second edition, 1992.

———. *Kangmei yuanchao jishi* [A Chronicle of the War to Resist America and Assist Korea]. Beijing: CCP Historical Materials Press, 1987.

Chaoxian wenti wenjian huibian [Selected Documents of the Korean Problem]. Beijing: People's Press, 1954.

Chen, Enhui. "An Important Conference for Strategic Decision-making: The CCP Politburo's September 1948 Conference." *Dangde wenxian*, (1989), no. 5.

Chen, Geng. *Chen Geng riji* [Chen Geng's Diaries]. 2 vols. Beijing: People's Liberation Army Press, 1984.

Chen, Guangxiang. "Why Did the PLA Fail to Liberate Shanghai Immediately after Crossing the Yangzi River." *Dangshi yanjiu ziliao*, (1992), no. 5.

———. "An Exploration of Stalin's Interference with the PLA's Plan to Cross the Yangzi River." *Zhonggong dangshi yanjiu* (1990), the Supplementary Issue on Relations Between the Soviet Union and the Chinese Revolution.

Chen, Hanbo. "Why China and the Soviet Union Should Participate in the [Korean] War." *Shijie zhishi,* July 14, 1950.

Chen, Jian. "China's Revolutionary Diplomacy versus America's Strategy of Containment: The Recognition Controversy, 1949–1950." In Wang Qingjia and Chen Jian eds. *Zhongxi lishi lunbianji* [Essays on Chinese and Western History by Chinese Historians in the United States]. Shanghai: Xuelin Press, 1992.

Chen, Jin. *Mao Zedong de wenhua xingge* [The Cultural Characters of Mao Zedong]. Beijing: The Press of Chinese Youth, 1991

Chen, Yan. ed. *Kangmei yuanchao lunwenji* [Essays on the War to Resist America and Assist Korea]. Shenyang: Liaoning People's Press, 1988.

Chen, Yun. *Chen Yun wenxuan, 1926–1949* [Selected Works of Chen Yun, 1926–1949]. Beijing: People's Press, 1984.

———. *Chen Yun wengao xuanbian, 1949–1956* [Selected Manuscripts of Chen Yun, 1949–1956]. Beijing: People's Press, 1984.

Cheng, Hua. ed. *Zhou Enlai he ta de mishumen* [Zhou Enlai and His Secretaries]. Beijing: Chinese Broadcasting and Television Press, 1992.

Chi, Aiping. "Mao Zedong's Strategic Direction of the New China's Diplomatic Affairs." *Dangde wenxian* (1992), no. 1.

"The Chinese People Are Watching Closely the Development of the Korean Situation." *Shijie zhishi,* August 26, 1950.

The Chinese Revolutionary Military Museum, comp. *Peng Dehuai yuanshuai fengbei yongcun* [The Monumental Achievements of Marshall Peng Dehuai Will Live Forever]. Shanghai: Shanghai People's Press, 1985.

Cui, Kezhi and Liu Huibo, eds. *Zhongguo waijiao sishinian* [The Forty Years of China's Diplomacy]. Shenyang: Shenyang Press, 1989.

Cui, Lun. "My Reminiscences of Chief Peng's Communication and Liaison Affairs After Our Troops' Entry into the Korean War." *Junshi lishi* (1989), no. 4.

Deng, Lifeng. *Xin zhongguo junshi huodong jishi, 1949–1959* [A Factual Record of the New China's Military Affairs]. Beijing: CCP Historical Materials Press, 1989.

Deng, Liqun. "Before and After Xinjiang's Peaceful Liberation: A Page of Sino-Soviet Relations." *Jindaishi yanjiu* (1989), no. 5.

Ding, Xuesong et al. "Recalling the Northeast Bureau's Special Office in North Korea During the War of Liberation in the Northeast." *Zhonggong dangshi ziliao,* 17 [March 1986]; a similar version of the article is published in *Liaoshen juezhan* [The Liaoshen Campaign]. Beijing: People's Liberation Army Press, 1988.

Du, Ping. *Zai zhiyuanjun zongbu: Du Ping huiyilu* [My Days at the Headquarters of the Chinese People's Volunteers: Du Ping's Memoirs]. Beijing: People's Liberation Army Press, 1988.

———. "The Brilliant Decision." *Xinghuo liaoyuan* (1985), no. 6.

Du, Ruo. "China's Liberation and Southeast Asia." *Shijie zhishi*, June 17, 1949.

The Editorial Committee and the History Department of Fudan University, eds. *Zhongmei guanxi lunwenji* [Essays on Sino-American Relations,] 3 vols. Chongqing: The Chongqing Press, 1985 and 1988; Nanjing: Nanjing University Press, 1992.

The Editorial Department of *Xinghuo liaoyuan* eds. *Jiefangjun jianglingzhuan* [A Collection of Biographies of PLA Commanders] 13 vols. Beijing: People's Liberation Army Press, 1987–1988.

The Editorial Group of the History of Chinese Military Advisory Group. *Zhongguo guwentuan yuanyue kangmei douzheng shishi* [A Factual History of Chinese Military Advisory Group in the Struggle of Assisting Vietnam and Resisting France]. Beijing: People's Liberation Army Press, 1990.

"Eight Documents on the PLA's Marching Toward the Fujian Province, May–October 1950." *Dangde wenxian* (1990), no. 2.

Fu, Ying. "The U.S. Imperialists are Beatable." *Xuexi* (1950) no. 11.

Gao, Yong et al. *Bujing de sinian* [Remember Him for Ever]. Beijing: The Central Press of Historical Documents, 1987.

Ge, Baoquan. "In Commemoration of Wang Jiaxiang, China's First Ambassador to the Soviet Union." In the Editorial Group of "Selected Works of Wang Jiaxiang" ed. *Huiyi Wang Jiaxiang* [In Commemoration of Wang Jiaxiang]. Beijing: People's Press, 1985.

Geng, Biao. *Geng Biao huiyilu* [Geng Biao's Memoirs]. Beijing: People's Liberation Army Press, 1991.

Gu, Junjie and Lu Xingdou et al. *Zhou Enlai he ta de shiye* [Zhou Enlai and His Cause]. Beijing: CCP History Press, 1990.

Hai, Fu. *Weisheme yibiandao* [Why Should We Lean to One Side]. Beijing: World Affairs Press, 1951.

Han, Huaizhi and Tan Jingqiao et al. *Dangdai zhongguo jundui de junshi gongzuo* [The Military Affairs of Contemporary Chinese Army] 2 vols. Beijing: Chinese Social Sciences Press, 1989.

Han, Nianlong et al. *Dangdai zhongguo waijiao* [Contemporary Chinese Diplomacy]. Beijing: Chinese Social Sciences Press, 1987.

He, Changgong. *He Changgong huiyilu* [He Changgong's Memoirs]. Beijing: People's Liberation Army Press, 1987.

He, Di. "The CCP's Policy Toward the United States, 1945–1949." *Lishi yanjiu* (1987), no. 3.

He, Jingxiu et al. *Mianhuai Liu Shaoqi* [In Commemoration of Liu Shaoqi]. Beijing: The Central Press of Historical Documents, 1988.

He, Long, *He Long junshi wenxuan* [Selected Military Papers of He Long]. Beijing: People's Liberation Army Press, 1989.

He, Xiaolu. *Yuanshuai waijiaojia* [A Marshal and a Diplomat]. Beijing: People's Liberation Army Literature Press, 1985.

Hoang, Van Hoan. *Canghai yisu: Hoang Van Hoan geming huiyilu* [A Drop in the Ocean: The Revolutionary Memoirs of Hoang Van Hoan]. Beijing: People's Liberation Army Press, 1987.

Hong, Xuezhi. *Kangmei yuanchao zhanzheng huiyi* [Recollections of the War to Resist America and Assist Korea]. Beijing: People's Liberation Army Literature Press, 1990.

———. "The Logistic Affairs in the War to Resist America and Assist Korea." *Junshi lishi* (1987), no. 1.

Hu, Guangzheng and Ma Shanying, eds. *Zhongguo renmin zhiyuanjun xulie* [The Organizations of the Chinese People's Volunteers]. Beijing: People's Liberation Army Press, 1987.

Hu, Guangzheng. "Brilliant Decision and Great Achievements." *Dangshi yanjiu* (1983), no. 1.

Hu, Guangzheng and Bao Mingrong. "Several Factual Corrections of Yan Xu's 'The Brilliant Decision to Resist America and Assist Korea.' " *Dangshi yanjiu* (1981), no. 3.

Hu, Hua et al. *Zhonggong dangshi renwu zhuan* [A Collection of Biographies of CCP's Historical Figures]. 50 vols. Xi'an: Shaanxi People's Press, 1979–1991.

Hu, Jiamuo. "A Factual Record of General Peng's Leading Troops to Korea." *Mingren zhuanji* (1990), no. 10.

Hu, Sheng et al. *Zhongguo gongchandang qishinian* [A Seventy Year History of the Chinese Communist Party]. Beijing: CCP History Press, 1991.

———. "How Did the United States Invade China in History." *Shishi shouce* (1950), no. 3.

Hu, Shiyan et al. *Chen Yi zhuan* [A Biography of Chen Yi]. Beijing: Contemporary China Press, 1991.

Hua, Qingzhao. *Cong yaerta dao banmendian: meiguo yu zhong, su, ying, 1945–1953* [From Yalta to Panmunjom: The United States, China, the Soviet Union, and Great Britain, 1945–1953]. Beijing: Chinese Social Sciences Press, 1992.

Huang, Hua. "My Contacts with Stuart after Najing's Liberation." In Pei Jianzhang et al. *Xinzhongguo waijiao fengyun*, listed below.

Huang, Yi. "Zhou Enlai: The Leader and Organizer of Strategic Logistic Affairs During the War to Resist America and Assist Korea." *Junshi shilin* (1989), nos. 5 and 6.

———. "Peng Dehuai's Great Contribution to the Logistic Affairs During the War to Resist America and Assist Korea." *Junshi shilin* (1989), no. 1.

Huang, Youlan. *Zhongguo renmin jiefang zhanzheng shi* [A History of the Chinese People's War of Liberation]. Beijing: Archives Press, 1992.

Huang, Zheng. *Hu Zhiming he zhongguo* [Ho Chi-minh and China]. Beijing: People's Liberation Army Press, 1987.

The Institute of Modern Chinese History at Fudan University, comp. *Zhongguo jindai duiwai guanxi shi ziliao xuanji* [Selected Historical Materials of the History of Modern Chinese International Relations]. Shanghai: Shanghai People's Press, 1977.

The Institute of Diplomatic History under the PRC's Foreign Ministry, ed. *Zhou Enlai waijiao huodong dashiji* [A Chronicle of Zhou Enlai's Diplomatic Activities]. Beijing: World Affairs Press, 1993.

Jiang, Yonghui. *38 jun zai chaoxian* [The 38th Army in Korea]. Shenyang: Liaoning People's Press, 1989.

Jin, Chongji et al. *Zhou Enlai zhuan, 1898–1949* [A Biography of Zhou Enlai]. Beijing: People's Press and the Central Press of Historical Documents, 1989.

Jing, Yu. "The Military Experience of Our Troops During the Korean War." *Junshi shiling* (1988), no. 5.

Ke, Bainian. "The New Democratic Foreign Policy." *Xuexi* (1949), no. 10.

———. "How Did the Soviet Union Struggle Against the Imperialists after the October Revolution." *Xuexi* (1949), no. 11.

Li, Changjiu and Shi Lujia, eds. *Zhongmei guanxi liangbainian* [Two Hundred Years of Sino-American relations]. Beijing: Xinhua Press, 1984.

Li, Jianwei et al. *Zhongguo gongchandang lishi* [A History of the Chinese Communist Party] 3 vols., Beijing: CCP Central Academy Press, 1990.

Li, Jükui. *Li Jükui huiyilu* [Li Jükui's Memoirs]. Beijing: People's Liberation Army Press, 1986.

———. "March Forward in the Face of Difficulties: Recalling the CPV's Logistic Affairs Before the Fifth Campaign." *Xinghuo liaoyuan* (1985), no. 5.

Li, Ping and Fang Ming et al, *Zhou Enlai nianpu, 1898- 1949* [A Chronology of Zhou Enlai, 1898–1949]. Beijing: The Central Press of Historical Documents and People's Press, 1989.

Li, Rui. "An Account on the Takeover of the Shenyang City." *Zhonggong dangshi ziliao* (1992), no. 40.

———. *Lushan huiyi shilu* [A Factual Account of the Lushan Conference]. Beijing: Chunqiu Press, 1989.

Li, Yinqiao. *Zai Mao zhuxi shenbian shiwunian* [With Chairman Mao for Fifteen Years]. Shijiazhuang: Hebei People's Press, 1991.

Li, Yueran. *Waijiao wutai shang de xinzhongguo lingxiu* [The Leaders of New China on the Diplomatic Scene]. Beijing: People's Liberation Army Press, 1989.

Liao, Gailong. "The Relations Between the Soviet Union and the Chinese Revolutionaries During the 1940s." *Zhonggong dangshi yanjiu*, Supplementary Issue on Relations Between the Chinese Revolution and the Soviet Union, 1990.

Lin, Fu et al. *Kongjun shi* [A History of the PLA's Air Force]. Beijing: People's Liberation Army Press, 1989.

Lin, Guliang. "A Brief Factual Description of the New China's Struggle Against Economic Blockade and Boycott." *Zhonggong dangshi ziliao* (1992), no. 42.

Lin, Yunhui et al. *Kaige xingjing de shiqi* [China from 1949 to 1989: The Period of Triumphant March]. Zhengzhou: Henan People's Press, 1989.

Liu, Guoguang et al. *Zhonghua renmin gongheguo jingji dang'an ziliao xuanbian, 1919–1952* [Selected Economic Archival Materials of the People's Republic of China, 1919–1952]. Beijing: Chinese Urban Economical Society Press, 1989.

Liu, Han et al. *Luo Ronghuan zhuan* [A Biography of Luo Ronghuan]. Beijing: Contemporary China Press, 1991.

Liu, Jiecheng. *Mao Zedong yu Sidalin* [Mao Zedong and Stalin]. Beijing: CCP Central Academy Press, 1993.

Liu, Shaoqi. *Liu Shaoqi xuanji* [Selected Works of Liu Shaoqi]. Beijing: The People's Press, 1984.

———. "On the Nature of China's New Democratic State and Government." *Wenxian yu yanjiu* (1982), no. 10.

———. "On Internationalism and Nationalism." *Renmin ribao*, November 7, 1948.

Liu, Wenxing and Li Yueqing. *Zhou Baozhong zhuan* [A Biography of Zhou Baozhong]. Harbin: Heilongjinag People's Press, 1987.

Liu, Wusheng et al. *Gongheguo zouguo de lu: jianguo yilai zhongyao wenxian zhuanti xuanji* [The Path the Republic Has Walked Through: A Selected Collection of Important Historical Documents Since the Establishment of the People's Republic, 1949–1952] 2 vols. Beijing: The Central Press of Historical Documents, 1991.

Liu, Xiao. *Chushi sulian banian* [Eight Years as Ambassador in the Soviet Union]. Beijing: CCP Historical Materials Press, 1986.

Liu, Zhen. *Liu Zhen huiyilu* [Liu Zhen's Memoirs]. Beijing: People's Liberation Army Press, 1990.

Liu, Zhi et al. *Xu Xiangqian zhuan* [A Biography of Xu Xiangqian]. Beijing: Contemporary China Press, 1991.

Lu, Dingyi. *Lu Dingyi wenji* [A Collection of Lu Dingyi's Works]. Beijing: People's Press, 1992.

———. "Explanations of Several Basic Problems Concerning the Postwar International Situation." *Jiefang ribao*, January 4 and 5, 1947.

Lü, Liping. *Tongtian zhilu* [The Path to the Sky]. Beijing: People's Liberation Army Press, 1989.

Luo, Guibo. "Comrade Liu Shaoqi Sent Me to Vietnam." In He Jingxiu et al. *Mianhuai Liu Shaoqi* [In Commemoration of Liu Shaoqi]. Beijing: The Central Press of Historical Documents, 1988.

Luo, Yingwen. "Two or Three Facts About General Deng Hua." *Renwu* (1985), no. 5.

Ma, Qibing and Chen Wenping et al. *Zhongguo gongchandang zhizheng sishinian* [The Chinese Communist Party as the Ruling Party for Forty Year]. Beijing: CCP Historical Materials Press, 1989.

Mao, Zedong. *Mao Zedong junshi wenji* [A Collection of Mao Zedong's Military Papers]. vols 5–6. Beijing: Military Science Press and the Central Press of Historical Documents, 1993.

———. *Jianguo yilai Mao Zedong wengao* [Mao Zedong's Manuscripts Since the Founding of the People's Republic]. vol.1, September 1949–December 1950, and vol.2, January 1951–December 1951. Beijing: The Central Press of Historical Documents, 1987, 1989.

———. *Mao Zedong shuxin xuanji* [Selected Correspondences of Mao Zedong]. Beijing: People's Press, 1983.

———. *Mao Zedong xinwen gongzuo wenxuan* [Selected Works of Mao Zedong on Journalistic Affairs]. Beijing: Xinhua Press, 1983.

———. *Mao Zedong junshi wenxuan* [Selected Military Works of Mao Zedong]. Beijing: Soldiers' Press, 1981.

———. *Mao Zedong xuanji* [Selected Works of Mao Zedong]. 5 vols. Beijing: People's Press, 1960, 1977.

Meng, Xianzhang et al. *Zhongsu maoyi shi ziliao* [Historical Materials of Sino-Soviet Trade Relations]. Beijing: Chinese Foreign Economy and Trade Press, 1991.

Meng, Zhaohui. "The Application and Development of Mao Zedong's Military Thought in the War to Resist America and Assist Korea." *Junshi lishi* (1991), no. 1.

———. "A Discussion of the Origins and Nature of the Korean War." *Junshi shilin* (1988), no. 1.

The Military Library of the Academy of Military Science eds. *Zhongguo renmin jiefangjun zuzhi he geji lingdao chengyuan minglu* [A List of the Historical Evolution of Organizations and Leading Members of the People's Liberation Army]. Beijing: Military Science Press, 1990.

Mo, Yang and Yao Jie et al. *Zhongguo renmin jiefangjun zhanshi* [The War History of the Chinese People's Liberation Army]. 3 vols. Beijing: Military Science Press, 1987.

Mu, Xin. *Chen Geng dajiang* [General Chen Geng]. Beijing: Xinhua Press, 1985.

National Defense University, Editorial Group. *Zhongguo renmin zhiyuanjun*

zhanshi jianbian [A Brief History of the Chinese People's Volunteers]. Beijing: People's Liberation Army Press, 1992.

Nie, Rongzhen. *Nie Rongzhen junshi wenxuan* [Selected Military Works of
Nie Rongzhen]. Beijing: People's Liberation Army Press, 1992.

———. *Nie Rongzhen huiyilu* [Nie Rongzhen's Memoirs]. Beijing: People's
Liberation Army Press, 1986.

Niu, Jun. *Cong Yanan zouxiang shijie: zhongguo gongchangdang duiwai guanxi
de qiyuan* [From Yanan to the World: The Origins of the CCP's External
Relations]. Fuzhou: Fujian People's Press, 1992.

———. *Cong heerli dao maxieer: meiguo tiaochu guogong maodun shimo* [From
Hurley to Marshall: American Mediation of the GMD-CCP Contradic-
tion]. Fuzhou: Fujian People's Press, 1988.

———. "The Origins of Mao Zedong's Revolutionary Diplomatic Strategy." *Jindaishi yanjiu* (1992), no. 6.

Pang, Xianzhi et al., *Mao Zedong nianpu, 1893–1949* [A Chronology of Mao
Zedong, 1893–1949]. 3 vols. Beijing: People's Press and the Central Press
of Historical Documents, 1993.

The Party History Institute under the CCP Central Committee, comp.
Zhonggong dangshi dashiji, 1919–1990 [A Chronicle of the History of the
Chinese Communist Party, 1919–1990]. Beijing: People's Press, 1991.

Pei, Jianzhang et al. *Xinzhongguo waijiao fengyun* [The Experiences of New
China's Diplomacy]. Beijing: World Affairs Press, 1990.

Peng, Dehuai. *Peng Dehuai junshi wenxuan* [Selected Military Works of Peng
Dehuai]. Beijing: The Central Press of Historical Documents, 1988.

———. *Peng Dehuai zishu* [The Autobiographical Notes of Peng Dehuai].
Beijing: People's Press, 1981.

Piao Doufu [Pak Tu-bok]. *Zhonggong canjia chaozhan yuanyin zhi yanjiu* [A
Study of the CCP's Participation in the Korean War]. Taipei: publisher
unclear, 1975.

The Political Department of the Chinese People's Volunteers. *Zhongguo renmin zhiyuanjun kangmei yuanchao zhanzheng zhengzhi gongzuo zongjie* [A
Summary of the Political Affairs of the Chinese People's Volunteers During the War to Resist America and Assist Korea]. Beijing: People's Liberation Army Press, 1985.

Qi, Dexue. "Zhou Enlai's Significant Contribution to the Guidance of the
War to Resist America and Assist Korea." *Junshi lishi* (1992), no. 1.

———. *Chaoxian zhanzheng juece neimu* [The Inside Story of the Decision-
making During the Korean War]. Liaoning: Liaoning University Press,
1991.

———. "A Survey of the CPV's Strategic Aims During the War to Resist
America and Assist Korea." *Zhonggong dangshi yanjiu* (1989), no. 6.

————. "A Distorted 'Factual Record': A Review of 'Heixue: A Historical Record of China's Entry into the Korean War.' " *Junshi lishi* (1989),
no. 6.

Qian, Jiang. *Zai Shenmi de zhanzheng zhong: Zhongguo junshi guwentuan fu
yuenan zhengzhan ji* [In the Course of a Misterious War: Chinese Military Advisory Group in Vietnam]. Zhengzhou: Henan People's Press,
1992.

"Selected Documents and Telegrams of the Campaign to Eliminate Bandits
in the Early Days of the PRC, November 1950–April 1951." *Dangde
wenxian* (1990), no. 6.

"Selected Documents of the CCP Central Committee Politburo's September 1948 Conference, September 8–11, 1948." *Dangde wenxian* (1989),
no. 5.

"Selected Telegrams of the PLA's Central-Southern Campaign." *Dangde
wenxian* (1991), no. 3.

"Selected Telegrams of the Deng Liqun Radio Station, August-December
1949." *Zhonggong dangshi ziliao* (1990), no. 36.

Shanghai Archives. *Shanghai jiefang* [Shanghai's Liberation]. Beijing:
Archives Press, 1989.

Shen, Zonghong and Meng, Zhaohui et al. *Zhongguo renmin zhiyuanjun
kangmei yuanchao zhanshi* [A History of the War to Resist America and
Assist Korea by the Chinese People's Volunteers]. Beijing: Military Science Press, 1988.

Shen, Zonghong, and Bi Jianzhong et al. *Zhongguo renmin jiefangjun liushin-
ian dashiji* [Important Events of the Chinese People's Liberation Army,
1927–1987]. Beijing: Military Science Press, 1988.

Shi, Yinhong. "From Confrontation to War: The Truman Administration's
Policy Toward the New China." Ph.D. Dissertation, Nanjing University,
1987.

Shi, Zhe. *Feng yu gu: Shi Zhe huiyilu* [High Peak and Deep Valley: Shi Zhe's
Memoirs]. Beijing: Red Flag Press, 1992.

————. *Zai lishi jüren shenbian: Shi Zhe huiyilu* [Together with Historical
Giants: Shi Zhe's Memoirs]. Beijing: The Central Press of Historical Documents, 1991.

————."I Accompanied Chairman Mao to the Soviet Union." *Renwu*
(1988), no. 5.

————. "Random Recollections of Comrade Liu Shaoqi." *Geming huiyilu*
(1983), supplementary issue no. 1.

Si, Mu. "The International Significance of the Victory of the Chinese People's Revolutionary War." *Shijie zhishi*, December 31, 1949.

Song, Renqiong. "Before and After Nanjing's Liberation." *Zhonggong dangshi ziliao* (1991), no. 38.

Su, Yu. *Su Yu zhanzheng huiyilu* [Su Yu's War Memoirs]. Beijing: People's Liberation Army Press, 1988.

Sun, Baoshen. "Mao Zedong Had Predicted that the Americans Would Land at Inchon." *Junshi shilin* (1990), no. 10.

Sun, Kejia. "The New Development of Mao Zedong's Thought of People's War During the War to Resist America and Assist Korea." *Junshi lishi* (1990), no. 5.

Sun, Qitai. "A Brief Summary of the Movement to Resist America and Assist Korea." *Zhonggong dangshi ziliao* (1990), no. 36.

Sun, Yaoshen and Cui Jingshan. "Winning Victory Not Just on the Battlefield: General Xie Fang in Korea." *Renwu* (1991), no. 1.

———. "General Xie Fang in the War to Resist America and Assist Korea." *Junshi lishi* (1990), no. 4.

Taiwan wenti wenjian [Documents on the Taiwan Problem]. Beijing: People's Press, 1955.

Tan, Jingqiao et al. *Kangmei yuanchao zhanzheng* [The War to Resist America and Assist Korea]. Beijing: Chinese Social Sciences Press, 1990.

Tan, Zheng. *Zhongguo renmin zhiyuanjun renwulu* [Biographical Records of Members of the Chinese People's Volunteers]. Beijing: CCP History Press, 1992.

Tao, Wenzhao. "The United States and China's Three Revolutions." *Zhonggong dangshi yanjiu* (1990), no. 2.

Tong, Xiaopeng et al. *Zhonggong zhongyang jiefang zhanzheng shiqi tongyi zhanxian wenjian xuanbian* [Selected United Front Documents of the CCP Central Committee During the War of Liberation]. Beijing: Archives Press, 1988.

———. et al. *Zhonggong zhongyang nanjing ju* [The CCP Central Committee's Nanjing Bureau]. Beijing: CCP History Press, 1990.

Wang, Binnan. *Zhongmei huitan jiunian huigu* [Nine Years of Sino-American Ambassadorial Talks]. Beijing: World Affairs Press, 1985.

Wang, Bo. *Peng Dehuai ru chao zuozhan jishi* [A Factual Account of Peng Dehuai's Leading Troops to Fight in Korea]. Shijiazhuang: Huashan Literature Press, 1992.

Wang, Dinglie et al. *Dangdai zhongguo kongjun* [Contemporary Chinese Air Force]. Beijing: Chinese Social Sciences Press, 1989.

Wang, Dongxing. *Wang Dongxing riji* [Wang Dongxing's Diaries]. Beijing: Chinese Social Sciences Presss, 1993.

Wang, Fangming. "We Should Respect the Truth and Think Independently: A Conversation with Chairman Mao in 1957." *Renmin ribao*, January 2, 1979.

Wang, Jianhua. "Brilliant Prediction, Great Decision, and Correct Action." *Wenxian yu yanjiu* (1985), no. 6.

Wang, Jianwei. "U.S. Policy Toward China around the Formation of the People's Republic of China." Master's thesis. Shanghai: Fudan University, 1985.

Wang, Jiaxiang. *Wang Jiaxiang xuanji* [Selected Works of Wang Jiaxiang]. Beijing: People's Press, 1989.

Wang, Runshen et al. *Kongjun: huiyi shiliao* [The Air Force: Reminisces and Recollections]. Beijing: People's Liberation Army Press, 1992.

Wang, Xianli and Li Ping et al. *Zhu De nianpu* [A Chronology of Zhu De]. Beijing: People's Press, 1986.

Wang, Yan et al. *Peng Dehuai zhuan* [A Biography of Peng Dehuai]. Beijing: Contemporary China Press, 1993.

Weida de kangmei yuanchao yundong [The Great Movement to Resist America and Assist Korea]. Beijing: People's Press, 1954.

Weng, Zhonger. "The Failure of America's Intervention in China and the Success of the War of Liberation." *Zhonggong dangshi ziliao* (1991), no. 38.

Wu, Xiuquan. *Huiyi yu huainian* [Recollections and Commemorations]. Beijing: CCP Central Academy Press, 1991.

———. *Wangshi cangsang: Wu Xiuquan huiyilu* [The Vicissitude of My Life: Wu Xiuquan's Memoirs]. Shanghai: Shanghai Literature Press, 1986.

———. *Zai waijiaobu bainian de jingli, 1950–1958* [Eight Years in the Ministry of Foreign Affairs, January 1950–October 1958]. Beijing: New World Press, 1984.

Xiang, Qing. "My Opinions on the Question Whether Stalin Had Advised Our Party Not to Cross the Yangzi River." *Dangde wenxian* (1989), no. 6.

Xiao, Jinguang. *Xiao Jinguang huiyilu* [Xiao Jinguang's Memoirs]. 2 vols. Beijing: People's Liberation Army Press, 1988 and 1989.

Xie Fang et al. *Kangmei yuanchao zhanzheng houqin jingyan zongjie* [Summaries of the Experiences of Logistical Affairs During the War to Resist America and Assist Korea] 5 vols. Beijing: Golden Shield Press, 1987.

Xie, Yixian. *Zhechong yu gongchu: xinzhongguo duiwai guanxi sishinian* [Confrontation and Coexistence: Forty Years of the New China's Foreign Policy]. Zhengzhou: Henan People's Press, 1990.

———. *Zhongguo waijiao shi, 1949–1979* [A History of Chinese Diplomacy, 1949–1979]. Zhengzhou: Henan People's Press, 1988.

Xu, Guangyi et al. *Dangdai zhongguo jundui de houqin gongzuo* [The Logistical Affairs of the Contemporary Chinese Army]. Beijing: Chinese Social Sciences Press, 1990.

Xu, Peilan and Zheng Pengfei. *Chen Geng jiangjun zhuan* [A Biography of General Chen Geng]. Beijing: People's Liberation Army Press, 1988.

Xu, Xiangqian. "The Great March to Win the Victory in the Whole Country." *Zhonggong dangshi ziliao* (1991), no. 38.

Xu, Yan. *Jinmen zhizhan* [The Battles for Jinmen]. Beijing: Chinese Broadcasting and Television Press, 1992.

———. "The Tortuous Process of Making the Final Decision to Enter the Korean War." *Dangshi yanjiu ziliao* (1991), no. 4.

———. *Diyici jiaoliang: kangmei yuanchao zhanzheng de lishi huigu yu fansi* [The First Test of Strength: A Historical Review and Evaluation of the War to Resist America and Assist Korea]. Beijing: Chinese Broadcasting and Television Press, 1990.

———. "How Did the CCP Central Committee Make the Decision to Dispatch Troops to Resist America and Assist Korea." Unpublished manuscript.

Yan, Changling. *Jingwei Mao zhuxi jishi* [Records of Guarding Chairman Mao]. Changchun: Jilin People's Press, 1992.

Yang, Chengwu. *Yang Chengwu huiyilu* [Yang Chengwu's Memoirs]. 2 vols. Beijing: People's Liberation Army Press, 1987, 1990.

Yang, Dezhi. *Yang Dezhi huiyilu* [Yang Dezhi's Memoirs]. Beijing: People's Liberation Army Press, 1992.

———. *Weile heping* [For the Sake of Peace]. Beijing: The Long March Press, 1987.

Yang, Fengan and Wang Tiancheng. *Jiayu chaoxian zhanzheng de ren* [The People Who Dominated the Korean War]. Beijing: CCP Central Academy Press, 1993.

Yang, Guoyu et al. *Dangdai zhongguo haijun* [Contemporary Chinese Navy]. Beijing: Chinese Social Sciences Press, 1987.

Yang, Kuisong. *Zhongjian didai de geming* [Revolution in the Intermediate Zone]. Beijing: CCP Central Academy Press, 1992.

———. "The GMD-CCP Negotiations and Marshall's Mission to China." *Lishi yanjiu* (1990), no. 5.

Yang, Wanqing. "Liu Yalou: The First Commander of the People's Air Force." *Zhonggong dangshi ziliao* (1992), no. 42.

Yang, Yunruo and Yang Kuisong. *Gongchan guoji he zhongguo geming* [The Comintern and the Chinese Revolution]. Shanghai: Shanghai People's Press, 1988.

Yang, Zhaoquan, ed. *Zhongchao guanxi lunwenji* [Essays on Chinese-Korean Relations]. Beijing: World Affairs Press, 1988.

Yao, Xu. *Cong yalujiang dao banmendian* [From the Yalu River to Panmunjom]. Beijing: People's Press, 1985.

———. "Comrade [Peng] Deng Hua in the War to Resist America and Assist Korea." *Hunan dangshi tongxun* (1985), nos. 3–4.

———. "Peng Dehuai's Contributions in Commanding the War to Resist America and Assist Korea." *Dangshi yanjiu ziliao* (1982), no. 1.

————. "The Brilliant Decision to Resist America and Assist Korea." *Dangshi yanjiu* (1980), no. 5.

Ye, Fei. *Ye Fei Huiyilu* [Ye Fei's Memoirs]. Beijing: People's Liberation Army Press, 1988.

Ye, Huoshen. "Understanding Several Fundamental Problems Concerning U.S. Invasion of Korea." *Xuexi* (1950), no. 9.

Ye, Yumeng. *Chubing chaoxian: kangmei yuanchao lishi jishi* [Entering the Korean War: A True Story of the History of Resisting America and Assisting Korea]. Beijing: October Literature Press, 1990.

Yu, Zhan and Zhang Guangyiu. "Had Stalin Advised the CCP Not to Cross the Yangzi River?" *Dangde wenxian* (1989), no. 1.

Zeng, Keling. *Rongma shengya de huiyi* [Recollections of My life in the Army]. Beijing: People's Liberation Army Press, 1992.

Zeng, Sheng. *Zeng Sheng huiyilu* [Zeng Sheng's Memoirs]. Beijing: People's Liberation Army Press, 1991.

Zhang, Baijia. "The New China's Foreign Policy," *Guoshi yanjiu ziliao* (1993), no. 2.

Zhang, Chengzong et al. *Jiefang zhanzheng shiqi de zhonggong zhongyang shanghaiju* [The Shanghai Bureau of the CCP Central Committee During the War of Liberation]. Shanghai: Xuelin Press, 1989.

Zhang, Hui. "The Contest of the Strategic Decision-making Between China and the United States." *Dangshi wenhui* (1988), no. 6.

Zhang, Lianzhong et al. *Haijun shi* [A History of the PLA's Navy]. Beijing: People's Liberation Army Press, 1989.

Zhang, Min. "A Survey of the Struggle to Suppress Counter-revolutionaries in the Early Years of the PRC." *Dangde wenxian* (1988), no. 2.

Zhang Pingkai. *Peng Dehuai shuaishi yuanchao* [Peng Dehuai Commanded Troops to Assist Korea]. Shenyang: Liaoning People's Press, 1990.

Zhang, Wentian. *Zhang Wentian Xuanji* [Selected Works of Zhang Wentian]. Beijing: People's Press, 1989.

Zhang, Xi. "The Sudden Cancellation of the CPV's Movement on the Eve of Its' Entry into Korea." *Dangshi yanjiu ziliao* (1993), no. 1.

————. "Before and After Peng Dehuai's Appointment to Command Troops in Korea." *Zhonggong dangshi ziliao* (1989), no. 31.

Zhang, Zhen. "The Third Field Army's Cross-Yangzi Campaign." *Zhonggong dangshi ziliao* (1990), no. 36.

Zhang Zhenglong. *Xuebai xuehong* [White Snow and Red Blood]. Beijing: People's Liberation Army Press, 1989.

Zhang, Zongxun. *Zhang Zongxun huiyilu* [Zhang Zongxun's Memoirs]. Beijing: People's Liberation Army Press, 1990.

Zhao, Dexin et al. *Zhonghua renmin gongheguo jingjishi* [An Economic History of the People's Republic of China, 1949–1966]. Zhengzhou: Henan People's Press, 1989.

Zhao, Nanqi and Wen Zhengyi, "The Korean Nationality People's Contribution to the War of Liberation in the Northeast," in Wu Xiuquan et al., *Liaoshen zhanyi* [The Liaoshen Campaign], vol. 2. Beijing: People's Press, 1992.

Zhao, Yongtian. *"Heixue*'s Serious Distortion of Historical Facts." *Junshi lishi*, (1989), no. 6.

Zhonggong dangshi jiaoxue cankao ziliao [Reference Materials for Teaching CCP History]. vols. 18–19 [1945–1953]. Beijing: National Defense University Press, 1986.

Zhonggong zhongyang wenjian xuanji [Selected Documents of the CCP Central Committee, internal edition]. 14 vols. Beijing: CCP Central Academy Press, 1983–1987.

Zhonggong zhongyang wenjian xuanji [Selected Documents of the CCP Central Committee, open edition]. 18 vols. Beijing: CCP Central Academy Press, 1989–1992.

Zhongguo renmin zhiyuanjun kangmei yuanchao zhanzheng zhengzhi gongzuo jingyan huibian [A Collection of Experience Summaries of the Political Affairs of the Chinese People's Volunteers During the War to Resist America and Assist Korea]. Beijing: People's Liberation Army Press, 1987.

Zhonghua renmin gongheguo duiwai guanxi wenjianji, 1949–1950 [Documents of Foreign Relations of the People's Republic of China, 1949–1950]. Beijing: World Affairs Press, 1957.

Zhonghua renmin gongheguo duiwai guanxi wenjianji, 1951–1953 [Documents of Foreign Relations of the People's Republic of China, 1951–1953]. Beijing: World Affairs Press, 1958.

Zhongmei guanxi ziliao huibian [A Collection of Materials concerning Sino-American Relations]. Beijing: World Affairs Press, 1957.

Zhou, Enlai. *Zhou Enlai waijiao wenxuan* [Selected Diplomatic Works of Zhou Enlai]. Beijing: The Central Press of Historical Documents, 1990.

———. *Zhou Enlai shuxin xuanji* [Selected Correspondences of Zhou Enlai]. Beijing: The Central Press of Historical Documents, 1988.

———. *Zhou Enlai xuanji* [Selected Works of Zhou Enlai] 2 vols. Beijing: People's Press, 1984.

———. *Zhou Enlai tongyi zhanxian wenxuan* [Selected United Front Works of Zhou Enlai]. Beijing: People's Press, 1984.

Zhou, Jun. "The Party Central Committee's Decision on the Strategic Transition from the War of Liberation to the War to Resist America and Assist Korea." *Dangshi yanjiu ziliao* (1992), no. 4.

———. "A Preliminary Exploration of Reasons for the People's Liberation

Army's Abortive Plan to Attack Taiwan after the Formation of the People's Republic." *Zhonggong dangshi yanjiu* (1991), no. 1.

Zhu, De. *Zhu De xuanji* [Selected Works of Zhu De]. Beijing: People's Press, 1983.

Zhu, Yuanshi. "Liu Shaoqi's Secret Visit to the Soviet Union in 1949." *Dangde wenxian* (1991), no. 3.

Zi, Zhongyun. *Meiguo duihua zhengce de yuanqi yu fazhan, 1945–1950* [The Origins and Development of U.S. Policy Toward China, 1945–1950]. Chongqing: Chongqing Press, 1987.

Japanese Language Sources

Hiramatsu, Shigeo. *China and the Korean War,* Tokyo: Keiso Book Store, 1988.

Kobayashi, Keiji. "Who Was the Initiators of the Korean War?" *Aera,* June 16, 1990.

Sakuyi, Lyoko. "The First Exposure of the Truth of the Korean War: Interview with Lee Sang-jo." *Spring and Autumn of Literature and Art* (1990), no. 6.

Zhu, Jianrong. *Mao Zedong's Korean War: China Crosses the Yalu.* Tokyo: Iwanami Book Store, 1991.

English Language Sources

Acheson, Dean. *Present at the Creation: My Years in the State Department.* New York: Norton, 1969.

Armstrong, J. D. *Revolutionary Diplomacy: Chinese Foreign Policy and The United Front Doctrine.* Berkeley and Los Angles: University of California Press, 1977.

Alexander, Bevin. *Korea: The First War We Lost.* New York: Hippocrene, 1986.

Appleman, Roy E. *Disaster in Korea: the Chinese Confront MacArthur.* College Station: Texas A & M University Press, 1989.

Baik, Bong. *Kim Il-sung: A Political Biography.* 3 vols. New York: Guardian Books Institution, 1977.

Barnett, A Doak. *China and the Major Powers in East Asia.* Washington, DC: Brookings Institution, 1977.

——. *Communist China and Asia: A Challenge to American Foreign Policy.* New York: Vintage Books, 1960.

Beloff, Max. *Soviet Policy in the Far East, 1944–1951.* London: Oxford University Press, 1953.

Bernstein, Barton J. "The Policy of Risk: Crossing the Thirty-Eighth Parallel and Marching to the Yalu." *Foreign Service Journal*, March 1977.

Blair, Clay. *The Forgotten War: America in Korea, 1950–1953.* New York: Times Books, 1987.

Blum, Robert M. *Drawing the Line: The Origins of the American Confrontation Policy in East Asia.* New York: Norton, 1982.

Bo, Yibo. "The Making of the 'Lean-to-one-side' Decision." trans. by Zhai Qiang, *Chinese Hsitorians* 5 (1992), no. 1.

Borg, Dorothy and Waldo Heinrichs, eds. *Uncertain Years: Chinese-American Relations, 1947–1950.* New York: Columbia University Press, 1980.

Bradley, Omar N. and Clay Blair. *A General's Life: An Autobiograph.* New York: Simon and Schuster, 1983.

Buhite, Russell D. "Major Interests: American Policy Toward China, Taiwan, and Korea, 1945–1950." *Pacific Historical Review* 47 (1978), no. 3.

———. "Missed Opportunities? American Policy and the Chinese Communists, 1949." *Mid-America*, 61 (1979).

Calingaert, Daniel. "Nuclear Weapons and the Korean War." *Journal of Strategic Studies* 11 (1988), no. 1.

Caridi, Ronald. *The Korean War and American Politics: The Republican Party as a Case Study.* Philadelphia: University of Pennsylvania Press, 1968.

Chaffee, Wilbur A. "Two Hypotheses of Sino-Soviet Relations as Concerns the Instigation of the Korean War." *Journal of Korean Affairs* 6 (1976–1977), nos. 3–4.

Chang, Gordon H. *Friends and Enemies: The United States, China, and the Soviet Union, 1948–1972.* Stanford, CA: Stanford University Press, 1990.

Chen, Jian. "China and the First Indochina War, 1950–1954." *The China Qaurterly* (1993), no. 133.

———. "China's Changing Aims During the Korean War." *The Journal of American-East Asian Relations* 1 (1992), no. 1.

———. "The Sino-Soviet Alliance and China's Entry Into the Korean War." Working paper no. 1, the Cold War International History Project. Washington, D.C.: Woodrow Wilson Center, December 1991.

———. "The Making of a Revolutionary Diplomacy: A Critical Study of Communist China's Policy Toward the United States, 1949–1950." *Chinese Historians* 3 (1990), no. 1.

Chen, Xiaolu. "China's Policy Toward the United States, 1949–1955." In Harry Harding and Yuan Ming, eds. *Sino-American Relations, 1945–1955*, listed below.

Choudhury, Golam W. "Reflections on the Korean War, 1950–1953." *Korean and World Affairs*, 14 (1990), no. 2.

Christensen, Thomas. "Domestic Mobilization and International Conflict:

Sino-American Relations in the 1950s." Ph.D. dissertation. New York: Columbia University, 1993.

———. "Threats, Assurances, and the Last Chance for Peace: The Lessons of Mao's Korean War Telegrams." *International Security,* 17 (Summer 1992), no. 1.

Clark, Mark W. *From the Danube to the Yalu.* New York: Harper, 1954.

Cohen, Warren I. *America's Response to China: An Interpretive History of Sino-American Relations.* 3rd ed. New York: Columbia University Press, 1990.

———. "Conversations with Chinese Friends: Zhou Enlai's Associates Reflect on Chinese-American Relations in the 1940s and the Korean War." *Diplomatic History* 11 (1987), no. 2.

Collins, J. Jawton. *War in Peacetime: The History and Lessons of Korea.* Boston: Houghton Mifflin, 1969.

Confidential U.S. State Department Central Files: People's Republic of China, *Foreign Affairs, 1950–1954.* Microfilm, University Publications of America.

Confidential U.S. State Department Central Files. *United States-China Relations, 1940–1949.* Microfilm, University Publication of America.

Cotton, James and Ian Neary, eds. *The Korean War in History.* Atlantic Highlands, NJ: Humanities International Press, 1989.

Cumings, Bruce. *The Origins of the Korean War.* 2 vols. Princeton: Princeton University Press, 1981, 1990.

———. ed. *Child of Conflict: The Korean-American Relationship, 1943–1953.* Seattle: University of Washington Press, 1983.

Dingman, Roger. "Reconsiderations at Forty-Plus: The Origins of the Korean War." *The Journal of American-East Asian Relations* 1 (1992), no. 1.

———. "Atomic Diplomacy During the Korean War." *International Security* 13 (1988/89), no. 3.

Domes, Jurgen. *Peng Te-huai: The Man and the Image.* Stanford: Stanford University Press, 1985.

Dulles, Foster Rhea. *American Policy Toward Communist China: The Historical Record, 1949–1969.* New York: Thomas Y. Crowell, 1972.

Eastman Lloyd. *Seeds of Destruction: North China in War and Revolution, 1937–1949.* Stanford, CA: Stanford University Press, 1984.

Esherick, Joseph S. ed. *Lost Chance in China: The World War II Dispatches of John S. Service.* New York: Random House, 1974.

Fairbank, John K. *The United States and China.* Cambridge: Harvard University Press, 1983.

———. ed. *The Chinese World Order.* Cambridge: Harvard University Press, 1968.

Farrar-Hockley, Anthony. "A Reminiscence of the Chinese People's Volunteers in the Korean War." *The China Quarterly* (1984), no. 98.

Fedorenko, Nikola. "The Stalin-Mao Summit in Moscow." *Far Eastern Affairs* [Moscow] (1989), no. 2.
———. "Recalling Zhou Enlai." *Far Eastern Affairs* [Moscow] (1989), no. 6.
Fitzgerald, Charles P. *The Chinese View of Their Place in the World.* London: Oxford University Press, 1964.
Foot, Rosemary. "Make the Unknown War Known: Policy Analysis of the Korean Conflict in the Last Decade." *Diplomatic History* 15 (1991), no. 3.
———. *A Substitute for Victory: The Politics of Peacemaking at the Korean Armistice Talks.* Ithaca: Cornell University Press, 1990.
———. *The Wrong War: American Policy and the Dimensions of the Korean Conflict, 1950–1953.* Ithaca: Cornell University Press, 1985.
Foreign Relations of the United States. Volumes for the years of 1948–1950, Washington, DC: Government Printing Office.
Futtrell, Robert Frank. *The United States Air Force in Korea, 1950–1953.* New York: Duell, Sloan, and Pearce, 1961.
Gaddis, John Lewis. *The Long Peace: Inquiries into the History of the Cold War.* New York: Oxford University Press, 1987.
———. *Strategies of Containment: A Critical Appraisal of Postwar American National Security Policy.* New York: Oxford University Press, 1982.
George, Alexander L. *The Chinese Communist Army in Action: The Korean War and Its Aftermath.* New York: Columbia University Press, 1967.
Gittings, John. *The World and China, 1922–1972.* London: Eyre Methuen, 1974.
———. *The Role of the Chinese Army.* London: Oxford University Press, 1967.
Goncharov, Sergei. "Stalin's Dialogue with Mao Zedong: I. V. Kovalev, Stalin's Representative, Answer Questions of Sinologist S. N. Goncharov." *Journal of Northeast Asian Studies* 10 (1991–92), no. 4.
———, John W. Lewis, and Xue Litai. *Uncertain Partners: Stalin, Mao, and the Korean War.* Stanford: Stanford University Press, 1993.
Goulden, Joseph C. *Korea: The Untold Story of the War.* New York: Times Books, 1982.
Gurtov, Melvin and Hwang, Byong-Moo. *China Under Threat: The Politics of Strategy and Diplomacy.* Baltimore: The Johns Hopkins University Press, 1980.
Harding, Harry. *Organizing China: The Problem of Bureaucracy, 1949–1976.* Stanford: Stanford University Press, 1981.
Harding, Harry and Yuan, Ming, eds. *Sino-American Relations, 1945–1955: A Joint Reassessment of a Critical Decade.* Wilmington, DE: Scholarly Resources, 1989.
Hasting, Max. *The Korean War.* New York: Simon and Schuster, 1987.

He, Di. "The Last Campaign to Unify China: The CCP's Unmaterialized Plan to Liberate Taiwan, 1949–1950." *Chinese Historians* 5 (1992), no. 1.

———. "The Most Respected Enemy: Mao Zedong's Perception of the United States." Unpublished paper.

Heo, Man-Ho. "From Civil War to an International War: A Dialectical Interpretation of the Origins of the Korean War." *Korea and World Affairs*, Summer 1990.

Hogan, Michael and Thomas Patterson. *Explaining the History of American Foreign Relations*. Cambridge: Cambridge University Press, 1991.

Hooper, Beverley. *China Stands Up: Ending the Western Presence, 1949–1950*. Sidney: Allen & Unwin, 1986.

Hoyt, Edwin P. *The Day the Chinese Attacked Korea, 1950*. New York: McGraw-Hill, 1990.

Huebner, Jon W. "The Abortive Liberation of Taiwan." *The China Quarterly* (1987), no. 110.

Hunt, Michael H. "Beijing and the Korean Crisis, June 1950–June 1951." *Political Science Quarterly* 107 (1992), no. 3.

———. "The Genesis of Chinese Communist Foreign Policy: Mao Zedong Takes Command, 1935–1949. Occasional paper. Washington, D.C.: Asian Program, the Woodrow Wilson Center, 1991.

———. and Odd Arne Westad. "The Chinese Communist Party and International Affairs: A Field Report on New Historical Sources and Old Research Problems." *The China Quarterly* (1990), no. 122.

———. *Ideology and U.S. Foreign Policy*. New Haven: Yale University Press, 1987.

———. "Korea and Vietnam: State-of-Art Surveys of Our Asian Wars." *Reviews in American History*, June 1987.

Iriye, Akira and Warren I. Cohen, eds. *American, Chinese, and Japanese Perspectives on Wartime Asia, 1931–1949*. Wilmington: Scholarly Resources, 1990.

Jervis, Robert. "The Impact of the Korean War on the Cold War." *Journal of Conflict Resolution*, December 1980.

———. *Perception and Misperception in International Politics*. Princeton: Princeton University Press, 1976.

Jia, Qing-guo. "Unmaterialized Rapprochement: Sino-American Relations in the Mid-1950s." Ph.D. dissertation. Ithaca: Cornell University, 1988.

Jiang, Arnold Xiangze. *The United States and China*. Chicago: The University of Chicago Press, 1988.

Kalicki, J. H. *The Pattern of Sino-American Crisis: Political-Military Interactions in the 1950s*. London: Cambridge University Press, 1975.

Kaufman, Burton I. *The Korean War: Challenges in Crisis, Credibility, and Command*. Philadelphia: Temple University Press, 1986.

Keith, Ronald C. *The Diplomacy of Zhou Enlai.* New York: St. Martin's, 1989.

Kennan, George. *Memoirs, 1925–1950.* Boston: Little, Brown, 1967.

———. *Memoir, 1950–1963.* Boston: Little, Brown, 1972.

Khrushchev, Nikita S. "Truth About the Korean War." *Far Eastern Affairs* [Moscow] (1991), no. 1.

———. *Khrushchev Remembers: The Glasnost Tapes.* trans. and ed. by Jettodld L. Schecter with Vyacheslav V. Luchkov, Boston: Little, Brown, 1990.

———. *Khrushchev Remembers.* tran. by Strobe Talbott, Boston: Little, Brown, 1970.

Kim, Chullbaum, ed. *The Truth About the Korean War: Testimony 40 Years Later.* Seoul: Eulyoo Publishing Co. 1991.

Kim, Chum-kon. *The Korean War, 1950–1953.* Seoul: Kwangmyong Publishing, 1980.

Kim, Hakjoon. "International Trends in Korean War Studies: A Review of the Documentary Literature." *Korea and World Affairs* 14 (1990), no. 2.

Kolko, Joyce, and Kolko, Gabriel. "To Root Out Those Among Them: A Response." *Pacific Historical Review* 42 (1973), no. 4.

LaFaber, Walter. *America, Russia, and the Cold War, 1945–1990.* 6th ed. New York: McGraw-Hill, 1991.

Levine, Steven I. *Anvil of Victory: The Communist Revolution in Manchuria, 1945–1948.* New York: Columbia University Press, 1987.

Lewis, John Wilson and Xue Litai. *China Builds the Bomb.* Stanford: Stanford University Press, 1988.

Li, Haiwen. "A Distortion of History: An Interview with Shi Zhe About Kovalev's Memoirs." *Chinese Historians* 5 (1992), no. 2.

———. "How and When did China Decide to Enter the Korean War?" trans. by Chen Jian, *Korea and World Affairs,* 18 (Spring 1994), no. 1.

Li, Xiaobing, Wang Xi and Chen Jian, trans. "Mao's Dispatch of Chinese Troops to Korea: Forty-six Telegrams, July-October 1950." *Chinese Historians* 5 (1992), no. 1.

Li, Xiaobing and Glenn Tracy, trans. "Mao's Telegrams During the Korean War, October-December 1950." *Chinese Historians* 5 (1992), no. 2.

Liao, Kuan-sheng. *Anti-Foreignism and Modernization in China, 1860–1980.* New York: St. Martin's, 1984.

Lim, Un. *The Founding of a Dynasty in North Korea: An Authentic Biography of Kim Il-sung.* Tokyo, 1982.

Lowe, Peter. *The Origins of the Korean War.* London: Longman, 1986.

MacArthur, Douglas A. *Reminiscences.* New York: McGraw-Hill, 1964.

MacDonald, Callum A. *Korea: The War Before Vietnam.* New York: Free Press, 1986.

MacFarquhar, Roderick ed. *Sino-American Relations, 1949–1971*. New York: Praeger, 1972.

McGlothlen, Ronald. "Acheson, Economics, and the American Commitment in Korea, 1947–1950." *Pacific Historical Review* 58 (1989), no. 1.

McGovern, James. *To the Yalu: From the Chinese Invasion of Korea to MacArthur's Dismissal*. New York: William Morrow, 1972.

McLean, David. "American Nationalism, the China Myth, and the Truman Doctrine: The Question of Accommodation with Peking, 1949–50." *Diplomatic History* 10 (1986), no. 1.

MacMahaon, Robert. "The Cold War in Asia: Toward a New Synthesis?" *Diplomatic History* 12 (1988), no. 2.

Mancall, Mark. *China at the Center: 300 Years of Foreign Policy*. New York: Fred Press, 1984.

———. "The Persistence of Tradition in Chinese Foreign Policy." *Annals of the American Academy of Political Social Science* (1963), no. 349.

Mandelbaum, Michael. *The Fate of Nations: The Search for National Security in the 19th and 20th Centuries*. Cambridge: Cambridge University Press, 1988.

Martin, Edwin W. *Divided Counsel: The Anglo-American Response to Communist Victory in China*. The University Press of Kentucky, 1986.

May, Ernest, ed. *American Cold War Strategy: Interpreting NSC 68*. Boston: St. Martin's, 1993.

Matray, James I. *The Reluctant Crusade: American Foreign Policy in Korea, 1941–1950*. Honolulu: University of Hawaii Press, 1985.

May, Ernest R. *The Truman Administration and China, 1945–1949*. Philadelphia: Lippincott, 1975.

Merrill, John. *Korea: the Peninsular Origins of the War*. Delaware University Press, 1989.

Misner, Maurice. *Mao's China and After: A History of the People's Republic*. New York: The Free Press, 1986.

Nakajima, Mineo. "Foreign Relations: from the Korean War to the Bandung Line." In R. MacFarquhar and J. K. Fairbank eds. *The Cambridge History of China*, vol.14, "The Emergence of Revolutionary China, 1949–1965," Cambridge: Cambridge University Press, 1987

———. "The Sino-Soviet Confrontation: Its Roots in the International Background of the Korean War." *Australian Journal of Chinese Affairs* (1979), no. 1.

Ness, Peter Van. *Revolution and Chinese Foreign Policy: Peking's Support for Wars of National Liberation*. Berkeley: University of California Press, 1970.

Paige, Glenn D. *The Korean Decision, June 24–30, 1950*. New York: The Free Press, 1968.

Panikkar, K.M. *In Two Chinas*. London: Allen and Unwin, 1955.

Pollack, Jonathan D. "The Korean War and Sino-American Relations." In
Harry Harding and Yuan Ming, eds. *Sino-American Relations, 1945–1955*,
listed above.

Purifoy, Lewis McCarroll. *Harry Truman's China Policy: McCarthyism and the
Diplomacy of Hysteria, 1947–1951*. New York: New Viewpoints, 1976.

Rees, David. *Korea: The Limited War*. New York: St. Martin's, 1964.

Reardon-Anderson, James. *Yenan and the Great Powers: The Origins of Chi-
nese-Communist Foreign Policy, 1944–1946*. New York: Columbia University Press, 1980.

Ryan, Mark A. *Chinese Attitude Toward Nuclear Weapons: China and the United States During the Korean War*. Armonk, NY: M. E. Sharpe, 1989.

Salisbury, Harrison E. *The New Emperors: China in the Era of Mao and Deng*.
Boston: Little, Brown, 1992.

Scalapino, Robert and Lee Chong-sik, *Communism in Korea*. 2 vols. Berkeley and Los Angeles, CA: University of California Press, 1972.

Schaller, Michael. *Douglas MacArthur: The Far Eastern General and American
Foreign Policy*. New York: Oxford University Press, 1989.

———. *American Occupation of Japan: The Origins of Cold War in Asia*. New
York: Oxford University Press, 1985.

———. *The U.S. Crusade in China, 1938—1945*. New York: Columbia
University Press, 1979.

Schram. Stuart R. *The Thought of Mao Tse-tung*. Cambridge: Cambridge
University Press, 1989.

Service, John S. *The Amerasia Papers: Some Problems in the History of U.S.-
China Relations*. Berkeley: University of California Press, 1971.

Shaw, Yu-ming. *An American Missionary in China: John Leighton Stuart and
Chinese-American Relations*. Cambridge: Harvard University Press, 1992.

———. "John Leighton Stuart and U.S.-Chinese Communist Rapprochement in 1949: Was There Another 'Lost Chance in China'?" *The China
Quarterly* (1982), no. 89.

Sheng, Michael S. "America's Lost Chance in China? A Reappraisal of Chinese Communist Policy Toward the United States Before 1945." *The
Australian Journal of Chinese Affairs* (1993), no. 29.

Shewmaker, Kenneth E. *Americans and Chinese Communists, 1927–1945, A
Persuading Encounter*. Ithaca: The Cornell University Press, 1971.

Shi, Zhe. "With Mao and Stalin: The Reminiscences of Mao's Interpreter."
trans. by Chen Jian, *Chinese Historians* (1992 and 1993) vol.5, no. 1 and
vol.6, no. 1.

Shum, Kui-Kwong. *Chinese Communists' Road to Power*. Hong Kong:
Oxford University Press, 1988.

Simmons, Robert R. *The Strained Alliance: Peking, Pyongyang, Moscow, and
the Politics of the Korean Civil War*. New York: Free Press, 1975.

Slavinsky, Boris. "The 1950–1953 Korean War in Retrospect." *Far Eastern Affairs* [Moscow] (1991), no. 3.

Smith, Gaddis. *Dean Acheson.* New York: Cooper Square, 1972.

Spanier, John W. *The Truman-MacArthur Controversy and the Korean War.* New York: Norton, 1965.

Spurr, Russell. *Enter the Dragon: China's Undeclared War Against the U.S. in Korea, 1950–1951.* Now York: Newmarket Press, 1988.

Staff of Soviet Foreign Ministry, "Background Report on the Korean War," August 9, 1966, trans. by Kathryn Weathersby. *The Journal of American-East Asian Relations,* 2 (1992), no. 4.

Stokesbury, James L. *A Short History of the Korean War.* New York: William Morrow, 1988.

Stuart, John Leighton. *Fifty Years in China: The Memoirs of John Leighton Stuart, Missionary and Ambassador.* New York: Random House, 1954.

Stueck, William Whitner, Jr. "The Korean War as International History." *Diplomatic History* 10 (Fall 1986), no 4.

———. *The Road to Confrontation: American Policy Toward China and Korea, 1947–1950.* Chapel Hill: The University of North Carolina Press, 1981.

———. "The Soviet Union and the Origins of the Korean War." *World Politics* (1976), no. 28.

Suh, Dae-sook. *The Korean Communist Movement, 1918–1948.* Princeton, NJ: Princeton University Press, 1967.

Syn, Song-Kil and Sin Sam-Soon. "Who Started the Korean War?" *Korea and World Affairs* 14 (1990), no. 2.

Teiwes, Fredrick. *Politics of Mao's Court: Gao Gang and Party Factionalism.* Armonk, N.Y.: M. E. Sharpe, 1990.

Thomson, James C. Jr. Stanley, Peter, and Perry, John Curtis. *Sentimental Imperialists: the American Experience in East Asia.* New York: Harper, 1981.

Tikhvinsky, S. "China in My Life." *Far Eastern Affairs* [Moscow] (1989), nos. 4–5.

Tozer, Warren W. "Lost Bridge to China: The Shanghai Power Company, the Truman Administration and the Chinese Communist Party." *Diplomatic History* 4 (Winter 1979), no. 1.

Truman, Harry S. *Memoirs.* 2 vols. Garden City, NY: Doubleday, 1956.

Tsou, Tang. *America's Failure in China, 1941–1950.* Chicago: University of Chicago Press, 1963.

Tsui, Chak Wing David. "Strategic Objectives of Chinese Military Intervention in Korea." *Korea and World Affairs* 16 (1992), no. 2.

Tucker, Nancy Bernkopf. "China and America: 1941–1991." *Foreign Affairs* 70 (1991/92), no. 5.

————. *Patterns in the Dust: Chinese- American Relations and the Recognition Controversy, 1949–1950*. New York: Columbia University Press, 1983..

Tuchman, Barbara. "If Mao Had Come to Washington: An Essay in Alternatives." *Foreign Affairs* 51(1971), no. 1.

United Nations. *Report of the United Nations Commission on Korea: Covering the Period from December 15, 1949 to September 4, 1950*. New York, 1950.

U.S. Congress, Senate Committee on Foreign Relations. *China and the United States: Today and Yesterday—Hearings Before the Committee on Foreign Relations*. 92nd Cong. 2nd sess. Washington, DC: Government Printing Office, 1972.

U.S. Congress, Senate Committee on Foreign Relations. *The United States and Communist China in 1949 and 1950: The Question of Rapprochement and Recognition*. Staff Study, Washington, DC: Government Printing Office, 1973.

The U.S. Imperialists Started the Korean War. Pyongyang: Foreign Language Publishing House, 1977.

Usov, Victor. "Who Sent the Chinese Volunteers?" *Far Eastern Affairs* [Moscow] (1991), no. 1.

Van Slyke, Lyman P. ed. *The China White Paper, August 1949*. Stanford: Stanford University Press, 1967.

Vladimirov, Peter. *The Vladimirov Diaries, Yenan, China: 1942–1945*. New York: Doubledays, 1975.

War Memorial Service-Korea. *The Historical Reillumination of the Korean War*. Seoul: Korean War Research Conference Committee, 1990.

Weathersby, Kathryn, "The Soviet Role in the Early Phase of the Korean War: New Documentary Evidence." *The Journal of American-East Asian Relations* 2 (1993), no. 4.

————. "Soviet Aims in Korea and the Origins of the Korean War, 1945–1950: New Evidence from Russian Archives." Working Paper no. 8, Cold War International History Project, Woodrow Wilson Center, Washington, D.C., November 1993.

Weiss, Lawrence S. "Storm Around the Cradle: The Korean War and the Early Years of the People's Republic of China, 1949–1953." Ph. D. dissertation. New York: Columbia University, 1981.

West, Philip. "Confronting the West: China as David and Goliath in the Korean War." *The Journal of American-East Asian Relations* 2 (1993), no. 1.

————. "Interpreting the Korean War." *American Historical Review* 94 (1989), no. 1.

Westad, Odd Arne. *Cold War and Revolution: Soviet-American Rivalry and the Origins of the Chinese Civil War, 1944–1946*. New York: Columbia University Press, 1992.

————. "Rethinking Revolution: The Cold War in the Third World." *Journal of Peace Research* 29 (1992), no. 4.

Whelan, Richard. *Drawing the Line: The Korean War, 1950–1953.* Boston: Little, Brown, 1990.

Whiting, Allen S. "The Sino-Soviet Split." In R. MacFarquhar and J. K. Fairbank eds. *The Cambridge History of China,* vol.14, "The Emergence of Revolutionary China, 1949–1965." Cambridge: Cambridge University Press, 1987.

————. *China Crosses the Yalu: the Decisions to Enter the Korean War.* New York: Macmillan, 1960.

Whitson, William W. with Huang, Chen-Hsia. *The Chinese High Command: A History of Communist Military Politics, 1927–1971.* New York: Praeger, 1973.

Xu, Yan. "China's Decision on the Military Intervention in the Korean War." Unpublished paper.

Yang, Kuisong. "The Soviet Factor and the CCP's Policy Toward the United States in the 1940s." *Chinese Historians* 5 (1992), no 1.

Yonhap Press. "N. K. Preemptive Strike Plan in '50 Made Public in Russia." *The Korean Herald,* August 30, 1992.

Young, Kenneth T. *Negotiating with the Chinese Communists: The United States Experience, 1953–1967.* New York: McGraw-Hill, 1968.

Yu, Song-chol. "My Testimony." *Foreign Broadcast Information Service: East Asia,* November 15 - December 27, 1990.

Zagoria, Donald S. "Choices in the Postwar World: Containment and China." In Charles Gati ed. *Caging the Bear: Containment and the Cold War.* Indianapolis: Bobbs-Merrill, 1974.

Zhai, Qiang. *The Dragon, the Lion, and the Eagle: Chinese-British-American Relations, 1949–1958.* Mansfield, OH: Kent State University Press, 1994.

Zhang, Shuguang. *Deterrence and Strategic Culture: Chinese-American Confrontations, 1949–1958.* Cornell University Press, 1992.

————. "Preparedness Eliminates Mishap: The CCP's Security Concerns in 1949–1950 and the Origins of Sino-American Confrontation." *The Journal of American-East Asian Relations* 1 (1992), no. 1.

Zhang, Xi. "Peng Dehuai and China's Entry into the Korean War." trans. by Chen Jian, *Chinese Historians* 6 (1993), no. 1.

Index